PROF. W. F. MURPHY
DEPARTMENT OF POLITICS
PRINCETON UNIVERSITY
PRINCETON, N. J. 08540

# OBLIGATION AND DISSENT

# Obligation and Dissent: An Introduction to Politics

EDITED BY

**DONALD W. HANSON**
*University of Utah*

**ROBERT BOOTH FOWLER**
*University of Wisconsin*

# LITTLE, BROWN AND COMPANY
*Boston*

COPYRIGHT © 1971, BY LITTLE, BROWN AND COMPANY (INC.)

ALL RIGHTS RESERVED. NO PART OF THIS BOOK MAY BE REPRODUCED IN ANY FORM OR BY ANY ELECTRONIC OR MECHANICAL MEANS INCLUDING INFORMATION STORAGE AND RETRIEVAL SYSTEMS WITHOUT PERMISSION IN WRITING FROM THE PUBLISHER, EXCEPT BY A REVIEWER WHO MAY QUOTE BRIEF PASSAGES IN A REVIEW.

LIBRARY OF CONGRESS CATALOG CARD NO. 70–151010

SECOND PRINTING

*Published simultaneously in Canada*
*by Little, Brown & Company (Canada) Limited*

PRINTED IN THE UNITED STATES OF AMERICA

# Contents

v

# General Introduction

## The Nature of Political Philosophy:
## Ideas, Argument, and the Necessity of Choice

DONALD W. HANSON

Political philosophy might be defined as reasoned argument about judgments of value and obligation in the public realm. Like any economical definition, however, this one requires considerable expansion before it will be helpful. Two problems demand consideration. One is to indicate more fully the nature of the problems of political philosophy, to articulate, in effect, a view of what political philosophy may be understood to be. The second is to distinguish political philosophy from a number of closely related forms of intellectual activity and judgment: political opinion, ideology, policy advice, and judgments of practicality or feasibility.

Political philosophy came into being because men differ profoundly about matters of politics — persistently and sometimes violently. But what are men differing about in their political disputes, or disputes in political philosophy, and what is the nature of their disagreement? At the highest level of abstraction, they are disagreeing not about what is or is not — however important — but rather about what "really matters" or should matter to men generally. This kind of disagreement normally involves an effort to supply standards by which men ought to judge the worth of other men, their actions, and their institutions. If the problem is left at this level, however, disputes of these kinds could be essentially religious or metaphysical, as well as political. One cannot always distinguish between these ideas with perfect clarity and precision; indeed, that has sometimes been the heart of sustained disagreement. But whatever the fundamental ideas, the suggestion that political philosophy arises from disagreement implies that it is in some way different from such disputes[1] and involves consideration of complex "boundary" problems. It is unnecessary to take the idea of boundaries too seriously, but it is useful to consider reasons for maintaining that political philosophy is a distinct kind of pursuit.

The chief aim of this essay, then, is to consider political philosophy, and how it differs from other types of intellectual activity which strive to form or express value judgments in politics. Before proceeding, however, we ought to understand that many possible definitions of political philosophy, including the one offered here, are compatible with a subject that tends to fall easily into two quite different sorts of inquiry and argument: the exclusively analytical, and the explicitly normative. Although we probably cannot isolate the two completely, it is not difficult to achieve a clear emphasis in one direction.[2] The emphasis in this book is normative; that is, we intend to present and, in a limited way, to discuss arguments in defense of explicit choices on a range of important and much debated topics. All these arguments depend in varying degrees upon analysis, that is, the explication and implications of crucial political concepts, and upon the ways in which they are put forth. But in most of the essays collected here the authors' intentions are clearly to present judgments of value and to defend them by argument.

Now we turn to the first of the general explanatory problems: to elucidate the concept of political philosophy. As we have mentioned, any reasonably brief definition requires explanation before it proves useful, unless (as in mathematics and the natural sciences) the meanings of the critical concepts are widely agreed upon. Since

---

[1] Throughout this discussion of the features that distinguish political philosophy from related intellectual activities, I would like to acknowledge my indebtedness to Judith N. Shklar, particularly to her "Facing Up to Intellectual Pluralism," in David Spitz, ed., *Political Theory and Social Change* (New York: Atherton Press, 1968), pp. 275–295.

[2] Some good examples of differing analytical emphases are Brian Barry, *Political Argument* (New York: Humanities Press, 1965); Richard E. Flathman, *The Public Interest* (New York: John Wiley, 1966); Antony Quinton, ed., *Political Philosophy* (New York: Oxford University Press, 1967); Felix E. Oppenheim, *Moral Principles in Political Philosophy* (New York: Random House, 1968).

this almost never occurs in the social sciences or humanities, exercises in terse, scrupulous definition are relatively useless. Such definitions do not and cannot settle problems. At most they can indicate the direction that inquiry might take.[3] In studying man in society, it is important to recognize the source of our disagreements, rather than to try to contrive adequate definitions to reduce or ultimately eliminate those disagreements. For the source of disagreement is that any definition involves emphasis, since it must select some and exclude other aspects of the phenomena to which it refers. In other words, definitions cannot help being the expression of some position regarding what is and is not significant, which is why definitions tend to become matters of argument. Although some of these disputes may have merit, the argument concerns judgments of comparative significance, that is, value.

Bearing in mind these problems and limitations, let us consider the expression "politics." Its meaning is notoriously debatable. Even a cursory survey of definitions would involve dozens of suggestions, but it is doubtful whether such a survey would be useful here. Any definition of politics is itself a philosophical problem. This will perhaps be clearer after we have explored the notion of the "philosophical." For the moment, it is enough to notice that a great many definitions of politics can be collected along a conceptual continuum. At one extreme are definitions that reduce politics to the phenomena of power and the struggle to acquire and maintain it. At the other extreme is a variety of definitions that identify the essence of political life with cooperation, communal solidarity, and obedience.[4] The sharp and fundamental contrast between these extremes has given rise historically to complex debates about the essence of politics. But there seems to be no compelling reason why the two extremes cannot be combined. Here, "politics" refers to varying degrees of both conflict and cooperation, to the phenomena of force and consent, to relationships of coercion and obligation. But this combination of vital elements is not enough, for it does not distinguish politics from any number of subpolitical activities that exhibit some mixture of conflict and cooper-

[3] This point has been well made in Stanley Hoffmann, ed., *Contemporary Theory in International Relations* (Englewood Cliffs, N.J.: Prentice-Hall, 1960), pp. 4–6.

[4] For an extended discussion of this contrast, see Ralf Dahrendorf, *Class and Class Conflict in Industrial Society* (Stanford: Stanford University Press, 1959).

ation. This frailty may be remedied by adding the proviso that these relationships refer to those matters recognized as "public," that is, generally shared problems and purposes. We have no reason to suppose that this or any other definition will put an end to debate, nor should it. Once again: to offer a definition of a critical concept cannot be an exclusively analytical exercise, because that which is finally at stake is the meaning and value that we are urged to attach to that part of our moral experience that we refer to as politics.

We must now identify what is meant by "philosophical." Let us recur to the definition of politics based on the idea of power, in order to question the nature of such statements. The most obvious difficulty here is that, though men certainly do engage in the struggle for power, they do not normally do so for the sake of power itself. In other words, the value of power is often sought for the sake of something else. Obviously this criticism rests on a statement of alleged fact, though it is a common sense observation, as distinguished from a verified proposition of social science. It is conceivable that the sponsor of such a definition could reply that common sense is deceived here. It might be argued that despite the appearance that politics is in part a matter of shared and conflicting purposes, it is "really" only a struggle for power. Precisely what such a contention means is far from clear. Does it mean that men's purposes are simply refined cloaks that obscure the realities of power? It might mean that even if purposes are genuinely entertained, men are mistaken in thinking that such values have a basis in reality. The world, in effect, is solely one of facts, among which is the fact that men embrace various values. This might mean that we are confronted with the task of describing and explaining the emotional life of man. In short, when we think we are discussing genuine moral problems, we are really issuing individual reports on our emotional states. Or again, it might mean that the effort to effectuate our purposes is an exercise in futility, for the one in power will always win. Finally, an advocate of power theory might present a straightforward value judgment: political struggle ought to be treated as a matter of power exclusively. This view contends that it is best to recognize politics as a matter of conflicting interests that can only be adversely affected by the intrusion of the "idealistic" elements represented by morality.

How is one to respond to these views — not how can they be refuted, but what would be an appropriate effort to defend or to criticize them? What kinds of considerations would be relevant to accepting or rejecting them? Beginning with definition, our initial response was that the definition of politics in terms of power was insufficient, on the common sense ground that politics includes purposes, some of which represent not merely instrumental values but ends that men embrace as values for their own sake. But the problem has advanced beyond the stage of definition to a philosophical one. The replies outlined above are not simple definitions, since they represent conscious efforts to penetrate beneath the surface of behavior, argument, and events to something "real." But are they, perhaps, scientific generalizations, or hypotheses that are susceptible to verification? If not, why not?

It is important to recognize a distinction between scientific and philosophical statements. We often characterize the latter as statements about "meaning," and therefore not as exclusively factual in any sense that would make them amenable to definitive settlement through empirical inquiry. In the first place, such statements are intended to say something about the nature of politics which is both true and perfectly general, and yet which defies ordinary understanding. Clearly a statement is not disqualified simply because it contradicts ordinary understanding, for solidly verified scientific laws often do precisely that, but statements like those we have been considering go beyond even a paradoxical scientific generalization. They purport to investigate the real but unobserved and unobservable nature and meaning of things. How could we *ever* verify or invalidate the contention that all our efforts to define our purposes in political life are doomed to frustration, because "right" has no meaning independent from discovering who has prevailed? The simplest objection would be that, disregarding the past, we have no way of knowing what the future holds. But this reply concedes far too much; or rather, it puts the problem on the wrong footing, since it concedes to it scientific plausibility. What this statement involves is not an unconfirmed hypothesis, but an interpretation of the meaning of politics with regard to its human significance. This can be easily illustrated by the profoundly different responses that can be made, for example, to the idea that power always wins, that might makes right. This view has sometimes been favorably received, and sometimes lamented. Such competing appraisals are enough to show that the question is not "what is politics?" in a descriptive sense, but rather "what is the significance of the facts of political life?" It is not, then, a matter of verifying the truth or falsity of an assertion, but one of gauging the moral adequacy of an outlook or an argument. This raises quite different questions: to what extent does such an assessment of the meaning of politics account for that segment of our moral experience? What kinds of reasons can be offered in criticism or defense? In short, does this idea illuminate our experience? The most likely answer might be, yes, within limits; this is normally true of interpretations, assessments, or judgments on the significance to us of a type of human behavior. It is a mistake, in other words, to treat judgments of this kind as if they were ordinary factual observations, except that they appear extraordinarily difficult to prove or disprove. For it is not a question of proof, but of justifiability, of significance, and, therefore, of worth. Some of the views mentioned involve an adverse judgment of the worth of what we normally understand by politics, which would be difficult to prove or disprove. Such arguments need not be depreciated, for we do not *discover* meaning and worth, we create and, more important, re-create them. Hence, these ideas are penetrating aids in the tasks of individual and collective self-understanding.

There is reason to dispute whether some familiar statements are philosophical in character, and whether they perform an intelligible and valuable intellectual function. However, we have not yet confronted the general problem of identifying a philosophical problem in the present context. The first thing to notice about this problem, in some ways its most perplexing aspect, is that to ask "what is a philosophical question?" is itself a philosophical question. This is not as paradoxical as it seems at first glance, for it is an important and recurrent problem in the history of philosophy. What is it that distinguishes a philosophical problem or statement from other statements, such as ordinary factual observations or scientific generalizations? More aggressively: why should we not consider that *all* questions, at least in principle, are susceptible to scientific inquiry and solution? One *can* adopt such a view, but in doing so he will have adopted a particular philosophical position, and so will not have settled the philosophical question at all. On the contrary, all that would be accomplished by this choice is that the chooser would have withdrawn himself from further consideration of philosophical problems; he would simply have abdicated from that aspect of intellectual inquiry. This view does nothing at all to remove the philosophical questions, and is sometimes supported by an argument that combines misreading of the history of philosophy with misunderstanding of the nature of philosophical questions. It supposes that the history of philosophy relates how each empirical discipline has been established by separating itself from the originally all-encompassing philosophical speculation, thus progressively narrowing the range and importance of philosophical inquiry. This view contains an important truth and an important misconception. The several natural and social sciences were once almost entirely subjects of speculation. Moreover, it is now well established that many questions are susceptible, at least in principle, to systematic empirical inquiry. It does not follow, however, that philosophy is, ever was, or ever will be in danger of extinction on this ground. For philosophical questions are not primarily misconceived or abortive empirical questions. In the first place, many of them have been analytical questions about our use of concepts and organizing ideas, arguments designed to show that a concept has unanticipated and, perhaps, undesirable implications. This is not just another empirical inquiry; it is not a matter of investigating what people mean when they use a problematical word, say, "justice," or "equality," or "liberty." To be sure, we may want to know this meaning, and as precisely as possible. But it is not the same as conceptual analysis. Moreover, analytical inquiry embraces more than one kind of question. Not only do we ask what is meant by our use of complex ideas, it is also possible to ask what we *can* mean; that is, questions about the requirements and limits of intelligible discourse. Further, we often ask of each other, what *should* we mean? What ought we to mean by, say, "justice"? We do not discover what justice means, or "really" means. On the contrary, the meaning of such a concept is a matter of discussion, argumentation, decision, choosing, intending, rather than discovery.

Second, however, we often want to consider questions that go substantially beyond the idea of conceptual analysis. For political philosophers have often wanted to make out as adequate a case as possible for a specific morality. An articulate political morality invites us not only to employ standards, but to consider (if not to adopt) an estimate of the meaning and significance of our moral and political experience. It invites one, in other words, to entertain judgments, for example, on the nature of man, on the significance of human history, and, more particularly, on man's propensity to organize himself politically and indulge in a great variety of efforts to preserve, alter, or eliminate the constraints that are implied by organized existence. This kind of argumentation is an effort to enhance individual and collective self-understanding, as well as to articulate goals and standards and is plainly an invitation to offer reasons justifying one's choice among several alternatives. Among the possible arguments, some might be resolved by an appeal to evidence. Here facts are clearly relevant and in some cases crucial, but no matter how extensively involved, facts cannot be decisive by themselves. No accumulation of factual data can possibly yield an answer to the questions, "what ought we to mean by 'equality,' " or "what ought we to do"? Nor are the facts decisive when the questions one is asking involve the adequacy of an argument's logical coherence.

At the level of meaning and of value, then, we are discussing choice and decision, rather than answers or solutions; of considered judgments, rather than doctrine; reasons, rather than formulas; argument rather than assertion or rhetoric, issuing in judgments of worth and obligation. It follows that philosophical questions cannot be definitively answered. Does this mean that philosophical questions are simply unresolvable, with the implication that it is therefore futile to ask them? We cannot settle such questions "once and for all." But, for that matter, what questions can we settle once and for all? Men can and do ignore these questions, but that does not mean that they vanish. The fundamental reason it is not possible to settle philosophical questions definitively is very simple and extremely important. Philosophical questions must be persistent because there are simply no limits to what men can mean when they employ language; the variety of possible meanings we intend to convey by signs and symbols is infinite. This does not mean that we must always ask the same questions, that we must ponder certain allegedly "perennial" questions. Perenniality is not a conclusive reason for considering a problem, for there is at least the possibility, that a perennial problem is no longer a real problem. Moreover, it is possible that common labels cover quite different problems. In part, we do not ask precisely the same questions, for the same reasons, as others have done. Our questions share with traditional problems in political philosophy the effort to marshal as sound an argument as possible on the questions of substantive political morality. As always, our capacity to create meanings deprives us of the possibility of definitive answers, but it does not relieve us of the necessity to go on choosing, making judgments about worth or obligation, for even the refusal to choose is inescapably a choice. All that must be assumed in order to recognize the worth of philosophical inquiry in politics is that reasoned argument, to some unknown degree, is apt to produce a more nearly adequate judgment than the failure to think.

Supposing that we are prepared to make this kind of wager on the uses of reasoned argument, we will now explore the second of the major problems indicated above: the distinctions that ought to be made between political philosophy and a variety of other sorts of intellectual activity bearing on politics. The most obvious of these can be identified as political opinion. Historically, political philosophy involves the claim that somehow it rises above the ordinary collisions of political opinion. But can we say anything more? As in many issues of this kind, it is a matter of degree, for a man's political opinions may be more or less articulate or sophisticated. But we do not insist that a man defend his opinion by sustained argument in order to be entitled to it, though this is a minimum requirement for a philosophical position. Further, a philosophical justification for a view requires what may be referred to as a self-consciously critical perspective, which involves awareness of arguments against one's views, countervailing considerations that have been taken into account in framing one's own argument. In other words, a critical perspective includes at least tacit dialogue with rival views. In this way, a political philosophy issues a general invitation to prosecute the argument. A political philosophy claims that its outcome is the result of following the comparatively impersonal demands of logic and evidence, in combination with the questions of value that are involved; it represents, ideally, an effort to follow the argument wherever it leads. Of course, the prosecution of this ideal is often less than complete, but human limitations do not involve the defeat of the principle. On the contrary, it is precisely the formation of alternative views that makes us aware of those limitations.

In sum, it seems clear that there are sufficient reasons for distinguishing sharply between political opinion and political philosophy. However, in dealing with that distinction, there is bound to be a difference between the ideal of political philosophy and the more or less extensive failure of some writers to fulfill the relevant expectations. Nor are such failings restricted to logical or factual error. They may also result from the unarticulated and undefended intrusion of the author's values, biases, interests and so on. It is this last possibility which gives rise to a more complicated problem than the one just considered, namely, the difference between political philosophy and ideology. This is a formidable problem for anyone maintaining the view that is being defended here — that political philosophy is a distinct kind of intellectual enterprise — because it is impossible to deny completely the influence of an author's biases on his theoretical work. On the other hand, stated in this way, the problem is manageable, in the sense that it does not create any general barrier. Alternative arguments supply a corrective here. But the problem has been sharply exacerbated by a much broader claim that descends from the Marxian concept of ideology.

In the last hundred years, many Western intellectuals have learned to treat ideas primarily, and some authors exclusively, in terms of the concept of ideology.[5] Whatever else may be said about it, this idea has been at once fruitful and damaging: fruitful in the sense that it has served to disarm a great deal of pretentious nonsense; damaging in the sense that it has produced an inclination to suppose that all social thought can be reduced to ideology, in the specific sense that it is determined by the social context in which it appears. It follows from this last, extreme view not merely that all judgments and the knowledge on which they rest are liable to distortion through the unacknowledged influence of bias, but that all knowledge is only relative, since it is inevitably the reflection of the thinker's place in history and society. This variant of ideology, known as the sociology of knowledge,[6] can be both illuminating and intellectually crippling. For on the one hand, valuable insights may be acquired by devoting sustained attention to the historical and social situation in which a theory arose. On the other hand, this emphasis is elevated to a perfectly general account of what must occur in the realm of social inquiry. From such a claim, it is only a short step from illumination

---

[5] See Judith N. Shklar, ed., *Political Theory and Ideology* (New York: Macmillan, 1966), "Introduction"; and Shklar, "Facing up to Intellectual Pluralism," in Spitz, ed., *Political Theory and Social Change*, pp. 275–295; George Lichtheim, *The Concept of Ideology and Other Essays* (New York: Vintage Books, 1967), pp. 3–46; Richard H. Cox, ed., *Ideology, Politics, and Political Theory* (Belmont, Calif.: Wadsworth, Inc., 1969).

[6] The classical expression of the sociology of knowledge may be found in Karl Mannheim, *Ideology and Utopia* (London: Kegan Paul, 1936).

to profound intellectual bafflement, for if knowledge of human affairs is necessarily relative in this way, the door is open to the most thoroughgoing skepticism. Fortunately, if the thesis of the sociology of knowledge is cast in this uncompromising way, it is possible to argue that it is self-defeating.

If it is true that all social thought is determined by some constellation of social factors that differ over time, then what is the status of the sociology of knowledge itself? If it is allowed to be socially determined in this way, then it is just as relative as any other body of social thought. In short, it cannot be true, in the sense of "objectively valid." On the other hand, if at least the sociology of knowledge is objectively true, this admits the possibility of objective knowledge in social inquiry, and if that is so in one case, why not in others? [7] In sum, the sociology of knowledge does not and cannot supply adequate evidence that social theory reduces to ideology. At most it supplies an emphasis that can be usefully employed, depending on the kind of inquiry being prosecuted.

We may conclude, then, that if the reduction of thought to ideology means what the sociology of knowledge alleges, it can be rejected. Of course, that does not eliminate the possibility that "ideology" may be intended to convey a quite different meaning. So, for instance, many uses of the phrase suggest nothing more than the observation that a man's theory reflects or embodies his political preferences. If that is the full meaning, there is no serious problem, for there is no reason men should not express their preferences, attempt to justify them, and try to persuade others of their merits. In short, the extreme claims advanced in the campaign to reduce thought to ideology fail, though claims that fall short of the extreme do not constitute any theoretical barriers to the kind of philosophical enterprise being explored here.

Thus far we have suggested that there are good reasons for insisting on the merits of recognizing and engaging in arguments designed to support judgments of value and obligation. Such decisions are among the most important elements in any debate about governmental policy. The question is, then, ought we to consider that normative political philosophy is ultimately indistinguishable from the ac-

[7] See Ernest Nagel, *The Structure of Science* (New York: Harcourt, Brace & World, 1961), pp. 498–502.

tivity of urging one or another choice at the level of public policy? A judgment on an issue of public policy can be recognized as an important undertaking, and it may be a part, or even the ultimate intention, of an individual's philosophical inquiry, without concluding that it is the same thing. In coming to this kind of decision, it is seldom necessary to engage in such arguments as whether there ought to be any coercive institutions at all, or whether the representatives of the people really ought to be invested with the authority to decide. Perhaps political decisions ought to be made by trained experts, or by those who possess an extraordinary degree of moral wisdom or, again, perhaps we ought to trust our natural impulses? These are some alternatives that have been repeatedly debated. In the ordinary course of policy choice, there is an understandable and quite reasonable inclination to assume a great many things as given, but it is precisely one of the primary functions of political philosophy to question those assumptions and the justifications supplied for them.

Similar considerations can be brought to the problem of distinguishing political philosophy from judgments of practicality or feasibility. To ask questions about "workability," of course, seems very hardheaded. But is this really so? At least two considerations are important here. To begin with, the view that the test of an idea's worth is its workability appears to assume that thought is an exclusively problem-solving activity. If the idea of problem-solving is made broad enough, it might be possible to characterize all thought in this way. But the price of expanding the idea to include everything would be the loss of its critical thrust, for it is designed, after all, to reproach some lines of thought. Moreover, unless it excludes some kinds of thinking, it is transformed into an uninformative tautology: thinking = problem-solving, therefore, thinking = thinking. Thus if the criterion of workability is to represent a distinctive intellectual outlook, it must exclude some considerations. The difficulty is the importance of what it excludes. Just as in the case of policy decisions, the idea of workability presumes that we both know and agree about the goals to be reached, that we agree about what is and what is not a problem, and which problems can and should be solved. In short, a problem-solving approach does not raise the question of whether a thing ought to be done at all. Furthermore, even supposing that some men engage in sustained debate concerning the worth of the ends in view, at least one important task remains: the utopian task. The point was made well by Nietzsche: "My aim is to disturb people." The idea of a utopian demand is that it lies beyond our power to attain it, but articulating it may nonetheless supply us with a new angle of vision, with moral illumination, as well as a worthy and demanding standard. This is surely not an instrumental task (though it might be defended on such grounds), and it is just as surely not an unworthy one.

We have now discussed the two major sorts of problems and briefly characterized and defended a view of the discipline of political philosophy; we shall conclude by indicating some limitations of this kind of intellectual activity. It is sometimes suggested that a truly adequate political philosophy ought to provide men with specific answers to concrete moral and political problems. This demand is excessive. For no system of principles, whether it is religious, philosophical, political, or ideological (defined as an image of the future and a strategy to attain it) — no system of principles can really provide these answers. It cannot, at any rate, if this demand is interpreted at all strictly, if what is meant is that the principles should provide automatic answers to the endless variety of situations in which men find themselves. It is understandable that men should desire such a system, but it is not attainable, for in the last resort neither facts, nor reasons, nor principles compel a single, unambiguous choice. Events do not appear wearing labels, indicating what they are. On the contrary, a man must decide that the facts ought to be characterized in a specific way, and then — and only then — can he apply whatever principles he has chosen to embrace. Even so, the decision to undertake a course of action may not be either automatic or easy. For each man must also resolve the problem of being involved in multiple and, perhaps, conflicting commitments and relations of obligation. Because a man may consider that he owes specific duties to family, friends, a variety of organizations, his country, or, perhaps, that his religion or his moral and political principles impose duties upon him, it follows that the decision as to which obligation shall take precedence must be an individual matter. Each of us, in short, has different obligations, as well as some that are shared, so that a general principle can provide only a guide, a criterion, and not an unequivocal answer. Nor is even this degree of complexity the end of the matter. One might conclude that a set of facts merited description as intolerable tyranny. Even supposing that he has successfully resolved the problems of multiple obligations, it does not follow that specific *actions* are justifiable, such as the decision to engage in some form of resistance. To begin with, he will have to consider the possibility that his fellow citizens may not agree with his assessment of the situation and may, indeed, feel that they must oppose him. Further, it might be that his judgment is very widely shared, but others may not agree that resistance is the appropriate response. For the judgment could be made that the force to be opposed is so formidable that resistance would be futile, or that it might merely worsen an already desperate situation. Decisions in such circumstances are among the most difficult that men can confront. It is only reasonable, therefore, that a political philosophy should involve consideration of them, of the problem of what men should consider as giving rise to obligations, of the problem of weighing different and conflicting duties, and of the cogency of the reasons offered for choice. But a political philosophy cannot produce an automatic reply. Individual responsibility for choice cannot be eliminated. Even if one has adopted a set of principles that includes detailed lists of appropriate responses, the individual still has had to adopt that set of principles. Thus, any attempt to elude the responsibility and difficulty of choice by appealing to the compulsion of general principles is bound to be an evasion. No conceivable political philosophy could accomplish this task for its proper function is not moral and intellectual tyranny, but illumination. It may provide criteria, considerations to be taken into account, perhaps even a full and logically coherent set of principles, but it is not and cannot be a substitute for thought and choice. All that a thought process can do, and it is not a little, is to make the choice more or less well informed.

Furthermore, reasons can be advanced for the view that it is a good thing that principles cannot coerce, rather than seeing it as something to be regretted. To pretend that the situation is otherwise, that some source of direction ought to exist that would relieve one of the responsibility for making a reasoned choice is just that — a pretense. To operate on such an assumption is to run a considerable risk; it is to risk dulling one's awareness, one's sense of critical appraisal as he confronts society and politics. In other words, if one supposes that such standards exist, he may awake from his critical slumber to find that he faces a hopeless situation. Further, and perhaps most important, the assumption that there are standards that are both general and yet compelling in specific circumstances deprives men of the ultimate source of their dignity — the freedom and the responsibility to choose for themselves.

# OBLIGATION AND DISSENT

# PART ONE

# POLITICAL OBLIGATION

# Introduction

The most important, probably the most exciting and most difficult problem in political theory is political obligation. It is the age-old problem of "when should I obey the State"? This question has reappeared today, as in the past, and many men and women have found themselves forced to ponder the possible answers.

It may well be that men think about this question seriously only in times in which consensus in a society or a civilization has eroded, conflict has risen, and doubt has spread about what one ought to do and to be in relation to one's political community. In any case, again and again the problem has appeared to face men in our time, and has lost none of its centrality or difficulty.

The problem of political obligation is fundamental to many of our contemporary moral and political disputes and agonies. It is not the only basis usually, but often it is the most important. Disputes over the proper limits of dissent and the grounds of revolution are, in part, over what men may do if they are, or if they are not, politically obligated. Disputes in particular over allegedly oppressed minorities and their proper political behavior also in part deal with political obligation and its nature and limits.

Similarly, disputes over the trials and treatment of political dissenters such as the Chicago Seven and the Black Panthers partially question who is an obligated citizen, what may he do, and what may be done to him if he is or is not obligated. The same applies to moral issues that arise in our time of war and dispute about war. Claims about pacifism, about conscientious objection and selective conscientious objection, all center on the moral question of the nature of political obligation and how it ought to be reconciled with other obligations.

Even these examples by no means exhaust the range of problems of our troubled time to which political obligation is essential. Even

3

if our times were perfectly placid and a citizen never found himself in actual or potential conflict with or in doubt about his relationship to his political community or his government, political obligation would remain a vital concern for any person seeking an understanding of himself and his world, and his proper place in it. The state looms over every man, sometimes near and sometimes remote, but always it is there. No one can — or should — avoid facing it and the question of the morally acceptable relationship between citizen and state.

Most theorists of political obligation seem to agree that the relationship between a citizen and his general political community, or his government alone, what we call political obligation, is one of moral duty. That is, political obligation is something that the citizen owes, if he is obligated. He may owe that obligation in return for nothing at all or he may owe it in return for clearly stated services or gains, reciprocities. He may owe it forever or for clearly stated limits of time, as a child, as an adult, or never. He may owe it because of or in spite of his conscience; or, he may not owe it if his conscience does not permit. He may owe it despite his other moral obligations to his family or friends, or because of them; or they may overrule his political obligation. The varied possibilities of understanding of political obligation and its conditions are endless, which is why the problem is so fascinatingly complex.

Political theorists have argued about all these varieties for several thousand years. But they have argued especially about the foundations of political obligation, about how a man becomes obligated and unobligated politically. This crucial matter will be explored in this first section of the book.

Several bases for political obligation have been advocated over the years. Some theorists have argued that men are obligated to their political communities according to the standards and limits provided for in divine law or universal natural laws. Others have stressed tradition or convention as the ultimate sources and guides for political obligation. Still others have made the key criterion individual or social utility. Most often in recent centuries, consent has been stressed as the basis of political obligation; a man is obligated to his political community if and only if he has consented or chosen to be. Since political obligation is a moral relationship, and choice is the essence of morality, one can be obligated only if one has made a choice.

More than any other works in the history of political philosophy Plato's *Crito* explores the complexities and dilemmas of political obligation and the grounds on which it may be justified or denied in a challenging way. This report of Socrates' discussion in prison before his death is actually a thorough consideration of the proper basis of political obligation. In his arguments Socrates considers most of the possible types of justification for political obligation in a context that brings alive the sometimes crucial and personal nature of the quest to understand.

The selections by professors Pitkin and Fowler are part of the lively contemporary dispute about the adequacy of the common consent basis for political obligation. These political theorists are responding to contemporary division and confusion about when men ought to obey; Professor Fowler in particular makes this clear by examining whether men are obligated to a military draft. Each attempts to meet opposing views of appropriate consent and obligation; and each is clearly in disagreement with the other. Professor Pitkin stresses the necessity of individual consent as a basis for political obligation and Professor Fowler the necessity for concern with "community-regardingness" as well as individual consent. In their dispute the theoretical issues are laid bare and clarified.

Certainly these three readings are the most difficult in the book, but they are the gateway to the specific problems of obligation, dissent, and enforcement that are often the focus of contemporary political morality. To elucidate specific moral problems in politics one must genuinely attempt to gain a solid theoretical foundation. These three readings begin that attempt.

# General Theories of Obligation

## Crito

### PLATO

PERSONS OF THE DIALOGUE

*Socrates.*        *Crito.*

*Scene:* The Prison of Socrates

*Socrates.* Why have you come at this hour, Crito? it must be quite early?

*Crito.* Yes, certainly.

*Soc.* What is the exact time?

*Cr.* The dawn is breaking.

*Soc.* I wonder that the keeper of the prisoner would let you in.

*Cr.* He knows me, because I often come, Socrates; moreover, I have done him a kindness.

*Soc.* And are you only just arrived?

*Cr.* No, I came some time ago.

*Soc.* Then why did you sit and say nothing, instead of at once awakening me?

*Cr.* I should not have liked myself, Socrates, to be in such great trouble and unrest as you are — indeed I should not: I have been watching with amazement your peaceful slumbers; and for that reason I did not awake you, because I wished to minimize the pain. I have always thought you to be of a happy disposition; but never did I see

From Plato, *The Last Days of Socrates,* translated by Hugh Tredennick. Reprinted by permission of Penguin Books Ltd.

anything like the easy, tranquil manner in which you bear this calamity.

*Soc.* Why, Crito, when a man has reached my age he ought not to be repining at the approach of death.

*Cr.* And yet other old men find themselves in similar misfortunes, and age does not prevent them from repining.

*Soc.* That is true. But you have not told me why you come at this early hour.

*Cr.* I come to bring you a message which is sad and painful; not, as I believe, to yourself, but to all of us who are your friends, and saddest of all to me.

*Soc.* What? Has the ship come from Delos, on the arrival of which I am to die?

*Cr.* No, the ship has not actually arrived, but she will probably be here to-day, as persons who have come from Sunium tell me that they left her there; and therefore tomorrow, Socrates, will be the last day of your life.

*Soc.* Very well, Crito; if such is the will of God, I am willing; but my belief is that there will be a delay of a day.

*Cr.* Why do you think so?

*Soc.* I will tell you. I am to die on the day after the arrival of the ship.

*Cr.* Yes; that is what the authorities say.

*Soc.* But I do not think that the ship will be here until to-morrow; this I infer from a vision which I had last night, or rather only just now, when you fortunately allowed me to sleep.

*Cr.* And what was the nature of the vision?

*Soc.* There appeared to me the likeness of a woman, fair and comely, clothed in bright raiment, who called to me and said: O Socrates,

"The third day hence to fertile Phthia shalt thou go." [1]

*Cr.* What a singular dream, Socrates!

*Soc.* There can be no doubt about the meaning, Crito, I think.

*Cr.* Yes; the meaning is only too clear. But, oh! my beloved Socrates, let me entreat you once more to take my advice and escape. For if you die I shall not only lose a friend who can never be replaced, but there is another evil: people who do not know you and me will

[1] Homer, Il. ix. 363.

believe that I might have saved you if I had been willing to give money, but that I did not care. Now, can there be a worse disgrace than this — that I should be thought to value money more than the life of friend? For the many will not be persuaded that I wanted you to escape, and that you refused.

*Soc.* But why, my dear Crito, should we care about the opinion of the many? Good men, and they are the only persons who are worth considering, will think of these things truly as they occurred.

*Cr.* But you see, Socrates, that the opinion of the many must be regarded, for what is now happening shows that they can do the greatest evil to any one who has lost their good opinion.

*Soc.* I only wish it were so, Crito; and that the many could do the greatest evil; for then they would also be able to do the greatest good — and what a fine thing this would be! But in reality they can do neither; for they cannot make a man either wise or foolish; and whatever they do is the result of chance.

*Cr.* Well, I will not dispute with you; but please to tell me, Socrates, whether you are not acting out of regard to me and your other friends: are you not afraid that if you escape from prison we may get into trouble with the informers for having stolen you away, and lose either the whole or a great part of our property; or that even a worse evil may happen to us? Now, if you fear on our account, be at ease; for in order to save you, we ought surely to run this, or even a greater risk; be persuaded, then, and do as I say.

*Soc.* Yes, Crito, that is one fear which you mention, but by no means the only one.

*Cr.* Fear not — there are persons who are willing to get you out of prison at no great cost; and as for the informers, they are far from being exorbitant in their demands — a little money will satisfy them. My means, which are certainly ample, are at your service, and if you have a scruple about spending all mine, here are strangers who will give you the use of theirs; and one of them, Simmias the Theban, has brought a large sum of money for this very purpose; and Cebes and many others are prepared to spend their money in helping you to escape. I say, therefore, do not hesitate on our account, and do not say, as you did in the court,[2] that you will have a difficulty in knowing what to do with yourself anywhere else. For men will love you in

[2] Cp. Apol. 37 C, D.

other places to which you may go, and not in Athens only; there are friends of mine in Thessaly, if you like to go to them, who will value and protect you, and no Thessalian will give you any trouble. Nor can I think that you are at all justified, Socrates, in betraying your own life when you might be saved; in acting thus you are playing into the hands of your enemies, who are hurrying on your destruction. And further I should say that you are deserting your own children; for you might bring them up and educate them; instead of which you go away and leave them, and they will have to take their chance; and if they do not meet with the usual fate of orphans, there will be small thanks to you. No man should bring children into the world who is unwilling to persevere to the end in their nurture and education. But you appear to be choosing the easier part, not the better and manlier, which would have been more becoming in one who professes to care for virtue in all his actions, like yourself. And, indeed, I am ashamed not only of you, but of us who are your friends, when I reflect that the whole business will be attributed entirely to our want of courage. The trial need never have come on, or might have been managed differently; and this last act, or crowning folly, will seem to have occurred through our negligence and cowardice, who might have saved you, if we had been good for anything; and you might have saved yourself, for there was no difficulty at all. See now, Socrates, how sad and discreditable are the consequences, both to us and you. Make up your mind, then, or rather have your mind already made up, for the time of deliberation is over, and there is only one thing to be done, which must be done this very night, and if we delay at all will be no longer practicable or possible; I beseech you therefore, Socrates, be persuaded by me, and do as I say.

*Soc.* Dear Crito, your zeal is invaluable, if a right one; but if wrong, the greater the  zeal the greater the danger; and therefore we ought to consider whether I shall or shall not do as you say. For I am and always have been one of those natures who must be guided by reason, whatever the reason may be which upon reflection appears to me to be the best; and now that this chance has befallen me, I cannot repudiate my own words: the principles which I have hitherto honoured and revered I still honour, and unless we can at once find other and better principles, I am certain not to agree with you; no, not even if the power of the multitude could inflict many more im- prisonments, confiscations, deaths, frightening us like children with hobgoblin terrors.[3] What will be the fairest way of considering the question? Shall I return to your old argument about the opinions of men? — we were saying that some of them are to be regarded, and others not. Now, were we right in maintaining this before I was condemned? And has the argument which was once good now proved to be talk for the sake of talking — mere childish nonsense? That is what I want to consider with your help, Crito: — whether, under my present circumstances, the argument appears to be in any way different or not; and is to be allowed by me or disallowed. That argument, which, as I believe, is maintained by many persons of authority, was to the effect, as I was saying, that the opinions of some men are to be regarded, and of other men not to be regarded. Now you, Crito, are not going to die to-morrow — at least, there is no human probability of this — and therefore you are disinterested and not liable to be deceived by the circumstances in which you are placed. Tell me, then, whether I am right in saying that some opinions, and the opinions of some men only, are to be valued, and that other opinions, and the opinions of other men, are not to be valued. I ask you whether I was right in maintaining this?

*Cr*. Certainly.

*Soc*. The good are to be regarded, and not the bad?

*Cr*. Yes.

*Soc*. And the opinions of the wise are good, and the opinions of the unwise are evil?

*Cr*. Certainly.

*Soc*. And what was said about another matter? Is the pupil who devotes himself to the practice of gymnastics supposed to attend to the praise and blame and opinion of every man, or of one man only — his physician or trainer, whoever he may be?

*Cr*. Of one man only.

*Soc*. And he ought to fear the censure and welcome the praise of that one only, and not of the many?

*Cr*. Clearly so.

*Soc*. And he ought to act and train, and eat and drink in the way which seems good to his single master who has understanding, rather than according to the opinion of all other men put together?

*Cr*. True.

[3] Cp. Apol. 30 C.

*Soc*. And if he disobeys and disregards the opinion and approval of the one, and regards the opinion of the many who have no understanding, will he not suffer?

*Cr*. Certainly he will.

*Soc*. And what will the evil be, whither tending and what affecting, in the disobedient person?

*Cr*. Clearly, affecting the body; that is what is destroyed by the evil.

*Soc*. Very good; and is not this true, Crito, of other things which we need not separately enumerate? In questions of just and unjust, fair and foul, good and evil, which are the subjects of our present consultation, ought we to follow the opinion of the many and to fear them; or the opinion of the one man who has understanding? ought we not to fear and reverence him more than all the rest of the world: and if we desert him shall we not destroy and injure that principle in us which may be assumed to be improved by justice and deteriorated by injustice; — there is such a principle?

*Cr*. Certainly there is, Socrates.

*Soc*. Take a parallel instance: — if, acting under the advice of those who have no understanding, we destroy that which is improved by health and is deteriorated by disease would life be worth having? And that which has been destroyed is — the body?

*Cr*. Yes.

*Soc*. Could we live, having an evil and corrupted body?

*Cr*. Certainly not.

*Soc*. And will life be worth having, if that higher part of man be destroyed, which is improved by justice and depraved by injustice? Do we suppose that principle, whatever it may be in man, which has to do with justice and injustice, to be inferior to the body?

*Cr*. Certainly not.

*Soc*. More honourable than the body?

*Cr*. Far more.

*Soc*. Then, my friend, we must not regard what the many say of us: but what he, the one man who has understanding of just and unjust, will say, and what the truth will say. And therefore you begin in error when you advise that we should regard the opinion of the many about just and unjust, good and evil, honourable and dishonourable. — "Well," some one will say, "but the many can kill us."

*Cr*. Yes, Socrates; that will clearly be the answer.

*Soc.* And it is true: but still I find with surprise that the old argument is unshaken as ever. And I should like to know whether I may say the same of another proposition — that not life, but a good life, is to be chiefly valued?

*Cr.* Yes, that also remains unshaken.

*Soc.* And a good life is equivalent to a just and honourable one — that holds also?

*Cr.* Yes, it does.

*Soc.* From these premises I proceed to argue the question whether I ought or ought not to try to escape without the consent of the Athenians: and if I am clearly right in escaping, then I will make the attempt; but if not, I will abstain. The other considerations which you mention, of money and loss of character and the duty of educating one's children, are, I fear, only the doctrines of the multitude, who would be as ready to restore people to life, if they were able, as they are to put them to death — and with as little reason. But now, since the argument has thus far prevailed, the only question which remains to be considered is, whether we shall do rightly either in escaping or in suffering others to aid in our escape and paying them in money and thanks, or whether in reality we shall not do rightly; and if the latter, then death or any other calamity which may ensue on my remaining here must not be allowed to enter into the calculation.

*Cr.* I think that you are right, Socrates; how then shall we proceed?

*Soc.* Let us consider the matter together, and do you either refute me if you can, and I will be convinced; or else cease, my dear friend, from repeating to me that I ought to escape against the wishes of the Athenians: for I highly value your attempts to persuade me to do so, but I may not be persuaded against my own better judgment. And now please to consider my first position, and try how you can best answer me.

*Cr.* I will.

*Soc.* Are we to say that we are never intentionally to do wrong, or that in one way we ought and in another way we ought not to do wrong, or is doing wrong always evil and dishonourable, as I was just now saying, and as has been already acknowledged by us? Are all our former admissions which were made within a few days to be thrown away? And have we, at our age, been earnestly discoursing with one another all our life long only to discover that we are no better than children? Or, in spite of the opinion of the many, and in spite of consequences whether better or worse, shall we insist on the truth of what was then said that injustice is always an evil and dishonour to him who acts unjustly? Shall we say so or not?

*Cr.* Yes.

*Soc.* Then we must do no wrong?

*Cr.* Certainly not.

*Soc.* Nor when injured in return, as the many imagine; for we must injure no one at all? [4]

*Cr.* Clearly not.

*Soc.* Again, Crito, may we do evil?

*Cr.* Surely not, Socrates.

*Soc.* And what of doing evil in return for evil, which is the morality of the many — is that just or not?

*Cr.* Not just.

*Soc.* For doing evil to another is the same as injuring him?

*Cr.* Very true.

*Soc.* Then we ought not to retaliate or render evil for evil to any one, whatever evil we may have suffered from him. But I would have you consider, Crito, whether you really mean what you are saying. For this opinion has never been held, and never will be held, by any considerable number of persons; and those who are agreed and those who are not agreed upon this point have no common ground, and can only despise one another when they see how widely they differ. Tell me, then, whether you agree with and assent to my first principle, that neither injury nor retaliation nor warding off evil by evil is ever right. And shall that be the premise of our argument? Or do you decline and dissent from this? For so I have ever thought, and continue to think; but, if you are of another opinion, let me hear what you have to say. If, however, you remain of the same mind as formerly, I will proceed to the next step.

*Cr.* You may proceed, for I have not changed my mind.

*Soc.* Then I will go on to the next point, which may be put in the form of a question: — Ought a man to do what he admits to be right, or ought he to betray the right?

*Cr.* He ought to do what he thinks right.

*Soc.* But if this is true, what is the application? In leaving the

---

[4] Cp. Rep. i. 355 E.

prison against the will of the Athenians, do I wrong any? or rather do I not wrong those whom I ought least to wrong? Do I not desert the principles which were acknowledged by us to be just — what do you say?

*Cr.* I cannot tell, Socrates; for I do not know.

*Soc.* Then consider the matter in this way: — Imagine that I am about to play truant (you may call the proceeding by any name which you like), and the laws and the government come and interrogate me: "Tell us, Socrates," they say; "what are you about? are you not going by an act of yours to overturn us — the laws, and the whole State, as far as in you lies? Do you imagine that a State can subsist and not be overthrown, in which the decisions of law have no power, but are set aside and trampled upon by individuals?" What will be our answer, Crito, to these and the like words? Any one, and especially a rhetorician, will have a good deal to say on behalf of the law which requires a sentence to be carried out. He will argue that this law should not be set aside; and shall we reply, "Yes; but the State has injured us and given an unjust sentence." Suppose I say that?

*Cr.* Very good, Socrates.

*Soc.* "And was that our agreement with you?" the law would answer; "or were you to abide by the sentence of the State?" And if I were to express my astonishment at their words, the law would probably add: "Answer, Socrates, instead of opening your eyes — you are in the habit of asking and answering questions. Tell us, — What complaint have you to make against us which justifies you in attempting to destroy us and the State? In the first place did we not bring you into existence? Your father married your mother by our aid and begat you. Say whether you have any objection to urge against those of us who regulate marriage?" None, I should reply. "Or against those of us who after birth regulate the nurture and education of children, in which you also were trained? Were not the laws, which have the charge of education, right in commanding your father to train you in music and gymnastic?" Right, I should reply. "Well, then, since you were brought into the world and nurtured and educated by us, can you deny in the first place that you are our child and slave, as your fathers were before you? And if this is true, you are not on equal terms with us; nor can you think that you have a right to do to us what we are doing to you. Would you have any right to strike or revile or do any other evil to your father or your master, if you had one, because you have been struck or reviled by him, or received some other evil at his hands? — you would not say this? And because we think right to destroy you, do you think that you have any right to destroy us in return, and your country as far as in you lies? Will you, O professor of true virtue, pretend that you are justified in this? Has a philosopher like you failed to discover that our country is more to be valued and higher and holier far than mother or father or any ancestor, and more to be regarded in the eyes of the gods and of men of understanding? also to be soothed, and gently and reverently entreated when angry, even more than a father, and either to be persuaded, or if not persuaded, to be obeyed? And when we are punished by her, whether with imprisonment or stripes, the punishment is to be endured in silence; and if she lead us to wounds or death in battle, thither we follow as is right; neither may any one yield or retreat or leave his rank, but whether in battle or in a court of law, or in any other place, he must do what his city and his country order him; or he must change their view of what is just: and if he may do no violence to his father or mother, much less may he do violence to his country." What answer shall we make to this, Crito? Do the laws speak truly, or do they not?

*Cr.* I think that they do.

*Soc.* Then the laws will say: "Consider, Socrates, if we are speaking truly that in your present attempt you are going to do us an injury. For, having brought you into the world, and nurtured and educated you, and given you and every other citizen a share in every good which we had to give, we further proclaim to any Athenian by the liberty which we allow him, that if he does not like us when he has become of age and has seen the ways of the city, and made our acquaintance, he may go where he pleases and take his goods with him. None of our laws will forbid him or interfere with him. Any one who does not like us and the city, and who wants to emigrate to a colony or to any other city, may go where he likes, retaining his property. But he who has experience of the manner in which we order justice and administer the State, and still remains, has entered into an implied contract that he will do as we command him. And he who disobeys us is, as we maintain, thrice wrong; first, because in disobeying us he is disobeying his parents; secondly, because we are the authors of his education; thirdly, because he has made an agreement with us that he will duly obey our commands; and he neither obeys them nor convinces us that our commands are unjust; and we do not rudely impose them, but give him the alternative of obeying or convincing us; — that is what we offer, and he does neither.

"These are the sort of accusations to which, as we were saying, you, Socrates, will be exposed if you accomplish your intentions; you, above all other Athenians." Suppose now I ask, why I rather than anybody else? they will justly retort upon me that I above all other men have acknowledged the agreement. "There is clear proof," they will say, "Socrates, that we and the city were not displeasing to you. Of all Athenians you have been the most constant resident in the city, which, as you never leave, you may be supposed to love.[5] For you never went out of the city either to see the games, except once when you went to the Isthmus, or to any other place unless when you were on military service; nor did you travel as other men do. Nor had you any curiosity to know other States or their laws: your affections did not go beyond us and our State; we were your special favourites, and you acquiesced in our government of you; and here in this city you begat your children, which is a proof of your satisfaction. Moreover, you might in the course of the trial, if you had liked, have fixed the penalty at banishment; the State which refuses to let you go now would have let you go then. But you pretended that you preferred death to exile,[6] and that you were not unwilling to die. And now you have forgotten these fine sentiments, and pay no respect to us, the laws, of whom you are the destroyer; and are doing what only a miserable slave would do, running away and turning your back upon the compacts and agreements which you made as a citizen. And, first of all, answer this very question: Are we right in saying that you agreed to be governed according to us in deed, and not in word only? Is that true or not?" How shall we answer, Crito? Must we not assent?

*Cr.* We cannot help it, Socrates.

*Soc.* Then will they not say: "You, Socrates, are breaking the covenants and agreements which you made with us at your leisure, not in any haste or under any compulsion or deception, but after you have had seventy years to think of them, during which time you were at liberty to leave the city, if we were not to your mind, or if our covenants appeared to you to be unfair. You had your choice, and

---

[5] Cp. Phaedr. 230 C.
[6] Cp. Apol. 37 D.

might have gone either to Lacedaemon or Crete, both which States are often praised by you for their good government, or to some other Hellenic or foreign State. Whereas you, above all other Athenians, seemed to be so fond of the State, or, in other words, of us, her laws (and who would care about a State which has no laws?), that you never stirred out of her; the halt, the blind, the maimed were not more stationary in her than you were. And now you run away and forsake your agreements. Not so, Socrates, if you will take our advice; do not make yourself ridiculous by escaping out of the city.

"For just consider, if you transgress and err in this sort of way, what good will you do either to yourself or to your friends? That your friends will be driven into exile and deprived of citizenship, or will lose their property, is tolerably certain; and you yourself, if you fly to one of the neighbouring cities, as, for example, Thebes or Megara, both of which are well governed, will come to them as an enemy, Socrates, and their government will be against you, and all patriotic citizens will cast an evil eye upon you as a subverter of the laws, and you will confirm in the minds of the judges the justice of their own condemnation of you. For he who is a corrupter of the law, is more than likely to be a corrupter of the young and foolish portion of mankind. Will you then flee from well-ordered cities and virtuous men? and is existence worth having on these terms? Or will you go to them without shame, and talk to them, Socrates? And what will you say to them? What you say here about virtue and justice and institutions and laws being the best things among men? Would that be decent of you? Surely not. But if you go away from well-governed States to Crito's friends in Thessaly, where there is great disorder and licence, they will be charmed to hear the tale of your escape from prison, set off with ludicrous particulars of the manner in which you were wrapped in a goatskin or some other disguise, and metamorphosed as the manner is of runaways; but will there be no one to remind you that in your old age you were not ashamed to violate the most sacred laws from a miserable desire of a little more life? Perhaps not, if you keep them in a good temper; but if they are out of temper you will hear many degrading things; you will live, but how? — as the flatterer of all men, and the servant of all men; and doing what? — eating and drinking in Thessaly, having gone abroad in order that you may get a dinner. And where will be your fine sentiments about justice and virtue? Say that you wish to live for the sake of your children —

you want to bring them up and educate them — will you take them into Thessaly and deprive them of Athenian citizenship? Is this the benefit which you will confer upon them? Or are you under the impression that they will be better cared for and educated here if you are still alive, although absent from them; for your friends will take care of them? Do you fancy that if you are an inhabitant of Thessaly they will take care of them, and if you are an inhabitant of the other world that they will not take care of them? Nay; but if they who call themselves friends are good for anything, they will — to be sure they will.

"Listen, then, Socrates, to us who have brought you up. Think not of life and children first, and of justice afterwards, but of justice first, that you may be justified before the princes of the world below. For neither will you nor any that belong to you be happier or holier or juster in this life, or happier in another, if you do as Crito bids. Now you depart in innocence, a sufferer and not a doer of evil, a victim, not of the laws but of men. But if you go forth returning evil for evil, and injury for injury, breaking the covenants and agreements which you have made with us and wronging those whom you ought least of all to wrong, that is to say, yourself, your friends, your country, and us, we shall be angry with you while you live, and our brethren, the laws in the world below, will receive you as an enemy; for they will know that you have done your best to destroy us. Listen, then, to us and not to Crito."

This, dear Crito, is the voice which I seem to hear murmuring in my ears, like the sound of the flute in the ears of the mystic; that voice, I say, is humming in my ears, and prevents me from hearing any other. And I know that anything more which you may say will be vain. Yet speak, if you have anything to say.

*Cr.* I have nothing to say, Socrates.

*Soc.* Leave me then, Crito, to fulfill the will of God, and to follow whither he leads.

---

# Obligation and Consent — II

## HANNA PITKIN

A reexamination of even the most venerable traditional problems of political theory can sometimes yield surprisingly new and relevant results.[1] The problem of political obligation, for example, and its most popular "solution," based on consent, turn out on reexamination to be rather different from what we have come to assume about them. The problem of political obligation resolves itself into at least four mutually related but partially independent questions:

    1. The limits of obligation ("*When* are you obligated to obey, and when not?")
    2. The locus of sovereignty ("*Whom* are you obligated to obey?")
    3. The difference between legitimate authority and mere coercion ("Is there *really* any difference; are you ever *really* obligated?")
    4. The justification of obligation ("*Why* are you ever obligated to obey even a legitimate authority?")

And the consent theory of obligation, as exemplified in Locke's *Second Treatise* and Joseph Tussman's *Obligation and the Body Politic,* turns out to yield a new formulation — perhaps a new interpretation of consent theory, perhaps an alternative to it — that might be labelled either the doctrine of the "nature of the government" or the doctrine of "hypothetical consent." [2]

    It teaches that your obligation depends not on any actual act of consenting, past or present, by yourself or your fellow-citizens, but on the character of the government. If it is a good, just government doing what a government should, then you must obey it; if it is a

From *The American Political Science Review* (March, 1966). Reprinted by permission of The American Political Science Association.
[1] This and part of the following paragraph are intended to summarize the argument of "Obligation and Consent — I," *American Political Science Review,* 59 (December, 1965), pp. 990–999.
[2] John Locke, *Second Treatise of Civil Government;* Joseph Tussman, *Obligation and the Body Politic* (New York: Oxford, 1960).

tyrannical, unjust government trying to do what no government may, then you have no such obligation. Or to put it another way, your obligation depends not on whether you have consented but on whether the government is such that you *ought* to consent to it, whether its actions are in accord with the authority a hypothetical group of rational men in a hypothetical state of nature would have (had) to give to any government they were founding. Having shown how this formulation emerges from Locke's and Tussman's ideas, I want now to defend it as a valid response to what troubles us about political obligation, and as a response more consonant than most with the moral realities of human decisions about obedience and resistance. At the same time the discussion should also demonstrate how many different or even conflicting things that one might want to call "consent" continue to be relevant — a fact which may help to explain the tenacity of traditional consent theory in the face of its manifest difficulties. Such a defense and demonstration, with detailed attention to such decisions, are difficult; the discussion from here on will be more speculative, and will raise more questions than it answers.

### THE THEORY APPLIED

Our new doctrine seems most obviously satisfactory as a response to question three, concerning the difference between legitimate authority and mere coercion. For it teaches that legitimate authority is precisely that which *ought* to be obeyed, to which one ought to consent, which deserves obedience and consent, to which rational men considering all relevant facts and issues would consent, to which consent can be justified. Anything or anyone else who tries to command us is then merely coercing, and is not entitled to our obedience. This answer to the question is essentially what Wittgenstein calls a "point of grammar"; it reminds us of the way concepts like "authority," "legitimacy," "law" are related in our language (and therefore in our world) to concepts like "consent" and "obedience." [3] To call something a legitimate authority is normally to imply that it ought to be obeyed. You cannot, without further rather elaborate

---

[3] Ludwig Wittgenstein, *Philosophical Investigations* (New York: Macmillan, 1953). See also Stanley Louis Cavell, "The Claim to Rationality" (Unpublished Ph.D. dissertation, Harvard University, 1961), esp. Chapter I.

explanation, maintain simultaneously *both* that this government has legitimate authority over you *and* that you have no obligation to obey it. Thus if you say that you consent to it (recognize it as an authority), that statement itself is normally a recognition of the obligation to obey, at least at the moment it is uttered. Part of what "authority" means is that those subject to it are obligated to obey. As an answer to question three, then, this doctrine tells us (something about) what legitimate authority *is* by reminding us of something about what "legitimate authority" *means*. But of course that is not yet to provide criteria for telling apart the two species — legitimate authority and mere coercion — when you encounter them in reality.

Thus, insofar as our *real* need is for a practical way of deciding whether to obey or resist this government right now, or which of two rival authorities to follow, our new theory seems less adequate. Its response to our question three does not seem immediately helpful with questions one and two; and surely those are of the most concern to real people confronted with decisions about action. It just does not seem very helpful to tell a man considering resistance to authority: you must obey if the government is such that you ought to obey. But neither is traditional consent theory very helpful to this man; indeed, one of its weaknesses has always been this matter of detailed application. Perhaps it is even a mistake to assume that a theory of political obligation is supposed to tell a man directly what to do in particular cases.[4]

One might argue, however, that such a theory should at least tell him what sorts of considerations are relevant to his decision, direct his attention and tell him where to look.[5] And in that regard, I suggest that traditional consent theory is defective, for it directs such a man's attention to the wrong place. It teaches him to look at himself (for his own consent) or at the people around him (for theirs), rather than at the merits of the government. Where it demands obedience, consent theory does so on the grounds that he or the majority have consented; where it justifies resistance, it does so

[4] See, for example, Margaret Macdonald, "The Language of Political Theory," in A. Flew, ed., *Logic and Language: First Series* (Oxford: Basil Blackwell, 1960), pp. 167–186.

[5] This suggestion is advanced, against Miss Macdonald's argument, in S. I. Benn and R. S. Peters, *Social Principles and the Democratic State* (London: George Allen & Unwin, 1959), pp. 299–301.

on the grounds that consent was never given or has been exceeded. Thus the man who must choose is directed to the question: have I (we) consented to this? The new doctrine formulated in this essay seems at least to have the virtue of pointing such a man in the right direction. For it tells him: look to the nature of the government — its characteristics, structure, activities, functioning. This is not much of a guide, but it is a beginning much more usefully related to what men need to think about when they make such choices.

Let us consider seriously what sorts of things people really think about when they confront a genuine decision about obedience and resistance, and what sorts of things they ought to think about. But anyone who undertakes to do that is immediately overwhelmed by the complexity and multiplicity of what seems relevant, and by the many different imaginable cases. We need to consider a list of specific cases at least as diverse as these:

Socrates, as presented in the *Crito* and the *Apology*.
An ordinary criminal.
An American student engaging in civil disobedience.
A Mississippi Negro who decides to join a revolutionary group.
A South African Negro who decides to join a revolutionary group.
A minor official in Nazi Germany, who continues to carry out his functions.

Even a brief review of such cases teaches at least this much: the occasions for contemplating and possibly engaging in disobedience are extremely varied; and a great many kinds of non-obedience are available, from flight through crime to attempted revolution.[6] Some forms of non-obedience are violent, others not; some are personal and others organized; some are isolated actions and others a systematic program of action; some are directed against a particular law or decree and others against an entire system of government. To a person confronted with a real decision about resistance or obedience, it makes an enormous difference what kind of action is contemplated. Circumstances that may justify escape or isolated refusal to obey a particular law may not suffice to justify revolution; indeed, some forms of resistance (like civil disobedience) may even be provided for within a political system.

[6] Something like this point is suggested by Tussman, *op cit.*, p. 43.

Next, we may notice that all of our examples are, or could reasonably be, people in conflict. Socrates may never have been in doubt as to what he would do, but his friends certainly disagreed with him at first; and he cast his own argument in the form of a confrontation between the desire "to play truant" and the admonitions of the laws. All of our examples (with the exception of the criminal?) might have good, serious reasons for resistance. None of them ought to feel entirely free to pursue those reasons without first weighing them against something else — his *prima facie* obligation to obey. One might say: all these men ought to feel a certain tie to their governments, their societies, in the sense in which Socrates feels such a tie, but some of them might nevertheless be justified in disobeying or resisting. That he does not sufficiently feel such a tie, that he has no (good) reason, no justification for disobedience, is precisely what makes the case of an "ordinary" criminal different from the rest. This is at least in accord with the formula offered by our new theory: normally law, authority, government are to be obeyed and resistance requires justification. You are not morally free to resist as a matter of whim.

The real person confronted by a problematic situation about obedience needs to know that, but he obviously needs to know much more. He needs to know much more specifically when resistance is justified and what might count as a justification. Does he learn this by thinking about his own past consent or that of his fellow-citizens, as traditional consent theory would suggest? Or does he learn it by assessing the nature and quality of the government?

Our cases of potential disobedience show an interesting division in this respect. Three of them — the student and the two Negroes — seem quite unlikely to think much about their own past consent — when and whether they consented, how often and how seriously, expressly or tacitly, and so on. What they are likely to think about is the "outrageous" conduct and "oppressive, unjust" structure of the government, and of the possible consequences of resistance. The criminal (since we have defined him as "ordinary") is not likely to think about either obligations to obey or justifications for his action. The Nazi might well cite his consent to the Fuehrer, his oath of office, pledges of absolute obedience, and so on, as a justification for continued obedience despite "certain unpleasant government measures that perhaps ought not to have been taken." And Socrates is passionately aware of his ties to the Athenian laws, the gratitude he owes them for past favors, the power of his past consent to them.

Thus both Socrates and the Nazi do seem to look to past consent rather than to the nature of the government. But the significance of this fact has yet to be assessed; for on closer examination, each of their cases reveals an important weakness in traditional consent theory. From the case of the Nazi we can learn that even express consent may not be enough; and from that of Socrates, the difficulties of applying past consent as a guide to action.

It might be tempting to say that of our six cases, only Socrates is truly moral, for only he thinks about his obligations and commitments to the laws. But the example of the Nazi saves us from this simplistic response, by showing that sometimes past promises and oaths are not enough to determine present obligations. Sometimes a man who cites even an express oath to obedience, is being not admirable but hypocritical, refusing to recognize where his real duty lies. We would not want to say that past oaths and promises count for nothing, that they can be ignored at will. We all feel the power of the argument that you ought to be consistent, that it isn't fair to pick up your marbles and go home just because it's your turn to lose under the rules you have accepted so far. But that is partly because such a partisan assessment of the rules is likely to be biased. If you can in fact show that the rules are really unfair, then any time is a good time to change them. Again, normally rules and authorities are to be obeyed; when occasions for questioning this obligation arise, what is ultimately needed is an assessment of the rules or authorities. Mere reference to your "going along with them" in the past is not enough.

No doubt if a man had no political obligation he could acquire one by a promise or contract. But that by no means proves that political obligation can be acquired *only* by promise or contract; it may be that a quite independent political obligation is sometimes reinforced by an oath to obey, at other times (partly) countered by a promise to resist. A personal past commitment to obey need not settle the matter.

Indeed, the case of the Nazi calls attention to something traditional consent theory seems to have overlooked: the duty to resist. There are times in human history when men are not merely free(d) from an obligation to obey, but positively obligated to oppose the powers that be. The authors of the Declaration of Independence recognized this, despite their heavy reliance on Locke; for they saw resistance to tyranny not merely as man's right but as his duty. Locke, and traditional consent theory in general, make no provision for such a duty, nor can it be easily accommodated within their framework. There is provision in Locke's system for majority resistance to a tyrannical government, and a duty to follow such a majority. But *individual* resistance has a highly ambiguous status at best, and is certainly *not* a duty.[7] For if political obligation arises from contract, the violation or overstepping of this contract leaves each individual free to do as he likes with regard to the tyranny. True, the individual is still then bound by natural law; but natural law does not command the punishment of offenders, it only permits it. And amending the Lockeian system on this score would obviously require fundamental changes in its individualistic presuppositions.

Similarly, traditional consent theory teaches that at times of civil war or successful revolution, when an old authority structure collapses, each individual is free to place his consent anew whereever he wishes and thinks best for himself. If he thinks fit to follow a highway robber then, he is free to do so. But when we contemplate real cases, would we not rather want to maintain that even in chaos there is responsibility, that even then the individual has some obligation to think of others as well as himself, the welfare of society or mankind as well as his own?

It seems that insufficient attention has been given to the failure of traditional consent theory to provide for any obligation to resist, or any obligation to choose responsibly when new authorities must be chosen. Indeed, divine right, prescription and utilitarianism can accommodate such obligations far more easily than a contract theory can. As for the "nature of the government" or "hypothetical consent" doctrine developed in this essay, it too would presumably require amendment on this score. An enlarged version might hold: your obligation is to obey what deserves obedience and consent, and to resist what deserves resistance and rejection (leaving the important possibility that many persons or agencies deserve neither obedience nor resistance). But it is not obvious to me whether the obligation to

---

[7] Locke, *op. cit.,* pars. 121, 149, 168, 203–4, 208–9, 211–12, 220, 232, 240–3.

resist tyranny should be construed as a part of political obligation at all, or as an occasional alternative to it. The question seems related to that of whether revolution is a special part of political life or a breakdown of the political.

### THE CASE OF SOCRATES

Though the Nazi may continue to obey on the grounds that he has sworn to do so, we may find that he thereby fails to perform his true obligations. Why, then, does Socrates' position — equally founded on past personal consent — strike us as so exemplary and moral? I would suggest that the distinguishing thing about Socrates' situation is this: he can find no fault with the Athenian laws, nor even with the Athenian way of administering them. Only his own particular conviction and sentence are (almost fortuitously) unjust. And his dialogue with the laws is essentially a way of expressing or establishing this fact. Socrates' past consent is not so much compelling in its own right, as it is a way of expressing and reinforcing his present judgment that there is nothing basically wrong with the system, no justification for resistance. What amazes us about him is not this judgment, nor the refusal to accept a single case of injustice as a justification for disobedience. These are relatively ordinary positions to take. What amazes us about him is that he construes disobedience so widely, to include even flight; and that he is willing to perform his obligation down to the minutest detail, even at the cost of his life.[8]

The suggestion is, then, that Socrates' focus on his past acceptance of the laws and his gratitude to them is in fact an evaluation of the Athenian government (or the expression of such an evaluation). We need to recall that this same moral Socrates refused to carry out an "authoritative" order given him in the time of the Thirty Tyrants, because it was unjust, and would apparently have refused to carry out injustice voted by a democratic majority as well.[9] In those earlier situations, one may suppose, what Socrates thought about was the injustice of what he had been ordered to do, and of those who issued the order, not his own (tacit?) consent to them.

To this line of argument a traditional consent theorist might respond: Socrates looks to his own past consent in order to find and

---

[8] Plato, *Crito* [50]: "are you not going by an act of yours to overturn us — the laws, and the whole state, as far as in you lies?" B. Jowett translation (New York: Random House, 1937).

[9] Plato, *Apology*, 32.

determine its limits, in order to see whether this new governmental action does not exceed what he had consented to. But if we take that seriously as a model of what the moral man must do when he contemplates resistance, we set him an extremely difficult task. How is Socrates to know *to what* he has consented, particularly if his consent has been tacit? Surely it is not enough to say that he has consented only to those precise things the government did in the past, so that any new or unprecedented action is automatically *ultra vires*. But if not that, then to what does one give tacit consent? Is it to the particular people then in authority, or to the authority of the office they hold, or to the laws that define and limit that office, or to the body that makes those laws, or to the Constitution that lays down rules and procedures for the making of laws, or to the principles behind that Constitution, or to the fellow-members of the society, or even to all of mankind? In particular cases, these various foci of loyalty may come into conflict; then knowing that one has consented to them all at a time when they were in agreement is no help for deciding what to do.

In short, though two of our examples do look to their own past consent in deciding what to do, one of them thereby fails to perform his true obligation, and the other seems to be using the language of the government. Furthermore, we have noted at least two disadvantages of personal consent as a criterion: the difficulty of knowing *to what* you have consented (especially if consent was tacit), and the fact that even an express oath to obey may sometimes be outweighed by an obligation to resist.

Besides an individual's personal consent, traditional consent theory offers as an alternative criterion the "consent of the governed," the consent of all, or a majority of one's fellow-citizens. Of such consent, too, we would have to say that it cannot simply be dismissed as irrelevant. Even our Negro in Mississippi or South Africa might think about how widely shared his grievances are. But again, the consent or dissent of the majority cannot by itself be decisive for defining your obligation. Majorities are sometimes wrong, and have been known to do evil. Resistance might be justified in Athens under the Thirty Tyrants or in Nazi Germany despite the majority.

But majority consent does enter the argument at another level, in a way quite different from the relevance of personal consent. Majority consent may be relevant as a *way* of assessing, as *evidence about* the nature of the government, given that the nature of the government bears on political obligation. In fact, a variety of considerations each of which we might want to call "consent of the governed" can be used in the process of evaluating a government. They may come into conflict with each other, and their relative weight and importance will be a matter of one's political values, of what kind of government he thinks desirable or even tolerable.

It is useful to distinguish here between the "procedural" criteria yielded by the consent of the governed for assessing a government, and the "substantive" ones. Procedural criteria are those which concern the institutional structure and political functioning of the government, the way in which it makes decisions and takes actions. To assess its nature, we want to know about the way a government functions in relation to the governed — whether it is responsive to them or forces its policies on them. Thus we look for machinery for the expression of popular desires; we look for the degree of popular participation in or control over decisions, for channels for the redress of grievances, for access to power. At the same time we look also for signs of repression, of propaganda, of coercion. We look, of course, not merely at the institutions defined on paper, but at their actual functioning in the largest social sense. Denial of suffrage to Negroes in South Africa is very different from denial of suffrage to women in Switzerland (and theorists would do well to think about why this is so). But roughly speaking, a government is likely to seem to us deserving if it is open to the governed, reprehensible if it rules them against their will. This general criterion may well be expressed by some formula like "the consent of the governed"; but that formula must not be taken too simply, and that criterion must not be regarded as our only one.

Besides this vague cluster of procedural criteria, we have in addition substantive ones. We may look also at the substance of what the government does — whether it pursues good, benevolent, justifiable policies. A government that systematically harms its subjects, whether out of misguided good intentions or simply for the selfish gain of the rulers, is to that extent illegitimate — even if the subjects do not know it, even if they "consent" to being abused. But even here "the consent of the governed" is *relevant* as important evidence, for one of the main ways we estimate whether people are being well treated is by whether they seem to like what they get. Only we may sometimes need to consider other evidence as well; the consent or dissent of the governed need not be decisive as to the goodness or justness of a government's policies.

It is the relationship between at least these two kinds of criteria that is likely to determine our assessment of a government, whether it deserves support or opposition. Thus we may all agree that a government pursuing very bad policies and forcing them on its subjects, so that it is obviously doing great harm to them and other countries, and doing so despite their attempts at protest and without their consent — such a government clearly is the occasion for resistance. Conversely, if we find a government that truly has the consent of its subjects although they have wide sources of information and true opportunities to dissent and criticize, and if that government pursues only the most praiseworthy policies, then few of us would urge revolution or resistance to it. The problematic cases are, of course, the ones in between, where procedure and substance are partly good, partly bad, and you need to make evaluations and decisions. Here it begins to be a matter of your metapolitics — how you think of men and societies, what positions you are willing to take and defend, and take responsibility for.

Suppose, for example, that a government is procedurally open, with genuine channels for controlling policy from below, but it engages in vicious policies. Then, one might want to say, the citizen is not free to engage in revolution; he has channels available and it is his duty to use them, to change the policy. But what if he tries to do so, and fails because the majority continues to approve of the wickedness? What if he is a member of a permanent minority group, being systematically abused and exploited by an eager, consenting majority? Then the seemingly open channels of consent are not truly open to him. Might there not come a point when violent minority resistance of some sort is justified?

Or suppose that a government is benevolent, so no one can criticize its actions, but in procedure it is simply autocratic and dictatorial. Is revolution justified against a benevolent dictatorship? This might be the case, for example, if men need political participation in order to be really well, in order to reach their full human potential. Then bad procedure would itself become a substantive grievance.

The theoretical complications possible here are legion, but at least this much seems clear: evaluating a government in order to decide whether it deserves obedience or resistance, requires attention both to the way it works and to what it does. In both cases something like consent is relevant; it may be a formula for expressing some rather

complex requirements concerning opportunities for dissent and participation, or it may be evidence of good policies. Thus even if we
adhere to the doctrine of hypothetical consent or the nature of government, majority consent may still be relevant in a subordinate capacity
for assessing a government, for working out more detailed answers to
our questions one and two about consent, the specific practical "when"
and "whom" of obedience. But here "the consent of the governed"
is not one simple thing, decisive for obligation; rather, it is relevant in
a number of different, potentially conflicting ways.

And all of these ways put together differ, in turn, not merely
from personal consent, but also from the doctrine of hypothetical
consent developed in this essay.[10] That legitimate authority is such
that one ought to consent to it is a precept built into English grammar, into the meanings of these terms. That a legitimate government
is one which has the consent of (a majority of) the governed — is
procedurally responsive to them or looks after their interests, or both
— is one particular position about what kind of government is desirable for men. More accurately, it is a cluster of positions, depending
on the relative weight given to procedural and substantive criteria.
Though these positions are very widely shared today, and though they
were shared by almost all traditional consent theorists, they are not
the only conceivable positions on this subject. Someone might undertake to argue, for example, that a government is legitimate only to
the extent that it fosters high culture, or to the extent that it promotes
the evolution of a master race. That would be to reject majority consent as any sort of criterion for assessing a government. But the doctrine of hypothetical consent holds even for someone taking such an
unorthodox position; even for him, a legitimate government would be
the one that deserves consent, to which everyone ought to consent.
Both the philosophical weakness and the historical persistence and
strength of traditional consent theory rest in its failure to distinguish
these very different arguments.

Finally, even if we succeed in evaluating a government, that does
not seem fully to settle how we must behave toward it. One final,
important consideration seems relevant: the action taken must be
appropriate. To the diversity of ways in which one can obey or sup-

___

[10] For the latter distinction, compare Benn and Peters, *op. cit.,* pp.
329–31.

port, resist or overthrow a government, there correspond a diversity of conditions when the various actions may be appropriate or justified. The fact that some action is justified, that some abuse has taken place, does not mean that just any action will do. A man mistreated by his superior may kick his dog. We can understand, and perhaps even sympathize, but surely the action is not justified. Not just any violation of law will qualify as civil disobedience or attempted revolution. This observation is presumably related to the traditional assertion of consent theorists, that it is necessary to "exhaust the remedies" available, to suffer "a long train of abuses" before violent resistance is justified. Where other actions are appropriate, revolution may not be called for.

Thus it begins to seem that a decision about obedience and resistance ought to be measured not merely against the character of the government, but against all the relevant social circumstances — what alternatives one can envision, and what consequences resistance is likely to have. Revolution would not seem justified, for example, if one had no hope of its being followed by an improvement in conditions. If it would simply substitute one tyranny for another, or if it would annihilate the human race through the resulting violence, then it does not seem justified.[11]

[11] One difficulty of this discussion is that it seems to make human decisions look excessively rational. Are any abstract principles of this kind really relevant to what real people think about when they must decide? Is a man on the point of rebellion or revolution not much more likely to be moved by strong emotion — by an overwhelming anger or sense of outrage?

But I would like to suggest that the human capacity for outrage is, as it were, the emotional correlate to rational moral principles. It is our inner, helpless response to a violation of principles of right and wrong, as we sense them, perhaps quite inarticulately. Outrage (unlike mere anger), is an emotion of principle. I take it that this is what Albert Camus means when he insists that "the act of rebellion is not, essentially, an egoistic act," even though it can, "of course" have "egoistic motives." *The Rebel* (New York: Vintage, 1956), p. 16. The rebel, the man who acts from a sense of outrage, says not merely "I don't want to put up with this," but "No man ought to have to put up with this." And by feeling "no man ought . . . " he acts, in a sense, on principle. Compare Tussman, *op. cit.,* pp. 78–79.

Of course a man's feeling that his situation is outrageous is one thing; whether the situation is in fact outrageous is another. A three-year-old may feel outraged at not being allowed to drink the detergent. We may sympathize with his feelings, but cannot condone the resulting violence. Not every feeling of outrage is a valid assessment of the world; but then, not every rational judgment that the limits of contractual obligation have been exceeded is valid either. No doubt rational judgments are more likely to be right; that is one advantage of rationality.

But a doctrine that casts its net so wide, making all social circumstances at least potentially relevant, that sees both an obligation to obey and an obligation to resist, and that stresses so much the individual burden of decision, seems very close to the social utilitarianism examined in the first half of this essay. It seems to say, with the social utilitarian, you are obligated to obey when that is best on the whole for society (all of mankind?), and obligated to resist when *that* is best on the whole. But that formula, and social utilitarianism, seem to neglect again the obligatory nature of law and authority in normal circumstances, the *prima facie* obligation to obey. Being subject to law, government, authority means precisely an obligation (normally) to do what *they* say is best, rather than judge the welfare of society for yourself and act on your private judgment. Yet there are times when you must resist in the name of something very like the welfare of society. Whether these two positions are compatible remains somehow problematic; but before we can make a final stab at the matter, we must finish applying our new doctrine to our four questions about political obligation.

### JUSTIFYING POLITICAL OBLIGATION

We come now to question four, the matter of justification: "why are you ever obligated to obey even legitimate authority?" Here again our "nature of the government" doctrine does not at first seem a very useful answer. For it can only say: because of the nature of the government, because the government is such that you ought to obey it and consent to it, because a rational man would do so. But that answer is not likely to still the question. For someone genuinely puzzled about obligation in this (philosophical) way is likely to persist: "how does that 'ought' bind me, *why* must I do what a rational man would do, what if I don't *want* to be rational?"

But the reader may have noticed by now that all of the theories and versions of theories we have considered are subject to this same difficulty to some extent. Some seem better designed to cope with it than others; yet we can always push the question further back: why must I do what God commands, why must I do what history teaches, why must I do what is best for me personally, why must I do what I have promised? Even traditional consent theory is liable to this difficulty; and it is remarkable that despite Hume's early criticism, we continue to believe in consent theory while ignoring this problem. For Hume had already told the consent theorist:

> You find yourself embarrassed when it is asked, *Why we are bound to keep our word?* Nor can you give any answer but what would, immediately, without any circuit, have accounted for our obligation to allegiance.[12]

The obligation to keep one's word is no more "natural" and self-evident and indubitable than political obligation itself; though either may sometimes reinforce the other, neither can give the other absolute justification. The two obligations are essentially separate and equal in status.[13] Why, then, does the traditional consent theorist, so doubtful about the validity of political obligation, take the obligation of keeping contracts as obvious? Why, if he imagines a state of nature, is it always stripped of political authority but inevitably equipped with a natural law that dictates the keeping of one's word? Hume uses these questions as a rhetorical device to attack consent theory, but they can also be taken seriously as a way of learning something more about the consent theorist.

For a theorist does not choose his beliefs and his doubts. The traditional consent theorist simply finds himself in doubt about (the justification of, or limits of, or validity of) political obligation; it just seems obvious to him that there is a problem about it. And he simply is not in doubt about promises or contracts; it just seems obvious to him that they oblige.

At one level one can argue that both the consent theorist's doubt and his assumption spring from the peculiar picture of man and society he seems to hold. If your picture of man in the abstract is of a man fully grown, complete with his own private needs, interests,

[12] David Hume, "Of the Original Contract," in Sir Ernest Barker, ed., *The Social Contract* (New York: Oxford, 1960), p. 161.

[13] This assertion is not about the relative claims that the two obligations — political obedience and promise-keeping — have on us, where they come into conflict. It seems obvious to me that no single, binding principle could be found to govern such a question. There are occasions when a vitally important promise is clearly a more important obligation than obedience to some minor law; on the other hand, the keeping of a minor promise is no excuse whatsoever for treason. But the assertion that the two obligations are separate and equal is not meant to bear on this question. It is meant only to say: there is no reason to suppose that promising is more "natural" or basic than obeying authority, and hence no reason to derive the latter from the former.

feelings, desires, beliefs and values, and if you therefore never think about how he grew up and became the particular person he became, then he may well seem to you an ineluctably *separate* unit, his ties to other individuals may seem mysterious or illusory and will require explanation. Given man as such a separate, self-contained unit, it does indeed seem strange that he might have obligations not of his own choosing, perhaps even without being aware of them, or even against his will. Furthermore, self-assumed obligations may then strike you as a way of overcoming this separateness. For it is easy to confuse the fact that promises and contracts are self-assumed, with the idea that the *obligation to keep* them is self-assumed as well. That is, the person who makes a promise seems to recognize and commit himself to the institution of promises; the person who makes a contract seems to acknowledge thereby the binding character of contracts, so that a later refusal to accept them as binding strikes one as a kind of self-contradiction. But of course this is a confusion. The making of particular promises or contracts presupposes the social institution of promising or contracts, and the obligation to keep promises cannot itself be founded on a promise.

In truth, there is something profoundly wrong with the consent theorist's picture of man. Every free, separate, adult, consenting individual was first shaped and molded by his parents and (as we say) society. It is only as a result of their influence that he becomes the particular person he does become, with his particular interests, values, desires, language and obligations. The only thing truly separate about us is our bodies; our selves are manifestly social. But surely even the consent theorist knows this, so the problem becomes why he nevertheless holds, or is held captive by, a different and peculiar picture. Could that picture be not so much the cause as the by-product of his philosophical doubt?

After all, consent theorists are not the only ones troubled about political obligation. Political theorists of other persuasions have also been led, or have led themselves sometimes to ask "why are you ever obligated to obey even legitimate authority?" But if none of the theories of political obligation is able to deal adequately with that question, it must be quite peculiar, not nearly as straightforward as it looks. Perhaps it is a question that cannot be fully answered in the ordinary way. But what sort of question is that; and if it cannot be answered, how should it be treated? Tussman rejects it as a symptom of "moral disorder"; I would suggest instead that it is a symptom of philosophical disorder, the product of a philosophical paradox. If so, it will not disappear — the theorist will not stop being bothered by it — unless we can show how and why it arises, why anyone should so much as suppose that political obligation in general needs (or can have) a general justification. But that would require a discussion of the nature of philosophical puzzlement far beyond the scope of this essay.

What can be done here is something much more limited and less effective. Having suggested that the status of political obligation and of the obligation to keep promises is essentially the same — that neither is more "natural" than or can serve as an absolute justification for the other — we can approach our question four about political obligation by first pursuing a parallel question about promises. For in the area of promises some extremely useful work has been done in philosophy in recent years — work which can be applied to the problem of political obligation.[14]

Philosophers have sometimes asked a question like our question four about promises: "why are you (ever) obligated to keep (any of) your promises (whatsoever); why do promises oblige?" This question, too, can be answered in terms of divine commandment or utilitarian consequences, social or individual; and here, too, the answers are less than satisfactory. "God commands you to keep your word" is no answer to the nonbeliever, nor to someone heretical enough to demand proof of God's will. The utilitarian response tends to dissolve the obligation altogether, so that your duty is always to do what produces the best results, quite apart from whether you have made any promises on the subject. And, of course, a consent argument is out of the question here ("you have promised to keep your promises"?).

What has been suggested by philosophers is this: "promise" is not just a word. Promising is a social practice, something we *do,* something children have to learn *how* to do. It has rules, penalties, roles, and moves almost in the way that games have them. Children

[14] See particularly J. L. Austin, *Philosophical Papers* (Oxford: Clarendon, 1961), chs. 3, 6 and 10; John Rawls, "Two Concepts of Rules," *Philosophical Review,* LXIV (January, 1955), 3–32; and S. L. Cavell, "Must We Mean What We Say?" in V. C. Chappell, *Ordinary Language* (Englewood Cliffs, N.J.: Prentice-Hall, 1964), esp. pp. 94–101.

do not learn what a promise is by having one pointed out to them; they learn gradually about what it means to "make a promise," "keep (or break) a promise," "be unable to promise but certainly intend to try," "have said something which, in the circumstances, amounted to a promise," and so on. Promising is not just producing certain sounds ("I promise"), for a phonograph might make those sounds, or a man rehearsing a play, or a philosopher explaining the practice, yet none of these would actually be promising. Promising, rather, is taking on an obligation. That is, "to promise" does not mean "to make certain sounds," but rather "to take on an obligation."

Now, of course, we do not always do what we have promised. Sometimes we act contrary to our obligations, and sometimes we are wholly or partly excused from performing what we had promised. If for example, keeping a promise would frustrate the purpose for which it was made, or would lead to great evil, or has become impossible, we may be excused from performing. So about any particular promise we have made it may sometimes be relevant to ask: am I still obligated to perform or not? That is, normally, in principle promises oblige; a promise is a certain kind of obligation. But sometimes, under certain circumstances, there is reason to question or withdraw or cancel that obligation in a particular case. In such circumstances we weigh the alternatives, the possible consequences of performance and failure to perform. But our obligations, including that of the promise, continue to be among the factors that must be weighed in the decision. The obligation of a promise does not simply disappear when there is occasion to question it; it only is sometimes outweighed.

But philosophers are sometimes led to wonder *categorically,* about *all* promises: do they oblige; what are the reasons pro and con; why am I ever obligated to keep any promise? And here, of course, there are no *particular* circumstances to weigh in the balance; the question is abstract and hypothetical. What sort of answer is possible to this question? First, that this is what a promise *is,* what "promise" means. A promise is a self-assumed obligation. If you *assume* an obligation and have not yet performed it, nor been excused from it, then you *have* an obligation; in much the same way as someone who puts on a coat, has a coat on.[15] To ask why promises oblige is to ask why (self-assumed) obligations oblige. And to the question why obli-

---

[15] Compare Cavell, "Must We Mean What We Say?" *op. cit.,* pp. 96, 99.

gations oblige the only possible answer would seem to be that this is what the words mean.

Beyond this one can only paraphrase Wittgenstein: there are a hundred reasons; there is no reason. There is no absolute, deductive answer to the question "why does any promise ever oblige?" beyond calling attention to the meaning of the words. There is no absolute, indubitable principle from which the obligation can be deduced. It is, to be sure, related to any number of other principles, obligations and values; but the relationship is more like a network (or patchwork) than like a hierarchical pyramid. It is simply a mistake to suppose that there might be such an absolute principle, such a deductive proof. We have no right to expect one. (Why, then, does the philosopher expect one; why can we ourselves be led to share his expectation when we are in a "philosophical mood"?)

John Rawls has pointed out that utilitarianism will not do as a criterion for the keeping of particular promises — as a standard for *when* promises oblige.[16] To say "keep your promises only when that maximizes pleasure and minimizes pain" is to miss precisely the *obligatory* nature of a promise; having once promised you are not free to decide what to do merely on utilitarian grounds. But, Rawls says, utilitarian considerations *are* relevant at a different level of argument, for assessing the social practice of promising. For we can ask "must we (should we) have an institution like promising and promise-keeping at all?" And here utilitarian reasons seem relevant; we may try to justify the social practice by its useful consequences.

Stanley Cavell has argued that this implies a degree of freedom of choice on our parts which we do not in fact have.[17] To evaluate the practice of promising pro and con, we would have to envision alternatives. And how shall we envision a society which knows no obligation to keep one's word? (For it is not, of course, the particular English locution "I promise" that is being assessed, but the practice of assuming obligations and holding people to their word.) We seem to have no choice about the pros and cons of such an institution. It is not socially useful; it is indispensable to the very concept of society and human life.

But even if we could and did evaluate as Rawls suggests, and

---

[16] *Op. cit.,* Part II.
[17] "The Claim to Rationality," Chapter VIII.

"decide" that the institution of promising is on balance socially useful, even this would not provide an absolute justification for the keeping of particular promises. For what are we to answer the man who says: "granted that we must have the practice of promising, and granted promising means taking on an obligation; still, why am *I* obliged to keep my promise? Why can't *I* be an exception?" To him we can only say, that is how obligation and promises work. Of course you *can* refuse to keep your promise, but then you are failing to perform an obligation.

Now the same line of reasoning can be applied to the question "why does even a legitimate government, a valid law, a genuine authority ever obligate me to obey?" As with promises, and as our new doctrine about political obligation suggests, we may say that this is what "legitimate government," "valid law," "genuine authority" *mean*. It is part of the concept, the meaning of "authority" that those subject to it are required to obey, that it has a right to command. It is part of the concept, the meaning of "law," that those to whom it is applicable are obligated to obey it. As with promises, so with authority, government and law: there is a *prima facie* obligation involved in each, and normally you must perform it. Normally a man is not free to decide on utilitarian grounds whether or not he will do a certain thing, if that thing happens to be against the law or required by law; he is not free to make a decision on his own the way he would be free where the law is silent. The existence of the law on this subject normally constitutes an obligation, just as having promised normally constitutes an obligation, so that one is not free to decide what to do just as if no promise had been made. (This is not, of course, to say that everything claiming to be law is law, that everyone claiming to have authority has it, that every statement alleged to be a promise is in fact one. It says only: *if* something is a promise, law, obligation, *then* normally it obliges.) This kind of response to question four is obviously almost the same as the one our doctrine of hypothetical consent yielded to question three: government and authority are concepts grammatically related to obligation and obedience. A legitimate government is one that you ought to obey and ought to consent to because that is what the words mean. But as before, this answer is likely to seem purely formal, and empty. It will not satisfy someone genuinely puzzled about the justification of political obligation.

But as with promises, all that one can say beyond calling attention to the meanings of the words, is that no absolute, deductive justification exists or is necessary. There are no absolute first principles from which this obligation could be derived. It is related to all kinds of other obligations in all kinds of ways, to be sure, but the relationship is not hierarchical and deductive. In particular, as we have seen, the obligatory nature of promises is no more or no less absolute and indubitable than the obligation to obey laws. Again, following Rawls' suggestion, one might attempt a utilitarian assessment of such institutions or practices as law, government and authority. And here, I suppose, there may be somewhat more room for discussion than with promises. For it is not at all obvious that government and law are indispensable to human social life. But can we conceive society without any such thing as authority? One function of the idea of the state of nature in classical consent theories does seem to be a kind of indirect demonstration of the utilitarian advantages of having governments and laws. If such things did not exist, Locke seems to argue, we would have to invent them.[18]

But as with promises, even a recognition of the necessity or utilitarian advantages of such things as authority, law and government is no absolute answer to the man who is questioning his particular obligation to obey, who wants to be an exception. There is no such absolute answer, and can be none. Nothing we say is absolutely beyond question. Again, you *can* disobey but in the absence of excuses or justification you violate an obligation when you do so.

The parallel between promises and authority as obligations is not perfect. For one thing, promises are explicitly taken on oneself; political obligation (I have argued) need not be. Furthermore, promises are normally made to particular persons, whereas political obligation is sometimes confounded by our question two, by the problem of rival authorities. We have noted the difficulty of determining to whom or what consent is given: particular officials, their positions, the laws, the Constitution, the people of the society. This means,

---

[18] It is significant, in this respect, that consent theorists so often speak of contracts or covenants, rather than simple promises or oaths. For of course the idea of a contract or covenant implies that you get something in return for the obligation you take on, and in a way at least suggests the informal additional ties of gratitude. But there are other differences as well, a contract being more formal and usually more explicit than a promise.

among other things, that political obligation is open to a kind of challenge not normally relevant to promises. We saw that, following Rawls, both promises and political obligation can be challenged at two very different levels: sometimes we may claim to be excused from performing in a particular case (for instance because of conflicting obligations or overwhelming difficulties). And sometimes we may want to challenge and assess the whole institution with the obligations it defines. But in addition, political obligation can be challenged also on a third level. Sometimes we may refuse to obey neither because our particular case is exceptional, nor because we question such obligation categorically, but because the one who is claiming authority over us does not in fact have it. We may resist a government that has become tyrannical not as a special, personal exception, and not because we are against government, but because *this* government no longer deserves obedience. Such a challenge is made on principle, *in accord* (as it were) with the "rules" of political obligation.

But the differences between promises and political obligation do not affect the point to be made here. That point concerns our question four, the search for a justification for having to obey (or having to keep a promise); and it is essentially twofold. First, we have said, "authority," "law," and "government" are grammatically, conceptually related to obligation, as is "promise." And beyond this, the quest for some "higher," absolute, deductive justification is misguided. Insofar, then, as the grammatical point does not seem to still the question, does not get at what someone philosophically puzzled wants to ask, what is needed is not a better justification, but an account of why the philosopher is driven to ask the question in the first place.

### THE DUALITY OF OBLIGATION

As Locke suggests in his preface, the consent theorist's purpose is a dual one. He wants both to show that men are sometimes justified in making revolutions, and to show that men are normally bound to obey governments and laws. And this is, indeed, what must be shown, since both these things are in fact true. The fact is that on one hand men are in some sense above or outside the institutions of their society, its laws, its government. They can measure and judge these institutions. Though they have not themselves made them they can change them; and sometimes even violent change may be justified. On the other hand, men are also part of and subject to their society, bound by its norms and authorities. Not every attempt at revolution is justified.

To say that men are both superior to their government and subject to it is to express a paradox. Because it seems so paradoxical, the traditional social contract theorists saw it instead as a temporal sequence: *first* men were free and could make a commonwealth, *then* they became bound by it (within the limits of a contract). We have seen some of the difficulties that result. Finding an accurate and un-paradoxical way to express this paradoxical truth seems to me the most interesting problem connected with political obligation, but it is important to notice that this problem is not confined to political obligation. We are both superior to and subject to *all* our obligations, and *that* is what requires an accounting. Discussing it will reveal one final, rather subtle way in which obligation both is and is not a matter of consent — but all obligation, not just the obligation to obey.

We are familiar enough from ethics with the view of a number of philosophers (notably Kant) that an action is not fully moral unless the actor knows what he is doing and does it for the right reasons. An action done for selfish motives but accidentally producing some charitable result is not (really, fully) a charitable action. A moral action is one taken *because* it is right, on principle. On analogy we might want to say that a man cannot (really, fully) obey an order unless he recognizes that it is an order, that the man issuing it has authority over him. He cannot (really, fully) obey a law or a govern-ment unless he recognizes it as valid law or legitimate government; only then will what he does (really, fully) *be* obeying. If I "order" a leaf to fall from a tree, and the leaf immediately does so, it is not obeying my order; if I silently and secretly "order" my neighbor to mow his lawn and he does so, he is not (really, fully) obeying my order. Even if he hears and understands what I am saying, he is not (really, fully) obeying me unless he recognizes what I say as an order, considers me as having authority to order him about, and mows the lawn *because* of my order.

Consequently, the capacity for this kind of awareness and inten-tion is a precondition for being fully obligated. This is why leaves cannot be obligated (except in storybooks, where they are anthropo-morphized), and children cannot fully do so. It may be right to punish or reward a child, but the child is not yet fully a moral agent capable of recognizing and therefore of having obligations.

It is not difficult to regard this kind of awareness and intention as a form of consenting to one's obligation. If (really, fully) obeying an order presupposes the recognition of it as an order and of the man who issues it as having authority, then surely that recognition resembles a kind of (perhaps tacit) consent to his authority. And then it becomes easy to take a final further step, and say you are not (really, fully) obligated unless you recognize, acknowledge, accept, acquiesce in, consent to that obligation. Such a line of reasoning undoubtedly has heightened the appeal of consent theory for a number of writers, and it clearly is the main basis for Tussman's stress on consent. He chooses agreement rather than force or habit as the nature of political association precisely because,

> "I have a duty to . . . " seems to follow from "I have agreed to" in a way that it does not follow from "I am forced to" or "I am in the habit of." This is sometimes expressed as the view that obligations are, or even must be voluntarily assumed.[19]

But even if one accepts these transitions and concludes that obligation in the full moral sense always requires consent, it by no means follows that obligation consists *only* of this inner awareness and intent. For that would imply that anyone failing or refusing to consent for any reason whatsoever is thereby excused from the obligation in question, does not have that obligation, cannot meaningfully be blamed or criticized for failing to perform it.[20] But no major ethical theorist, least of all Kant, would be willing to accept that consequence, any more than Tussman is willing to let the morally unaware clods in society disobey laws whenever they please.

It is necessary to recognize that obligation has not one, but two fundamental aspects — the inner, "awareness" aspect stressed by Tussman, and an outer aspect having to do with the way others see what we do, how it looks objectively. These two aspects of obligation may be seen as corresponding to two familiar strains in ethical theory: the teleological, concerned with the consequences of action, and the deontological, concerned with its motives.[21] The former deals pri-

---

[19] *Op. cit.,* p. 8.

[20] Benn and Peters, *op. cit.,* p. 322.

[21] This and the next three paragraphs lean heavily on Cavell, "The Claim to Rationality," p. 323 and all of Part II.

marily in the outer, shared world of facts and events, and takes as fundamental the concept of the *good:* the latter deals primarily in the inner, personal world of thoughts and feelings, and takes as fundamental the concept of *right.* I would suggest, following Cavell, that both are a necessary part of any valid account of morality and obligation, that neither can be ignored outright in assessing action.

Those moral philosophers who have stressed the deontological side of moral appraisal have been concerned particularly with the matter of giving praise: a person does not deserve full credit for an act of charity, of courage, of obedience, unless his intentions were charitable, courageous, obedient. He should not get full credit for an action that merely looks charitable "from the outside," if his own perception of what he was doing was quite otherwise. To a lesser extent this is also true of blame: you are responsible for the damage you do, no matter how good your intentions were, but good intentions may be a *partial excuse.* Those philosophers who have stressed the teleological orientation of moral appraisal have been more concerned with blame or responsibility, but most particularly with duty. Your duty is not merely to intend good behavior, but to behave well; the performance and its results are what define your duty.

But in a way this dichotomization — deontology for praise, teleology for duty — misses the point. For the real difficulty is in determining *what* action has been performed, what actually was done. It is naming the action (correctly) that is the problem: was it, should we call it, an act of charity, an act of obedience, considering what took place, considering his intentions? Having put it that way, one wants to say that the two modes of assessment are always both relevant, but not equally relevant to all actions. To the assessment of certain actions, inner intention  is much more revelant; to the assessment of others, outer events will seem decisive. Lying is more a matter of inner intent, deceiving more a matter of outward results. Moreover it may be that, in a broader sense, whole categories of action vary in this respect. It may be, for example, that inner awareness is categorically more relevant in face-to-face, personal relationships than in public, political conduct. We do care more about motive and intention in assessing personal relationships and actions — love, anger and forgiveness — than in assessing political actions in the public realm.

If this is so, it deserves more attention than it has received from political theorists. No doubt it has something to do with the fact that in personal morality there is no umpire, no arbiter or judge; it is of the essence of morality that we confront each other directly. In the political, public realm, on the other hand, the normal situation is one where official "interpreters" are supplied by the society to tell the individual what the law or Constitution says, whether he has or has not committed grand larceny. But what happens at times of resistance or revolution is precisely that these normal official interpreters are themselves called into question. We are both bound by, and yet sometimes free to challenge or change all our obligations; but political obligation has an additional complexity, in that its *content* seems to be a subordination to the judgment of others.[22]

But if normally law and authority oblige and resistance requires justification, and if normally judgment is to some extent subordinated to that of the authorities, and if revolutionary situations are precisely the ones that are not normal in these respects, then the crucial question seems to be: *who is to say?* [23] Who is to say what times are normal and what times are not, when resistance is justified or even obligatory? If we say "each individual must decide for himself," we seem to deny

[22] Compare Tussman, *op. cit.,* pp. 86–95. It is tempting to construe the problem in relation to Hannah Arendt's discussion of action: *The Human Condition* (1958), Part V. The human situation is precarious, and human action fallible in unpredictable ways. Both privately as individuals, and collectively as a society, we try to some extent to overcome this uncertainty, this fallibility. We make commitments, tie ourselves down for the future. As individuals, for example, we make promises. As a society, for example, we try to act and plan beyond the lifetimes of individuals, through the education of our children, or through the establishment of laws and institutions. As we reduce the uncertainty of private future action by telling others what we will do so that they can count on it, so we reduce the uncertainty of public future action by telling others and ourselves what we will do and how, so that we all can count on it. Yet in both private and collective action, uncertainty remains and things go wrong. We do not always live up to our commitments, and promised actions do not always accomplish their intended purpose. Institutions do not always function as intended either; they produce quite different goals, pursue other principles than those they were supposed to embody. Thus sometimes we need to review, replace or reject commitments we have made; sometimes it must be right for us to do so.

And where do human beings get the standards by which on such occasions they assess their government and find it wanting? Well, surely from the very society which they criticize with these standards. That this is possible — that we learn both the existing rules and criteria for assessing rules *together,* and yet can use the latter on occasion to criticize the former — may well be the most important single fact about social life.

[23] Compare Tussman, *op. cit.,* pp. 44–6.

the normally binding character of the law and authority. If we say "society" or "the majority" or "the duly constituted authorities decide," then we seem to deny the right to resist, since it may be the majority or the authorities themselves that need to be challenged. Yet these seem to be the only two alternatives.

The matter is very difficult, though the question seems so simple. This essay will only briefly indicate a direction in which a solution might be sought. What needs to be said seems to be this: the decision both is and is not up to each individual. Each individual does and must ultimately decide for himself and is responsible for his decision; but he may make a wrong decision and thereby fail to perform his obligations. But then who is to say someone has made a wrong decision? Anyone can say, but not everyone who cares to say will judge correctly; he may be right or wrong. And who decides that?

Each person decides for himself what to say and do; yet people sometimes speak and act in ways that are cowardly or cruel, thoughtless or irresponsible. And it is not merely up to the actor to assess his own action in this respect. Other people who want or need to assess the action may also do so; each of them will make a decision for which he bears responsibility, yet none of these decisions is absolutely definitive. The judge trying a would-be rebel makes a decision; the foreign onlooker asked to give money for a revolutionary cause makes a decision; the historian examining the record in a later generation makes a decision.[24] Each of us who talks or thinks or acts with regard to the situation assesses it, and no theory or God or Party can get us off that hook.

But that does not mean that all judgments are arbitrary or merely a matter of personal preference or whim. Some decisions are made arbitrarily or whimsically or selfishly or foolishly; others are made on principle, rationally, responsibly. These are ways or modes of deciding; none of them characterizes decision as such. And an individual's decision does not become rational, responsible or right merely because

---

[24] Thus not only citizens, but also bystanders and commentators may need to decide about a government. Their problems are not the same, to be sure. The citizen must decide whether to obey or resist; the bystander never had an obligation to obey, so he at most must decide whether or whom to assist; the commentator only makes a judgment. Therefore the evaluation of governments as to their legitimacy, their entitlement-to-be-obeyed-by-their-subjects, is a topic that ranges beyond problems of political obligation.

he thinks it is, merely because he urgently wants it to be. What is ultimately needed here is a better understanding of the role played in our language and our lives by assessments like "he was right," "he made a bad decision," "he betrayed the cause," and the like.

Who is to say? I want to answer, each person who cares to, will say — not merely the one who acts, not merely his associates, not merely those in authority over him, not merely the detached historian or observer. No one has the last word because there is no last word. But in order to make that clear, one would have to say a great deal more about how language functions, and why we are so persistently inclined to suppose that there must be a last word.

---

# Political Obligation and the Draft

ROBERT BOOTH FOWLER

In recent years, a great and growing controversy about the nature and functioning of the Selective Service System in the United States has raged over such issues as the cost and effect of the draft, the wisdom of selecting by lottery, deferments, the possibilities of a volunteer army, the advantage of local boards versus central administration.[1] Generally, however, the arguments have been in a context that too rarely questioned whether all American young men owe an obligation to the United States political community in the form of military service. Nor is there much question about the specific form of consent theory that is the basis for that alleged obligation. In this article I propose to inspect that general premise of owed obligation and its basis, to ask whether a case for such an obligation can be made satisfactorily and, if so, on what grounds.

The host of difficult political and philosophical problems this matter involves makes it understandable why here neither the nature of political obligation in general nor the complex matter of the appar-

[1] A fine treatment of the basic issues is in James Davis and Kenneth Dolbeare, *Little Groups of Neighbors* (Chicago: Markham Publishing Co., 1968).

ent operational theory of political obligation in America and its historical justifications can be considered in detail.

For the same reason, I will not enter deeply into the most basic assumption, that political obligation is good. Those who reject this assumption are essentially anarchistic, and although their radical individualism may well be legitimate, this essay does not concern that perspective.

By political obligation I mean what is owed by an individual to the general political community or its agents. Political obligation can exist only in a situation in which an individual has freedom, that is, choice, and he must choose an obligation. Where there is no choice there can be no political obligation because obligation is a moral concept and morality cannot be practiced in a situation of no choice. This means that only a consent-based form of political obligation is satisfactory.

Although I assume that every person has free will to some degree, this is a moot question, which is not crucial to dispute here. My notion of choice simply refers to external constraints and/or heavy unwanted consequences as the limiters of choice. Since the degree of choice is always involved, there is no free choice in an absolute sense, nor any situation of absolutely no choice. But the greater the absence of external restraints and the more even the negative consequences between two or more paths to be chosen, the greater the choice, and, therefore, the greater the consequent obligation, political or otherwise.

The reverse also applies, of course, but all this should not be taken to mean more than it does. The hard moral choices in life are not likely to be made in situations of high free choice or low costs because of the choice made. If they are not, this does not at all eliminate them as moral choices; it simply weakens their moral weight. A "difficult" choice or a "costly" choice, is still one that counts morally, though it may not count very much.

One other characteristic is important in determining the moral weight to assign a choice, and that is its degree of willfulness. A choice must be knowingly made, with a conception of what is involved or it really is not a choice in any ordinary sense of the word. The more a choice is willful and conscious, the more it is binding; this applies as well to a chosen obligation. Inherited obligations of an individual would, for example, count for nothing.[2]

[2] Cf. Michael Walzer, "The Duty to Disobey," in Spitz, ed., *Political Theory and Social Change* (New York: Atherton, 1967).

The recognition of the necessity of willfulness is the essential strength of Joseph Tussman's argument about political obligation. Though he uses harsh terms, he is justified in insisting that those who do not consciously know what they are doing when they choose — however choose is meant — cannot be considered obligated.[3]

In addition to the precondition of choice, political obligation involves moral requirement; that is, political obligation, once incurred, is a binding moral duty toward the political community. Finally, it is assumed that political obligation takes place only in a situation of mutuality; that is, there can be no political obligation where a society and most of its individuals do not constitute a political community or where they do not accept the idea that they may ever be in any mutual relationship to the political community; obligation is always obligation to someone or some group. This does not necessarily imply that political obligation involves reciprocity, for that would depend upon the specific theory of obligation.

It is also important to understand that the political community as used here refers to the political state, the people in a nation state in their political aspect. It does not refer to any other community of people within the nation state even if that community includes all the people in it nor to such communities as the family or the church or even such particularistic political communities as a political party or a political movement. Indeed, unless there is a willingness to accept specified conditions, it makes no sense to talk of political obligation at all. To renounce community-regardingness in the sense here delineated, is to renounce the possibility of political obligation to a nation state, a defensible position perhaps, but not one under inspection here.

Of course most men and women live in a social world of multiple obligations, of which the political is only one. But commitment to a sense of community-regardingness requires that one's political obligation to the national political community or its agents, if owed, must be placed first, at least in some conceivable and carefully specified conditions. Otherwise, there is no basis for an affirmation of community-regardingness, only vague rhetoric.[4]

Unquestionably, the prudent, and, very likely, the humane,

---

[3] Joseph Tussman, *Obligation and the Body Politic* (New York: Oxford University Press, 1965), pp. 36–37.

[4] For the problem of multiple obligations see Morton Grodzins, *The Loyal and the Disloyal* (Chicago: University of Chicago Press, 1956).

political community will seek to avoid situations that demand the primacy of owed political obligation among its citizens. There are wise provisions in the present United States Selective Service Act that are examples of this humane prudence, provisions regarding conscientious objection, the last surviving son, and sole support of one's family. Yet there will surely be times in the historical life of a political community and possibly in the life of an obligated citizen within the community when the primacy of the political obligation will be insisted upon, and properly so.

The paradox of its necessary primacy is that for many, perhaps most, the willfulness of choice leading to political obligation is weak, particularly when compared to such intense obligations as family and friends. Yet unless the political obligation is upheld as first, in the end, then the political community whose very existence is the usual precondition for the fulfillment of other, more willful, choices and obligations is threatened. Obviously this constitutes a crucial assumption behind my entire obligation argument.

Now it has been suggested that political obligation to the political community may exist only through the intermediacy of obligation to one's primary social groups; that is, that a threat to the political community since it amounts to a threat to these groups obligates one to the political community and to its defense.[5] But while this may be the operational reality, with men it will often not provide a moral basis for political obligation to the political community. For there is no choice here to become obligated to the political community; a prudent policy for many men is, instead, elevated into a moral relationship.

The matter before us, then, is whether the consent basis of political obligation is sufficient to sustain the proposition that service in the United States army (or any army) is owed by a citizen of the United States (or any state).[6] My argument shall be that if an adequate definition of consent is employed such an obligation is indeed owed by most adult American males, but that at the same time it is not owed by those American males now being drafted.

The central problem for us lies in the determination of to what a consent foundation for political obligation amounts. The answer is that it can be many different things. And what definition or theory is

---

[5] A theory advanced by my student Ronald McLean.
[6] I am not concerned with anyone but formal, legal citizens.

adequate is crucial to this or any argument over whether the presently drafted have given consent and are thus obligated. In short, accepting a vague consent grounding for obligation as in America does not get us very far until we decide much more precisely what consent ought to involve in this vital matter.

My contention is that the standard of consent which comes closest to an adequate basis for political obligation is a form of tacit consent; specifically, the possession of meaningful opportunity to politically participate amounts to consent and confers political obligation.

My argument shall proceed in two parts. First, I shall argue for my standard, presenting its strengths and considering its weaknesses. Second, I shall look at alternative theories of consent and explain why I find them ultimately less satisfactory.

Basically, the case for the opportunity to participate test is that it best fulfills the conditions necessary for a genuine political obligation. Clearly enough, it is genuinely community-regarding for two reasons. First, this test is based around an opportunity concerned with the public political realm, with the realm of the political community. But, more uniquely, it is a test that makes possible the achievements of obligation realistically for most Americans and for most citizens in any polity, if structured correctly. It is not, then, a test like several we will examine below which set such high criteria that they in effect promise to eliminate the possibility of political obligation for most men under most situations, thus in effect vitiating the idea of political obligation itself.

Contention with my test, however, is not based on concern with and provision for community-regardingness. Rather, it is based on whether it provides the reality of choice so central and so crucial to any notion of political obligation. It has been argued that my theory ought not to be called a consent theory at all because there is no consent here. In America for instance, this theory might be taken to mean that one is born into political obligation or, at least, that one automatically becomes obligated upon assuming legal adulthood. Where would there be any choice? [7]

---

[7] Cf. Gary Goodman, "Political Obligation and Consent Theory," unpublished essay, University of Wisconsin.

Another contention is that the opportunity test cannot be considered to involve choice because choice involves an *act* and yet there is no act here, unlike if the test were simply political participation instead of referring to mere opportunity.[8]

These objections are very serious, but they are not fatal. They do, however, require that we make clear again with this as with any test for political obligation based upon consent that willfulness must be present. That is, people must know what they are doing if it may result in their incurring political obligation; therefore, adoption of my opportunity test would be immoral unless its implications were made fully clear to the general citizenry and especially clear to the prospective citizenry. They would have to know beforehand that the general community and its agent, government, would consider the provision of opportunity to politically participate to citizens to politically obligate them and that failure to reject this opportunity would be taken as consent.

If this were done, and alternative choices provided, much of the complaint about the absence of choice and/or an act of choice would lose its power. To be sure, for those, surely most people in most circumstances, who became politically obligated in this way there still would be no direct act of choice. The choice would be passive and tacit. But why must we assume that choice to be choice must be active and direct? As long as it is conscious and alternatives are provided it is still choice; and, indeed, paradoxical as it may seem, a willful passive choice probably is more meaningful than a ritualistic direct act of choice, as I argue below in rejecting the value of direct consent. Moreover, undoubtedly a more passive choice is more community-regarding than a direct one; and we must not forget that the best form of consent theory combines choice and community-regardingness. As we shall see, as often as not in consent theory either choice or community-regardingness is exalted far above the other criterion, an easy if false solution. Here in the opportunity test there is a genuine, if troublesome, attempt at reconciliation.

Of course other choices must be provided. The first and most obvious other choice is allowing departure from the political society with which one is concerned. Not simply must this possibility be permitted, as it is so sadly not permitted for draft-aged men in America,

---

[8] A point made to me by my colleague, Professor Donald Hanson.

but it must be financially provided for so that it will constitute more than a paper choice.

Unquestionably, making departure one of the important choices is disturbing to many concerned with political obligation. Many believe this is not a realistic choice even if it is financially supported.[9] This belief is understandable, but it is erroneous for two reasons. First, the facts of human history belie it. Leaving their country of birth has been a real choice for millions in human history. Much of the story of man has been his movement, his migration. Certainly no American can read the history of the immigration to his country and deny that many have made choices that have involved movement from their nation of origin to the United States. Even today some thousands of American young men have emigrated to Canada to avoid the draft.

Second, moving, even if it is possible, is never an easy choice and often it is a very difficult one. This is often emphasized.[10] Yet what does this fact imply? Choices are still choices even if they are difficult or not equal in undesirable consequences. Of course the mere presence of a formal alternative may not mean that one has a real choice, for example if that formal alternative is death. In any case death is far indeed from an alternative that involves moving. In sum, surely it is naive to believe that important choices will always be easy and without cost; indeed, they will often be the opposite. But choice will be there nonetheless.

Moreover, the only alternative the opportunity test provides is not necessarily leaving. Any member or any group or any whole citizenry which is not given the opportunity to politically participate of course is not obligated. This does not necessarily mean that, for example, revolution would be a justified choice in that situation, since that would depend upon other factors as well, including the individual's or group's assessment of the proper strategy to follow and upon questions of general community interest. But certainly it might well be a defensible alternative. In any case, resistance to demands justified by alleged political obligation would be sanctioned.

Yet even if this standard for consent is arguably adequate in

---

[9] A point frequently pressed on me by my students in Political Science 109, The University of Wisconsin.
[10] *Ibid.*

terms of combining choice with community-regardingness, a substantial problem remains; for the test sets up the criterion of meaningful opportunity, and this is by no means clear. It is not clear, first of all, just what the need is for insisting that the opportunity be meaningful. Why does this stipulation matter? It matters because if the citizen does not have meaningful opportunity to politically participate then the opportunity is really nothing. Yet it is because the opportunity to politically participate best meets the conditions for political obligation that the test has been advanced here as the most adequate; therefore, if this is to be the test, then opportunity to politically participate must really exist, not to be a mere formality. Thus it must be "meaningful."

This leads us quickly to the second and greater problem of clarity, a satisfactory definition for "meaningful." [11] Certainly mere endorsement of meaningfulness gets us nowhere; there must be standards. But there is no essence to our key word and all that one can offer is a judgment about what would be satisfactory criteria.

There is unquestionably much room for argument here, but a start can be made by suggesting the utility of two measures, depth and length of opportunity. Depth would have to include the opportunity to affect decision-making by participation in such actions as voting, campaigning, lobbying, and so on. Merely having the opportunity to vote is not enough depth since its relation to affecting decision-making is in individual terms essentially nonexistent, basically a ritualistic act. Moreover, a broad range of political opportunities for participation must be matched by a roughly equal opportunity to politically participate in depth.

There is no real depth of opportunity for a man if in fact other men have far greater opportunity. Fulfilling this norm may not be easy, and certainly cannot be precise, in any political society, but keeping it in mind at the least suggests that in the United States, for instance, greater equalization of political resources between the average white man and the average black man is needed.

On the other hand, depth of opportunity, to affect decision-making, need not guarantee anything in terms of success in one's policy aims within a political system. Just as one could have the

---

[11] On no matter have I found greater concern and disputation among colleagues and students with whom I have argued political obligation. It is a crucial matter.

requisite opportunity and not use it and be obligated politically, so one could use the opportunity and lose in the political system and still be obligated, as long as roughly equal opportunity to politically participate remains. Democracy cannot and need not promise that we will have our wishes realized; all it can and should promise is that they will be heard, felt, and counted roughly equally with the wishes of all others.

The length of opportunity criterion is simpler. It suggests that if we add to a depth criterion one that amounts to an insistence that one have had the opportunity to politically participate for some time then we have progressed to a definite standard for measuring opportunity. But how long is meaningful length? Clearly any specific period is rather arbitrary here, but perhaps one could reasonably claim that after five years one has genuinely had meaningful opportunity to politically participate. Voting in one election certainly ought not to yield up maximum political obligation, but perhaps the opportunity to participate in depth in politics over five years might. At the least it is evidently a greater, more meaningful opportunity than one vote or the opportunity for one vote.

Now if we take this proposed standard for political obligation, that one is politically obligated if he has the opportunity to politically participate in a meaningful way, as defined, then the drafting of most men in the United States could be legitimate; certainly it would be if one could be surer that they understand that their obligation has its proper basis in the political opportunities here and if there were a greater equalization of political resources in America.

But, at the same time, most of those currently being drafted are probably not obligated to serve. Arguably, this would not be true for men on the older end of the eighteen to twenty-six age spectrum of men currently subject to the draft. Yet to suggest that those on the younger side of the spectrum might be obligated seems wrong on the basis of the length standard alone, and in most cases on the depth standard, too. In short, it makes no sense to claim that eighteen-year-olds, and not they alone, are obligated and thus may be drafted. For they have had little, if any, opportunity to politically participate in a meaningful way; that is, they have had little chance to give tacit consent or to depart. Therefore, I conclude that the drafting of many, perhaps all, of the men now being called ought to cease because they are not obligated to serve.

One may resist this conclusion and yet employ the same test for political obligation, arguing that political obligation may be imposed on the basis of future opportunity to politically participate and thus the late teenagers may be drafted. This is a serious contention.[12] But the answer to it is to insist again and again that obligation founded on a promise about the future is too community-regarding, sacrificing choice in the process; there is a delicate balance to be maintained between these two requisites, as we have seen, and this standard errs too far in the one direction. For promises can always be made if that is all that is needed to politically obligate. Yet promises are not enough in this serious business; performance — in this case opportunity of performance — is more substantial, more meaningful, and thus more adequate to defend heavy political obligations like the draft.

My argument here does not deal at all with the practical problems of finding men for those armies which are raised by immorally drafting unobligated men. This omission may make it somehow less than "realistic;" [13] but realism, we should have learned by now, is not a word which in a specific situational context is clearly defined, and, in any case, one can easily argue that the actual realists are those who are aware that something serious is eroding the sense of political obligation among a portion of our young men in America, an erosion which my argument justifies. Yet nothing could be both more dangerous and more disturbing if one still believes that the American ideal of constitutional government by consent of the governed remains a worthy value and a worthy basis of political obligation.

Lastly, my discussion does not provide the basis for a conclusion that the unobligated are free to obey or not obey more ordinary and less consequential everyday regulations such as traffic lights and laws against theft. Obedience of these is easily justifiable in terms of general social utility and in terms of the specific self-interest of the unobligated as well as the obligated. It is much less easy to defend any draft on such a basis except in times of severe and direct community threat.

The second part of my theory of obligation and the draft involves the consideration of opposing arguments. For no obligation theory

---

[12] This argument was first made to me by my colleague, Professor Henry Hart.

[13] This seems to vitiate my argument somewhat to some readers, a position argued best and most usefully by my colleague, Professor Crawford Young.

is fully satisfactory, far from it. Part of the argument I wish to present for my theory is a treatment of the relatively greater weaknesses of the differing, contending consent theories.

Since there are many of these we can look at several, though not all, and we can begin almost anywhere. I will start by looking at the idea of direct consent, the notion that to be obligated politically one must give public and specific consent to the general political community.

If we mean by consent, direct consent, then political obligation of any sort, much less a major political obligation like serving in the military, cannot be justified for many in America or elsewhere. For who has so directly consented? Except for a few who have gone through the citizenship process and in doing so have formally, publicly, and legally given direct consent by taking an oath of citizenship plus others who at one time or another have sworn oaths of allegiance, few Americans have given direct consent. That the Founding Fathers did give this direct consent is clear, but there is no inherent reason why this should be binding on later generations; nor is it clear that even those who have given direct consent at one time or another are presently obligated, since it is a most serious question how long consent once given may impose future political obligation.

In brief, direct consent cannot now be used as a justified basis for political obligation in America to sustain the draft or anything else allegedly owed. Some who are enthusiastic about direct consent would happily conclude, therefore, that few, if any, men are obligated, and take the anarchistic conclusions most willingly.

But also most naively. Direct consent is something which can be instituted without much effort or pain in any society with ultimate effects that are far from anarchistic. All that would be needed to fulfill the conditions for direct consent would be a regularized process of having the citizenry take oaths of direct consent periodically, for example in the local postoffice.

The real problem with direct consent lies elsewhere. Even if people do directly consent it is not an adequate foundation for political obligation, despite, or indeed because of, its very directness. As a test for consent it would be too formalistic and not sufficiently meaningful in terms of people's lives to justify the consequences of such an obligation test, including service in the military. Signing a statement or swearing an oath is too ritualistic an act to indicate adequately deep and abiding consent. The truth is that the form which one might casually assume to be the strongest, direct consent, is in fact weak and inadequate.

Though direct consent does not appear to be a satisfactory justification for political obligation this by no means exhausts the types of consent theory. For example, there are several forms of tacit consent besides my own which have been advanced. But before examining their adequacy, one other consent theory must be examined, one that lies between direct and tacit theories. This is the deserved theory of consent. It maintains that if one would give consent to the government and its policies then one is obligated politically, and vice versa. The question can only be individually posed; and one's personal reply to whether the government and its policies deserve consent solely determines one's political obligation.[14]

As the primary proponent of this theory, Professor Hanna Pitkin stresses that the test must combine a judgment on both the form of government and its general policies. But is this theory adequate and especially should policies be included in any judgment about whether a government deserves consent? The answers appear to be in the negative.

To be sure, the Pitkin test seeks to provide as much consent as possible, by substituting for direct consent, nonformal, continuing individual decision about consent. Still, the problems with the deserved theory are many. It leaves too much to conscious judgment. By so doing it over-rationalizes men's behavior and would tend in practice to obligate automatically the less educated and/or the less aware much more than the educated and/or the more aware. Moreover, it leaves too much to individual judgment; it allows the individual to decide himself whether a government in form and in policy meets *his* standards of the satisfactory. One need not be considered cynical to suggest that the result, except in times of widely-recognized national emergencies, might be that many men might make very, perhaps impossibly, high, the standards government and government policies had to meet before they would give consent and as a result be available for military service.

Indeed, this theory can be seen as covertly hostile to the idea

[14] See the splendid articles on obligation and consent by Hanna Pitkin, *American Political Science Review,* vols. LIX, no. 4 and LX, no. 1.

of achieving political obligation, at least in practice. That is, it might well work out this way because the willingness to be community-regarding, so important to any acceptable system of political obligation in theory and in practice, is strongly and unfortunately de-emphasized here.

In any case, further problems remain. The necessarily individual standards pose another difficulty besides their potential for being employed in ways not community-regarding; in being individual they are likely to be far from uniform and equalitarian. Is this defensible? Most traditional consent theories have considered a man as a man, which, too, is part of the theory of American political ideals. There is no obvious reason this standard should be brushed aside and there is the practical reason it might be highly confusing if one did so.

Another problem with the deserved theory of consent is its inclusion of policies as well as the form of government as part of what is to be judged. This raises the requirements consent theories traditionally have held necessary in order for political obligation to exist. Tradition is hardly a final argument against the deserved consent theory; nonetheless, this inclusion of governmental policies reminds us how heavily the community-regarding side is downgraded here in order to maximize another necessary condition for political obligation, choice.

The inclusion of policies should not be accepted even though it is not always easy to distinguish between the form of government and its policies, nor is it evident that they ought to be distinguished when considering consent theories of political obligation. Regarding the former problem, some would urge that the fundamental procedures stemming directly from a constitutional form of government are not part of that form of government, but are rather the heart of its policies. In this case, how could form and policy be separated? Certainly at the margin there are cases where the two may blur, as for example in provision for civil liberties in liberal constitutional regimes; but generally the ordinary language distinction between policy, referring to the substance of legislative outputs of a governmental system, and the government itself seems real enough. Medicare or pollution laws are not the form of government in the United States or elsewhere.

The form of government is what ought to count. Indeed, the alternative or companion, consent based on policy, seems to concern political convenience rather than political obligation. If one likes the present outputs of a political system one will play along; if not, one will refuse. Yet the point of political obligation, once incurred, is that it must hold men to their obligations even in circumstances in which they wish not to be obligated. To include among such circumstances dislike of policy outputs that do not threaten roughly equal opportunity to politically participate, is to all but abandon the idea that men may be obligated against their momentary will, again a sacrifice of community-regardingness.

The final objection is directly raised here: that the Pitkin test of consent for political obligation is oriented strictly toward the present. In this sense, it is the opposite of the theory that because our government was, at least for some Americans at the time, founded on direct consent, centuries later we are still politically obligated. While the latter obviously errs in making the past too binding on the present, the Pitkin theory goes too far in ignoring the relevance of the past on one's present obligation. How can it be that our past actions are irrelevant to whether we are presently obligated? Again, this proviso has only one effect, weakening political obligations.

At some point, if the standards become too high and the obstacles too many, political obligation as a concept or certainly as an achievable reality will tend to disappear. Is this not what would happen if the deserved consent standard were adopted? This is not indefensible, but here we have assumed that, under specified conditions, achieving political obligation is good; therefore, deserved consent becomes a dubious basis.

Of course this is not to say that the only acceptable standard is one that will lead to the conclusion that all Americans, or all citizens of any country, are obligated. My own standard most definitely does not lead in that direction. This point is made clearer, however, by a discussion of another alternative consent theory, the Lockeian type. Little need be said about this classic view. In its several versions it holds that if one travels the highways, inherits property, and in general simply lives in a country and can leave, then one has tacitly given consent and is politically obligated.

This is a much too sweeping consent theory. Mere residence is in no sense, even a tacit one, a giving of consent, unless consent is entirely empty. If so, as it need not be just because it is a form of tacit consent, why bother with the charade of political obligation based on consent at all? Why not just say that residence obligates one and not pretend that residence says anything about consent?

It seems evident that the Lockeian theory is the grounds, in practice, for political obligation in the United States, and elsewhere, regarding the draft. If so, this does not change the contention here that to call residence a satisfactory test of consent is little more than a verbal game. To found obligation on such a verbal game is really to threaten to undermine both the ideals of consent and of obligation itself, for disillusion with games can be costly.

Because this form of tacit consent appears unsatisfactory does not mean that the longtime, if vague, American basis of political obligation on the general ground of tacit consent is also; but to be satisfactory, tacit consent must have content, as some other non-Lockeian forms besides my own do. For example, political participation is sometimes proposed as a better indicator of tacit consent. According to this view, if one has politically participated then in effect one has given tacit consent and must accept the consequent political obligation.

But in fact using this test would leave so substantial a proportion of the population without any political obligation — in America and elsewhere — that most governments would have to be declared to be operating without the consent of the governed; in America, at least, even in these years of serious internal conflict, this result does not make sense.

For instance, if we took as our test of political participation presidential voting, in America this would mean that about forty per cent of the adult population is not consenting and is therefore not obligated. Yet there is not any major other reason to assume that this is so. This all is complicated by the fact that evidence of consent, especially as a justification for such a substantial obligation as military service, must involve greater depth and length of political participation than presidential voting or even voting in general. As I have already argued, consent must be meaningful if it is to lead to obligation and voting is simply not a very meaningful political act. Yet if more active participation tests are sought, none can be found in America that begin to compare in popular involvement with the relatively widespread act of voting.[15]

One may conclude that the vast proportion of the population has not given consent and is not politically obligated. But I would

[15] Angus Campbell, et al., *The American Voter* (New York: John Wiley & Sons, 1960) has the basic data here.

contend that this foundation, too, is not sufficiently community regarding, that it in effect abolishes political obligation and its reasonable possibility by making the standards for consent too high. Another society than those about us, one like Rousseau's of *The Social Contract* or, less extremely, one whose politics were much more decentralized and participatory is the only kind in which this test could be meant as a serious basis for political obligation. One can advocate this kind of major change, or attempts to achieve this kind of major change, but I do not think this test is adequate for any existent and probably for any achievable society, partly because its standards of consent are too high for known national human practice.

Another problem with the political participation test concerns the establishment of standards and the measuring of individual cases within those standards, which would be no modest task. Probably, indeed, it would be an all but impossible task.

A third and much worse standard that has been proposed for tacit consent is the benefit theory or the socio-economic participatory test. It holds that one is obligated politically to the degree that one has gained socially and economically from living in a society.

The difficulties with this test are manifold. First of all, how can a test for political obligation be made on the grounds of nonpolitical criteria?[16] To contend that there is no distinction between the political and the nonpolitical in a society and that my distinction here is invalid has been argued by many political philosophies. But it is the essence of the liberalism of consent theory that such a distinction can and must be made unless the individual is to be totally absorbed into and destroyed by the political; politics need not be all.

Neither does it appear clear how one could possibly measure socio-economic benefit; indeed, devising standards would inevitably be too arbitrary. More important than these two problems, however, is the fact that young men of the upper socio-economic classes, presumably those who would be the first drafted under this arrangement, would be held liable for the "sins" of their fathers. That is, they could have had little choice by draft age regarding their socio-economic standing in society. Where there has been no choice, surely there can be no obligation.

---

[16] A point contributed to my argument by my colleague, Professor Donald Hanson.

It should also be pointed out that this test, if employed, would imply a substantial rearrangement of the present operations of the draft in America. It seems to be implicitly advocated as a test by those who constantly attack the draft system as discriminatory against the poor. The evidence is solid that the draft system in America does work a disproportionately heavy burden on the lower classes, especially the lower middle.[17] In our context this is not quite the point since the test is inadequate even though it might be "fairer" to the less advantaged.

In the end one is led back to my opportunity-to-politically-participate-tacit-consent test for political obligation, partially because of the flaws of the major alternatives.

The opportunity test will definitely not satisfy those who are convinced that the relationship between the individual and his political community that we call political obligation can never exist. It will not satisfy those whose moral inclinations are fundamentally anarchistic. But it may be said with confidence that an obligation system with heavy consequences like the draft, that is increasingly and rightly recognized as morally illegitimate by many among the draft-aged in America, is much more likely to produce anarchistic perspectives than one that is adequately grounded morally as I have argued that my opportunity test is. It is, therefore, not only morality but also prudence that dictates the necessity for revision in the accepted criterion for political obligation.

[17] Cf. the arguments of Davis and Dolbeare here.

# PART TWO

---

# MORALITY, LAW, AND ENFORCEMENT

# Introduction

Why do we punish people? This is the provocative question at the center of the issues raised in this section. Lively controversy has accompanied the political and moral problems raised by punishment since the beginning of political argument in antiquity, and there are no signs that the debate has ended. From the normative perspective adopted here, the question is intended to invite consideration, not of the psychological question of fact — what features of the personality prompt human beings to inflict on each other the injuries or deprivations we call punishment — but of this question: what, if anything, justifies the acts we refer to as punishment?

As always in such discussions, there must be a point of departure. One could obtain wide agreement on at least this: the deliberate but purposeless injury of another is never morally justifiable, for it would be impossible to offer any defense. Of course, men's purposes vary enormously, and one could find it extraordinarily difficult to obtain complete agreement on the question of which purposes constituted plausible and defensible reasons for punishment. Nevertheless, at the level of morality, punishment is not an end in itself. Rather, it is a means to something else. But what exactly? Even if the end in view is clearly established, one still might ask whether the means is appropriate.

Beneath controversy over the justification of punishment, there is a prior question. The presumption behind theories of punishment is that it is necessary or desirable (or both) to maintain the rules for acceptable behavior that a social order has developed. But a moment's reflection on this presumption leads one to a collection of difficult and fundamental problems in political theory. As J. D. Mabbott has argued, it would appear impossible to obtain intellectual clarity here unless one distinguishes the separate questions at stake.

To begin with, is it either necessary or desirable that there be rules at all? Comparatively few theorists have argued against the general idea of some system of rules, some legal, publically enforceable standards. Several forms of anarchism in the history of political reflection illustrate that some men have dreamt of a rule-less existence. Or at least, it has been argued that since oppressive, indeed unnatural rules, are a result of government, the abolition of government would eliminate rules sustained in the last resort by coercion. In the broadest terms, there have been two replies to this line of argument. First, it has been argued that the assumptions of anarchism are much too broad and too easy, perhaps impossibly optimistic. They depend upon two crucial assumptions that have been repeatedly questioned. First, the argument depends on the view that the anti-social behavior of men is not native to them but is the result of coercive institutions that distort human nature. It has been replied to this that it is human nature that gives rise to the institutions, either because it is intrinsically anti-social, or because the human condition irresistibly creates mutual uncertainty, fear and, therefore, the kinds of competition that produce both politics and the necessity of organized restraints. Second, much anarchist argument presumes that all coercion is either directly governmental or is fostered and protected by government. The response to this has usually been that coercive relationships develop at all levels of life, from the family to the state, and so cannot be eliminated merely by removing government.

Further, there is a positive response to the anarchist view: that the idea of some recognized and publicly enforced rules possesses a high degree of value in itself. The contention is that the existence of a body of enforceable rules affords men at least a minimum of stable expectations in their dealings with each other. In short, it can be argued that the chief value of a legal system is a stability of expectations that cannot be obtained in any other way; it enables men to anticipate behavior and its consequences with some confidence and accuracy. Further, one can argue that a legal system is indispensable to justice; whatever its defects, such as excessive generality and rigidity, it is superior in practice to the risks of arbitrariness that appear intrinsic to one-man rule, or to spontaneous justice at the hands of instruments such as people's courts.

Even supposing it is widely agreed that there ought to be *some* system of enforceable rules, there remains a second range of scarcely less important questions. What specific rules should there be? Which values and interests should be promoted? Which forms of conduct should be rewarded and protected and which prohibited? Finally, at a third level of concern, what ought to be done when the rules are violated and why? Some behavior will have to be punished, because without sanctions for failure to obey rules, it could hardly be claimed that they exist at all.

In recent years considerable debate has developed on the problem of what rules ought to be publicly enforced, whether there ought to be established limits to political rule-making power, and if so, where these should lie and why. The segment of readings on law and morals thus raises some of the crucial issues involved in the first two levels of questions just mentioned. Lord Devlin presents the view that the generally accepted morality of the society is the only appropriate standard and, therefore, ought to be legally enforced. The arguments of both Hart and Wollheim are intended to demonstrate the frailties of Devlin's view and to defend a more restricted vision of appropriate legal standards.

Supposing one has developed a defensible view of the principles in terms of which to discuss the scope of law, the question remains, to what end and for what reasons do we punish lawbreakers? The history of political thought contains three major theories on these questions. One view, most often referred to as the retributive theory, is that the idea of punishment ought to be narrowly construed, that properly speaking it has only to do with violation of the existing rules. The heart of this view is that punishment ought to be inflicted if, but only if a specific person has been duly found guilty of violating an established rule. One version of this theory is presented in the essay by J. D. Mabbott.

A second major view, often associated with a utilitarian political and moral theory, is normally referred to as the deterrence theory. This view shifts the primary focus of discussion from an individual to a social level, arguing that what is important here is what social consequences can be expected from punishment. The principal point of the deterrence theory is protection of the social order by attempting to discourage or to prevent specified forms of behavior by attaching deprivations to that conduct. Deterrence theorists often argue that the "warning" of penalties and their actual execution dissuades others from engaging in similar forms of misconduct. A utilitarian view is defended here in the essay by Quinton.

The third major perspective is that the point of punishment ought not to be deprivation due to individual behavior, or the effort to restrain illegal impulses by a system of warnings, but rather to be the rehabilitation or cure of the offender. Here, of course, the offender becomes a patient, whose primary need is treatment for some emotional disability. In some versions of the curative approach to legal offenses, the argument is extended farther: punishment is said to be a mistake, for men cannot help themselves. On the contrary, as Weihofen argues in his essay, human behavior is determined; hence, individual guilt and responsibility are equally inapplicable to human conduct. In some versions of this general outlook, behavior is the irresistible result of familial and social environments; other versions suggest that criminal misconduct is the result of biological defect. In either case, the individual is not responsible. Not all those who adopt a curative theory of punishment, however, are willing to embrace determinism, or to reject the idea of responsibility. Some of the issues involved in this position are developed in the article by Halleck. Pointed questions concerning the validity of the idea of mental illness generally and, hence, the idea of treating offenders against law as patients, are raised in the essay by Szasz.

# Law and Morals

## Morals and the Criminal Law

### PATRICK DEVLIN

The Report of the Committee on Homosexual Offenses and Prostitution, generally known as the Wolfenden Report, is recognized to be an excellent study of two very difficult legal and social problems. But it has also a particular claim to the respect of those interested in jurisprudence; it does what law reformers so rarely do; it sets out clearly and carefully what in relation to its subjects it considers the function of the law to be.[1] Statutory additions to the criminal law are too often made on the simple principle that "there ought to be a law against it." The greater part of the law relating to sexual offences is the creation of statute and it is difficult to ascertain any logical relationship between it and the moral ideas which most of us uphold. Adultery, fornication, and prostitution are not, as the Report[2] points out, criminal offences: homosexuality between males is a criminal offence, but between females it is not. Incest was not an offence until it was declared so by statute only fifty years ago. Does the legislature select these offences haphazardly or are there some

---

From *The Enforcement of Morals,* by Lord Devlin, published by Oxford University Press.

[1] The Committee's "statement of juristic philosophy" (to quote Lord Pakenham) was considered by him in a debate in the House of Lords on 4 December 1957, reported in *Hansard Lords Debates,* vol. ccvi at 738; and also in the same debate by the Archbishop of Canterbury at 753 and Lord Denning at 806. The subject has also been considered by Mr. J. E. Hall Williams in the *Law Quarterly Review,* January 1958, vol. lxxiv, p. 76.

[2] Para. 14.

principles which can be used to determine what part of the moral law should be embodied in the criminal? There is, for example, being now considered a proposal to make A.I.D., that is, the practice of artificial insemination of a woman with the seed of a man who is not her husband, a criminal offence; if, as is usually the case, the woman is married, this is in substance, if not in form, adultery. Ought it to be made punishable when adultery is not? This sort of question is of practical importance, for a law that appears to be arbitrary and illogical, in the end and after the wave of moral indignation that has put it on the statute book subsides, forfeits respect. As a practical question it arises more frequently in the field of sexual morals than in any other, but there is no special answer to be found in that field. The inquiry must be general and fundamental. What is the connexion between crime and sin and to what extent, if at all, should the criminal law of England concern itself with the enforcement of morals and punish sin or immorality as such?

The statements of principle in the Wolfenden Report provide an admirable and modern starting-point for such an inquiry. In the course of my examination of them I shall find matter for criticism. If my criticisms are sound, it must not be imagined that they point to any shortcomings in the Report. Its authors were not, as I am trying to do, composing a paper on the jurisprudence of morality; they were evolving a working formula to use for reaching a number of practical conclusions. I do not intend to express any opinion one way or the other about these; that would be outside the scope of a lecture on jurisprudence. I am concerned only with general principles; the statement of these in the Report illuminates the entry into the subject and I hope that its authors will forgive me if I carry the lamp with me into places where it was not intended to go.

Early in the Report [3] the Committee put forward:

> Our own formulation of the function of the criminal law so far as it concerns the subjects of this enquiry. In this field, its function, as we see it, is to preserve public order and decency, to protect the citizen from what is offensive or injurious, and to provide sufficient safeguards against exploitation and corruption of others, particularly those who are specially vulnerable because they are young, weak in

[3] Para. 13.

body or mind, inexperienced, or in a state of special physical, official or economic dependence.

It is not, in our view, the function of the law to intervene in the private lives of citizens, or to seek to enforce any particular pattern of behaviour, further than is necessary to carry out the purposes we have outlined.

The Committee preface their most important recommendation [4]

that homosexual behaviour between consenting adults in private should no longer be a criminal offence, [by stating the argument [5]] which we believe to be decisive, namely, the importance which society and the law ought to give to individual freedom of choice and action in matters of private morality. Unless a deliberate attempt is to be made by society, acting through the agency of the law, to equate the sphere of crime with that of sin, there must remain a realm of private morality and immorality which is, in brief and crude terms, not the law's business. To say this is not to condone or to encourage private immorality.

Similar statements of principle are set out in the chapters of the Report which deal with prostitution. No case can be sustained, the Report says, for attempting to make prostitution itself illegal.[6] The Committee refer to the general reasons already given and add: "We are agreed that private immorality should not be the concern of the criminal law except in the special circumstances therein mentioned." They quote[7] with approval the report of the Street Offenses Committee,[8] which says: "As a general proposition it will be universally accepted that the law is not concerned with private morals or with ethical sanctions." It will be observed that the emphasis is on *private* immorality. By this is meant immorality which is not offensive or injurious to the public in the ways defined or described in the first passage which I quoted. In other words, no act of immorality should be made a criminal offense unless it is accompanied by some other feature such as indecency, corruption, or exploitation. This is

---

[4] Para. 62.
[5] Para. 61.
[6] Para. 224.
[7] Para. 227.
[8] Cmd. 3231 (1928).

clearly brought out in relation to prostitution: "It is not the duty of the law to concern itself with immorality as such . . . it should confine itself to those activities which offend against public order and decency or expose the ordinary citizen to what is offensive or injurious."[9]

These statements of principle are naturally restricted to the subject-matter of the Report. But they are made in general terms and there seems to be no reason why, if they are valid, they should not be applied to the criminal law in general. They separate very decisively crime from sin, the divine law from the secular, and the moral from the criminal. They do not signify any lack of support for the law, moral or criminal, and they do not represent an attitude that can be called either religious or irreligious. There are many schools of thought among those who may think that morals are not the law's business. There is first of all the agnostic or free-thinker. He does not of course disbelieve in morals, nor in sin if it be given the wider of the two meanings assigned to it in the *Oxford English Dictionary* where it is defined as "transgression against divine law or the principles of morality." He cannot accept the divine law; that does not mean that he might not view with suspicion any departure from moral principles that have for generations been accepted by the society in which he lives; but in the end he judges for himself. Then there is the deeply religious person who feels that the criminal law is sometimes more of a hindrance than a help in the sphere of morality, and that the reform of the sinner — at any rate when he injures only himself — should be a spiritual rather than a temporal work. Then there is the man who without any strong feeling cannot see why, where there is freedom in religious belief, there should not logically be freedom in morality as well. All these are powerfully allied against the equating of crime with sin.

I must disclose at the outset that I have as a judge an interest in the result of the inquiry which I am seeking to make as a jurisprudent. As a judge who administers the criminal law and who has often to pass sentence in a criminal court, I should feel handicapped in my task if I thought that I was addressing an audience which had no sense of sin or which thought of crime as something quite different. Ought one, for example, in passing sentence upon a female

---

[9] Para. 257.

abortionist to treat her simply as if she were an unlicensed midwife? If not, why not? But if so, is all the panoply of the law erected over a set of social regulations? I must admit that I begin with a feeling that a complete separation of crime from sin (I use the term throughout this lecture in the wider meaning) would not be good for the moral law and might be disastrous for the criminal. But can this sort of feeling be justified as a matter of jurisprudence? And if it be a right feeling, how should the relationship between the criminal and the moral law be stated? Is there a good theoretical basis for it, or is it just a practical working alliance, or is it a bit of both? That is the problem which I want to examine, and I shall begin by considering the standpoint of the strict logician. It can be supported by cogent arguments, some of which I believe to be unanswerable and which I put as follows.

Morals and religion are inextricably joined — the moral standards generally accepted in Western civilization being those belonging to Christianity. Outside Christendom other standards derive from other religions. None of these moral codes can claim any validity except by virtue of the religion on which it is based. Old Testament morals differ in some respects from New Testament morals. Even within Christianity there are differences. Some hold that contraception is an immoral practice and that a man who has carnal knowledge of another woman while his wife is alive is in all circumstances a fornicator; others, including most of the English-speaking world, deny both these propositions. Between the great religions of the world, of which Christianity is only one, there are much wider differences. It may or may not be right for the State to adopt one of these religions as the truth, to found itself upon its doctrines, and to deny to any of its citizens the liberty to practise any other. If it does, it is logical that it should use the secular law wherever it thinks it necessary to enforce the divine. If it does not, it is illogical that it should concern itself with morals as such. But if it leaves matters of religion to private judgement, it should logically leave matters of morals also. A State which refuses to enforce Christian beliefs has lost the right to enforce Christian morals.

If this view is sound, it means that the criminal law cannot justify any of its provisions by reference to the moral law. It cannot say, for example, that murder and theft are prohibited because they are immoral or sinful. The State must justify in some other way the punishments which it imposes on wrongdoers and a function for the criminal law independent of morals must be found. This is not difficult to do. The smooth functioning of society and the preservation of order require that a number of activities should be regulated. The rules that are made for that purpose and are enforced by the criminal law are often designed simply to achieve uniformity and convenience and rarely involve any choice between good and evil. Rules that impose a speed limit or prevent obstruction on the highway have nothing to do with morals. Since so much of the criminal law is composed of rules of this sort, why bring morals into it at all? Why not define the function of the criminal law in simple terms as the preservation of order and decency and the protection of the lives and property of citizens, and elaborate those terms in relation to any particular subject in the way in which it is done in the Wolfenden Report? The criminal law in carrying out these objects will undoubtedly overlap the moral law. Crimes of violence are morally wrong and they are also offences against good order; therefore they offend against both laws. But this is simply because the two laws in pursuit of different objectives happen to cover the same area. Such is the argument.

Is the argument consistent or inconsistent with the fundamental principles of English criminal law as it exists today? That is the first way of testing it, though by no means a conclusive one. In the field of jurisprudence one is at liberty to overturn even fundamental conceptions if they are theoretically unsound. But to see how the argument fares under the existing law is a good starting-point.

It is true that for many centuries the criminal law was much concerned with keeping the peace and little, if at all, with sexual morals. But it would be wrong to infer from that that it had no moral content or that it would ever have tolerated the idea of a man being left to judge for himself in matters of morals. The criminal law of England has from the very first concerned itself with moral principles. A simple way of testing this point is to consider the attitude which the criminal law adopts towards consent.

Subject to certain exceptions inherent in the nature of particular crimes, the criminal law has never permitted consent of the victim to be used as a defence. In rape, for example, consent negates an essential element. But consent of the victim is no defence to a charge of murder. It is not a defence to any form of assault that the victim thought his punishment well deserved and submitted to it; to make a good defence the accused must prove that the law gave him the right to chastise and that he exercised it reasonably. Likewise, the victim may not forgive the aggressor and require the prosecution to desist; the right to enter a *nolle prosequi* belongs to the Attorney-General alone.

Now, if the law existed for the protection of the individual, there would be no reason why he should avail himself of it if he did not want it. The reason why a man may not consent to the commission of an offence against himself beforehand or forgive it afterwards is because it is an offence against society. It is not that society is physically injured; that would be impossible. Nor need any individual be shocked, corrupted, or exploited; everything may be done in private. Nor can it be explained on the practical ground that a violent man is a potential danger to others in the community who have therefore a direct interest in his apprehension and punishment as being necessary to their own protection. That would be true of a man whom the victim is prepared to forgive but not of one who gets his consent first; a murderer who acts only upon the consent, and maybe the request, of his victim is no menace to others, but he does threaten one of the great moral principles upon which society is based, that is, the sanctity of human life. There is only one explanation of what has hitherto been accepted as the basis of the criminal law and that is that there are cerain standards of behaviour or moral principles which society requires to be observed; and the breach of them is an offence not merely against the person who is injured but against society as a whole.

Thus, if the criminal law were to be reformed so as to eliminate from it everything that was not designed to preserve order and decency or to protect citizens (including the protection of youth from corruption), it would overturn a fundamental principle. It would also end a number of specific crimes. Euthanasia or the killing of another at his own request, suicide, attempted suicide and suicide pacts, duelling, abortion, incest between brother and sister, are all acts which can be done in private and without offence to others and need not involve the corruption or exploitation of others. Many people think that the law on some of these subjects is in need of reform, but no one hitherto has gone so far as to suggest that they should all be left outside the criminal law as matters of private morality. They can be brought within it only as a matter of moral principle. It must be remembered also that although there is much immorality that is not punished by the law, there is none that is condoned by the law. The law will not allow its processes to be used by those engaged in immorality of any sort. For example, a house may not be let for immoral purposes; the lease is invalid and would not be enforced. But if what goes on inside there is a matter of private morality and not the law's business, why does the law inquire into it at all?

I think it is clear that the criminal law as we know it is based upon moral principle. In a number of crimes its function is simply to enforce a moral principle and nothing else. The law, both criminal and civil, claims to be able to speak about morality and immorality generally. Where does it get its authority to do this and how does it settle the moral principles which it enforces? Undoubtedly, as a matter of history, it derived both from Christian teaching. But I think that the strict logician is right when he says that the law can no longer rely on doctrines in which citizens are entitled to disbelieve. It is necessary therefore to look for some other source.

In jurisprudence, as I have said, everything is thrown open to discussion and, in the belief that they cover the whole field, I have framed three interrogatories addressed to myself to answer:

1. Has society the right to pass judgement at all on matters of morals? Ought there, in other words, to be a public morality, or are morals always a matter for private judgement?

2. If society has the right to pass judgement, has it also the right to use the weapon of the law to enforce it?

3. If so, ought it to use that weapon in all cases or only in some; and if only in some, on what principles should it distinguish?

I shall begin with the first interrogatory and consider what is meant by the right of society to pass a moral judgement, that is, a judgement about what is good and what is evil. The fact that a majority of people may disapprove of a practice does not of itself make it a matter for society as a whole. Nine men out of ten may disapprove of what the tenth man is doing and still say that it is not their business. There is a case for a collective judgement (as distinct from a large number of individual opinions which sensible people may even refrain from pronouncing at all if it is upon somebody else's private affairs) only if society is affected. Without a collective judgement there can be no case at all for intervention. Let me take as an illustration the Englishman's attitude to religion as it is now and as it has been in the past. His attitude now is that a man's religion is his private affair; he may think of another man's religion that it is right or wrong, true or untrue, but not that it is good or bad. In earlier times that was not so; a man was denied the right to practise what was thought of as heresy, and heresy was thought of as destructive of society.

The language used in the passages I have quoted from the Wolfenden Report suggests the view that there ought not to be a collective judgement about immorality per se. Is this what is meant by "private morality" and "individual freedom of choice and action?" Some people sincerely believe that homosexuality is neither immoral nor unnatural. Is the "freedom of choice and action" that is offered to the individual, freedom to decide for himself what is moral or immoral, society remaining neutral; or is it freedom to be immoral if he wants to be? The language of the Report may be open to question, but the conclusions at which the Committee arrive answer this question unambiguously. If society is not prepared to say that homosexuality is morally wrong, there would be no basis for a law protecting youth from "corruption" or punishing a man for living on the "immoral" earnings of a homosexual prostitute, as the Report recommends.[10] This attitude the Committee make even clearer when they come to deal with prostitution. In truth, the Report takes it for granted that there is in existence a public morality which condemns homosexuality and prostitution. What the Report seems to mean by private morality might perhaps be better described as private behaviour in matters of morals.

This view — that there is such a thing as public morality — can also be justified by *a priori* argument. What makes a society of any sort is community of ideas, not only political ideas but also ideas about the way its members should behave and govern their lives; these latter ideas are its morals. Every society has a moral structure as well as a political one: or rather, since that might suggest two independent systems, I should say that the structure of every society is made up both of politics and morals. Take, for example, the

[10] Para. 76.

institution of marriage. Whether a man should be allowed to take more than one wife is something about which every society has to make up its mind one way or the other. In England we believe in the Christian idea of marriage and therefore adopt monogamy as a moral principle. Consequently the Christian institution of marriage has become the basis of family life and so part of the structure of our society. It is there not because it is Christian. It has got there because it is Christian, but it remains there because it is built into the house in which we live and could not be removed without bringing it down. The great majority of those who live in this country accept it because it is the Christian idea of marriage and for them the only true one. But a non-Christian is bound by it, not because it is part of Christianity but because, rightly or wrongly, it has been adopted by the society in which he lives. It would be useless for him to stage a debate designed to prove that polygamy was theologically more correct and socially preferable; if he wants to live in the house, he must accept it as built in the way in which it is.

We see this more clearly if we think of ideas or institutions that are purely political. Society cannot tolerate rebellion; it will not allow argument about the rightness of the cause. Historians a century later may say that the rebels were right and the Government was wrong and a percipient and conscientious subject of the State may think so at the time. But it is not a matter which can be left to individual judgement.

The institution of marriage is a good example for my purpose because it bridges the division, if there is one, between politics and morals. Marriage is part of the structure of our society and it is also the basis of a moral code which condemns fornication and adultery. The institution of marriage would be gravely threatened if individual judgements were permitted about the morality of adultery; on these points there must be a public morality. But public morality is not to be confined to those moral principles which support institutions such as marriage. People do not think of monogamy as something which has to be supported because our society has chosen to organize itself upon it; they think of it as something that is good in itself and offering a good way of life and that it is for that reason that our society has adopted it. I return to the statement that I have already made, that society means a community of ideas; without shared ideas on politics, morals, and ethics no society can exist. Each one of us has ideas about what is good and what is evil; they cannot be kept private from the society in which we live. If men and women try to create a society in which there is no fundamental agreement about good and evil they will fail; if, having based it on common agreement, the agreement goes, the society will disintegrate. For society is not something that is kept together physically; it is held by the invisible bonds of common thought. If the bonds were too far relaxed the members would drift apart. A common morality is part of the bondage. The bondage is part of the price of society; and mankind, which needs society, must pay its price.

Common lawyers used to say that Christianity was part of the law of the land. That was never more than a piece of rhetoric as Lord Sumner said in *Bowman v. The Secular Society*.[11] What lay behind it was the notion which I have been seeking to expound, namely that morals — and up till a century or so ago no one thought it worth distinguishing between religion and morals — were necessary to the temporal order. In 1675 Chief Justice Hale said: "To say that religion is a cheat is to dissolve all those obligations whereby civil society is preserved."[12] In 1797 Mr. Justice Ashurst said of blasphemy that it was "not only an offence against God but against all law and government from its tendency to dissolve all the bonds and obligations of civil society."[13] By 1908 Mr. Justice Phillimore was able to say: "A man is free to think, to speak and to teach what he pleases as to religious matters, but not as to morals."[14]

You may think that I have taken far too long in contending that there is such a thing as public morality, a proposition which most people would readily accept, and may have left myself too little time to discuss the next question which to many minds may cause greater difficulty: to what extent should society use the law to enforce its moral judgements? But I believe that the answer to the first question determines the way in which the second should be approached and may indeed very nearly dictate the answer to the second question. If society has no right to make judgements on morals, the law must find some special justification for entering the field of morality: if homosexuality and prostitution are not in themselves wrong, then

[11] (1917), A.C. 406, at 457.
[12] *Taylor's Case,* 1 Vent. 293.
[13] *R. v. Williams,* 26 St. Tr. 653, at 715.
[14] *R. v. Boulter,* 72 J.P. 188.

the onus is very clearly on the lawgiver who wants to frame a law against certain aspects of them to justify the exceptional treatment. But if society has the right to make a judgement and has it on the basis that a recognized morality is as necessary to society as, say a recognized government, then society may use the law to preserve morality in the same way as it uses it to safeguard anything else that is essential to its existence. If therefore the first proposition is securely established with all its implications, society has a prima facie right to legislate against immorality as such.

The Wolfenden Report, notwithstanding that it seems to admit the right of society to condemn homosexuality and prostitution as immoral, requires special circumstances to be shown to justify the intervention of the law. I think that this is wrong in principle and that any attempt to approach my second interrogatory on these lines is bound to break down. I think that the attempt by he Committee does break down and that this is shown by the fact that it has to define or describe its special circumstances so widely that they can be supported only if it is accepted that the law *is* concerned with immorality as such.

The widest of the special circumstances are described as the provision of "sufficient safeguards against exploitation and corruption of others, particularly those who are specially vulnerable because they are young, weak in body or mind, inexperienced, or in a state of special physical, official or economic dependence." [15] The corruption of youth is a well-recognized ground for intervention by the State and for the purpose of any legislation the young can easily be defined. But if similar protection were to be extended to every other citizen, there would be no limit to the reach of the law. The "corruption and exploitation of others" is so wide that it could be used to cover any sort of immorality which involves, as most do, the co-operation of another person. Even if the phrase is taken as limited to the categories that are particularized as "specially vulnerable," it is so elastic as to be practically no restriction. This is not merely a matter of words. For if the words used are stretched almost beyond breaking-point, they still are not wide enough to cover the recommendations which the Committee make about prostitution.

Prostitution is not in itself illegal and the Committee do not

[15] Para. 13.

think that it ought to be made so.[16] If prostitution is private immorality and not the law's business, what concern has the law with the ponce or the brothel-keeper or the householder who permits habitual prostitution? The Report recommends that the laws which make these activities criminal offences should be maintained or strengthened and brings them (so far as it goes into principle; with regard to brothels it says simply that the law rightly frowns on them) under the head of exploitation.[17] There may be cases of exploitation in this trade, as there are or used to be in many others, but in general a ponce exploits a prostitute no more than an impresario exploits an actress. The Report finds that "the great majority of prostitutes are women whose psychological makeup is such that they choose this life because they find in it a style of living which is to them easier, freer and more profitable than would be provided by any other occupation. . . . In the main the association between prostitute and ponce is voluntary and operates to mutual advantage." [18] The Committee would agree that this could not be called exploitation in the ordinary sense. They say: "It is in our view an over-simplification to think that those who live on the earnings of prostitution are exploiting the prostitute as such. What they are really exploiting is the whole complex of the relationship between prostitute and customer; they are, in effect, exploiting the human weaknesses which cause the customer to seek the prostitute and the prostitute to meet the demand." [19]

All sexual immorality involves the exploitation of human weaknesses. The prostitute exploits the lust of her customers and the customer the moral weakness of the prostitute. If the exploitation of human weaknesses is considered to create a special circumstance, there is virtually no field of morality which can be defined in such a way as to exclude the law.

I think, therefore, that it is not possible to set theoretical limits to the power of the State to legislate against immorality. It is not possible to settle in advance exceptions to the general rule or to define inflexibly areas of morality into which the law is in no circumstances to be allowed to enter. Society is entitled by means of its laws

[16] Paras. 224, 285, and 318.
[17] Paras. 302 and 320.
[18] Para. 223.
[19] Para. 306.

to protect itself from dangers, whether from within or without. Here again I think that the political parallel is legitimate. The law of treason is directed against aiding the king's enemies and against sedition from within. The justification for this is that established government is necessary for the existence of society and therefore its safety against violent overthrow must be secured. But an established morality is as necessary as good government to the welfare of society. Societies disintegrate from within more frequently than they are broken up by external pressures. There is disintegration when no common morality is observed and history shows that the loosening of moral bonds is often the first stage of disintegration, so that society is justified in taking the same steps to preserve its moral code as it does to preserve its government and other essential institutions.[20] The suppression of vice is as much the law's business

---

[20] It is somewhere about this point in the argument that Professor Hart in *Law, Liberty and Morality* discerns a proposition which he describes as central to my thought. He states the proposition and his objection to it as follows (p. 51). "He appears to move from the acceptable proposition that *some* shared morality is essential to the existence of any society [this I take to be the proposition on p. 12] to the unacceptable proposition that a society is identical with its morality as that is at any given moment of its history, so that a change in its morality is tantamount to the destruction of society. The former proposition might be even accepted as a necessary rather than an empirical truth depending on a quite plausible definition of society as a body of men who hold certain moral views in common. But the latter proposition is absurd. Taken strictly, it would prevent us saying that the morality of a given society had changed, and would compel us instead to say that one society had disappeared and another one taken its place. But it is only on this absurd criterion of what it is for the same society to continue to exist that it could be asserted without evidence that any deviation from a society's shared morality threatens its existence." In conclusion (p. 82) Professor Hart condemns the whole thesis in the lecture as based on "a confused definition of what a society is."

I do not assert that *any* deviation from a society's shared morality threatens its existence any more than I assert that *any* subversive activity threatens its existence. I assert that they are both activities which are capable in their nature of threatening the existence of society so that neither can be put beyond the law.

For the rest, the objection appears to me to be all a matter of words. I would venture to assert, for example, that you cannot have a game without rules and that if there were no rules there would be no game. If I am asked whether that means that the game is "identical" with the rules, I would be willing for the question to be answered either way in the belief that the answer would lead to nowhere. If I am asked whether a change in the rules means that one game has disappeared and another has taken its place, I would reply probably not, but that it would depend on the extent of the change.

Likewise I should venture to assert that there cannot be a contract

as the suppression of subversive activities; it is no more possible to define a sphere of private morality than it is to define one of private subversive activity. It is wrong to talk of private morality or of the law not being concerned with immorality as such or to try to set rigid bounds to the part which the law may play in the suppression of vice. There are no theoretical limits to the power of the State to legislate against treason and sedition, and likewise I think there can be no theoretical limits to legislation against immorality. You may argue that if a man's sins affect only himself it cannot be the concern of society. If he chooses to get drunk every night in the privacy of his own home, is any one except himself the worse for it? But suppose a quarter or a half of the population got drunk every night, what sort of society would it be? You cannot set a theoretical limit to the number of people who can get drunk before society is entitled to legislate against drunkenness. The same may be said of gambling. The Royal Commission of Betting, Lotteries, and Gaming took as their test the character of the citizen as a member of society. They said: "Our concern with the ethical significance of gambling is confined to the effect which it may have on the character of the gambler as a member of society. If we were convinced that whatever the degree of gambling this effect must be harmful we should be inclined to think that it was the duty of the state to restrict gambling to the greatest extent practicable." [21]

---

without terms. Does this mean that an "amended" contract is a "new" contract in the eyes of the law? I once listened to an argument by an ingenious counsel that a contract, because of the substitution of one clause for another, had "ceased to have effect" within the meaning of a statutory provision. The judge did not accept the argument; but if most of the fundamental terms had been changed, I daresay he would have done.

The proposition that I make in the text is that if (as I understand Professor Hart to agree, at any rate for the purposes of the argument) you cannot have a society without morality, the law can be used to enforce morality as something that is essential to a society. I cannot see why this proposition (whether it is right or wrong) should mean that morality can never be changed without the destruction of society. If morality is changed, the law can be changed. Professor Hart refers (p. 72) to the proposition as "the use of legal punishment to freeze into immobility the morality dominant at a particular time in a society's existence." One might as well say that the inclusion of a penal section into a statute prohibiting certain acts freezes the whole statute into immobility and prevents the prohibitions from ever being modified.

These points are elaborated in the sixth lecture at pp. 115–16.

[21] (1951) Cmd. 8190, para. 159.

In what circumstances the State should exercise its power is the third of the interrogatories I have framed. But before I get to it I must raise a point which might have been brought up in any one of the three. How are the moral judgements of society to be ascertained? By leaving it until now, I can ask it in the more limited form that is now sufficient for my purpose. How is the law-maker to ascertain the moral judgements of society? It is surely not enough that they should be reached by the opinion of the majority; it would be too much to require the individual assent of every citizen. English law has evolved and regularly uses a standard which does not depend on the counting of heads. It is that of the reasonable man. He is not to be confused with the rational man. He is not expected to reason about anything and his judgement may be largely a matter of feeling. It is the viewpoint of the man in the street — or to use an archaism familiar to all lawyers — the man in the Clapham omnibus. He might also be called the right-minded man. For my purpose I should like to call him the man in the jury box, for the moral judgement of society must be something about which any twelve men or women drawn at random might after discussion be expected to be unanimous. This was the standard the judges applied in the days before Parliament was as active as it is now and when they laid down rules of public policy. They did not think of themselves as making law but simply as stating principles which every right-minded person would accept as valid. It is what Pollock called "practical morality," which is based not on theological or philosophical foundations but "in the mass of continuous experience half-consciously or unconsciously accumulated and embodied in the morality of common sense." He called it also "a certain way of thinking on questions of morality which we expect to find in a reasonable civilized man or a reasonable Englishman taken at random." [22]

Immorality then, for the purpose of the law, is what every right-minded person is presumed to consider to be immoral. Any immorality is capable of affecting society injuriously and in effect to a greater or lesser extent it usually does; this is what gives the law its *locus standi*. It cannot be shut out. But — and this brings me to the third question — the individual has a *locus standi* too; he cannot be expected to surrender to the judgement of society the whole conduct

[22] *Essays in Jurisprudence and Ethics* (1882), Macmillan, pp. 278 and 353.

of his life. It is the old and familiar question of striking a balance between the rights and interests of society and those of the individual. This is something which the law is constantly doing in matters large and small. To take a very down-to-earth example, let me consider the right of the individual whose house adjoins the highway to have access to it; that means in these days the right to have vehicles stationary in the highway, sometimes for a considerable time if there is a lot of loading or unloading. There are many cases in which the courts have had to balance the private right of access against the public right to use the highway without obstruction. It cannot be done by carving up the highway into public and private areas. It is done by recognizing that each have rights over the whole; that if each were to exercise their rights to the full, they would come into conflict; and therefore that the rights of each must be curtailed so as to ensure as far as possible that the essential needs of each are safeguarded.

I do not think that one can talk sensibly of a public and private morality any more than one can of a public or private highway. Morality is a sphere in which there is a public interest and a private interest, often in conflict, and the problem is to reconcile the two. This does not mean that it is impossible to put forward any general statements about how in our society the balance ought to be struck. Such statements cannot of their nature be rigid or precise; they would not be designed to circumscribe the operation of the law-making power but to guide those who have to apply it. While every decision which a court of law makes when it balances the public against the private interest is an ad hoc decision, the cases contain statements of principle to which the court should have regard when it reaches its decision. In the same way it is possible to make general statements of principle which it may be thought the legislature should bear in mind when it is considering the enactment of laws enforcing morals.

I believe that most people would agree upon the chief of these elastic principles. There must be toleration of the maximum individual freedom that is consistent with the integrity of society. It cannot be said that this is a principle that runs all through the criminal law. Much of the criminal law that is regulatory in character — the part of it that deals with *malum prohibitum* rather than *malum in se* — is based upon the opposite principle, that is, that the choice of the individual must give way to the convenience of the many.

But in all matters of conscience the principle I have stated is generally held to prevail. It is not confined to thought and speech; it extends to action, as is shown by the recognition of the right to conscientious objection in war-time; this example shows also that conscience will be respected even in times of national danger. The principle appears to me to be peculiarly appropriate to all questions of morals. Nothing should be punished by the law that does not lie beyond the limits of tolerance. It is not nearly enough to say that a majority dislike a practice; there must be a real feeling of reprobation. Those who are dissatisfied with the present law on homosexuality often say that the opponents of reform are swayed simply by disgust. If that were so it would be wrong, but I do not think one can ignore disgust if it is deeply felt and not manufactured. Its presence is a good indication that the bounds of toleration are being reached. Not everything is to be tolerated. No society can do without intolerance, indignation, and disgust;[23] they are the forces behind the moral law, and indeed it can be argued that if they or something like them are not present, the feelings of society cannot be weighty enough to deprive the individual of freedom of choice. I suppose that there is hardly anyone nowadays who would not be disgusted by the thought of deliberate cruelty to animals. No one proposes to relegate that or any other form of sadism to the realm of private morality or to allow it to be practised in public or in private. It would be possible no doubt to point out that until a comparatively short while ago nobody thought very much of cruelty to animals and also that pity and kindliness and the unwillingness to inflict pain are virtues more generally esteemed now than they have ever been in the past. But matters of this sort are not determined by rational argument. Every moral judgement, unless it claims a divine source, is simply a feeling that no right-minded man could behave in any other way without admitting that he was doing wrong. It is the power of a common sense and not the power of reason that is behind the judgements of society. But before a society can put a practice beyond the limits of tolerance there must be a deliberate judgement that the practice is injurious to society. There is, for example, a general abhorrence of homosexuality. We should ask ourselves in

[23] These words, which have been much criticized, are considered again in the Preface at p. viii.

the first instance whether, looking at it calmly and dispassionately, we regard it as a vice so abominable that its mere presence is an offence. If that is the genuine feeling of the society in which we live, I do not see how society can be denied the right to eradicate it. Our feeling may not be so intense as that. We may feel about it that, if confined, it is tolerable, but that if it spread it might be gravely injurious; it is in this way that most societies look upon fornication, seeing it as a natural weakness which must be kept within bounds but which cannot be rooted out. It becomes then a question of balance, the danger to society in one scale and the extent of the restriction in the other. On this sort of point the value of an investigation by such a body as the Wolfenden Committee and of its conclusions is manifest.

The limits of tolerance shift. This is supplementary to what I have been saying but of sufficient importance in itself to deserve statement as a separate principle which law-makers have to bear in mind. I suppose that moral standards do not shift; so far as they come from divine revelation they do not, and I am willing to assume that the moral judgements made by a society always remain good for that society. But the extent to which society will tolerate — I mean tolerate, not approve — departures from moral standards varies from generation to generation. It may be that over-all tolerance is always increasing. The pressure of the human mind, always seeking greater freedom of thought, is outwards against the bonds of society forcing their gradual relaxation. It may be that history is a tale of contraction and expansion and that all developed societies are on their way to dissolution. I must not speak of things I do not know; and anyway as a practical matter no society is willing to make provision for its own decay. I return therefore to the simple and observable fact that in matters of morals the limits of tolerance shift. Laws, especially those which are based on morals, are less easily moved. It follows as another good working principle that in any new matter of morals the law should be slow to act. By the next generation the swell of indignation may have abated and the law be left without the strong backing which it needs. But it is then difficult to alter the law without giving the impression that moral judgement is being weakened. This is now one of the factors that is strongly militating against any alteration to the law on homosexuality.

A third elastic principle must be advanced more tentatively. It is that as far as possible privacy should be respected. This is not an idea that has ever been made explicit in the criminal law. Acts or words done or said in public or in private are all brought within its scope without distinction in principle. But there goes with this a strong reluctance on the part of judges and legislators to sanction invasions of privacy in the detection of crime. The police have no more right to trespass than the ordinary citizen has; there is no general right of search; to this extent an Englishman's home is still his castle. The Government is extremely careful in the exercise even of those powers which it claims to be undisputed. Telephone tapping and interference with the mails afford a good illustration of this. A Committee of three Privy Councillors who recently inquired [24] into these activities found that the Home Secretary and his predecessors had already formulated strict rules governing the exercise of these powers and the Committee were able to recommend that they should be continued to be exercised substantially on the same terms. But they reported that the power was "regarded with general disfavour."

This indicates a general sentiment that the right to privacy is something to be put in the balance against the enforcement of the law. Ought the same sort of consideration to play any part in the formation of the law? Clearly only in a very limited number of cases. When the help of the law is invoked by an injured citizen, privacy must be irrelevant; the individual cannot ask that his right to privacy should be measured against injury criminally done to another. But when all who are involved in the deed are consenting parties and the injury is done to morals, the public interest in the moral order can be balanced against the claims of privacy. The restriction on police powers of investigation goes further than the affording of a parallel; it means that the detection of crime committed in private and when there is no complaint is bound to be rather haphazard and this is an additional reason for moderation. These considerations do not justify the exclusion of all private immorality from the scope of the law. I think that, as I have already suggested, the test of "private behaviour" should be substituted for 'private morality' and the influence of the factor should be reduced from that of a definite limitation to that of a matter to be taken into account. Since the gravity of the crime is also a proper consideration, a distinction might well be made in the

[24] (1957) Cmd. 283.

case of homosexuality between the lesser acts of indecency and the full offence, which on the principles of the Wolfenden Report it would be illogical to do.

The last and the biggest thing to be remembered is that the law is concerned with the minimum and not with the maximum; there is much in the Sermon on the Mount that would be out of place in the Ten Commandments. We all recognize the gap between the moral law and the law of the land. No man is worth much who regulates his conduct with the sole object of escaping punishment, and every worthy society sets for its members standards which are above those of the law. We recognize the existence of such higher standards when we use expressions such as "moral obligation" and "morally bound." The distinction was well put in the judgement of African elders in a family dispute: "We have power to make you divide the crops, for this is our law, and we will see this is done. But we have not power to make you behave like an upright man."[25]

It can only be because this point is so obvious that it is so frequently ignored. Discussion among law-makers, both professional and amateur, is too often limited to what is right or wrong and good or bad for society. There is a failure to keep separate the two questions I have earlier posed — the question of society's right to pass a moral judgement and the question of whether the arm of the law should be used to enforce the judgement. The criminal law is not a statement of how people ought to behave; it is a statement of what will happen to them if they do not behave; good citizens are not expected to come within reach of it or to set their sights by it, and every enactment should be framed accordingly.

The arm of the law is an instrument to be used by society, and the decision about what particular cases it should be used in is essentially a practical one. Since it is an instrument, it is wise before deciding to use it to have regard to the tools with which it can be fitted and to the machinery which operates it. Its tools are fines, imprisonment, or lesser forms of supervision (such as Borstal and probation) and — not to be ignored — the degradation that often follows upon the publication of the crime. Are any of these suited to

---

[25] A case in the Saa-Katengo Kuta at Lialiu, August 1942, quoted in *The Judicial Process among the Barotse of Northern Rhodesia* by Max Gluckman, Manchester University Press, 1955, p. 172.

the job of dealing with sexual immorality? The fact that there is so much immorality which has never been brought within the law shows that there can be no general rule. It is a matter for decision in each case; but in the case of homosexuality the Wolfenden Report rightly has regard to the views of those who are experienced in dealing with this sort of crime and to those of the clergy who are the natural guardians of public morals.

The machinery which sets the criminal law in motion ends with the verdict and the sentence; and a verdict is given either by magistrates or by a jury. As a general rule, whenever a crime is sufficiently serious to justify a maximum punishment of more than three months, the accused has the right to the verdict of a jury. The result is that magistrates administer mostly what I have called the regulatory part of the law. They deal extensively with drunkenness, gambling, and prostitution, which are matters of morals or close to them, but not with any of the graver moral offences. They are more responsive than juries to the ideas of the legislature; it may not be accidental that the Wolfenden Report, in recommending increased penalties for solicitation, did not go above the limit of three months. Juries tend to dilute the decrees of Parliament with their own ideas of what should be punishable. Their province of course is fact and not law, and I do not mean that they often deliberately disregard the law. But if they think it is too stringent, they sometimes take a very merciful view of the facts. Let me take one example out of many that could be given. It is an offence to have carnal knowledge of a girl under the age of sixteen years. Consent on her part is no defence; if she did not consent, it would of course amount to rape. The law makes special provision for the situation when a boy and girl are near in age. If a man under twenty-four can prove that he had reasonable cause to believe that the girl was over the age of sixteen years, he has a good defence. The law regards the offence as sufficiently serious to make it one that is triable only by a judge at assizes. "Reasonable cause" means not merely that the boy honestly believed that the girl was over sixteen but also that he must have had reasonable grounds for his belief. In theory it ought not to be an easy defence to make out but in fact it is extremely rare for anyone who advances it to be convicted. The fact is that the girl is often as much to blame as the boy. The object of the law, as judges repeatedly tell juries, is to protect young girls against themselves; but juries are not impressed.

The part that the jury plays in the enforcement of the criminal law, the fact that no grave offence against morals is punishable without their verdict, these are of great importance in relation to the statements of principle that I have been making. They turn what might otherwise be pure exhortation to the legislature into something like rules that the law-makers cannot safely ignore. The man in the jury box is not just an expression; he is an active reality. It will not in the long run work to make laws about morality that are not acceptable to him.

This then is how I believe my third interrogatory should be answered — not by the formulation of hard and fast rules, but by a judgement in each case taking into account the sort of factors I have been mentioning. The line that divides the criminal law from the moral is not determinable by the application of any clear-cut principle. It is like a line that divides land and sea, a coastline of irregularities and indentations. There are gaps and promontories, such as adultery and fornication, which the law has for centuries left substantially untouched. Adultery of the sort that breaks up marriage seems to me to be just as harmful to the social fabric as homosexuality or bigamy. The only ground for putting it outside the criminal law is that a law which made it a crime would be too difficult to enforce; it is too generally regarded as a human weakness not suitably punished by imprisonment. All that the law can do with fornication is to act against its worst manifestations; there is a general abhorrence of the commercialization of vice, and that sentiment gives strength to the law against brothels and immoral earnings. There is no logic to be found in this. The boundary between the criminal law and the moral law is fixed by balancing in the case of each particular crime the pros and cons of legal enforcement in accordance with the sort of considerations I have been outlining. The fact that adultery, fornication, and lesbianism are untouched by the criminal law does not prove that homosexuality ought not to be touched. The error of jurisprudence in the Wolfenden Report is caused by the search for some single principle to explain the division between crime and sin. The Report finds it in the principle that the criminal law exists for the protection of individuals; on this principle fornication in private between consenting adults is outside the law and thus it becomes logically indefensible to bring homosexuality between consenting adults in private within it. But the true principle is that the law exists for the protection of society. It does not discharge its function by protecting the individual from injury, annoyance, corruption, and exploitation; the law must protect also the institutions and the community of ideas, political and moral, without which people cannot live together. Society cannot ignore the morality of the individual any more than it can his loyalty; it flourishes on both and without either it dies.

I have said that the morals which underly the law must be derived from the sense of right and wrong which resides in the community as a whole; it does not matter whence the community of thought comes, whether from one body of doctrine or another or from the knowledge of good and evil which no man is without. If the reasonable man believes that a practice is immoral and believes also — no matter whether the belief is right or wrong, so be it that it is honest and dispassionate — that no right-minded member of his society could think otherwise, then for the purpose of the law it is immoral. This, you may say, makes immorality a question of fact — what the law would consider as self-evident fact no doubt, but still with no higher authority than any other doctrine of public policy. I think that that is so, and indeed the law does not distinguish between an act that is immoral and one that is contrary to public policy. But the law has never yet had occasion to inquire into the differences between Christian morals and those which every right-minded member of society is expected to hold. The inquiry would, I believe, be academic. Moralists would find differences; indeed they would find them between different branches of the Christian faith on subjects such as divorce and birth-control. But for the purpose of the limited entry which the law makes into the field of morals, there is no practical difference. It seems to me therefore that the free-thinker and the non-Christian can accept, without offence to his convictions, the fact that Christian morals are the basis of the criminal law and that he can recognize, also without taking offence, that without the support of the churches the moral order, which has its origin in and takes its strength from Christian beliefs, would collapse.

This brings me back in the end to a question I posed at the beginning. What is the relationship between crime and sin, between the Church and the Law? I do not think that you can equate crime with sin. The divine law and the secular have been disunited, but they are brought together again by the need which each has for the other. It is not my function to emphasize the Church's need of the secular law; it can be put tersely by saying that you cannot have a ceiling without a floor. I am very clear about the law's need for the Church. I have spoken of the criminal law as dealing with the minimum standards of human conduct and the moral law with the maximum. The instrument of the criminal law is punishment; those of the moral law are teaching, training, and exhortation. If the whole dead weight of sin were ever to be allowed to fall upon the law, it could not take the strain. If at any point there is a lack of clear and convincing moral teaching, the administration of the law suffers. Let me take as an illustration of this the law on abortion. I believe that a great many people nowadays do not understand why abortion is wrong. If it is right to prevent conception, at what point does it become sinful to prevent birth and why? I doubt if anyone who has not had a theological training would give a satisfactory answer to that question. Many people regard abortion as the next step when by accident birth-control has failed; and many more people are deterred from abortion not because they think it sinful or illegal but because of the difficulty which illegality puts in the way of obtaining it. The law is powerless to deal with abortion *per se;* unless a tragedy occurs or a "professional" abortionist is involved — the parallel between the "professional" in abortions and the "professional" in fornication is quite close — it has to leave it alone. With one or other of these features the crime is rarely detected; and when detected, the plea *ad misericordiam* is often too strong. The "professional" abortionist is usually the unskilled person who for a small reward helps girls in trouble; the man and the girl involved are essential witnesses for the prosecution and therefore go free; the paid abortionist generally receives a very severe sentence, much more severe than that usually given to the paid assistant in immorality, such as the ponce or the brothel-keeper. The reason is because unskilled abortion endangers life. In a case in 1949 [26] Lord Chief Justice Goddard said: "It is because the unskilful attentions of ignorant people in cases of this kind often result in death that attempts to produce abortion are regarded by the law as very serious offences." This gives the law a twist which disassociates it from morality and, I think, to some extent from sound sense. The act is being punished

[26] *R. v. Tate, The Times,* 22 June 1949.

because it is dangerous, and it is dangerous largely because it is illegal and therefore performed only by the unskilled.

The object of what I have said is not to criticize theology or law in relation to abortion. That is a large subject and beyond my present scope. It is to show what happens to the law in matters of morality about which the community as a whole is not deeply imbued with a sense of sin; the law sags under a weight which it is not constructed to bear and may become permanently warped.

I return now to the main thread of my argument and summarize it. Society cannot live without morals. Its morals are those standards of conduct which the reasonable man approves. A rational man, who is also a good man, may have other standards. If he has no standards at all he is not a good man and need not be further considered. If he has standards, they may be very different; he may, for example, not disapprove of homosexuality or abortion. In that case he will not share in the common morality; but that should not make him deny that it is a social necessity. A rebel may be rational in thinking that he is right but he is irrational if he thinks that society can leave him free to rebel.

A man who concedes that morality is necessary to society must support the use of those instruments without which morality cannot be maintained. The two instruments are those of teaching, which is doctrine, and of enforcement, which is the law. If morals could be taught simply on the basis that they are necessary to society, there would be no social need for religion; it could be left as a purely personal affair. But morality cannot be taught in that way. Loyalty is not taught in that way either. No society has yet solved the problem of how to teach morality without religion. So the law must base itself on Christian morals and to the limit of its ability enforce them, not simply because they are the morals of most of us, nor simply because they are the morals which are taught by the established Church — on these points the law recognizes the right to dissent — but for the compelling reason that without the help of Christian teaching the law will fail.

---

# Immorality and Treason

### H. L. A. HART

The Wolfenden Committee on Homosexual Offences and Prostitution recommended by a majority of 12 to 1 that homosexual behaviour between consenting adults in private should no longer be a criminal offence. One of the Committee's principal grounds for this recommendation was expressed in its report in this way: "There must remain a realm of private morality and immorality which in brief and crude terms is not the law's business." I shall call this the liberal point of view: for it is a special application of those wider principles of liberal thought which John Stuart Mill formulated in his essay on Liberty. Mill's most famous words, less cautious perhaps than the Wolfenden Committee's, were:

> The only purpose for which power can be rightfully exercised over any member of a civilized community against his will is to prevent harm to others. His own good, either physical or moral, is not a sufficient warrant. He cannot rightfully be compelled to do or forbear . . . because in the opinion of others to do so would be wise or even right.

### REPUDIATION OF THE LIBERAL POINT OF VIEW

The liberal point of view has often been attacked, both before and after Mill. I shall discuss here the repudiation of it made by Sir Patrick Devlin, in his recent lecture, which has now been published.[1] This contains an original and interesting argument designed to show that "*prima facie* society has the right to legislate against immorality as such" and that the Wolfenden Committee were mistaken in thinking that there is an area of private immorality which is not the law's business. Sir Patrick's case is a general one, not

From *The Listener,* July 30, 1959, pp. 162–163. Reprinted by permission of author and publisher.

[1] *The Enforcement of Morals. Proceedings of the British Academy: Maccabaean Lecture in Jurisprudence* (Oxford).

confined to sexual immorality, and he does not say whether or not he is opposed to the Wolfenden Committee's recommendation on homosexual behaviour. Instead he gives us a hypothetical principle by which to judge this issue. He says: "If it is the genuine feeling of our society that homosexuality is a vice so abominable that its mere presence is an offence," society has the right to eradicate it by the use of the criminal law.

The publication by Sir Patrick of his lecture is in itself an interesting event. It is many years since a distinguished English lawyer delivered himself of general reasoned views about the relationship of morality to the criminal law. The last to do so with comparable skill and clarity was, I think, the great Victorian judge James Fitzjames Stephen. It is worth observing that Stephen, like Sir Patrick, repudiated the liberal point of view. Indeed his gloomy but impressive book *Liberty, Equality, Fraternity* was a direct reply to Mill's essay *On Liberty*. The most remarkable feature of Sir Patrick's lecture is his view of the nature of morality — the morality which the criminal law may enforce. Most previous thinkers who have repudiated the liberal point of view have done so because they thought that morality consisted either of divine commands or of rational principles of human conduct discoverable by human reason. Since morality for them had this elevated divine or rational status as the law of God or reason, it seemed obvious that the state should enforce it, and that the function of human law should not be merely to provide men with the opportunity for leading a good life, but actually to see that they lead it. Sir Patrick does not rest his repudiation of the liberal point of view on these religious or rationalist conceptions. Indeed much that he writes reads like an abjuration of the notion that reasoning or thinking has much to do with morality. English popular morality has no doubt its historical connexion with the Christian religion: "That," says Sir Patrick, "is how it got there." But it does not owe its present status or social significance to religion any more than to reason.

What, then, is it? According to Sir Patrick it is primarily a matter of feeling. "Every moral judgment," he says, "is a feeling that no right-minded man could act in any other way without admitting that he was doing wrong." Who then must feel this way if we are to have what Sir Patrick calls a public morality? He tells us that it is "the man in the street," "the man in the jury box," or (to use the phrase so familiar to English lawyers) "the man on the Clapham omnibus." For the moral judgments of society so far as the law is concerned are to be ascertained by the standards of the reasonable man, and he is not to be confused with the rational man. Indeed, Sir Patrick says "he is not expected to reason about anything and his judgment may be largely a matter of feeling."

### INTOLERANCE, INDIGNATION, AND DISGUST

But what precisely are the relevant feelings, the feelings which may justify use of the criminal law? Here the argument becomes a little complex. Widespread dislike of a practice is not enough. There must, says Sir Patrick, be "a real feeling of reprobation." Disgust is not enough either. What is crucial is a combination of intolerance, indignation, and disgust. These three are the forces behind the moral law, without which it is not "weighty enough to deprive the individual of freedom of choice." Hence there is, in Sir Patrick's outlook, a crucial difference between the mere adverse moral judgment of society and one which is inspired by feeling raised to the concert pitch of intolerance, indignation, and disgust.

This distinction is novel and also very important. For on it depends the weight to be given to the fact that when morality is enforced individual liberty is necessarily cut down. Though Sir Patrick's abstract formulation of his views on this point is hard to follow, his examples make his position fairly clear. We can see it best in the contrasting things he says about fornication and homosexuality. In regard to fornication, public feeling in most societies is not now of the concert-pitch intensity. We may feel that it is tolerable if confined: only its spread might be gravely injurious. In such cases the question whether individual liberty should be restricted is for Sir Patrick a question of balance between the danger to society in the one scale, and the restriction of the individual in the other. But if, as may be the case with homosexuality, public feeling is up to concert pitch, if it expresses a "deliberate judgment" that a practice as such is injurious to society, if there is "a genuine feeling that it is a vice so abominable that its mere presence is an offence," then it is beyond the limits of tolerance, and society may eradicate it. In this case, it seems, no further balancing of the claims of individual liberty is to be done, though as a matter of prudence the legislator should remember that the popular limits of tolerance may shift: the concert pitch feeling may subside. This may produce a dilemma for the law; for the law may then be left without the full moral backing that it needs, yet it cannot be altered without giving the impression that the moral judgment is being weakened.

If this is what morality is — a compound of indignation, intolerance, and disgust — we may well ask what justification there is for taking it, and turning it as such, into criminal law with all the misery which criminal punishment entails. Here Sir Patrick's answer is very clear and simple. A collection of individuals is not a society; what makes them into a society is among other things a shared or public morality. This is as necessary to its existence as an organized government. So society may use the law to preserve its morality like anything else essential to it. "The suppression of vice is as much the law's business as the suppression of subversive activities." The liberal point of view which denies this is guilty of "an error in jurisprudence": for it is no more possible to define an area of private morality than an area of private subversive activity. There can be no "theoretical limits" to legislation against immorality just as there are no such limits to the power of the state to legislate against treason and sedition.

Surely all this, ingenious as it is, is misleading. Mill's formulation of the liberal point of view may well be too simple. The grounds for interfering with human liberty are more various than the single criterion of "harm to others" suggests: cruelty to animals or organizing prostitution for gain do not, as Mill himself saw, fall easily under the description of harm to others. Conversely, even where there is harm to others in the most literal sense, there may well be other principles limiting the extent to which harmful activities should be repressed by law. So there are multiple criteria, not a single criterion, determining when human liberty may be restricted. Perhaps this is what Sir Patrick means by a curious distinction which he often stresses between theoretical and practical limits. But with all its simplicities the liberal point of view is a better guide than Sir Patrick to clear thought on the proper relation of morality to the criminal law: for it stresses what he obscures — namely, the points at which thought is needed before we turn popular morality into criminal law.

## SOCIETY AND MORAL OPINION

No doubt we would all agree that a consensus of moral opinion on certain matters is essential if society is to be worth living in. Laws against murder, theft, and much else would be of little use if they were not supported by a widely diffused conviction that what these laws forbid is also immoral. So much is obvious. But it does not follow that everything to which the moral vetoes of accepted morality attach is of equal importance to society; nor is there the slightest reason for thinking of morality as a seamless web: one which will fall to pieces carrying society with it, unless all its emphatic vetoes are enforced by law. Surely even in the face of the moral feeling that is up to concert pitch — the trio of intolerance, indignation, and disgust — we must pause to think. We must ask a question at two different levels which Sir Patrick never clearly enough identifies or separates. First, we must ask whether a practice which offends moral feeling is harmful, independently of its repercussion on the general moral code. Secondly, what about repercussion on the moral code? Is it really true that failure to translate this item of general morality into criminal law will jeopardize the whole fabric of morality and so of society?

We cannot escape thinking about these two different questions merely by repeating to ourselves the vague nostrum: "This is part of public morality and public morality must be preserved if society is to exist." Sometimes Sir Patrick seems to admit this, for he says in words which both Mill and the Wolfenden Report might have used, that there must be the maximum respect for individual liberty consistent with the integrity of society. Yet this, as his contrasting examples of fornication and homosexuality show, turns out to mean only that the immorality which the law may punish must be generally felt to be intolerable. This plainly is no adequate substitute for a reasoned estimate of the damage to the fabric of society likely to ensue if it is not suppressed.

Nothing perhaps shows more clearly the inadequacy of Sir Patrick's approach to this problem than his comparison between the suppression of sexual immorality and the suppression of treason or subversive activity. Private subversive activity is, of course, a contradiction in terms because "subversion" means overthrowing government, which is a public thing. But it is grotesque, even where moral feeling against homosexuality is up to concert pitch, to think of the homosexual behaviour of two adults in private as in any way like treason or sedition either in intention or effect. We can make it *seem* like treason only if we assume that deviation from a general moral code is bound to affect that code, and to lead not merely to its modification but to its destruction. The analogy could begin to be plausible only if it was clear that offending against this item of morality was likely to jeopardize the whole structure. But we have ample evidence for believing that people will not abandon morality, will not think any better of murder, cruelty, and dishonesty, merely because some private sexual practice which they abominate is not punished by the law.

Because this is so the analogy with treason is absurd. Of course "No man is an island": what one man does in private, if it is known, may affect others in many different ways. Indeed it may be that deviation from general sexual morality by those whose lives, like the lives of many homosexuals, are noble ones and in all other ways exemplary will lead to what Sir Patrick calls the shifting of the limits of tolerance. But if this has any analogy in the sphere of government it is not the overthrow of ordered government, but a peaceful change in its form. So we may listen to the promptings of common sense and of logic, and say that though there could not logically be a sphere of private treason there is a sphere of private morality and immorality.

Sir Patrick's doctrine is also open to a wider, perhaps a deeper, criticism. In his reaction against a rationalist morality and his stress on feeling, he has I think thrown out the baby and kept the bath water; and the bath water may turn out to be very dirty indeed. When Sir Patrick's lecture was first delivered *The Times* greeted it with these words: "There is a moving and welcome humility in the conception that society should not be asked to give its reason for refusing to tolerate what in its heart it feels intolerable." This drew from a correspondent in Cambridge the retort: "I am afraid that we are less humble than we used to be. We once burnt old women because, without giving our reasons, we felt in our hearts that witchcraft was intolerable."

This retort is a bitter one, yet its bitterness is salutary. We are not, I suppose, likely, in England, to take again to the burning of old women for witchcraft or to punishing people for associating with those of a different race or colour, or to punishing people again for adultery. Yet if these things were viewed with intolerance, indignation, and disgust, as the second of them still is in some countries, it seems that on

Sir Patrick's principles no rational criticism could be opposed to the claim that they should be punished by law. We could only pray, in his words, that the limits of tolerance might shift.

### CURIOUS LOGIC

It is impossible to see what curious logic has led Sir Patrick to this result. For him a practice is immoral if the thought of it makes the man on the Clapham omnibus sick. So be it. Still, why should we not summon all the resources of our reason, sympathetic understanding, as well as critical intelligence, and insist that before general moral feeling is turned into criminal law it is submitted to scrutiny of a different kind from Sir Patrick's? Surely, the legislator should ask whether the general morality is based on ignorance, superstition, or misunderstanding; whether there is a false conception that those who practise what it condemns are in other ways dangerous or hostile to society; and whether the misery to many parties, the blackmail and the other evil consequences of criminal punishment, especially for sexual offences, are well understood. It is surely extraordinary that among the things which Sir Patrick says are to be considered before we legislate against immorality these appear nowhere; not even as "practical considerations," let alone "theoretical limits." To any theory which, like this one, asserts that the criminal law may be used on the vague ground that the preservation of morality is essential to society and yet omits to stress the need for critical scrutiny, our reply should be: "Morality, what crimes may be committed in thy name!"

As Mill saw, and de Tocqueville showed in detail long ago in his critical but sympathetic study of democracy, it is fatally easy to confuse the democratic principle that power should be in the hands of the majority with the utterly different claim that the majority, with power in their hands, need respect no limits. Certainly there is a special risk in a democracy that the majority may dictate how all should live. This is the risk we run, and should gladly run; for it is the price of all that is so good in democratic rule. But loyalty to democratic principles does not require us to maximize this risk: yet this is what we shall do if we mount the man in the street on the top of the Clapham omnibus and tell him that if only he feels sick enough about what other people do in private to demand its suppression by law no theoretical criticism can be made of his demand.

# Crime, Sin, and Mr. Justice Devlin

## RICHARD WOLLHEIM

It was to a most evidently impressed gathering of people that on March 18th of this year Sir Patrick Devlin delivered his lecture on *The Enforcement of Morals.* The audience was not on the face of it an impressionable one: part professional lawyers, part professional lecture-goers, it seemed as hard a nut to crack as any. But the lecturer was up to it; within a few minutes of being introduced to his audience he had clearly established his ascendency. Everything about his manner and his appearance he pressed into the service of his performance, and everything scored: the thin, slightly hunched body with an air at once of scholarship and of youth, the arms crossed in front of him revealing long and delicate wrists, the collected voice and the even flow of perfectly constructed sentences, the regular movement of the hands reaching out to turn over the notes on the lectern, page by page, without the eye ever bothering to fall on them, and the one single gesture that he permitted himself, that of occasionally running his fore-finger round the line of his right ear as if to brush away the ends of a wig that were tickling him. There was little in the lecture in the way of decoration or rhetoric or surprise, but the lack of these things only increased the magisterial, the authoritative effect of the exposition. As a lecturer Sir Patrick, one felt, stood to other lecturers rather like an electric clock stands to other clocks: he offered considerably less to the senses, but as long as he went at all, he couldn't, it seemed, go wrong; his only mistake would be to stop.

But when he stopped, as he eventually had to, the effect of his skill persisted. One went away impressed. And as if to prove one right, the *Times* the next morning took the unusual step of devoting both an article and a leader to the lecture. Sir Patrick's views about sin and crime were well on the way, it seemed, to becoming at any rate one kind of orthodoxy. The only disturbing thing — leading to further disturbing thoughts — was that Sir Patrick Devlin's argument

From *Encounter,* vol. 13 (November, 1959), pp. 34–40. Reprinted by permission of author and publisher.

as it appeared in *The Times* bore little relation to Sir Patrick Devlin's argument as it survived in the memory of at least one member of his audience.

Now that the text of this remarkable lecture is available,[1] it is a good moment to pass in review the whole incident. What did Sir Patrick Devlin really say before the British Academy on March 18th on the subject of law and morals? Is what he said true, as at the time it seemed to so many? If it is true, is it the whole truth — and if it isn't true, where does the error lie? Direct and by no means easy questions: but surely for all of us questions worth the answering. There are, I believe, few subjects on which we *ought* to hold an opinion. But this subject of laws and morals is surely one of them. Always important, it has recently gained topicality. Sir Patrick referred frequently — from the original sub-title of his lecture onwards — to the Wolfenden Report as giving the subject a present claim on our attention: but he could equally well have mentioned other issues of the day like obscenity, or artificial insemination, or divorce by mutual consent, or euthanasia, and thereby only over-established his case. If, then, the subject of Sir Patrick's lecture is all that significant, what more suitable way could there be of making an entry into it than through the examination of some concise but distinguished opinion on the matter?

*The Enforcement of Morals,* it should be pointed out, is likely to present two difficulties to the understanding of the general reader. In the first place — and this is criticism — for all its careful composition the organisation of material within the lecture is not totally satisfactory: this I shall try to bring out later. Secondly — and this is warning, not criticism — Mr. Justice Devlin sticks, with an austerity that may be rather puzzling to the layman, to the narrow track of jurisprudence. He confines himself to the principles to which law should conform, and utters no view on the law itself: and even when examining the principles of law, his interests are more what may be called *formal* than *substantive* — he asks how such principles are to be justified or validated, and when he controverts any such principle it is on account of its incoherence or inconsistency with better-grounded principles rather than on the score of its falsehood.

[1] The Hon. Sir Patrick Devlin, *The Enforcement of Morals, Maccabaean Lecture in Jurisprudence of the British Academy, 1959.* Oxford University Press.

The content of *The Enforcement of Morals* is given in the form of answers to three questions that Devlin poses: he considers that between them these questions "cover the whole field," and since they occupy so central a place in his exposition it would perhaps be fairest to give them in his own words:

> 1. Has society the right to pass judgment at all on matters of morals? Ought there, in other words, to be a public morality, or are morals always a matter for private judgment?
> 2. If society has the right to pass judgment, has it also the right to use the weapon of the law to enforce it?
> 3. If so, ought it to use that weapon in all cases or only in some; and if only in some, on what principles should it distinguish?

To the first question Devlin answers *Yes,* and he regards this answer as a necessary condition for supposing there to be a case at all for intervention on the part of law in the life of the individual. And he arrives at his answer by an a priori argument which takes as its starting-point the nature of a society. A society to be a society — as opposed, presumably, to some looser association of men — requires the existence of a community of ideas between its members, and these ideas include not merely political ideas but also ideas about how people should behave and govern their lives, i.e., moral ideas. From this it follows not merely that society may pass moral judgments, but that it must: for in so far as it fails to pass them, it ceases to be in the true acceptance of the word a society.

To the second question, whether society has the right to enforce its moral judgments by means of the law, Devlin again returns an affirmative answer, and he thinks this answer is "very nearly dictated" by the answer to the previous question. For if it is part of the nature or essence of a society to possess a common morality, then society may properly use the law to enforce this morality just as it may use it to safeguard anything else essential to its existence. And this right, it further follows, is unconditional, or has no "theoretical limits" set to it: in other words, *whatever else may be the case* society has the right to enforce morality, and it is not true that — as many moralists and jurists have maintained — some further condition must exist before society can rightfully invoke the aid of the law. It is not true, for instance (as Mill maintained) that the immorality must be of an "other-regarding" character or that (as the Wolfenden Committee maintained) it must affect those who are "specially vulnerable" before it can be proceeded against. The unconditionality of society's right to prosecute morality is, according to Devlin, evident from the way that any formulation or definition of the condition on which this right might be thought to depend, has to be made so flexible before it is found generally acceptable that by that time it excludes nothing; it becomes, in effect, a standing condition of society.

But though society has the right to deal with immorality *as such,* the question arises when should the State exercise this right? Ought it to exercise it in all cases, or only in some? This brings us to the third and last of the questions that Devlin sets himself, and his answer is that the State ought to exercise its right only in some cases, and he then advances a number of "elastic" or "practical" principles which between them determine the range of human behaviour that is at once immoral and yet to be tolerated. The first principle, and the most important, is that there should be toleration of "the maximum individual freedom that is consistent with the integrity of society"; another is that "in any new matter of morals the law should be slow to act"; another is that "as far as possible privacy should be respected"; and finally there is the principle that "the law is concerned with the minimum and not with the maximum."

•   •   •

Let us now turn to consider the various stages in Devlin's argument. First, the argument for a right inherent in society — as opposed to the individuals who constitute it — to pass moral judgments. An initial difficulty here is to see what in Devlin's eyes makes a moral judgment a judgment of society, a public not a private judgment. A moral judgment, he insists, is *not* made public by receiving the support of most members of the society in which it is passed. Its publicity seems to depend upon its being essential or internal to the nature of that society. Now if this is so, then the argument from the nature of society to the existence of public judgments of morality is clearly valid — for a society, it will be remembered, is partially defined in terms of a common morality. Wherever we have a society, we *must* have a common morality. Accordingly, the interest of the argument now focuses on its premiss; the conception of society as a community of ideas.

The conception is not novel. But over the last three hundred years it has been characteristic of the civilised parts of Europe — their pride, some would say — to develop a theory of politics which is in radical contrast to Devlin's. According to this theory the identity, and the continuity, of a society resides not in the common possession of a single morality but in the mutual toleration of different moralities. This theory is called Liberalism. It has been attacked often enough; it has formidable and uncompromising rivals in doctrines like Communism and Catholicism: but it still is the theory of most "uncommitted" thinkers in mid-twentieth-century Europe, for whom the problem seems not so much to demonstrate the acceptability or consistency of the theory as to establish exactly to what degree it can ever be realised and how great is the strain that it imposes upon human nature.

To some it might seem that the contrast between Liberalism and the political theory underlying *The Enforcement of Morals* is superficial. For toleration is a moral principle or idea, and why should we not therefore, in accordance with Devlin's theory, characterise the Liberal society as a society that finds its moral identity in the common or generally accepted principle of toleration? The suggestion is ingenious. But it won't work. It won't work, because though toleration *is* a moral principle, it is not so in the sense required by Devlin. For he requires of the common morality of a society that it should be rich and comprehensive enough for conformity to it to result in behaviour of a uniform kind over a fairly large area of human activity. Morality must be of this kind, else the problem of law and morals, as envisaged in *The Enforcement of Morals,* does not arise. For this problem is just how much of this behaviour is to be enforced by law. Now it is fairly clear that toleration cannot be seen as a morality conformity to which issues in uniform behaviour. A society can be marked by universal toleration and yet display no common pattern of behaviour: for what is tolerated may in each case be different. Accordingly, Devlin's insistence that it is in the nature of a society to possess a community of moral ideas is certainly incompatible with Liberalism; and therefore those who find Liberalism for one reason or another acceptable must reject the conception of society on which the whole of Devlin's argument depends.

But even if one were to accept Devlin's idea of society as what, I believe, used to be called "a moral entity," one might well want to object to his rather peculiar interpretation of this idea. For, as we have seen, Devlin not merely expounds what he considers to be the rôle of morality in society, he also has something to say about the nature of morality itself. And this is of an extreme subjectivist kind. It would be a negligible exaggeration of Devlin's moral philosophy to say that for him what is wrong is what makes "the man on the Clapham omnibus" sick. To ask whether the man is justified in being sick or whether he is sick on a false assumption or sick mistakenly or with no good reason (questions that we normally think it perfectly all right to raise about a moral judgment) is an evident absurdity. If he is sick, he is sick, and the best we can do is to see that he has no cause for being sick again. Reasons, justification, argument are at best persuasive tricks, at worst they are sophistries that obscure the intimate connection between the moral judgment and its emotional ground.

Such a totally irrationalist conception of morals can surely make little direct appeal, and the main interest of it must lie in the motives that prompted Devlin to embrace it; and from this point of view his case is of more than local interest. For he demonstrates in a peculiarly clear way a paradox that is recurrent in the history of ideas. We find, time and time again, a man setting out in the full intention of establishing morality on a basis that will make it at once independent of, and superior to, the individual judgments of individual men: of endowing it with an authority that is to be higher and more impersonal than the mere private conscience. And then when we look at the outcome of his efforts, we find that morality has been made to rest on what we would ordinarily think to be everything most arbitrary and unreliable in human nature; that is to say, feeling in its most primitive reaches. This is the paradox: on the one hand, morality is ascribed an objectivity that goes far beyond ordinary demands; on the other hand, what it is provided with is a grounding in total subjectivity. And yet there is a curious kind of logic, or unity of vision, that does unite these two apparently contrasted conceptions of morality, the extreme "objective" and the extreme "subjective," and accounts for the fact that they are not infrequently — though none the less uncomfortably — yoked together. For both these two conceptions share in the desire to place morality outside the forum of discussion, to make its distinctions not the fit subject for reasoning and its verdicts something that cannot be overturned in argument. Indeed it may be said with justice that both extreme objectivism and extreme subjectivism in ethics are best to be understood in terms of what they exclude; and they exclude much the same.

It is, moreover, a further fact that what they exclude is what it has been the triumph of civilisation to establish: the taming of the conscience by reason.

It is now time to turn to the last lap in Devlin's argument — the last lap, I say advisedly, because, as we have already seen, it is quite unjustified to separate, as he does, the second from the third enquiry: it is wrong to ask, first, whether society has a right to punish immorality, and, then (as though it were a quite separate question) whether this right is qualified or not. So let us now ask: Is it correct to move from society's right to pass judgments of a moral character to its right (qualified or unqualified) to enforce these judgments with the weapon of the law?

I think that the case may perhaps be argued; but what I am certain of is that it can't be argued as Devlin argues it. For he makes the transition by introducing the further premiss — which he regards as all but self-evident and therefore no real introduction into the argument — that society has a right to secure its own self-preservation. From this right society's right to enforce its own morality is supposed directly to follow. Now, society's right to self-preservation is something that, implicitly or explicitly, meets with fairly general acceptance. The right can, of course, be abused: as in the Moscow purges or the South African "treason trials." And even when exercised within due limits it is never popular. But only an anarchist could consistently deny it. Furthermore, to ground the right, as Devlin does, on the mere *existence* of society has traditional backing: it is, for instance, typical of Spinoza to argue from a thing's existence to its right to maintain itself in existence. And, arguing like this, Spinoza enjoys popular as well as traditional support.

But, I suggest, both the right of society to preserve itself and the argument that would derive this right from society's mere existence seem plausible and are acceptable only when "self-preservation" is understood in a far narrower sense than that in which it figures in Devlin's argument. For whereas in the popular understanding, self-preservation is contrasted with destruction or decay, Devlin contrasts it with change itself and makes no distinction between different kinds of change. Against corruption and against amelioration alike society is entitled to invoke the right to preserve itself. The moral identity of a democratic society is threatened by storm-troopers; the moral identity of a cannibal society is threatened by missionaries; the moral identity of Franco's Spain is threatened by Protestant bible-pedlars. If we argue with Devlin, we must concede that in all these cases the moral right of society to suppress those who would "subvert" it enjoys the same standing. Now, I doubt if this is what is meant by most of those who ordinarily talk of, and accept, society's right of self-preservation.

But even if we accept the right of self-preservation in this extended sense, it is by no means clear that it follows from it and the fact that society's morality is essential to its existence, that society has a right to enforce its morality. What *does* follow is that society has a right to preserve its morality. But are the enforcement and the preservation of morality one and the same thing? It is not obvious that they are. It is, for instance, arguable that a morality, if enforced, ceases to be respected, and once it loses respect its existence is in danger. And, again, it can be argued that for a code of morals to preserve respect, it must sometimes be broken, and if it is rigorously enforced it runs the risk of never being broken. Historical examples confirm this abstract reasoning. Sumptuary laws may provide a reasonable system of taxation, but they have done little to inculcate a moral aversion to waste and extravagance; and the relation between Prohibition and Temperance has been the inverse of that desired by reformers.

Of course there is a conclusion to be drawn from Devlin's premises, but that conclusion is not merely unacceptable but *so* unacceptable that in itself it is a powerful argument against the truth of the premises that necessitate it. And that is the proposition that society can use any method at its disposal to suppress criticism of its prevailing moral ideas. For there can be no reasonable doubt that what really places a moral code in jeopardy is the free diffusion of ideas inimical to it. For unless the code is uselessly rudimentary, or the criticism of it extremely incompetent, sooner or later some of its leading ideas are going to be very roughly handled. And then the code really will be endangered. A moral code can survive a great deal in the way of contravention; what, I submit, it can survive very little of is controversion. Is Devlin really prepared to hand over to society the right to preserve its morality from the minds of its members? Devlin's dilemma is that either he must follow the argument where it really leads him, or else he must find another argument for remaining where he wishes to be.

I think then that *The Enforcement of Morals,* for all its great literary merits and its air of extreme clarity, contains little reasoning that is at once valid and acceptable. Of course the ultimate position may be correct: in the history of ideas as many bad arguments have been produced for true conclusions as for false ones.

But there may well be those who, reading *The Enforcement of*

*Morals,* are led not merely to reject it but to reject in advance any argument of a similar kind. They may feel that any attempt to draw a line between sin and crime that makes reference to notions like the moral community or society's unqualified right to self-preservation is doomed to be unacceptable, and equally that any discussion of the subject that fails to mention human fallibility and the self-development of the individual and his faculties must be miserably incomplete. To those who feel like this I would lend a sympathetic ear. But I must, regretfully, point out that nothing I have set down here, none of the limited and local argument I have used against Devlin, can increase, to any measurable degree, the authority of what they say.

# Punishment and Responsibility

## Retribution Is Obsolete

### HENRY WEIHOFEN

Professor Bodenheimer states his thesis in such fair-minded terms that one must seem churlish to disagree with him. He admits all the objections to a retributive approach to crime and actually ends up with what I would call the utilitarian view; yet throughout his paper, he gives the over-all impression that he is criticizing that view and making defense for retribution.[1]

The first question that suggests itself is: Why should a decent and kindly philosopher like Edgar Bodenheimer feel impelled to try so hard to find something good to say about the irrational, primitive urge for vengeance? That is what he defends, and he says so. He defines the term punishment as he uses it as "an unpleasant act which society imposes as a *requital for a wrong* committed." Requital. An eye for an eye, a tooth for a tooth. He who sins must suffer.

This vindictive concept of justice is a legacy from our primitive ancestors. Every step of progress that we have made in dealing with crime and criminals has been *away* from this concept. And every step has been over violent, emotional opposition of the advocates of vengeance. This urge to punish remains today the greatest single obstacle to the adoption of a decent, rational penal program. Whenever we fail to solve the maladjustments of our society, there is the constant impulse to turn in our impatience and anger to vindictive

From Carl J. Friedrich, ed., *Responsibility* (New York: The Liberal Arts Press, 1960), pp. 116–127. By permission of the American Society for Political and Legal Philosophy.

[1] See Edgar Bodenheimer, "Is Punishment Obsolete?" Carl J. Friedrich, ed., *Responsibility* (New York: Liberal Arts Press, 1960), pp. 87–105.

punishment and terror. What we very much need is greater understanding of the irrationality and self-defeating nature of this atavistic
urge. What we do not need are philosophical efforts to sugarcoat it
with respectability.

My fundamental criticism of Professor Bodenheimer's paper,
therefore, is his emphasis on a dichotomy between "punishment" and
what he calls a utilitarian point of view and his apparent conclusion
that there is something to be said for both. I say apparent conclusion,
because, as Professor Brandt points out, his actual conclusion is not
really different from the utilitarian viewpoint, and the ends he seeks
could be achieved just as well if he took a stand against "requital."

The utilitarian approach, as Professor Bodenheimer says, has
two ends: to protect society and reform the criminal. That is all
the criminal law can do and should do — to apprehend lawbreakers
and keep them under constraint as long as public safety requires, and
in the meantime try to rehabilitate them so that they may be returned
to society as soon as it is safe to do so. Bodenheimer himself actually
comes to exactly that conclusion, when he says that an equilibrium
must be found "between the concerns of society in the repression of
crime and the delinquent's interest in being readmitted into the fold
of the community at the earliest possible opportunity."

Professor Brandt is right in saying that it only complicates one's
theory of criminal justice to add to these objectives a demand for
"requital." It does worse than complicate it; it makes utter hash of it,
as G. B. Shaw said many years ago:

> To propose to punish and reform people by the same operation
> is exactly as if you were to take a man suffering from pneumonia,
> and attempt to combine punitive and curative treatment. Arguing
> that a man with pneumonia is a danger to the community, and that
> he need not catch it if he takes proper care of his health, you resolve
> that he shall have a severe lesson, both to punish him for his
> negligence and pulmonary weakness and to deter others from follow-
> ing his example. You therefore strip him naked, and in that condition
> stand him all night in the snow. But as you admit the duty of
> restoring him to health if possible and discharging him with sound
> lungs, you engage a doctor to superintend the punishment and
> administer cough lozenges, made as unpleasant to the taste as
> possible so as not to pamper the culprit.[2]

[2] Preface to Sidney and Beatrice Webb, *English Prisons under Local
Government* (1922), p. xiv.

If we are to impose punishment for its own sake, we must decide how much to inflict. Bodenheimer says, "There must be at least a rough proportionality between the deed and the punishment." The Mikado said it more melodiously, but I am not at all sure Bodenheimer would approve the Mikado's methods of making the punishment fit the crime. Nor would people ever agree on any formula for application. Crime and punishment are different things, and cannot be equated. You can take a life for a life, but beyond that there is practically no room for the principle of equation to operate. You can't impose a rape for a rape, forgery for forgery. An eye for an eye is not impossible, but does Bodenheimer or anyone else today seriously suggest putting out the eye of a man guilty of hitting another in the eye in a felonious assault?

The nearest we could come to achieving "proportionality" between crime and punishment would be to rank crimes in what we decide, somehow, is their order of seriousness, and also rank punishments in order of their unpleasantness, and then try to correlate the two lists. Professor Brandt has discussed some of the quagmire this gets us into. Even if it could be done, the question would remain, how far up or down the scale of possible severity should the whole list of punishments be pegged? Should you start with the death penalty, or with a maximum of twenty years' imprisonment? This is a question of public policy which can only be answered intelligently on the basis of some utilitarian objectives, the reformatory (or demoralizing) effects of long prison terms, the *in terrorem* (or brutalizing) effect of executions, etc. It cannot be answered by trying to find "proportionality" between the deed and the punishment. The seriousness of a crime is a matter of value judgment, which will depend upon the cultural premises of the judge. Different cultures vary enormously in their ranking of offenses. There is certainly no universal standard. Even within our own American culture, there are surprising variations. An offense punishable by twenty years' imprisonment in one state may carry a maximum sentence of one year in another. Older statutes may reflect a view of the seriousness of a crime that is no longer current today. Such statutes will therefore prescribe punishments quite different not only from those prescribed by more recent enactments in neighboring states, but different also from the current popular standard of that state itself. Nor could this situation be met by trying to bring such statutes up to date so as to reflect current popular standards. The day is past in our society when the great majority of people accepted the same cultural norms. Ours is a heterogeneous society, and it would be impossible to achieve anything like a consensus on the relative seriousness of different crimes and the "just" punishment.[3]

For these and many other reasons, all of this abstract philosophizing about punishment as requital for crime has a musty smell about it, a smell of the professor's study. It does not breathe the air of reality, of the criminal courts, or the prisons or the institutes for psychopathic offenders. No working criminologist, or judge, or prison warden, talks this way. The people who have the responsibility for fighting crime and dealing with criminals have learned that it is pointless to talk about "how much punishment" is deserved. In the nineteenth century, when sociological and economic laws were supposed to operate automatically, standardization of punishments to fit the crime had its appeal, but experience has since led to a critical re-evaluation of the entire process. The modern behavioral sciences have shown that arm-chair abstractions about the "justice" of retribution by philosophers who reject human experience[4] are sadly defective in human understanding, not to say human sympathy. The retributive approach is too subjective and too emotional to solve problems that have their roots in social conditions and the consequent impact on individual personality. Such an approach can only obstruct the job of evolving techniques for social control utilizing what we now know about the forces that control human behavior.

But, as Professor Bodenheimer says, there are those who, though they themselves may reject retribution in theory as "only vengeance in disguise," nevertheless say that we must be realistic in recognizing that the desire for vengeance is strong in men, and we must not offend this "instinctive sense of justice." But if this so-called sense of justice is unsound, then we should reject it, and not condone it. The law

---

[3] A few years ago, a group of university students were asked to rank in seriousness 13 different crimes defined by the California statutes, including arson, bigamy, forgery, theft, assault with a deadly weapon, and attempted burglary. The students rated as deserving of most punishment the serious beating by a father of a small child. Of a group of California prisoners serving sentence for these various crimes, the actual average punishment meted out for this offence was *less* than for all but one other of the 13 crimes. The crime for which the longest average sentence was actually served was injuring electric or telephone lines, an offense which the students rated as twelfth in seriousness. Rose and Prell, "Does the Punishment Fit the Crime? A Study in Social Valuation," *American Journal of Sociology,* 61 (1955), 247.

[4] E.g., Immanuel Kant, *Philosophy of Law* (1887), p. 243, trans. Hastie.

today is strong enough to do what is right. Furthermore, I deny that there is any evidence to support the idea that we must "come to terms with" or "yield to" this anti-social aggressiveness. There is no proof that the public is as thirsty for vengeance as this notion assumes. There is no proof of any "unbridgeable gap" between public opinion and the objectives of modern criminology. Public opinion during the past two hundred years has been rather less retributive than the law itself. It was public opinion that forced the law to become humane — to abandon capital punishment for scores of offenses, to recognize mitigating circumstances, to treat juveniles differently from adults. Juries today have almost wholly abolished capital punishment in fact, even though it remains on the books in all but nine states. As an actual operating part of our penal program the death penalty has almost ceased to exist (48 executions in the whole country in 1958, as against some 7,000 murders) — and this because and not in spite of public opinion. It isn't often one meets an argument that can be called both base and baseless at the same time, but that is what we can call the sounding of a retreat before the unreal specter of an irresistible mob baying for blood.

Professor Bodenheimer discusses two criticisms of the utilitarian view. The first is that it "has a tendency to play down the claims of justice." What he means by this is that "unless it is tempered by non-utilitarian considerations it may lead to unnecessary harshness and severity in the treatment of offenders." Every utilitarian would agree that *unnecessary* harshness should be avoided; almost by definition, what is unnecessary is not utilitarian. The danger of unduly harsh treatment of offenders is a real one, but the problem is one of balancing two utilitarian concepts — respect for the interests of the individual against concern for the interests of the group. These interests are likely to be more or less opposed; releasing a prisoner now, to give him another chance, may be the most promising way to rehabilitate him, but it takes a chance with the safety of society. All we can do is to put the responsibility for making the choice into the hands of the most competent people we can find, and give them elbow room to make the wisest decisions they can. I might point out that if there is one basic difference between our political system and that of the totalitarianisms, it is that we are relatively more willing to take a chance in favor of the individual, whereas a police state is more likely to give primacy to state security. No utilitarian I know questions the soundness of that value judgment.

This problem of weighing the interests of the individual against the interests of society could not be solved in any degree by adopting Professor Bodenheimer's suggestions that we temper *both* these utilitarian objectives "by non-utilitarian considerations." On the contrary, the non-utilitarian concept of requital is much more often the *source* of unnecessarily harsh treatment of the individual than it is a protection against it. Those who clamor for "justice" usually mean that they want *harsher* penalties inflicted than utilitarian considerations justify. What does a man mean when he says that a certain crime (for example, certain Nazi atrocities) is so heinous that "justice" demands severe punishment? He means merely that the acts create such feelings of antagonism in himself that he wants to see the wrongdoer suffer, and suffer much. This is a common human reaction — but the fact that a certain feeling is frequently found among men does not mean that it is commendable or justified. That a person who has suffered at the hands of the Nazis should feel that no punishment is too bad for them is understandable. But this does not make such hatred a "just" or worthy sentiment. Rather, we should say that the creation of such hatred is among the worst of the wrongs that can be laid against the Nazis. Our ideal should be, and for 2,000 years our ideal has been, to overcome such hatred, and to treat even such criminals with decency; to do what needs to be done to protect ourselves against them, without hate and without the deliberate infliction of unnecessary cruelty. Playfair and Sington, in a recent book, *The Offenders,* report that the Van der Hoeven Clinic in Holland has as a patient a man who worked for the German occupation forces as a concentration-camp guard and committed atrocities, including probably homicide, against his fellow Dutchmen.[5] In Holland, it has apparently come to

---

[5] Playfair and Sington devote a chapter to the story of Irma Grese, the "blond beastess" of Belsen, as the newspapers called her. They trace the childhood of this simple peasant girl, the influence of Nazi indocrination about the lower breeds, her romantic devotion to what she had been taught was her duty to the German race. Her hanging, conclude the authors, "like all the other executions for war crimes — seems to have been useless as well as barbaric." It has not deterred other potential war criminals, as events in Korea and even in Germany itself have shown. On the contrary, it has done political harm. For some Germans, her story became a legend — not a healthy legend, but one that emphasized the callous side of the British occupation. "A civilized attitude would have seen Irma Grese as a psychological casualty of war, like many of the young soldiers in all countries, who, having been trained as 'killers,' became a social problem in postwar years." G. Playfair and D. Sington, *The Offenders: The Case Against Legal Vengeance* (1957), pp. 167–211.

be realized that the proper approach even to so-called "crimes against humanity" is the curative one. England during the war created a center where young German prisoners of war indoctrinated with Nazism could discover liberal, tolerant ways of life. The experiment was so successful that it was continued for ten years after the war. If those whose own homelands were overrun or bombed by the Nazis and whose countrymen and perhaps family and friends were the main victims of these atrocities can find it in their hearts to offer a chance for rehabilitation to the "corrupted generation," we in America should be willing to do the same for our own criminals. And I believe we shall, if only well meaning professors will leave off giving aid and comfort to the peddlers of hatred.

There is nothing special about "war criminals" that justifies treating them differently from others. Those who try to make a case for retribution by appealing to hate and fury can also find plenty of peace-time atrocities to point to. Thus one writer invites the reader to "picture that your daughter or favorite niece was ruthlessly raped and then her belly torn open by a neurotic assailant." [6] Another asks, what of "the three monsters . . . who literally fried to death a schoolteacher who lived alone. . . ?" [7]

But as one eminent psychiatrist has said in answer to such arguments, "While the impulse to punish such persons is easy to understand, it is hardly a rational basis for determining how the criminal law shall function in order to protect society. We cannot exceed the community's willingness to be "understanding" and "loving" in relation to acts committed against it. However, the professionals who are to shed light on questions of *why* these acts were committed, as well as to find ways permanently to protect society from further depredations by such individuals, must not be hampered in their efforts by rules which are predicated on ancient and atavistic concepts of protection." [8]

Professor Bodenheimer's second objection to the utilitarian approach is, strangely enough, the very opposite of the first. Not only may it lead to undue harshness; it may also lead to undue softness. "By focusing its attention exclusively on the individual offender . . .

---

[6] H. A. Davidson, *Irresistible Impulse and Criminal Responsibility, in Crime and Insanity* (1958), p. 40.

[7] Mr. Justice Mackay of the Court of Appeals of Ontario, quoted in H. Weihofen, *The Urge to Punish* (1956), p. 155.

[8] Dr. Andrews S. Watson, Book Review, *University of Pennsylvania Law Review,* 107 (1959), 898.

it may lead to a sentimentalism which jeopardizes society's interest in crime prevention." But the utilitarian view does not focus its attention exclusively on the offender; Professor Bodenheimer himself admits this. It is concerned also for the interests of society. As already said, individual and group interests are likely to be more or less opposed. As also already said, in balancing those interests our social system favors the individual more than do some others. But that is a long way from saying that Americans generally or utilitarians in particular are concerned exclusively with the individuals and care nothing about protection of the public.

In their concern for the rehabilitation of the offender, modern criminologists do not take the position that punishment can never have a reformative or deterrent effect. No one denies in toto the validity of the pleasure-pain principle of learning. On the contrary, psychologists would say that punishment calmly devised and administered has therapeutic value and is an important factor in personality development. What we do say is: first, our faith in the deterrent effect of inflicting unpleasant consequences as a response to criminality is exaggergated; second, punishment should therefore not be used indiscriminately (or absolutely, as a mystically, transcendentally required requital for crime), but only where, upon expert diagnosis, it promises to do some good; and third, other methods of treatment are at least as effective in many cases, and punishment should therefore be considered as only one part of a well-rounded preventive-therapeutic program.

Even if we indulge our urge for "requital" in the *sentencing* of the offender, our *prison* programs must be rehabilitative in purpose. We cannot and do not want to keep all these men locked up for life. The overwhelming majority must be released eventually, and we certainly do not want to turn them out wholly unregenerated. We cannot avoid addressing ourselves to the need to do what we can to see that this steady stream of men comes out less dangerous than when they went in.

The extent to which punishment actually serves this need seems to be of no concern to those who see it only as a necessary requital for wrongdoing. But one who relies on principles to decide specific cases cannot avoid defending those principles by showing that they lead to proper consequences. Those who know tell us that punishment has some undesirable consequences that may outweigh all that can be said in its favor. It isolates the individual and is more likely to con-firm his anti-social attitude than to reform him. More important, punishment can deter only by appealing to selfish fear, not to insight or moral conviction. When it succeeds, it is a victory for cowardice. At best, it can achieve only a sterile conformity, a blind obedience, not a healthy adjustment to society. We want more than merely to repress. We want to help the unsocialized child or adult to become a self-reliant, self-respecting, co-operative member of the human race.

But punishment usually stops any such constructive efforts. Hav-ing imposed punishment, we are likely to feel with smug satisfaction that we have taken care of the problem. The criminal is taken away, locked up and forgotten. We assume that he will be kept there for a long time, and that when he does come out, he will have learned his lesson.

But even if he is remorseful and resolved to reform, he needs help to carry that good intention into effect. Motivation, stimulation, suggestions, ideals, and patterns of conduct must be provided. He must be given a chance to carry his resolves and ideals into practice in social relations with other human beings. All this calls for indi-vidualized thought and effort on the part of a trained and competent staff.

The experts who deal with the problem first hand know this. The judge, the prosecuting attorney, the police officer, the probation officer, these are not usually the ones calling for harsher punishments. Any of you who have ever attended a forum or conference at which crime or juvenile delinquency is discussed have perhaps seen the pat-tern. These experts emphasize the need for understanding what kind of people get into trouble — the fact that 10 per cent of juvenile delinquents come from families where one or both parents have schizo-phrenia; that 20 per cent to 40 per cent are mentally backward, due either to heredity or to poor environment; that their parents, if not actually psychotic, are themselves delinquent, or immature, drunken, or absent. The experts emphasize the need for competent and skilled probation workers to work with these youngsters, the need for clinical and institutional facilities, if they are to be redeemed. It is always some ignorant member of the audience who then rises to say that the whole problem could be solved if you take them out to the wood shed — give them a taste of jail — or jail their parents. Prompt to second this view is the fundamentalist hellfire and brimstone preacher.

It is unfortunate when professorial musings over a supposed transcendental necessity for punishment are used to lend a cloak of decency to the performance.

Crime and criminal responsibility are not mere interesting abstractions for philosophers to amuse themselves by, dreaming up metaphysical constructs out of them. Crime is a reality, an ever-present danger which in some cases is literally a matter of life and death.

The voices of ignorance and hate are loud enough now, angrily trying to shout down almost every effort to improve criminal administration by substituting rational for irrational solutions, a rehabilitative for a punitive approach. The rationale of these programs calls for an understanding of the sociological, economic, and cultural sources of criminality, and for an understanding of the psychology of criminals and of our reactions to criminality. We need the help of all those who have the education and the insights to understand; we need them to stand up for reason and decency, and to teach and preach and fight for it. We need you.

I resent the apostles of "punishment for its own sake" arrogating to themselves words like "moral" and "justice," and implying in consequence that those who scorn their metaphysics are amoral or at least unconcerned with moral values. Surely the feeling of concern for the offender as a human being, the desire to save him from a criminal career and to help him redeem himself as a member of the human family, and the even wider concern to prevent others from falling into criminality by searching out the influences and conditions that produce those frustrating and embittering defeats, degradations, and humiliations of the human spirit that turn a man against his fellow men; the effort, therefore, to give men those advantages that will help them to keep their feet on the right path — better education, healthier dwellings, readier aid for the motherless and the widowed, and more systematic provision for the casualties of sickness, accident, and failure of employment — surely this is not a less moral ideal than that which knows only one measure of morality: an eye for an eye and a tooth for a tooth.

Half a century ago, Winston Churchill said, in essence (I do not have his exact words):

> The mood and temper of the public toward crime and criminals is one unfailing test of the civilization of any country. A desire to

rehabilitate those who have committed crime, tireless efforts toward the discovery of curative and regenerative processes, and an unfaltering belief that there is worth, if you can but find it, in the heart of every man — these are the symbols that mark and measure the stored-up strength of the nation.

Yes; and I would add, these are the sign and proof of its morality.

---

# The Psychiatrist and the Legal Process

### SEYMOUR HALLECK

In a society dominated by change, complexity and respect for humanistic values, the theories and practices of psychiatry are becoming increasingly relevant to a multitude of legal issues. The most controversial relationship of psychiatry to the law arises in those situations in which the psychiatrist is asked to help the society deal with emotionally troubled citizens who also happen to be troubling the community. When the psychiatrist assists in the determination of the sanity of accused offenders, or judges the mental competency of offenders to stand trial, or recommends involuntary commitment of noncriminal patients to mental hospitals, he participates in legal processes which have profound social consequences. These are processes in which the psychiatrist's opinions and actions influence the amount of control or restriction of freedom which society imposes upon its deviant members.

It is ironic that practitioners of medicine, a profession dominated by respect for individual values, should have become so deeply involved in problems of social control. Nobody is very comfortable with this situation. In order to deal with the conflict in values generated by psychiatric involvement in such areas, both the medical and legal professions have conducted an agonized search for humane and

Reprinted from *Psychology Today* Magazine, February, 1969. Copyright © Communications/Research/Machines/Inc.

rational rules which would govern the control of emotionally disturbed individuals. Sometimes new rules are made and both the society and the deviant person benefit. More often the rules remain the same or the benefits of widely heralded changes in the rules turn out to be more illusory than real.

Before considering the theoretical and practical problems of deriving rules it would be useful to point out that we would not have to be so preoccupied with rules if our legal and mental-health-service systems were adequate. If our system of correctional justice were fully devoted to protecting the community and to rehabilitating offenders, and were not so preoccupied with the goal of punishment, psychiatry and the law would not have to search for means of excusing insane offenders. We would be certain that they would receive proper treatment irrespective of their legal designation. If we knew that every offender was going to be treated rationally and humanely regardless of his emotional condition, we would also be less in conflict over the need to ascertain that each offender is emotionally equipped to defend himself in the courtroom. Similar considerations are relevant to the issue of civil commitment. If our mental hospitals were fully adequate there would be less fear of the trauma of hospitalization and probably less need for involuntary commitment. And if community mental-health resources were adequate, even the need for hospitalization, voluntary or involuntary, would be minimal.

There is probably no legal proceeding in our society which generates the excitement and interest of the insanity trial. It deals with an issue that is crucial to any humane society, namely whether there are some individuals who are too emotionally disturbed to be responsible for their criminal actions. The psychiatrist's testimony in such proceedings may be decisive in determining the guilt or innocence of the alleged offender.

Sometimes psychiatric testimony frees the accused of the burden of institutionalization. More often, even if the accused is found not guilty by reason of insanity, it does not. But whatever happens to the offender the actual insanity trial always provides superb emotional and intellectual diversion for the public.

Unfortunately the stimulation provided by the insanity trial is rarely accompanied by any sense of humanistic accomplishment. Ultimately every participant in the proceedings is frustrated. Psychiatrists find themselves forced to take theoretical positions which contradict the conceptual basis of their practices outside of the courtroom. Lawyers and judges find psychiatric pronouncements confusing and sometimes unintelligible. And the disturbed offender rarely receives the kind of treatment that would enable him to return to society as a free and useful citizen.

The psychiatrist's problems begin with his willingness to participate in the process of assigning responsibility. To be useful to the courts in an insanity trial the psychiatrist must make a judgment as to the responsibility of an offender for a particular act. Yet, there is no body of fact or theory in the behavioral sciences which offers the psychiatrist any guidance in this task. Rather, assignment of responsibility primarily involves philosophical considerations. In this area every citizen has an opinion and it is unlikely that the psychiatrist's training or experience makes him more of an expert.

In some ways the psychiatrist's philosophical plight is more complex than that of the ordinary citizen. As a scientist, the psychiatrist may be a "hard" determinist, but in his day-to-day practice he knows that if he is ever going to help people overcome their difficulties he must constantly implore them to assume responsibility for their actions. When attempting to treat his patients the psychiatrist assumes that neither mental illness nor unconsciously determined behavior absolves one of responsibility. In actual practice, he tries to teach all of his patients to be totally accountable for their thoughts, acts and dreams. It is only when he enters the courtroom that he is asked questions which tempt him to forget his own teachings.

What seems to happen in the  criminal insanity trial is that psychiatrists of different value orientations examine the same patient and agree about psychiatric questions but disagree about philosophical questions. Psychiatrists generally agree when asked about the nature of the offender's disturbance and about the kind of treatment which might lead to rehabilitation. When they are asked to comment upon the questions of the offender's responsibility for his behavior, however, psychiatrists answer this question in terms of their own values. Although there are some exceptions, it is generally true that the psychiatrist who is politically liberal, psychoanalytically oriented and deeply concerned with social justice will be more likely to find a given offender nonresponsible than the psychiatrist who is more politically conservative, more biologically oriented and more concerned with individual rights and privileges.

The legal rules which guide the psychiatrist and the court in assessing the responsibility of the offender were created to find some means of relating the highly complex concept of mental illness to the philosophical concept of responsibility. There is a presumption in each rule that mental illness is a clearly definable entity. It is not. In this decade some psychiatrists consider mental illness a biological disorder while others think of it as a social role or as a convenient metaphor for describing maladaptive behavior. Most psychiatrists probably adopt the latter position. Yet, the rules for assessing responsibility are based on assumptions that mental illness is an affliction, something superimposed upon an individual's personality. The M'Naughten rule focuses upon the extent to which mental illness precludes the offender's knowing the nature and quality of his act or knowing its rightness or wrongness. The assumption that those we call mentally ill either regularly or even occasionally do not recognize the moral or legal implications of their behavior has no foundation in reality. I have examined hundreds of extremely disturbed inmates of civil hospitals and hospitals for the criminally insane and with one or two exceptions find that they always appreciate the criminality of their actions. Attempts to liberalize the M'Naughten rule by invoking the concept of "emotional knowing" as opposed to "intellectual knowing" simply lead to totally unscientific estimation as to the extent to which one "really" knows what he is doing. Value judgments rather than science or logic are the dominant factor in such determinations.

The Durham decision, which excuses an offender if his crime is believed to be a product of mental illness, also has serious theoretical limitations. It again is based on a questionable concept of mental illness. The idea that an illness can by itself absolve one of responsibility for behavior can, if followed literally, lead to some absurd conclusions. It has been pointed out by one observer, for example, that by invoking a holistic, stress theory of behavior, an individual might not, according to Durham, be guilty of some criminal acts if he were suffering from a psychosomatic illness such as asthma. Insofar as the Durham decision fails to define what is meant by mental illness, it may also put the psychiatrist in a position where he must invoke circular thinking. Whenever a psychiatrist bases his diagnosis of mental illness upon the peculiarity or unreasonableness of the criminal act, he is defining illness in terms of the crime and in effect arguing that the cause and effect are similar or identical. The American Law

Institute ruling, the irresistible impulse clause and other rulings may sometimes make it easier for a psychiatrist to testify, but insofar as they are based on the same erroneous assumption about mental illness as M'Naughten and Durham they do not solve the problem.

I have criticized the theoretical basis of psychiatric testimony and have emphasized the deficiency of legal tests of criminal responsibility. It must also be noted that many practical inconsistencies and injustices arise through psychiatric participation in such legal procedure. Specifically I wish to emphasize four points.

First, for any legal procedure to be just and effective it must be consistently applied to all men regardless of race, or social or economic status. In practice the issue of criminal responsibility is raised with unusual selectivity. It is rarely invoked unless there has been a spectacular crime involving murder or extreme violence. Much depends not only on the circumstance of the crime, but on the availability of forensic psychiatrists, the laws of the state, the attitude of the community and the offender's social and economic class. In many jurisdictions, for example, it would be quite unlikely that an uneducated Negro would plead insanity and even more unlikely that he would be found not guilty by reason of insanity. It would seem that the degree of emotional disturbance should be the major if not the only factor in selecting those who plead insanity. Yet, selection is just as likely to be based upon far more arbitrary factors.

Second, implied in any legal determination of criminal responsibility is an assumption that to find a man not guilty by reason of insanity and to send him to a state hospital is a merciful and humane act. In practice this is a highly questionable assumption. Most offenders found not guilty by reason of insanity are committed to a hospital for the criminally insane. A few of these hospitals are adequate; most are not. Many of the men who are sent to hospitals for the criminally insane are retained for as long a period or longer than they would have been if given a criminal commitment. In some instances psychiatric treatment facilities at the state or federal prison where the offender would have been sent if he had been found guilty are more advanced and comprehensive than those at the corresponding hospitals.

Third, effective utilization of the plea of criminal insanity implies psychiatrists will come to eventual agreement on a workable definition of terms such as psychosis or mental illness. This is highly unlikely.

The criminal offender does not fit easily into psychiatric classifications. When he does he is usually put into one of the borderline categories. Because of the enormous psychological impact of his crime, his incarceration, his confinement to hospital's and prisons, and his trial, his emotional state is constantly changing. Most psychiatrists, while agreeing as to psychodynamics, have difficulty in applying psychiatric labels to the offender. This difficulty is compounded by the shifting adaptation of the offender as he is examined in various pretrial settings.

Finally, the most serious problem with psychiatric participation in the insanity trial is that such activity exerts a pernicious influence upon the psychiatric profession itself. The efforts of psychiatrists to deal with unresolvable legal and philosophical issues must be viewed as a waste of psychiatric energy and talent.

The futility of searching for a means for helping the emotionally disturbed offender by discovering the "proper" test of responsibility is dramatized by legal struggles underlying the use of the Durham decision in the District of Columbia. The Durham decision was greeted with a wave of enthusiasm for the possibility of humane treatment of offenders. Many believed that Durham would allow psychiatrists to testify more rationally and that it would result in more emotionally disturbed offenders receiving freedom and treatment rather than punishment. For a while things looked hopeful, but as more offenders were declared nonresponsible, as mental-health facilities began to become overcrowded and as the willingness of psychiatrists to participate in the responsibility trial failed to grow, enthusiasm for Durham gradually waned. Federally employed psychiatrists began finding more and more of their subjects responsible and judges began putting more restrictions upon the interpretation of the Durham principle. At this point Judge David Bazelon's laudable effort to create a rule of law which would serve the well-being of the emotionally disturbed offender shows little promise of having any beneficial impact on the psychiatric or legal status quo.

The history of the criminal-insanity issue suggests some psychiatrists and some attorneys have, out of humanistic zeal, sought a liberal solution, a compromise in which efforts were made to temper the harshness of punishment for a few mentally disturbed offenders but in which the plight of the mass offenders was ignored. Like most compromises with unreasonable systems it has failed to yield such humanistic gain. By investing an incredible amount of energy in trying to help a small number of emotionally disturbed offenders, psychiatrists have done little more than lend our correctional system a deceptive façade of decency. When psychiatrists help the insane offender escape punishment they actually strengthen the current system of correctional justice. The public, spared the agony of watching the mentally ill be punished, is more willing to tolerate the merciless and irrational punishment of the ordinary offender.

It can be asserted here that an enlightened correctional system would employ psychiatrists for only two purposes: (1) to help to diagnose, treat and rehabilitate all classes of offenders; and (2) to help control dangerous offenders. If punishment were not the major issue, all offenders, including those believed to be emotionally disturbed, would be tried in court for the sole purpose of determining if they had actually committed an illegal act. Mental illness would not mitigate criminal intent. All persons found to have committed a crime (except where *mens rea* does not exist for reasons other than mental illness) would be considered fully responsible. Psychiatrists and other behavioral scientists would be able to confine their role to assisting in the determination of what is to be done with the individual offender.

If it were assumed that the goal of society is to rehabilitate all offenders who could be helped and to control all those who remained dangerous to the society, the psychiatrist could be used as a resource whose advice would serve the judge or jury in the  question of disposition. The offender whose behavior was felt to represent a public danger would also receive treatment, but his behavior would be subjected to greater control.

Any radical change in our legal system would be subjected to vigorous scrutiny and, if adopted, would be done cautiously. It is unlikely that a complete abolishment of the insanity plea would be easily accepted by many segments of our society. Assuming such changes are years away, there are nevertheless less radical changes, which could be made immediately, which would allow the psychiatrist to assist the judicial process without involving himself in the unresolvable question of man's responsibility. These changes would not tamper with the concept of *mens rea* as applied to the seriously emotionally disturbed.

The psychiatrist is the only expert witness who is asked to present opinions as to man's responsibility and man's punishability. The toxicologist may testify as to the amount of poison in a victim's body and give an opinion as to whether it was sufficient to cause death. The orthopedic surgeon testifies as to the degree of motor incapacitation and its possible causes. The fingerprint or ballistics experts give opinions which are strictly limited to their fields of competence. None of these experts is ever asked to give an opinion as to the guilt or responsibility of the offender. Only the psychiatrist is asked to testify and answer questions which go beyond his own training or competence.

There is no rational reason why the psychiatrist couldn't be allowed to testify like other expert witnesses, i.e., present all the information available as to why a man committed a certain crime and as to the extent of his psychological impairment, without having to ponder whether the offender knew right from wrong or if one of his behaviors was the product of another. Under such a directive the psychiatrist could describe in detail the emotional state of the offender at the time of the crime without answering the impossible questions posed by M'Naughten or Durham. The judge or jury could then make up their own minds as to whether the offender possessed evil intent and should be punished. In making such decisions, they would be assisted only by psychiatric fact and opinion and would not be influenced by the philosophical speculations of a single professional discipline. Ultimately, if the decision of responsibility is to be made at all, it must be entirely in the hands of the judge or jury.

It could, of course, be argued that jurists are not capable of deciding upon the responsibility of mentally ill offenders without receiving considerable direction from psychiatrists. Yet if the community wishes to punish some and excuse others, it could just as easily make such decisions itself without forcing the problem upon the psychiatrist.

Although the issue of criminal responsibility has consumed most of the interest of forensic psychiatrists, the question of mental competency to stand trial may be of far greater importance both in terms of the number of individuals involved and in terms of the more disturbing potentiality for competency rulings to lead to deprivation of civil rights. Because it is unlikely that the confused or disorganized person could adequately defend himself in court, our society often elects to delay the trial of such an offender until he has recovered his emotional stability. If an alleged offender is unable to understand the charges against him or is unable to understand the proceedings which are to be invoked or is unable to assist his counsel, he is usually judged incompetent to stand trial. The practice in most jurisdictions is to commit such individuals to a hospital or prison unit for the criminally insane until they regain their competency.

A number of psychiatrists and social scientists have pointed out the potential hazards of such commitments. Confinement to an institution for the criminally insane represents a serious restriction of freedom. If the offender does not recover he can spend a great deal of time in confinement even though he has not been convicted of the crime. Hospitals for the criminally insane may be so deplorably understaffed that opportunities for recovery are sorely limited. The offender is then deprived of his constitutional guarantee of a speedy trial. He is also placed in a kind of double jeopardy since the time he spends in the hospital is not considered a part of his future sentence.

The psychiatrist approaches the task of determining competency of accused offenders with benevolent motivations but there is always a serious danger his efforts might result in arbitrary confinement of an individual who has never even been convicted of a crime. Part of the problem lies in the vagueness of terms such as ability to understand charges, ability to understand legal proceedings or ability to assist counsel. These terms can only be defined arbitrarily. There has been a deplorable tendency among psychiatrists to expect too much of man before they call him competent. Many offenders who are now being judged incompetent could probably do an adequate job of protecting their own interests in the courtroom.

Actually, if hospitals for the criminally insane were updated to levels possible in modern psychiatry, the great majority of incompetent offenders could be provided with enough help so that they would be well enough to return to court in a few weeks or a few months. The only major exception to this statement would be brain-damaged offenders or severely defective offenders.

Until the day arrives when hospitals for the criminally insane are able to provide high levels of psychiatric care, psychiatrists would do better to define incompetency only in the most severe cases of deficiency, confusion or disorganization. They might also consider utilizing the advice of attorneys in what is often a crucial part of the competency determination, namely, the ability of the offender to assist his counsel. It may well be that attorneys are better equipped to make such judgments than are psychiatrists. It is also true that many individuals found incompetent to stand trial do not have to be hospitalized. The treatment which restores their competency could just as easily be conducted in an outpatient setting. This would still leave the problem of dealing with the severely disturbed, with the relatively small proportion of chronically psychotic and severely retarded offenders who would not be in a position to defend their case but who would also be unlikely to improve rapidly with any sort of treatment. A solution for this group might be civil commitment. If such commitment were conducted under the guiding principles I will outline in a second essay many of these individuals who could probably function in a protected setting outside the hospital would be free to do so.

---

# Mental Illness Is a Myth

THOMAS S. SZASZ

On Feb. 28, 1966, the United States Court of Appeals for the Second Circuit handed down a decision which displaced the time-honored M'Naghten Rule as a test of criminal insanity, and substituted for it a new rule recommended by the American Law Institute.

The M'Naghten Rule dates from 1843, when one Daniel M'Naghten shot and killed a man named Drummond, the private secretary of Sir Robert Peel, whom M'Naghten had intended to kill. At M'Naghten's trial, evidence was introduced showing that he "was laboring under an insane delusion" of being hounded by enemies, among them Peel. The jury found him "not guilty, on the ground of insanity."

*De jure,* M'Naghten was acquitted; *de facto,* he was sentenced to life imprisonment in an insane asylum. He died in 1865, having been incarcerated for the last 22 years of his life.

The new ruling (binding on Federal courts in New York, Connecticut and Vermont) provides that: "A person is not responsible for

© 1966 by the New York Times Company. Reprinted by permission.

criminal conduct if at the time of such conduct as a result of mental disease or defect he lacks substantial capacity either to appreciate the wrongfulness of his conduct or to conform his conduct to the requirements of law."

Both of these tests — and others, whatever their semantic differences — rest on the premise that the human mind may become "diseased," and that a person who has a "diseased mind" may, because of it, commit criminal acts unintentionally, not know the difference between right and wrong, or be unable to restrain himself from engaging in conduct prohibited by law. The value of all psychiatric tests of criminal responsibility thus hinges on the soundness of this underlying concept of "mental disease."

But what exactly is mental disease? If it is an illness, what kind is it? And if it is not an illness, what is it and why is it called an illness? Because of the frequency with which issues of mental health and illness arise not only in criminal cases but in matters of everyday life, it is important that we ask these questions and intelligently debate various possible answers to them.

I submit that mental illness is a myth. Bodies are physical objects; minds, whatever they may be, are not physical objects. Accordingly, mental diseases (such as depression or schizophrenia) cannot exist in the sense in which bodily diseases (such as broken bones or ulcerated skins) exist.

My disbelief in mental illness does not mean that I reject any facts of human behavior. "A myth," says the British philosopher Gilbert Ryle, "is not a fairy story. It is the presentation of facts belonging in one category in the idiom belonging to another. To explode a myth is accordingly not to deny facts, but to reallocate them." To say that mental illness is a myth is therefore not to *deny* facts (such as sadness or fear) but to *reallocate* them (from the category of mental illness to the category of personal conduct). Insofar as men are human beings, not machines, they always have some choice in how they act — hence, they are always responsible for their conduct. There is method in madness, no less than in sanity.

As long ago as the early nineteen-twenties, George H. Mead formulated the thesis that social situations — and human behavior in them — are analogous to games which must be played by certain "rules." In life, the games are infinite. As social conditions undergo rapid change, old games are constantly scrapped and new ones started.

But most people are totally unprepared to shift from one type of game playing to another. They have early in life learned one set of rules — or, at most, a few — and find themselves forced to play new games by the old rules. This fundamental conflict leads to various problems in living — some severe enough to be commonly diagnosed as "mental illness" or "disease." It is these problems in living that the psychiatrist is usually called on to treat.

"But surely," someone might say, "a dope fiend, a rapist, or a Lee Harvey Oswald is not a *normal* person. What difference does it make whether we call him sick or something else? "

It makes, of course, all the difference in the world, for what we call things, and especially people, will shape our attitudes and justify our actions toward them. For example, when socially threatening behavior is called "witchcraft," it is handled by means of theological sanctions; when it is called "crime," it is handled by means of judicial sanctions, and when it is called "mental illness," it is handled by means of psychiatric sanctions.

The practices of modern American psychiatrists originate from two principal sources: hospital psychiatry and psychoanalysis.

Institutions for the care of the insane have existed since antiquity. However, the systematic confinement of madmen in buildings labeled "hospitals" did not begin until the middle of the 17th century. For about 250 years, from 1650 to 1900, the psychiatrist worked almost exclusively in the mental hospital. The alienist, as he was then called, was employed by an institution — a private or, more often, a public insane asylum.

The historical model and social prototype of the modern mental hospital is the French Hôpital Général. According to the distinguished medical historian George Rosen, the purposes of this institutional system were threefold: "In part they were economic: to increase [the] manufacture [of goods], provide productive work for the able-bodied, and to end unemployment; in part social: to punish willful idleness, restore public order, and rid Paris of beggars; and in part, religious and moral: to relieve the needy, the ill and suffering, to deal with immorality and antisocial behavior, and to provide Christian instruction."

A few years after its foundation, the Hôpital Général of Paris alone contained 6,000 persons, or about 1 per cent of the population. Who were these "mentally ill" people? According to regulations issued in 1680, "children of artisans and other poor inhabitants of Paris up to the age of 25 . . . girls who were debauched or in evident danger of being debauched . . . [and] wayward children . . ." were among those listed as proper subjects for confinement. In addition, old people, persons with venereal diseases, epileptics, vagrants, prostitutes — in brief, all of society's *"misérables"* — were incarcerated in the Hôpital Général. Michel Foucault, a French student of psychiatric history, thus concludes: "The Hôpital Général is not a medical establishment. It is rather a sort of semijudicial structure, an administrative entity which, along with already constituted powers, and outside the courts, decides, judges and executes."

The facts I have cited are important in showing us one of the roles of the psychiatrist — indeed, his traditional role: He is a physician working in a mental hospital, employed, as a rule, by the state, and charged with the task of confining and "treating" people who are considered "insane." Although some of his methods have changed, the social role of the institutional psychiatrist has remained what it has always been.

Nor is its importance diminished. At the present time in the United States, approximately 750,000 persons are incarcerated in mental hospitals — 90 per cent of them against their will. This is about three times the number of persons imprisoned in jails.

The mental hospital is also important for the psychiatrist: Of 15,200 practicing psychiatrists in the United States, approximately 50 per cent are in institutional practice, most of them in mental hospitals, or in related administrative positions.

I do not imply that the hospital psychiatrist does not try to help his patient, but rather that his interpretation of "helping" is different from the patient's. If one person has the power to confine another, and uses it, it seems inevitable that the confined person will consider the other his jailer. This point of view, often held by mental patients, was expressed by Valentine Alamazov, the protagonist of Valeriy Tarsis's autobiographical novel, "Ward 7." Finding himself incarcerated in a mental hospital, Alamazov had this to say to his psychiatrist:

"I don't regard you as a doctor. You call this a hospital, I call it a prison. . . . So, now, let's get everything straight. I am your prisoner, you are my jailer, and there isn't going to be any nonsense about my health . . . or about examination and treatment."

It was Sigmund Freud who created the second major form of contemporary American psychiatric practice — psychoanalysis.

In the eighteen-eighties, when Freud was a young physician, to be a psychiatrist was to be an alienist or hospital psychiatrist. Traditionally, the psychiatrist was called in by a "mentally healthy" member of the family to treat one of its "mentally sick" members; often this meant removing the sick member from the family and putting him in a mental hospital as a "patient."

Freud departed from this traditional approach. Instead of acting as the agent of the family — ostensibly caring for the patient, but actually protecting the family from him — Freud created a new professional role — the agent of the patient.

He did not accept the situation as it was presented to him, usually by the patient's family. Instead, he listened at length to the patient to ascertain how he perceived his problem; and he tried to help him realize his own aspirations and goals, even if these brought the patient, or Freud himself, into even greater conflict with the family or with society.

Thus, ethically, Freud acted like other physicians, but unlike other psychiatrists: He tried to help his patient, not someone else. By systematically refusing to "treat" patients who did not want to be treated by him, Freud departed from the accepted psychiatric methods of his day. Many psychoanalysts still adhere to this principle in treating patients. Most hospital psychiatrists do not.

It is important to note also that Freud characterized psychoanalytic treatment in humanistic and pedagogic terms and did not regard his work as medical. Psychoanalysis was never intended to make "sick" people "well" again. The analyst's task, in Freud's words, was "to serve the patient . . . as a teacher and educator."

Freud was emphatic that the analyst — and hence also the psychotherapist who only listens and talks and uses no "medical" methods — does not cure disease. Indeed, although the three great pioneers of psychoanalysis — Freud, Adler and Jung — had little good to say about one another's doctrines and methods in later years, they all agreed on one thing: that psychological methods of therapy are *not* medical procedures.

We are now ready to reconsider the question: What is mental illness? In order to do this, it is necessary to understand the principal uses of the concept of mental illness and their social consequences.

First, the term "mental illness" is used to refer to certain types of bodily diseases — that is, to diseases of the brain whose predominant symptoms are abnormalities of behavior (for example, neurosyphilis). According to one school of psychiatric thought, all mental diseases are of this type. Those who hold this view assume that some metabolic, genetic or neurological defect — perhaps a very subtle one — will ultimately be found to explain all disorders of thinking and behavior now called "mental illness."

No one would deny that, like any other part of the body, the brain may be injured or become diseased. Nor are there, to my knowledge, any psychiatrists who would deny that some of the people nowadays diagnosed as mentally ill (and free of demonstrable organic disease) might actually be suffering from the effects of as yet undiscovered neurologic or metabolic disease processes. But for those who regard mental illness as a type of brain disease, the concept of mental illness is unnecessary and misleading. If they mean that people labeled mentally ill suffer from diseases of the brain, it would seem better for the sake of clarity to say that and not something else.

The second major use of the term "mental illness" is to denote a "functional" or "psychological" disorder. Proponents of this view admit that patients called "mentally ill" do not suffer from bodily diseases, but they maintain that such individuals exhibit defects or deformations of their personalities so severe as to justify calling them "ill."

When physicians (or others) label people as "sick" merely because their actions differ from those of their fellows, they speak metaphorically — as poets, not scientists. To be sure, this kind of metaphoric use of the term "sick" is not limited to psychiatry: People also say that our economy is "sick," that a joke is "sick" or that someone they dislike makes them "sick." Yet only in connection with mental illness do we systematically act as if figure of speech were fact. No one believes that "sick economies" require medical help, but nearly everyone believes that "sick minds" do.

The power to name, or to classify, is the basis for the third use of the term "mental illness" — that is, to denote a deviant social role. For our purposes it is necessary only to distinguish between two types of social roles: those that are assumed voluntarily, such as husband or graduate student, and those that are ascribed to a person against his will, such as draftee or convicted criminal.

Roles are social artifacts. Role deviance, therefore, has meaning only in the context of specific social customs and laws. The criminal is deviant because he breaks the law; the homosexual because most people are heterosexuals; the atheist because most people believe — or say they believe — in God. In the same way, the so-called "potential killer" (who, however, has not yet killed anyone) is considered deviant because he appears to be more dangerous than most people; and so is the chronically withdrawn mental-hospital patient, because most people are — and are expected to be — socially more responsive. (I shall say more about the problems that such persons pose for those about them, and for society in general, later on.)

But which kinds of social deviance constitute "mental illness"? The answer is: that conduct which deviates from psychiatrically defined rules of mental health.

However obvious this may be, its implications for our understanding of mental illness seem to be vastly unappreciated. The fact is that every time psychiatrists formulate a new rule of mental health they create a new class of mentally sick individuals. For example, the proposition that prejudice against Jews or Negroes is a manifestation of psychopathology — one of many instances in the contemporary inflation of the concept of mental illness — is nothing but an attempt to expand the category of people who can be legitimately classified as psychologically sick.

Since the consequences of being labeled mentally ill include such penalties as personal degradation, loss of employment, loss of the right to drive a car, to vote, to make valid contracts or to stand trial — and, last but not least, incarceration in a mental hospital, possibly for life — the expansion of the category of people who can be so designated is useful for the increased employment of psychiatric methods of social control.

Labeling someone mentally ill is a special kind of name-calling. In other fields name-calling may constitute libel, but calling someone "mentally sick" does not. The main reason for this is that the psychiatrist who makes a diagnosis of mental illness (especially on an involuntary patient) has more social power than the person he diagnoses.

The role of power in the psychiatric diagnostic process becomes obvious only when the potential patient is a Very Important Person. When someone like Secretary of Defense Forrestal disturbs people by his ideas and actions, it is difficult to get a psychiatrist to label him mentally ill. The reason for this is that by casting the individual in a socially deviant role the psychiatric diagnostician imparts a negative, debased identity to that person. This he cannot do if his intended "patient" is socially more powerful than he is. When a mental-hospital superintendent in Louisiana tried to incarcerate and "treat" Gov. Earl Long, the Governor fired the doctor — and walked out of the hospital.

One of the traditional problems of legal psychiatry, as we saw at the outset, is the determination of criminal insanity. Lawyers and psychiatrists persist in trying to distinguish between "sane" and "insane" criminals, and in finding a "scientific" basis for determining which offenders ought to be "punished" with imprisonment and which "treated" with involuntary mental hospitalization.

I submit that criminal insanity is a metaphorical and strategic concept just as civil insanity is. The effort to distinguish, by psychiatric methods, among different classes of criminals is really an exercise in second-order classification: Having labeled some persons as "criminals," we have the option of labeling them also as "mentally healthy," and dealing with them by means of penal sanctions, or as "mentally ill" (that is, as "criminally insane"), and dealing with them by means of psychiatric sanctions.

I do not believe that insanity should be an "excusing condition" for crime. Lawbreakers, irrespective of their "mental health," ought to be treated as offenders.

Another classic dilemma of psychiatry is the problem of what society should do with its "insane" citizens who, while having committed no crime, lack "insight" into their "illness" and hence do not seek "treatment." Here we should distinguish between two fundamentally different types of psychiatric practice. The person who decides to consult a psychiatrist and pays him for his services is like a graduate student pursuing a course of study: he assumes the role of mental patient (if we wish so to label his role) *voluntarily* and is free to cast it off. By contrast, the person who is coerced into psychiatric treatment by his relatives or by the law, and who does not pay the psychiatrist for his services, is like a prisoner sentenced to a term of servitude; he is placed in the role of mental patient *against his will* and is not free to cast it off.

The psychiatrist thus has a choice between doing something *to* his patient and doing something *for* him. One of the things the psychiatrist can do to his patient is to prescribe certain life games, with the expectation that these will pacify the patient's family and social environment — and perhaps also "help" the patient. Since this kind of treatment is carried out against the wishes of the patient, it requires coercion.

One of the things the psychiatrist can do for his patient is to analyze his life games, with the expectation that this understanding will help the client to lead a life more free and responsible. To do this, however, requires a voluntary, cooperating client. Coercion has no place whatever in this type of psychiatric work. Such a psychiatrist aspires to be on tap, not on top.

The reader who finds this thesis persuasive might wonder about its practical application. If we look upon mental illness as a metaphor and a social role, rather than as a disease, how will this affect what we *do?*

For work with voluntary clients the consequences would be mainly professional and economic: The humanistic view of mental illness would open opportunities for training nonmedical persons (psychologists, social workers and others) in psychotherapy and psychoanalysis, and would eliminate the rationale for preventing such persons from engaging in the independent practice of these skills.

For work with involuntary clients the consequences would be mainly legal and social: The humanistic view of mental illness would remove the justification for involuntary mental hospitalization and treatment; accordingly, it would require the mobilization of fresh personal efforts and social resources to cope with problems now dealt with by means of traditional psychiatric methods.

It would be impossible suddenly to empty out our mental hospitals and to stop all commitments — though, to be sure, I consider these desirable goals. To attain them, however, we must provide suitable alternatives to the present social functions of involuntary mental hospitalization. I must limit myself here to mentioning only a few such alternatives, each directed toward ameliorating a specific type of human problem.

The usual justification for commitment is that the person whose confinement is sought is "dangerous to himself or others." My position is based on a principle enunciated more than 100 years ago by John Stuart Mill: "The only purpose for which power can be rightfully exercised over any member of a civilized community, against his will, is to prevent harm to others. His own good, either physical or moral, is not sufficient warranty."

Suicide, for example, should be recognized as a basic human right. The threat of suicide, or an attempt at suicide, should not be ground for involuntary mental hospitalization. (This does not mean that a physician should not treat a person who, say, is unconscious as a result of an overdose of barbiturates. It does mean that, after the patient has regained consciousness, he should not be confined in a hospital against his will.)

While being "dangerous to oneself" should never be considered a legitimate reason for depriving a person of his liberty, being "dangerous to others" — if it involves breaking the law — is the best reason for doing so. One of the main functions of society is to prevent violence among its members. Thus, if individuals commit violence, or threaten to do so, they should be treated for what they are — law-breakers.

Judicial sentencing of lawbreakers does not deprive us of the opportunity of also trying to help them. If we truly believe that some lawbreakers are "mentally ill," we could offer them psychiatric help in prison. As always, the clients ought to be free to accept or reject such help.

The social control, by means of psychiatric sanctions, of dangerous behavior is complicated by the fact that people often disagree on what constitutes "dangerousness," and, even if they agree on it, on how such "dangerousness" is to be established. Thus, one group of persons now often committed is composed of individuals who manage their lives more or less adequately, but who break certain laws or social customs, and are therefore considered "dangerous" and treated as involuntary patients.

If we wish to avoid using coercive psychiatric measures against persons of this type, we have two basic options. Instead of constantly proliferating legislation prohibiting various kinds of personal conduct not directly injurious to others (as we now do), we might consider repealing and eschewing such legislation. We would thereby eliminate many types of "crime" and hence the need to define such criminals (as "dope addicts," "homosexuals" and so forth) as mentally sick. Or, if we wish to persist in our efforts to control private behavior by means of criminal sanctions, we might decide that it is more humane to punish persons who transgress these prohibitions by means of penal rather than psychiatric sanctions; the result would be the jailing of many individuals now committed to mental hospitals. (The desirability of confining lawbreakers in mental hospitals rather than in prisons is sometimes advocated on the allegedly humanitarian ground that conditions in mental hospitals are better than in jails. Even if this were true — and as a rule it is not — it would not justify redefining lawbreakers as patients. The proper remedy for inadequate prisons is prison reform.)

In addition to persons whose dangerousness is actual, established by what they have done, there are those whose dangerousness is potential, who are feared for what they might do. We often hear of "potential trouble-makers" who, however, have broken no laws, and hence could not be convicted of crime, but whom many would like to "diagnose" as "deranged" and restrain in mental hospitals.

We cannot eat our cake and have it, too: we cannot have a free society and imprison — in jails *or* mental hospitals — people who have broken no law. This does not mean that some people might not be "potentially" dangerous to others (indeed, many, like drunken drivers, are very dangerous); it means only that we cannot restrain such people through our mental-hygiene laws without gravely injuring the entire fabric of our society.

Another large group of persons confined involuntarily in mental hospitals is the aged; in some public mental hospitals as many as one-third of the inmates fall into this group. Yet, even hospital psychiatrists admit that many of these patients do not need mental-hospital care. "Only 50 per cent of the [elderly] patients . . . hospitalized required hospitalization in a mental institution," testified Dr. Dale C. Cameron, superintendent of St. Elizabeth's Hospital in Washington, before a House committee. "For many older patients," he added, "the primary need was found to be for physical rather than psychiatric care."

The fact that public mental hospitals accept geriatric patients — whose "mental illness" is so clearly a strategic concept designed to justify their forcible removal to places of custody — diminishes the pressure on society to provide suitable accommodations for them.

Still another group of involuntarily hospitalized patients is composed of individuals who present so-called psychiatric emergencies. Examples are the young man who becomes uncommunicative, does not leave his room, refuses to eat, perhaps even soils himself; or the young woman who faints and thereafter remains unresponsive and acts as if she were unconscious.

Patients of this type do not object to being hospitalized or to receiving medical care. Moreover, some of them suffer from bodily illness — brain tumor, head injury, uncontrolled diabetes. Others develop medical problems as a result of their behavior — severe dehydration because of failure to eat and drink, for example. Such patients should therefore be hospitalized in medical, not mental, hospitals, and should be treated as medical emergencies. Consent for hospitalization and treatment should be given by relatives, and confinement should last only until the patient has regained his powers.

The application of these principles to the care of the chronic mental patients would help us to avoid coercion in their care as well. Regardless of the cause — subtle malfunctions of the brain, the effect of prolonged institutionalization or flight from communal existence into a world of private dreams — people who are almost completely unable to cope with their problems of living will no doubt always be with us. Such "nondangerous" but gravely disabled individuals could be dealt with by offering them care — good and attractive enough so that they would willingly accept it — while leaving them free to make other choices.

In short, the abolition of involuntary mental hospitalization and treatment would mean that psychiatric help, like medical, would (on the whole) have to be restricted to voluntary clients. Furthermore, some persons who are now cast in the role of involuntary mental patients would, if they broke laws, have to be dealt with as offenders, not as patients.

The nominal aim of psychiatry is the study and treatment of mental disorders. The consequences of subscribing to this apparently harmless, conventional definition of "mental-health" work, are, in our present age, momentous. Accepting the existence of a class of phenomena called "mental diseases", rather than inquiring into the conditions under which some persons may designate others as "mentally ill," has been the decisive step in embracing what I call the mental-health ethic. In so doing, the study of a large part of human behavior is subtly transformed from ethics to psychiatry, from the free marketplace of ideas to the closed wards of the mental hospital.

The psychiatrist deals with moral and social problems, not with medical diseases. Hence he cannot help being embroiled in the moral conflicts of his patient and of his society. The psychiatrist's role as moral legislator and social engineer is obscured, however, by the rhetoric of mental health and illness which makes his work appear as a species of medical therapy. This evasion of ethical judgments and choices may be reassuring to the laity and comforting to the profession. But can we, as individuals, afford it?

The individual can never escape the moral burden of his existence. He must choose between obedience to authority and responsibility to himself. Moral decisions are often hard and painful to make. The temptation to delegate this burden to others is therefore ever-present. Yet, as all history teaches us, those who would take from man his moral burdens — must also take from him his liberty and hence his very humanity.

A humanistic psychiatry must, therefore, repudiate its seemingly therapeutic mandate, the pursuit of which often results, intentionally or unwittingly, in moral tranquility gained at the expense of freedom and responsibility. Instead of trying to diminish man's moral burdens, such a psychiatrist must aim at increasing his powers and so making him equal to his task.

And what is this task? No one has stated it better than Albert Camus when he wrote: "The aim of life can only be to increase the sum of freedom and responsibility to be found in every man and in the world. It cannot, under any circumstances, be to reduce or suppress that freedom, even temporarily."

---

# On Punishment

### ANTHONY M. QUINTON

There is a prevailing antinomy about the philosophical justification of punishment. The two great theories — retributive and utilitarian — seem, and at least are understood by their defenders, to stand in open and flagrant contradiction. Both sides have arguments at their

From *Analysis,* vol. 14, 1954. Reprinted by permission of publisher.

disposal to demonstrate the atrocious consequences of the rival theory. Retributivists, who seem to hold that there are circumstances in which the infliction of suffering is a good thing in itself, are charged by their opponents with vindictive barbarousness. Utilitarians, who seem to hold that punishment is always and only justified by the good consequences it produces, are accused of vicious opportunism. Where the former insists on suffering for suffering's sake, the latter permits the punishment of the innocent. Yet, if the hope of justifying punishment is not to be abandoned altogether, one of these apparently unsavoury alternatives must be embraced. For they exhaust the possibilities. Either punishment must be self-justifying, as the retributivists claim, or it must depend for its justification on something other than itself, the general formula of "utilitarianism" in the wide sense appropriate here.

In this paper I shall argue that the antinomy can be resolved, since retributivism, properly understood, is not a moral but a logical doctrine, and that it does not provide a moral justification of the infliction of punishment but an elucidation of the use of the word. Utilitarianism, on the other hand, embraces a number of possible moral attitudes towards punishment, none of which necessarily involves the objectionable consequences commonly adduced by retributivists, provided that the word "punishment" is understood in the way that the essential retributivist thesis lays down. The antinomy arises from a confusion of modalities, of logical and moral necessity and possibility, of "must" and "can" with "ought" and "may." In brief, the two theories answer different questions: retributivism the question "when (logically) *can* we punish?" utilitarianism the question "when (morally) *may* we or *ought* we to punish?" I shall also describe circumstances in which there is an answer to the question "when (logically) *must* we punish?" Finally, I shall attempt to account for this difference in terms of a distinction between the establishment of rules whose infringement involves punishment from the application of these rules to particular cases.

### THE RETRIBUTIVE THEORY

The essential contention of retributivism is that punishment is only justified by guilt. There is a certain compellingness about the repudiation of utilitarianism that this involves. We feel that whatever other considerations may be taken into account, the primary and indispensable matter is to establish the guilt of the person to be punished. I shall try to show that the peculiar outrageousness of the rejection of this principle is a consequence, not of the brutality that such rejection might seem to permit, but of the fact that it involves a kind of lying. At any rate the first principle of retributivism is that it is necessary that a man be guilty if he is to be punished.

But this doctrine is normally held in conjunction with some or all of three others which are logically, if not altogether psychologically, independent of it. These are that the function of punishment is the negation or annulment of evil or wrongdoing, that punishment must fit the crime (the *lex talionis*) and that offenders have a right to punishment, as moral agents they ought to be treated as ends not means.

The doctrine of "annulment," however carefully wrapped up in obscure phraseology, is clearly utilitarian in principle. For it holds that the function of punishment is to bring about a state of affairs in which it is as if the wrongful act had never happened. This is to justify punishment by its effects, by the desirable future consequences which it brings about. It certainly goes beyond the demand that only the guilty be punished. For, unlike this demand, it seeks to prescribe exactly what the punishment should be. Holding that whenever wrong has been done it must be annulled, it makes guilt — the state of one who has done wrong — the sufficient as well as the necessary condition of punishment. While the original thesis is essentially negative, ruling out the punishment of the innocent, the annulment doctrine is positive, insisting on the punishment and determining the degree of punishment of the guilty. But the doctrine is only applicable to a restricted class of cases, the order of nature is inhospitable to attempts to put the clock back. Theft and fraud can be compensated, but not murder, wounding, alienation of affection or the destruction of property or reputation.

Realizing that things cannot always be made what they were, retributivists have extended the notion of annulment to cover the infliction on the offender of an injury equal to that which he has caused. This is sometimes argued for by reference to Moore's theory of organic wholes, the view that sometimes two blacks make a white. That this, the *lex talionis,* revered by Kant, does not follow from the original thesis is proved by the fact that we can always refrain from punishing the innocent but that we cannot always find a punishment to fit the crime. Some indeed would argue that we can never fit punishment to wrongdoing, for how are either, especially wrongdoing, to be measured? (Though, as Ross has pointed out, we can make ordinal judgments of more or less about both punishment and wrongdoing.)

Both of these views depend on a mysterious extension of the original thesis to mean that punishment and wrongdoing must necessarily be somehow equal and opposite. But this is to go even further than to regard guilt and punishment as necessitating one another. For this maintains that only the guilty are to be punished and that the guilty are always to be punished. The equal and opposite view maintains further that they are to be punished to just the extent that they have done wrong.

Finally retributivism has been associated with the view that if we are to treat offenders as moral agents, as ends and not as means, we must recognize their right to punishment. It is an odd sort of right whose holders would strenuously resist its recognition. Strictly interpreted, this view would entail that the sole relevant consideration in determining whether and how a man should be punished is his own moral regeneration. This is utilitarian and it is also immoral, since it neglects the rights of an offender's victims to compensation and of society in general to protection. A less extreme interpretation would be that we should never treat offenders merely as means in inflicting punishment but should take into account their right to treatment as moral agents. This is reasonable enough; most people would prefer a penal system which did not ignore the reformation of offenders. But it is not the most obvious correlate of the possible view that if a man is guilty he ought to be punished. We should more naturally allot the correlative right to have him punished to his victims or society in general and not to him himself.

## THE RETRIBUTIVIST THESIS

So far I have attempted to extricate the essentials of retributivism by excluding some traditional but logically irrelevant associates. A more direct approach consists in seeing what is the essential principle which retributivists hold utilitarians to deny. Their crucial charge is that utilitarians permit the punishment of the innocent. So their fundamental thesis must be that only the guilty are to be punished, that guilt is a necessary condition of punishment. This hardly lies open to the utilitarian countercharge of pointless and vindictive barbarity, which could only find a foothold in the doctrine of annulment and in the *lex talionis*. (For that matter, it is by no means obvious that the charge can be sustained even against them, except in so far as the problems of estimating the measure of guilt lead to the adoption of a purely formal and external criterion which would not distinguish between the doing of deliberate and accidental injuries.)

Essentially, then, retributivism is the view that only the guilty are to be punished. Excluding the punishment of the innocent, it permits the other three possibilities: the punishment of the guilty, the nonpunishment of the guilty and the nonpunishment of the innocent. To add that guilt is also the sufficient condition of punishment, and thus to exclude the nonpunishment of the guilty, is another matter altogether. It is not entailed by the retributivist attack on utilitarianism and has none of the immediate compulsiveness of the doctrine that guilt is the necessary condition of punishment.

There is a very good reason for this difference in force. For the necessity of not punishing the innocent is not moral but logical. It is not, as some retributivists think, that we *may* not punish the innocent and *ought* only to punish the guilty, but that we *cannot* punish the innocent and *must* only punish the guilty. Of course, the suffering or harm in which punishment consists can be and is inflicted on innocent people, but this is not punishment, it is judicial error or terrorism or, in Bradley's characteristically repellent phrase, "social surgery." The infliction of suffering on a person is only properly described as punishment if that person is guilty. The retributivist thesis, therefore, is not a moral doctrine, but an account of the meaning of the word "punishment." Typhoid carriers and criminal lunatics are treated physically in much the same way as ordinary criminals; they are shut up in institutions. The essential difference is that no blame is implied by their imprisonment, for there is no guilt to which the blame can attach. "Punishment" resembles the word "murder;" it is infliction of suffering on the guilty and not simply infliction of suffering, just as murder is wrongful killing and not simply killing. Typhoid carriers are no more (usually) criminals than surgeons are (usually) murderers. This accounts for the flavour of moral outrage attending the notion of punishment of the innocent. In a sense a contradiction in terms, it applies to the common enough practice of inflicting the suffering involved in punishment on innocent people and of sentencing them to punishment with a lying imputation of their responsibility and guilt. Punishment *cannot* be inflicted on the innocent; the suffering associated with punishment *may* not be inflicted on them, firstly, as brutal and secondly, if it is represented as punishment, as involving a lie.

This can be shown by the fact that punishment is always *for* something. If a man says to another "I am going to punish you" and is asked "what for?" he cannot reply "nothing at all" or "something you have not done." At best, he is using "punish" here as a more or less elegant synonym for "cause to suffer." Either that or he does not understand the meaning of "punish." "I am going to punish you for something you have not done" is as absurd a statement as "I blame you for this event for which you were not responsible." "Punishment implies guilt" is the same sort of assertion as "ought implies can." It is not *pointless* to punish or blame the innocent, as some have argued, for it is often very useful. Rather the very conditions of punishment and blame do not obtain in these circumstances.

### AN OBJECTION

But how can it be useful to do what is impossible? The innocent can be punished and scapegoats are not logical impossibilities. We do say "they punished him for something he did not do." For A to be said to have punished B it is surely enough that A thought or said he was punishing B and ensured that suffering was inflicted on B. However innocent B may be of the offence adduced by A, there is no question that, in these circumstances, he has been punished by A. So guilt cannot be more than a *moral* precondition of punishment.

The answer to this objection is that "punish" is a member of that now familiar class of verbs whose first-person-present use is significantly different from the rest. The absurdity of "I am punishing you for something you have not done" is analogous to that of "I promise to do something which is not in my power." Unless you are guilty I am no more in a position to punish you than I am in a position to promise what is not in my power. So it is improper to say "I am going to punish you" unless you are guilty, just as it is improper to say "I promise to do this" unless it is in my power to do it. But it is only *morally* improper if I do not *think* that you are guilty or that I can do the promised act. Yet, just as it is perfectly proper to say of another "he promised to do this," whether he thought he could do it or not, provided that he *said* "I promise to do this," so it is perfectly proper to say "they punished him," whether they thought him guilty or not, provided that they *said* "we are going to punish you" and inflicted suffering on him. By the first-person-present use of these verbs we *prescribe* punishment and *make* promises; these activities involve the satisfaction of conditions over and above what is required for *reports* or *descriptions* of what their prescribers or makers represent as punishments and promises.

Understandably "reward" and "forgive" closely resemble "punish." Guilt is a precondition of forgiveness, desert — its contrary — of reward. One cannot properly say "I am going to reward you" or "I forgive you" to a man who has done nothing. Reward and forgiveness are always *for* something. But, again, one can say "they rewarded (or forgave) him for something he had not done." There is an interesting difference here between "forgive" and "punish" or "reward." In this last kind of assertion "forgive" seems more peculiar, more inviting to inverted commas, than the other two. The three undertakings denoted by these verbs can be divided into the utterance of a more or less ritual formula and the consequences authorized by this utterance. With punishment and reward the consequences are more noticeable than the formula, so they come to be sufficient occasion for the use of the word even if the formula is inapplicable and so improperly used. But, since the consequences of forgiveness are negative, the absence of punishment, no such shift occurs. To reward involves giving a reward, to punish inflicting a punishment, but to forgive involves no palpable consequence, e.g. handing over a written certificate of pardon.

Within these limitations, then, guilt is a *logically* necessary condition of punishment and, with some exceptions, it might be held, a morally necessary condition of the infliction of suffering. Is it in either way a sufficient condition? As will be shown in the last section there are circumstances, though they do not obtain in our legal system, nor generally in extra-legal penal systems (e.g. parental), in which guilt is a logically sufficient condition of at least a sentence of punishment. The parallel moral doctrine would be that if anyone is guilty of wrongdoing he ought morally to be punished.

This rather futile rigourism is not embodied in our legal system with its relaxations of penalties for first offenders. Since it entails that offenders should never be forgiven it is hardly likely to commend itself in the extra-legal sphere.

## THE UTILITARIAN THEORY

Utilitarianism holds that punishment must always be justified by the value of its consequences. I shall refer to this as "utility" for convenience without any implication that utility must consist in pleasure. The view that punishment is justified by the value of its consequences is compatible with any ethical theory which allows meaning to be attached to moral judgments. It holds merely that the infliction of suffering is of no value or of negative value and that it must therefore be justified by further considerations. These will be such things as prevention of and deterrence from wrongdoing, compensation of victims, reformation of offenders and satisfaction of vindictive impulses. It is indifferent for our purposes whether these are valued as intuitively good, as productive of general happiness, as conducive to the survival of the human race or are just normatively laid down as valuable or derived from such a norm.

Clearly there is no *logical* relation between punishment and its actual or expected utility. Punishment *can* be inflicted when it is neither expected, nor turns out, to be of value and, on the other hand, it can be foregone when it is either expected, or would turn out, to be of value.

But that utility is the morally necessary or sufficient condition, or both, of punishment are perfectly reputable moral attitudes. The first would hold that no one should be punished unless the punishment would have valuable consequences; the second that if valuable consequences would result punishment ought to be inflicted (without excluding the moral permissibility of utility-less punishment). Most people would no doubt accept the first, apart from the rigorists who regard guilt as a morally sufficient condition of punishment. Few would maintain the second except in conjunction with the first. The first says when you may not but not when you ought to punish, the second when you ought to but not when you may not.

Neither permits or encourages the punishment of the innocent, for this is only logically possible if the word "punishment" is used in an unnatural way, for example as meaning any kind of deliberate infliction of suffering. But in that case they cease to be moral doctrines about punishment as we understand the word and become moral doctrines (respectively platitudinous and inhuman) about something else.

So the retributivist case against the utilitarians falls to the ground as soon as what is true and essential in retributivism is extracted from the rest. This may be unwelcome to retributivists since it leaves the moral field in the possession of the utilitarians. But there is a compensation in the fact that what is essential in retributivism can at least be definitely established.

RULES AND CASES

So far what has been established is that guilt and the value or utility of consequences are relevant to punishment in different ways. A further understanding of this difference can be gained by making use of a distinction made by Sir David Ross in the appendix on punishment in *The Right and the Good*. This will also help to elucidate the notion of guilt which has hitherto been applied uncritically.

The distinction is between laying down a rule which attaches punishment to actions of a certain kind and the application of that rule to particular cases. It might be maintained that the utilitarian theory was an answer to the question "What kinds of action should be punished?" and the retributive theory an answer to the question "On what particular occasions should we punish?" On this view both punishment and guilt are defined by reference to these rules. Punishment is the infliction of suffering attached by these rules to certain kinds of action, guilt the condition of a person to whom such a rule applies. This accounts for the logically necessary relation holding between guilt and punishment. Only the guilty can be punished because unless a person is guilty, unless a rule applies to him, no infliction of suffering on him is properly called punishment, since punishment is infliction of suffering as laid down by such a rule. *Considerations of utility, then, are alone relevant to the determination of what in general, what kinds of action, to punish.* The outcome of this is a set of rules. Given these rules, the question of whom in particular to punish has a definite and necessary answer. Not only will guilt be the logically necessary but also the logically sufficient condition of punishment or, more exactly, of a sentence of punishment. For declaration of guilt will be a declaration that a rule applies and, if the rule applies, what the rule enjoins — a sentence of punishment — applies also.

The distinction between setting up and applying penal rules helps to explain the different parts played by utility and guilt in the justification of punishment, in particular the fact that where utility is a moral, guilt is a logical, justification. Guilt is irrelevant to the setting up of rules, for until they have been set up the notion of guilt is undefined and without application. Utility is irrelevant to the application of rules, for once the rules have been set up punishment is determined by guilt; once they are seen to apply, the rule makes a sentence of punishment necessarily follow.

But this account is not an accurate description of the very complex penal systems actually employed by states, institutions and parents. It is, rather, a schema, a possible limiting case. For it ignores an almost universal feature of penal systems (and of games, for that matter, where penalties attend infractions of the rules) — discretion. For few offences against the law is one and only one fixed and definite punishment laid down. Normally only an upper limit is set. If guilt, the applicability of the rule, is established no fixed punishment is entailed but rather, for example, one not exceeding a fine of forty shillings or fourteen days' imprisonment. This is even more evident in the administration of such institutions as clubs or libraries and yet more again in the matter of parental discipline. The establishment of guilt does not close the matter; at best it entails some punishment or other. Precisely how much is appropriate must be determined by reference to considerations of utility. The variety of things is too great for any manageably concise penal code to dispense altogether with discretionary judgment in particular cases.

But this fact only shows that guilt is not a logically *sufficient* condition of punishment; it does not affect the thesis that punishment entails guilt. A man cannot be guilty unless his action falls under a penal rule and he can only be properly said to be punished if the rule in question prescribes or permits some punishment or other. So all applications of the notion of guilt necessarily contain or include all applications of the notion of punishment.

# Punishment

### J. D. MABBOTT

I propose in this paper to defend a retributive theory of punishment and to reject absolutely all utilitarian considerations from its justification. I feel sure that this enterprise must arouse deep suspicion and hostility both among philosophers (who must have felt that the retributive view is the only moral theory except perhaps psychological hedonism which has been definitely destroyed by criticism) and among practical men (who have welcomed its steady decline in our penal practice).

The question I am asking is this. Under what circumstances is the punishment of some particular person justified and why? The theories of reform and deterrence which are usually considered to be the only alternatives to retribution involve well-known difficulties. These are considered fully and fairly in Dr. Ewing's book, *The Morality of Punishment,* and I need not spend long over them. The central difficulty is that both would on occasion justify the punishment of an innocent man, the deterrent theory if he were believed to have been guilty by those likely to commit the crime in future, and the reformatory theory if he were a bad man though not a criminal. To this may be added the point against the deterrent theory that it is the threat of punishment and not punishment itself which deters, and that when deterrence seems to depend on actual punishment, to implement the threat, it really depends on publication and may be achieved if men believe that punishment has occurred even if in fact it has not. As Bentham saw, for a Utilitarian apparent justice is everything, real justice is irrelevant.

Dr. Ewing and other moralists would be inclined to compromise with retribution in the face of the above difficulties. They would admit that one fact and one fact only can justify the punishment of this man, and that is a *past* fact, that he has committed a crime. To this extent reform and deterrence theories, which look only to the consequences, are wrong. But they would add that retribution can determine only *that*

From *Mind,* vol. 49 (1939). Reprinted by the author's permission.

a man should be punished. It cannot determine how or how much, and here reform and deterrence may come in. Even Bradley, the fiercest retributionist of modern times, says "Having once the right to punish we may modify the punishment according to the useful and the pleasant, but these are external to the matter; they cannot give us a right to punish and nothing can do that but criminal desert." Dr. Ewing would maintain that the whole estimate of the amount and nature of a punishment may be affected by considerations of reform and deterrence. It seems to me that this is a surrender which the upholders of retribution dare not make. As I said above, it is publicity and not punishment which deters, and the publicity though often spoken of as "part of a man's punishment" is no more part of it than his arrest or his detention prior to trial, though both these may be also unpleasant and bring him into disrepute. A judge sentences a man to three years' imprisonment not to three years *plus* three columns in the press. Similarly with reform. The visit of the prison chaplain is not part of a man's punishment nor is the visit of Miss Fields or Mickey Mouse.

The truth is that while punishing a man and punishing him justly, it is possible to deter others, and also to attempt to reform him, and if these additional goods are achieved the total state of affairs is better than it would be with the just punishment alone. But reform and deterrence are not modifications of the punishment, still less reasons for it. A parallel may be found in the case of tact and truth. If you have to tell a friend an unpleasant truth you may do all you can to put him at his ease and spare his feelings as much as possible, while still making sure that he understands your meaning. In such a case no one would say that your offer of a cigarette beforehand or your apology afterwards are modifications of the truth still less reasons for telling it. You do not tell the truth in order to spare his feelings, but having to tell the truth you also spare his feelings. So Bradley was right when he said that reform and deterrence were "external to the matter," but therefore wrong when he said that they may "modify the punishment." Reporters are admitted to our trials so that punishments may become public and help to deter others. But the punishment would be no less just were reporters excluded and deterrence not achieved. Prison authorities may make it possible that a convict may become physically or morally better. They cannot ensure either result; and the punishment would still be just if the criminal took no advantage of their arrangements and their efforts failed. Some moralists see this and exclude these "extra" arrangements for deterrence and reform. They say that it must be the punishment *itself* which reforms and deters. But it is just my point that the punishment *itself* seldom reforms the criminal and never deters others. It is only "extra" arrangements which have any chance of achieving either result. As this is the central point of my paper, at the cost of laboured repetition I would ask the upholders of reform and deterrence two questions. Suppose it could be shown that a particular criminal had not been improved by a punishment and also that no other would-be criminal had been deterred by it, would that prove that the punishment was unjust? Suppose it were discovered that a particular criminal had lived a much better life after his release and that many would-be criminals believing him to have been guilty were influenced by his fate, but yet that the "criminal" was punished for something he had never done, would these excellent results prove the punishment just?

It will be observed that I have throughout treated punishment as a purely legal matter. A "criminal" means a man who has broken a law, not a bad man; an "innocent" man is a man who has not broken the law in connection with which he is being punished, though he may be a bad man and have broken other laws. Here I dissent from most upholders of the retributive theory — from Hegel, from Bradley, and from Dr. Ross. They maintain that the essential connection is one between punishment and moral or social wrong-doing.

My fundamental difficulty with their theory is the question of *status*. It takes two to make a punishment, and for a moral or social wrong I can find no punisher. We may be tempted to say when we hear of some brutal action "that ought to be punished"; but I cannot see how there can be duties which are nobody's duties. If I see a man ill-treating a horse in a country where cruelty to animals is not a legal offence, and I say to him "I shall now punish you," he will reply, rightly, "What has it to do with you? Who made you a judge and a ruler over me?" I may have a duty to try to stop him and one way of stopping him may be to hit him, but another way may be to buy the horse. Neither the blow nor the price is a punishment. For a moral offence, God alone has the *status* necessary to punish the offender; and the theologians are becoming more and more doubtful whether even God has a duty to punish wrongdoing.

Dr. Ross would hold that not all wrong-doing is punishable, but only invasion of the rights of others; and in such a case it might be thought that the injured party had a right to punish. His right, however, is rather a right to reparation, and should not be confused with punishment proper.

This connection, on which I insist, between punishment and crime, not between punishment and moral or social wrong, alone accounts for some of our beliefs about punishment, and also meets many objections to the retributive theory as stated in its ordinary form. The first point on which it helps us is with regard to retrospective legislation. Our objection to this practice is unaccountable on reform and deterrence theories. For a man who commits a wrong before the date on which a law against it is passed, is as much in need of reform as a man who commits it afterwards; nor is deterrrence likely to suffer because of additional punishments for the same offence. But the orthodox retributive theory is equally at a loss here, for if punishment is given for moral wrong-doing or for invasion of the rights of others, that immorality or invasion existed as certainly before the passing of the law as after it.

My theory also explains, where it seems to me all others do not, the case of punishment imposed by an authority who believes the law in question is a bad law. I was myself for some time disciplinary officer of a college whose rules included a rule compelling attendance at chapel. Many of those who broke this rule broke it on principle. I punished them. I certainly did not want to reform them; I respected their characters and their views. I certainly did not want to drive others into chapel through fear of penalties. Nor did I think there had been a wrong done which merited retribution. I wished I could have believed that I would have done the same myself. My position was clear. They had broken a rule; they knew it and I knew it. Nothing more was necessary to make punishment proper.

I know that the usual answer to this is that the judge enforces a bad law because otherwise law in general would suffer and good laws would be broken. The effect of punishing good men for breaking bad laws is that fewer bad men break good laws.

[*Excursus on Indirect Utilitarianism.* The above argument is a particular instance of a general utilitarian solution of all similar problems. When I am in funds and consider whether I should pay my debts or give the same amount to charity, I must choose the former because repayment not only benefits my creditor (for the benefit to him might be less than the good done through charity) but also up-holds the general credit system. I tell the truth when a lie might do more good to the parties directly concerned, because I thus increase general trust and confidence. I keep a promise when it might do more immediate good to break it, because indirectly I bring it about that promises will be more readily made in future and this will outweigh the immediate loss involved. Dr. Ross has pointed out that the effect on the credit system of my refusal to pay a debt is greatly exaggerated. But I have a more serious objection of principle. It is that in all these cases the indirect effects do not result from my wrong action — my lie or defalcation or bad faith — but from the publication of these actions. If in any instance the breaking of the rule were to remain un-known then I could consider only the direct or immediate conse-quences. Thus in my "compulsory chapel" case I could have con-sidered which of my culprits were law-abiding men generally and unlikely to break any other college rule. Then I could have sent for each of these separately and said "I shall let you off if you will tell no one I have done so." By these means the general keeping of rules would not have suffered. Would this course have been correct? It must be remembered that the proceedings need not deceive everybody. So long as they deceive would-be lawbreakers the good is achieved.

As this point is of crucial importance and as it has an interest beyond the immediate issue, and gives us a clue to what I regard as the true general nature of law and punishment, I may be excused for expanding and illustrating it by an example or two from other fields. Dr. Ross says that two men dying on a desert island would have duties to keep promises to each other even though their breaking them would not affect the future general confidence in promises at all. Here is certainly the same point. But as I find that desert-island morality always rouses suspicion among ordinary men I should like to quote two instances from my own experience which also illustrate the problem.

1.   A man alone with his father at his death promises him a private and quiet funeral. He finds later that both directly and in-directly the keeping of this promise will cause pain and misunder-standing. He can see no particular positive good that the quiet funeral will achieve. No one yet knows that he has made the promise nor need anyone ever know. Should he therefore act as though it had never been made?

2.   A college has a fund given to it for the encouragement of a subject which is now expiring. Other expanding subjects are in great need of endowment. Should the authorities divert the money? Those who oppose the diversion have previously stood on the past, the promise. But one day one of them discovers the "real reason" for this slavery to a dead donor. He says "We must consider not only the value of this money for these purposes, since on all direct consequences it should be diverted at once. We must remember the effect of this diversion on the general system of benefactions. We know that benefactors like to endow special objects, and this act of ours would discourage such benefactors in future and leave learning worse off." Here again is the indirect utilitarian reason for choosing the alternative which direct utilitarianism would reject. But the immediate answer to this from the most ingenious member of the opposition was crushing and final. He said, "Divert the money but keep it dark." This is obviously correct. It is not the act of diversion which would diminish the stream of benefactions but the news of it reaching the ears of benefactors. Provided that no possible benefactor got to hear of it no indirect loss would result. But the justification of our action would depend entirely on the success of the measures for "keeping it dark." I remember how I felt and how others felt that whatever answer was right this result was certainly wrong. But it follows that indirect utilitarianism is wrong in all such cases. For its argument can always be met by "Keep it dark."]

The view, then, that a judge upholds a bad law in order that law in general should not suffer is indefensible. He upholds it simply because he has no right to dispense from punishment.

The connection of punishment with law-breaking and not with wrong-doing also escapes moral objections to the retributive theory as held by Kant and Hegel or by Bradley and Ross. It is asked how we can measure moral wrong or balance it with pain, and how pain can wipe out moral wrong. Retributivists have been pushed into holding that pain *ipso facto* represses the worse self and frees the better, when this is contrary to the vast majority of observed cases. But if punishment is not intended to measure or balance or negate moral wrong then all this is beside the mark. There is the further difficulty of reconciling punishment with repentance and with forgiveness. Repentance is the reaction morally appropriate to moral wrong and punishment added to remorse is an unnecessary evil. But if punishment is associated with law-breaking and not with moral evil the punisher is not entitled to consider whether the criminal is penitent any more than he may consider whether the law is good. So, too, with forgiveness. Forgiveness is not appropriate to law-breaking. (It is noteworthy that when, in divorce cases, the law has to recognize forgiveness it calls it "condonation," which is symptomatic of the difference of attitude.) Nor is forgiveness appropriate to moral evil. It is appropriate to personal injury. No one has any right to forgive me except the person I have injured. No judge or jury can do so. But the person I have injured has no right to punish me. Therefore there is no clash between punishment and forgiveness since these two duties do not fall on the same person nor in connection with the same characteristic of my act. (It is the weakness of vendetta that it tends to confuse this clear line, though even there it is only by personifying the family that the injured party and the avenger are identified. Similarly we must guard against the plausible fallacy of personifying society and regarding the criminal as "injuring society," for then once more the old dilemma about forgiveness would be insoluble.) A clergyman friend of mine catching a burglar red-handed was puzzled about his duty. In the end he ensured the man's punishment by information and evidence, and at the same time showed his own forgiveness by visiting the man in prison and employing him when he came out. I believe any "good Christian" would accept this as representing his duty. But obviously if the punishment is thought of as imposed *by* the victim or *for* the injury or immorality then the contradiction with forgiveness is hopeless.

So far as the question of the actual punishment of any individual is concerned this paper could stop here. No punishment is morally retributive or reformative or deterrent. Any criminal punished for any one of these reasons is certainly unjustly punished. The only justification for punishing any man is that he has broken a law.

In a book which has already left its mark on prison administration I have found a criminal himself confirming these views. *Walls Have Mouths,* by W. F. R. Macartney, is prefaced, and provided with appendices to each chapter, by Compton Mackenzie. It is interesting to notice how the novelist maintains that the proper object of penal servitude should be reformation,[1] whereas the prisoner himself accepts the view I have set out above. Macartney says "To punish a man is to

---

[1] W. F. R. Macartney, *Walls Have Mouths,* p. 97.

treat him as an equal. To be punished *for an offense against rules* is a sane man's right."[2] It is striking also that he never uses "injustice" to describe the brutality or provocation which he experienced. He makes it clear that there were only two types of prisoner who were *unjustly* imprisoned, those who were insane and not responsible for the acts for which they were punished[3] and those who were innocent and had broken no law.[4] It is irrelevant, as he rightly observes, that some of these innocent men were, like Steinie Morrison, dangerous and violent characters, who on utilitarian grounds might well have been restrained. That made their punishment no whit less unjust.[5] To these general types may be added two specific instances of injustice. First, the sentences on the Dartmoor mutineers. "The Penal Servitude Act . . . lays down specific punishments for mutiny and incitement to mutiny, which include flogging. . . . Yet on the occasion of the only big mutiny in an English prison, men are not dealt with by the Act specially passed to meet mutiny in prison, but are taken out of gaol and tried under an Act expressly passed to curb and curtail the Chartists — a revolutionary movement."[6] Here again the injustice does not lie in the actual effect the sentences are likely to have on the prisoners (though Macartney has some searching suggestions about that also) but in condemning men for breaking a law they did not break and not for breaking the law they did break. The second specific instance is that of Coulton, who served his twenty years and then was brought back to prison to do another eight years and to die. This is due to the "unjust order that no lifer shall be released unless he has either relations or a job to whom he can go: and it is actually suggested that this is really for the lifer's own good. Just fancy, you admit that the man in doing years upon years in prison had expiated his crime: but, instead of releasing him, you keep him a further time — perhaps another three years — because you say he has nowhere to go. Better a ditch and hedge than prison! True, there are abnormal cases who want to stay in prison, but Lawrence wanted to be a private soldier, and men go into monasteries. Because occasionally a man wants to stay in prison, must every lifer who has lost his family

[2] *Ibid.*, p. 165. My italics.
[3] *Ibid.*, p. 165–166.
[4] *Ibid.*, p. 298.
[5] *Ibid.*, p. 301.
[6] *Ibid.*, p. 255.

during his sentence (I was doing only ten years and I lost all my family) be kept indefinitely in gaol after he has paid his debt?" [7] Why is it unjust? Because he has paid his debt. When that is over it is for the man himself to decide what is for his own good. Once again the reform and utilitarian arguments are summarily swept aside. Injustice lies not in bad treatment or treatment which is not in the man's own interest, but in restriction which, according to the law, he has not merited.

It is true that Macartney writes, in one place, a paragraph of general reflection on punishment in which he confuses, as does Compton Mackenzie, retribution with revenge and in which he seems to hold that the retributive theory has some peculiar connection with private property. "Indeed it is difficult to see how, in society as it is to-day constituted, a humane prison system could function. All property is sacred, although the proceeds of property may well be reprehensible, therefore any offence against property is sacrilege and must be punished. Till a system eventuates which is based not on exploitation of man by man and class by class, prisons must be dreadful places, but at least there might be an effort to ameliorate the more savage side of the retaliation, and this could be done very easily."[8] The alternative system of which no doubt he is thinking is the Russian system described in his quotations from *A Physician's Tour in Soviet Russia,* by Sir James Purves-Stewart, the system of "correctional colonies" providing curative "treatment" for the different types of criminal.[9] There are two confusions here, to one of which we shall return later. First, Macartney confuses the retributive system with the punishment of one particular type of crime, offences against property, when he must have known that the majority of offenders against property do not find themselves in Dartmoor or even in Wandsworth. After all his own offence was not one against property — it was traffic with a foreign Power — and it was one for which in the classless society of Russia the punishment is death. It is surely clear that a retributive system may be adopted for any class of crime. Secondly, Macartney confuses injustice within a penal system with the wrongfulness of a penal system. When he pleads for "humane prisons" as if

---

[7] *Ibid.,* p. 400.
[8] *Ibid.,* pp. 166, 167.
[9] *Ibid.,* p. 229.

the essence of the prison should be humanity, or when Compton Mackenzie says the object of penal servitude should be reform, both of them are giving up punishment altogether, not altering it. A Russian "correctional colony," if its real object is curative treatment, is no more a "prison" than is an isolation hospital or a lunatic asylum. To this distinction between abolishing injustice in punishment and abolishing punishment altogether we must now turn.

It will be objected that my original question "Why ought X to be punished?" is an illegitimate isolation of the issue. I have treated the whole set of circumstances as determined. X is a citizen of a state. About his citizenship, whether willing or unwilling, I have asked no questions. About the government, whether it is good or bad, I do not enquire. X has broken a law. Concerning the law, whether it is well-devised or not, I have not asked. Yet all these questions are surely relevant before it can be decided whether a particular punishment is just. It is the essence of my position that none of these questions is relevant. Punishment is a corollary of law-breaking by a member of the society whose law is broken. This is a static and an abstract view but I see no escape from it. Considerations of utility come in on two quite different issues. Should there be laws, and what laws should there be? As a legislator I may ask what general types of action would benefit the community, and, among these, which can be "standardized" without loss, or should be standardized to achieve their full value. This, however, is not the primary question since particular laws may be altered or repealed. The choice which is the essential *prius* of punishment is the choice that there should be laws. The choice is not Hobson's. Other methods may be considered. A government might attempt to standardize certain modes of action by means of advice. It might proclaim its view and say "Citizens are requested" to follow this or that procedure. Or again it might decide to deal with each case as it arose in the manner most effective for the common welfare. Anarchists have wavered between these two alternatives and a third — that of doing nothing to enforce a standard of behaviour but merely giving arbitrational decisions between conflicting parties, decisions binding only by consent.

I think it can be seen without detailed examination of particular laws that the method of law-making has its own advantages. Its orders are explicit and general. It makes behaviour reliable and predictable. Its threat of punishment may be so effective as to make punishment unnecessary. It promises to the good citizen a certain security in his life. When I have talked to business men about some inequity in the law of liability they have usually said "Better a bad law than no law, for then we know where we are."

Someone may say I am drawing an impossible line. I deny that punishment is utilitarian; yet now I say that punishment is a corollary of law and we decide whether to have laws and which laws to have on utilitarian grounds. And surely it is only this corollary which distinguishes law from good advice or exhortation. This is a misunderstanding. Punishment is a corollary not of law but of law-breaking. Legislators do not choose to punish. They hope no punishment will be needed. Their laws would succeed even if no punishment occurred. The criminal makes the essential choice: he "brings it on himself." Other men obey the law because they see its order is reasonable, because of inertia, because of fear. In this whole area, and it may be the major part of the state, law achieves its ends without punishment. Clearly, then, punishment is not a corollary of law.

We may return for a moment to the question of amount and nature of punishment. It may be thought that this also is automatic. The law will include its own penalties and the judge will have no option. This, however, is again an initial choice of principle. If the laws do include their own penalties then the judge has no option. But the legislature might adopt a system which left complete or partial freedom to the judge, as we do except in the case of murder. Once again, what are the merits (regardless of particular laws, still more of particular cases) of fixed penalties and variable penalties? At first sight it would seem that all the advantages are with the variable penalties; for men who have broken the same law differ widely in degree of wickedness and responsibility. When, however, we remember that punishment is not an attempt to balance moral guilt this advantage is diminished. But there are still degrees of responsibility; I do not mean degrees of freedom of will but, for instance, degrees of complicity in a crime. The danger of allowing complete freedom to the judicature in fixing penalties is not merely that it lays too heavy a tax on human nature but that it would lead to the judge expressing in his penalty the degree of his own moral aversion to the crime. Or he might tend on deterrent grounds to punish more heavily a crime which was spreading and for which temptation and opportunity were frequent. Or again on deterrent grounds he might "make examples" by punishing ten times as heavily those criminals who are detected in cases in which nine out of ten evade detection. Yet we should revolt from all such punishments if they involved punishing theft more heavily than blackmail or negligence more heavily than premeditated assault. The death penalty for sheep-stealing might have been defended on such deterrent grounds. But we should dislike equating sheep-stealing with murder. Fixed penalties enable us to draw these distinctions between crimes. It is not that we can say how much imprisonment is right for a sheep-stealer. But we can grade crimes in a rough scale and penalties in a rough scale, and keep our heaviest penalties for what are socially the most serious wrongs regardless of whether these penalties will reform the criminal or whether they are exactly what deterrence would require. The compromise of laying down maximum penalties and allowing judges freedom below these limits allows for the arguments on both sides.

To return to the main issue, the position I am defending is that it is essential to a legal system that the infliction of a particular punishment should *not* be determined by the good *that particular punishment* will do either to the criminal or to "society." In exactly the same way it is essential to a credit system that the repayment of a particular debt should not be determined by the good that particular payment will do. One may consider the merits of a legal system or of a credit system, but the acceptance of either involves the surrender of utilitarian considerations in particular cases as they arise. This is in effect admitted by Ewing in one place where he says "It is the penal system as a whole which deters and not the punishment of any individual offender."[10]

To show that the choice between a legal system and its alternatives is one we do and must make, I may quote an early work of Lenin in which he was defending the Marxist tenet that the state is bound to "wither away" with the establishment of a classless society. He considers the possible objection that some wrongs by man against man are not economic and therefore that the abolition of classes would not *ipso facto* eliminate crime. But he sticks to the thesis that these surviving crimes should not be dealt with by law and judicature. "We are not Utopians and do not in the least deny the

10 A. C. Ewing, *The Morality of Punishment* (London: Routledge and Kegan Paul, Ltd., 1929), p. 66.

possibility and inevitability of excesses by *individual persons,* and equally the need to suppress such excesses. But for this no special machine, no special instrument of repression is needed. This will be done by the armed nation itself as simply and as readily as any crowd of civilized people even in modern society parts a pair of combatants or does not allow a woman to be outraged." [11] This alternative to law and punishment has obvious demerits. Any injury not committed in the presence of the crowd, any wrong which required skill to detect or pertinacity to bring home would go untouched. The lynching mob, which is Lenin's instrument of justice, is liable to error and easily deflected from its purpose or driven to extremes. It must be a mob, for there is to be no "machine." I do not say that no alternative machine to ours could be devised but it does seem certain that the absence of all "machines" would be intolerable. An alternative machine might be based on the view that "society" is responsible for all criminality, and a curative and protective system developed. This is the system of Butler's "Erewhon" and something like it seems to be growing up in Russia except for cases of "sedition."

We choose, then, or we acquiesce in and adopt the choice of others of, a legal system as one of our instruments for the establishment of the conditions of a good life. This choice is logically prior to and independent of the actual punishment of any particular persons or the passing of any particular laws. The legislators choose particular laws within the framework of this predetermined system. Once again a small society may illustrate the reality of these choices and the distinction between them. A Headmaster launching a new school must explicitly make both decisions. First, shall we have any rules at all? Second, what rules shall he have? The first decision is a genuine one and one of great importance. Would it not be better to have an "honour" system, by which public opinion in each house or form dealt with any offence? (This is the Lenin method.) Or would complete freedom be better? Or should he issue appeals and advice? Or should he personally deal with each malefactor individually, as the case arises, in the way most likely to improve his conduct? I can well imagine an idealistic Headmaster attempting to run a school with one of these methods or with a combination of several of them and therefore without punishment. I can even imagine that with a small school

[11] *The State and Revolution* (Eng. trans.), p. 93. Original italics.

of, say, twenty pupils all open to direct personal psychological pressure from authority and from each other, these methods involving no "rules" would work. The pupils would of course grow up without two very useful habits, the habit of having some regular habits and the habit of obeying rules. But I suspect that most Headmasters, especially those of large schools, would either decide at once, or quickly be driven, to realize that some rules were necessary. This decision would be "utilitarian" in the sense that it would be determined by consideration of consequences. The question "what rules?" would then arise and again the issue is utilitarian. What action must be regularized for the school to work efficiently? The hours of arrival and departure, for instance, in a day school. But the one choice which is now no longer open to the Headmaster is whether he shall punish those who break the rules. For if he were to try to avoid this he would in fact simply be returning to the discarded method of appeals and good advice. Yet the Headmaster does not decide to punish. The pupils make the decision there. He decides actually to have rules and to threaten, but only hypothetically, to punish. The one essential condition which makes actual punishment just is a condition he *cannot* fulfil — namely that a rule should be broken.

I shall add a final word of consolation to the practical reformer. Nothing that I have said is meant to counter any movement for "penal reform" but only to insist that none of these reforms have anything to do with punishment. The only type of reformer who can claim to be reforming the system of punishment is a follower of Lenin or of Samuel Butler who is genuinely attacking the *system* and who believes there should be no laws and no punishments. But our great British reformers have been concerned not with punishment but with its accessories. When a man is sentenced to imprisonment he is not sentenced also to partial starvation, to physical brutality, to pneumonia from damp cells and so on. And any movement which makes his food sufficient to sustain health, which counters the permanent tendency to brutality on the part of his warders, which gives him a dry or even a light and well-aired cell, is pure gain and does not touch the theory of punishment. Reformatory influences and prisoners' aid arrangements are also entirely unaffected by what I have said. I believe myself that it would be best if all such arrangements were made optional for the prisoner, so as to leave him in these cases a freedom of choice which would make it clear that they are not part of his punishment. If it is said that every such reform lessens a man's punishment, I think that is simply muddled thinking which, if it were clear, would be mere brutality. For instance, a prisoners' aid society is said to lighten his punishment, because otherwise he would suffer not merely imprisonment but also unemployment on release. But he was sentenced to imprisonment, not imprisonment *plus* unemployment. If I promise to help a friend and through special circumstances I find that keeping my promise will involve upsetting my day's work, I do not say that I really promised to help him and to ruin my day's work. And if another friend carries on my work for me I do not regard him as carrying out part of my promise, nor as stopping me from carrying it out myself. He merely removes an indirect and regrettable consequence of my keeping my promise. So with punishment. The Prisoners' Aid Society does not alter a man's punishment nor diminish it, but merely removes an indirect and regrettable consequence of it. And anyone who thinks that a criminal cannot make this distinction and will regard all the inconvenience that comes to him as punishment, need only talk to a prisoner or two to find how sharply they resent these wanton additions to a punishment which by itself they will accept as just. Macartney's chapter on "Food" in the book quoted above is a good illustration of this point, as are also his comments on Clayton's administration. "To keep a man in prison for many years at considerable expense and then to free him charged to the eyes with uncontrollable venom and hatred generated by the treatment he has received in gaol, does not appear to be sensible." Clayton "endeavoured to send a man out of prison in a reasonable state of mind. 'Well, I've done my time. They were not too bad to me. Prison is prison and not a bed of roses. Still they didn't rub it in. . . .' " [12] This "reasonable state of mind" is one in which a prisoner on release feels he has been punished but not *additionally* insulted or ill-treated. I feel convinced that penal reformers would meet with even more support if they were clear that they were *not* attempting to alter the system of punishment but to give its victims "fair play." We have no more right to starve a convict than to starve an animal. We have no more right to keep a convict in a Dartmoor cell "down which the water trickles night and day" [13] than we have to keep a child in such a place. If our reformers

[12] *Op. cit.,* p. 152.
[13] *Ibid.,* p. 258.

really want to alter the system of punishment, let them come out clearly with their alternative and preach, for instance, that no human being is responsible for any wrong-doing, that all the blame is on society, that curative or protective measures should be adopted, forcibly if necessary, as they are with infection or insanity. Short of this let them admit that the essence of prison is deprivation of liberty for the breaking of law, and that deprivation of food or of health or of books is unjust. And if our sentimentalists cry "coddling of prisoners," let us ask them also to come out clearly into the open and incorporate whatever starvation and disease and brutality they think necessary *into the sentences they propose.*[14] If it is said that some prisoners will prefer such reformed prisons, with adequate food and aired cells, to the outer world, we may retort that their numbers are probably not greater than those of the masochists who like to be flogged. Yet we do not hear the same "coddling" critics suggest abolition of the lash on the grounds that some criminals may like it. Even if the abolition from our prisons of all maltreatment other than that imposed by law results in a few down-and-outs breaking a window (as O. Henry's hero did) to get a night's lodging, the country will lose less than she does by her present method of sending out her discharged convicts "charged with venom and hatred" because of the additional and unconvenanted "rubbing it in" which they have received.

I hope I have established both the theoretical importance and the practical value of distinguishing between penal reform as we know and approve it — that reform which alters the accompaniments of punishment without touching its essence — and those attacks on punishment itself which are made not only by reformers who regard criminals as irresponsible and in need of treatment, but also by every judge who announces that he is punishing a man to deter others or to protect society, and by every juryman who is moved to his decision by the moral baseness of the accused rather than by his legal guilt.

---

[14] "One of the minor curiosities of jail life was that they quickly provided you with a hundred worries which left you no time or energy for worrying about your sentence, long or short. . . . Rather as if you were thrown into a fire with spikes in it, and the spikes hurt you so badly that you forget about the fire. But then your punishment would *be* the spikes not the fire. Why did they pretend it was only the fire, when they knew very well about the spikes?" (From *Lifer* by Jim Phelan, p. 40.)

# PART THREE

---

# THE FORMS AND
# LIMITS OF DISSENT

# Introduction

The readings presented in Part One introduced some of the complexities involved in framing a general theory of obligation. Such a theory is intended to provide a standard by which one may judge the adequacy of the reasons men offer for affirming or denying that they, or others, are obligated to the political community under specified circumstances. In Part Two, two groups of the chief controversies were raised in response to the general problem of obligation. First, which rules should be publicly enforced, and according to what standards and for what reasons? Second, what purposes should that enforcement serve? Just as the problems of rules and their enforcement in many ways presuppose a theory of political obligation, so do the problems of dissent introduced in this section. Whatever general theory of obligation one considers most nearly satisfactory, and whatever broad views one finds acceptable concerning the merits or defects, the scope, and the purposes of public enforcement of standards for behavior, there must logically remain the possibility that an individual or a group, under some circumstances, may be able to justify some form of dissent. In short, a theory of obligation necessarily implies limitation. Since such a theory attempts to specify the reasons for, and the circumstances in which men ought to consider themselves obligated, a situation may always arise in which that rationale may no longer apply. On the other hand, just as the effort to articulate principles of obligation implies limits, so does the effort to formulate theories of justifiable dissent.

The readings in this section concern debates on particular modes of dissent, disobedience and resistance. Perhaps the most extensively discussed form in recent years has been civil disobedience, particularly non-violent civil disobedience. The essay of Bedau is a painstaking effort to clarify the meaning of civil disobedience and the issues at stake, while Thoreau's now classical piece affirms the justifiability of disobedience in connection with a specific issue. Normally, an important element in the argument that civil disobedience is sometimes a legitimate recourse is the claim that it is a nonviolent political technique. But the article by Prosch argues that this claim cannot always be supported, and, therefore, raises serious questions about its justifiability. In any case, the usual presumption behind the idea of legitimate civil disobedience is that the citizen's general obligation to his political community remains in tact, so that the question of loyalty to the system as a whole does not really arise. On the contrary, the argument normally is that a particular law or policy constitutes either a violation of the more general legal system or, especially in the United States, some principle of the Constitution, or that it frustrates the very values it is supposed to serve. In short, the normal democratic processes are not called into question; rather, civil disobedience most often is seen as an effort to reinforce them in those instances in which they have failed to operate.

More acute problems, however, are raised by considering the position of social groups who are consistently disadvantaged by existing laws and institutions. An important element in the successful functioning of a democratic process is accepting that one's own values and interests, or those of the groups with which he identifies, may lose in electoral processes or in the effort to affect policy decisions. The idea, of course, is that one's interests also win sometimes, or at least receive enough recognition that obligation based upon consent is not an unreasonable interpretation of the political system. But how is one to deal with questions of obligation and obedience if there are groups — presumably minorities — that lose *consistently?* What is to be said about source or the scope and limits of their obligations? Are extraordinary measures of dissent justifiable in such cases? Would it then be possible to argue that even the use of political violence by or on behalf of such groups might be justifiable? While the article by Bay might as easily have been employed in the preceding section, it seems appropriate here, also, because he raises difficult questions about unresponsive institutions and inherited practices which may no longer be appropriate, and suggests that genuine democracy may be unobtainable under contemporary conditions without recourse to a generalized idea of civil disobedience. From quite another perspective, Wolff argues that disputes about legitimate disobedience or, indeed, legitimate recourse to violence are idle, because legitimate political authority is impossible to achieve. This essay, in short, presents the case for political anarchism, and so bears on virtually all the issues canvassed here.

Just as it is possible that active resistance by oppressed minorities may be justifiable, so it is that under some, presumably extreme circumstances revolutionary resistance may be justifiable. Because revolutionary violence involves such high risks for human life, and because it normally aims at the institutionalization of alternative values for the entire social order, much more controversy has always accompanied the fundamental question whether revolution is *ever* justified. The essay by Marcuse argues both that revolution can be justified, and that it is possible to reconcile the costs involved with the demands of ethics. The excerpt from Hook, on the other hand, suggests that in a democratic system, at least, revolutionary activity involves a more demanding theory of justification than is always recognized.

It is clear that the kinds of dissent are so numerous, and the issues involved so difficult, that it is not possible to explore them all here. Nevertheless, in considering the major alternatives illustrated in this section, some general points may be helpful to bear in mind. One major consideration has already been alluded to in passing: one's judgment on an issue of dissent cannot help being conditioned by the form it takes, its scope, and its intent. As a beginning, one might distinguish four broad levels. At the most narrow level, is what might be called legal forms of dissent. In contemporary America, it is frequently said that if an individual is persuaded that he must follow his own conscientious decision, rather than the law, he is free to do so, but that he ought then to accept whatever penalty accompanies that violation. This view appears to amount to the paradoxical contention that a person can simultaneously obey both his conscience and the law, both obey and not obey. If the purposes of the dissenter are narrow, for instance, if he wishes merely to register his disagreement in a striking way, he may be content to leave the issue at that level. What is suggested by this is that there is involved no charge that the law in question is in some way not lawful; hence, the form, scope and intent of such disobedience are all sharply confined.

At a second level, however, we might identify disobedience that is plainly intended to be illegal, with unwillingness to accept punishment. Such a situation might arise because a person is persuaded that a law, or a public policy, or a governmental institution is itself involved in illegality, injustice, or frustration of the social values that it is supposed to protect. Presumably, this contention would be a major part of the justification offered. The important point here is whether or not those dissenting confine their disobedience to the offending law or policy, and whether the actions taken can be considered reasonably suited to the objective. It is not easy to see how, for example, indiscriminate violence could be justified if the original complaint (supposing, for the sake of the argument, that that was justifiable) is narrow. However complex such situations may be, the general point is simple. It is much more likely that justification can be achieved if the actions taken remain closely tied to the specific objection.

In the third place, it may be appropriate to distinguish forms of dissent that aim, not at a specific complaint, but at a general reform of the society's institutions. At this level the intent is much more comprehensive and so, most likely, would be the actions and their scope. But the important point for present purposes is that the difficulty of justification is correspondingly magnified; hence, one's judgment must be more demanding. At a final level, it seems useful to distinguish revolutionary intent. Here it is no longer a question of even general reform, but of the desirability of organizing a society on alternative principles and values. Accordingly, the task of justification becomes immensely more complex, involving the highest political stakes and very high risks for large numbers of people.

Especially at the last two levels, particularly acute problems arise in a society that is intended to be organized in terms of democratic values. On the one hand, some may think that society is violating its own principles, although it may be unable, by accepted means at least, to obtain the necessary changes. In such a case, individuals who remain firmly committed to the values of their society find themselves in an immensely painful dilemma. On the other hand, there may be those who contend that the society is not in fact a democracy but ought to be. They may be persuaded that their assessment of the situation is correct, but, finding themselves unable to persuade the majority, are faced with a similar dilemma: whether to acquiesce to the majority view, or to attempt in some way to impose their interpretation on the recalcitrant majority. The most acute difficulty here is different from the first case, in which the dissenters intend to rectify a discrepancy between value and practice, but do not maintain that the political system in general simply is not what it is supposed to be. In the second case, however, the problem is the gap between a revolutionary proposal that claims to aim at a democratic result, and the kind of anti-democratic elitism that may be necessary before the new order is achieved, for this involves serious damage to the justification offered for the revolutionary proposal in the first place. The general observation, however, holds: as the scope of actions and intent contemplated becomes wider, and, therefore, the interests, values and concerns of more persons are liable to be affected, the more one ought to require that the justification be fully developed.

It may often be necessary to distinguish between justifiable complaint and justifiable action. It is possible that a dissenting assessment of a situation may be quite correct, but it does not follow that one ought to undertake specific actions. Imagine a case in which it is widely agreed that the vast majority of people is suffering the impositions of political tyranny. One might easily agree that resistance would be abundantly justified, but not necessarily agree that specific actions were rightly undertaken. Suppose that acts of resistance had the effect of provoking large scale retaliation on innocent persons, as happened in the resistance to Nazism in the ghettos of occupied Europe during the Second World War. Surely here there is matter for the most serious debate and disagreement. The illustration admittedly concerns an extreme case, but the point seems generally applicable.

Further, in one's effort to develop his own standards of judgment, it would seem possible for someone to acknowledge that another person, under given circumstances, had supplied an adequate justification for what he chose to do, but not necessarily share the other's judgment. Particularly in a society that takes pride in not merely tolerating, but acknowledging the worth of differing and competing values, there is always the possibility that legitimate interests and values may differ enough to lead to profoundly different judgments. It follows that though one may understand, and what is more, endorse another's judgment, he need not share or support it.

# Civil Disobedience

## Civil Disobedience

HENRY DAVID THOREAU

I heartily accept the motto, — "That government is best which governs least;" and I should like to see it acted up to more rapidly and systematically. Carried out, it finally amounts to this, which also I believe, — "That government is best which governs not at all;" and when men are prepared for it, that will be the kind of government which they will have. Government is at best but an expedient; but most governments are usually, and all governments are sometimes, inexpedient. The objections which have been brought against a standing army, and they are many and weighty, and deserve to prevail, may also at last be brought against a standing government. The standing army is only an arm of the standing government. The government itself, which is only the mode which the people have chosen to execute their will, is equally liable to be abused and perverted before the people can act through it. Witness the present Mexican war, the work of comparatively a few individuals using the standing government as their tool; for, in the outset, the people would not have consented to this measure.

This American government, — what is it but a tradition, though a recent one, endeavoring to transmit itself unimpaired to posterity, but each instant losing some of its integrity? It has not the vitality and force of a single living man; for a single man can bend it to his will. It is a sort of wooden gun to the people themselves. But it is not the less necessary for this; for the people must have some complicated machinery or other, and hear its din, to satisfy that idea of government which they have. Governments show thus how successfully men can be imposed on, even impose on themselves, for their own advantage.

It is excellent, we must all allow. Yet this government never of itself furthered any enterprise, but by the alacrity with which it got out of its way. *It* does not keep the country free. *It* does not settle the West. *It* does not educate. The character inherent in the American people has done all that has been accomplished; and it would have done somewhat more, if the government had not sometimes got in its way. For government is an expedient by which men would fain succeed in letting one another alone; and, as has been said, when it is most expedient, the governed are most let alone by it. Trade and commerce, if they were not made of India-rubber, would never manage to bounce over the obstacles which legislators are continually putting in their way; and, if one were to judge these men wholly by the effects of their actions and not partly by their intentions, they would deserve to be classed and punished with those mischievous persons who put obstructions on the railroads.

But, to speak practically and as a citizen, unlike those who call themselves no-government men, I ask for, not at once no government, but *at once* a better government. Let every man make known what kind of government would command his respect, and that will be one step toward obtaining it.

After all, the practical reason why, when the power is once in the hands of the people, a majority are permitted, and for a long period continue, to rule is not because they are most likely to be in the right, nor because this seems fairest to the minority, but because they are physically the strongest. But a government in which the majority rule in all cases cannot be based on justice, even as far as men understand it. Can there not be a government in which majorities do not virtually decide right and wrong, but conscience? — in which majorities decide only those questions to which the rule of expediency is applicable? Must the citizen ever for a moment, or in the least degree, resign his conscience to the legislator? Why has every man a conscience, then? I think that we should be men first, and subjects afterward. It is not desirable to cultivate a respect for the law, so much as for the right. The only obligation which I have a right to assume is to do at any time what I think right. It is truly enough said, that a corporation has no conscience; but a corporation of conscientious men is a corporation *with* a conscience. Law never made men a whit more just; and, by means of their respect for it, even the well-disposed are daily made the agents of injustice. A common and natural result of an undue respect for law is, that you may see a file of soldiers, colonel, captain, corporal, privates, powder-monkeys, and all, marching in admirable order over hill and dale to the wars, against their wills, ay, against their common sense and consciences, which makes it very steep marching indeed, and produces a palpitation to the heart. They have no doubt that it is a damnable business in which they are concerned; they are all peaceably inclined. Now, what are they? Men at all? or small movable forts and magazines, at the service of some unscrupulous man in power? Visit the Navy-Yard, and behold a marine, such a man as an American government can make, or such as it can make a man with its black arts, — a mere shadow and reminiscence of humanity, a man laid out alive and standing, and already, as one may say, buried under arms with funeral accompaniments, though it may be, —

> Not a drum was heard, not a funeral note,
>     As his corse to the rampart we hurried;
> Not a soldier discharged his farewell shot
>     O'er the grave where our hero we buried.

The mass of men serve the state thus, not as men mainly, but as machines, with their bodies. They are the standing army, and the militia, jailors, constables, posse comitatus, etc. In most cases there is no free exercise whatever of the judgment or of the moral sense; but they put themselves on a level with wood and earth and stones; and wooden men can perhaps be manufactured that will serve the purpose as well. Such command no more respect than men of straw or a lump of dirt. They have the same sort of worth only as horses and dogs. Yet such as these even are commonly esteemed good citizens. Others — as most legislators, politicians, lawyers, ministers, and office-holders — serve the state chiefly with their heads; and, as they rarely make any moral distinctions, they are as likely to serve the Devil, without *intending* it, as God. A very few, as heroes, patriots, martyrs, reformers in the great sense, and *men,* serve the state with their consciences also, and so necessarily resist it for the most part; and they are commonly treated as enemies by it. A wise man will only be useful as a man, and will not submit to be "clay," and "stop a hole to keep the wind away," but leave that office to his dust at least: —

> I am too high-born to be propertied,
> To be a secondary at control,

Or useful serving-man and instrument
To any sovereign state throughout the world.

He who gives himself entirely to his fellow-men appears to them useless and selfish; but he who gives himself partially to them is pronounced a benefactor and philanthropist.

How does it become a man to behave toward this American government to-day? I answer, that he cannot without disgrace be associated with it. I cannot for an instant recognize that political organization as *my* government which is the *slave's* government also.

All men recognize the right of revolution; that is, the right to refuse allegiance to, and to resist, the government, when its tyranny or its inefficiency are great and unendurable. But almost all say that such is not the case now. But such was the case, they think, in the Revolution of '75. If one were to tell me that this was a bad government because it taxed certain foreign commodities brought to its ports, it is most probable that I should not make an ado about it, for I can do without them. All machines have their friction; and possibly this does enough good to counterbalance the evil. At any rate, it is a great evil to make a stir about it. But when the friction comes to have its machine, and oppression and robbery are organized, I say, let us not have such a machine any longer. In other words, when a sixth of the population of a nation which has undertaken to be the refuge of liberty are slaves, and a whole country is unjustly overrun and conquered by a foreign army, and subjected to military law, I think that it is not too soon for honest men to rebel and revolutionize. What makes this duty the more urgent is the fact that the country so overrun is not our own, but ours is the invading army.

Paley, a common authority with many on moral questions, in his chapter on the "Duty of Submission to Civil Government," resolves all civil obligation into expediency; and he proceeds to say, "that so long as the interest of the whole society requires it, that is, so long as the established government cannot be resisted or changed without public inconveniency, it is the will of God that the established government be obeyed, and no longer. . . . This principle being admitted, the justice of every particular case of resistance is reduced to a computation of the quantity of the danger and grievance on the one side, and of the probability and expense of redressing it on the other." Of this, he says, every man shall judge for himself. But Paley appears never to have contemplated those cases to which the rule of expediency does not apply, in which a people, as well as an individual, must do justice, cost what it may. If I have unjustly wrested a plank from a drowning man, I must restore it to him though I drown myself. This, according to Paley, would be inconvenient. But he that would save his life, in such a case, shall lose it. This people must cease to hold slaves, and to make war on Mexico, though it cost them their existence as a people.

In their practice, nations agree with Paley; but does any one think that Massachusetts does exactly what is right at the present crisis?

> A drab of state, a cloth-o'-silver slut,
>> To have her train borne up, and her soul trail in the dirt.

Practically speaking, the opponents to a reform in Massachusetts are not a hundred thousand politicians at the South, but a hundred thousand merchants and farmers here, who are more interested in commerce and agriculture than they are in humanity, and are not prepared to do justice to the slave and to Mexico, *cost what it may*. I quarrel not with far-off foes, but with those who, near at home, coöperate with, and do the bidding of, those far away, and without whom the latter would be harmless. We are accustomed to say, that the mass of men are unprepared; but improvement is slow, because the few are not materially wiser or better than the many. It is not so important that many should be as good as you, as that there be some absolute goodness somewhere; for that will leaven the whole lump. There are thousands who are *in opinion* opposed to slavery and to the war, who yet in effect do nothing to put an end to them; who, esteeming themselves children of Washington and Franklin, sit down with their hands in their pockets, and say that they know not what to do, and do nothing; who even postpone the question of freedom to the question of free-trade, and quietly read the prices-current along with the latest advices from Mexico, after dinner, and, it may be, fall asleep over them both. What is the price-current of an honest man and patriot to-day? They hesitate, and they regret, and sometimes they petition; but they do nothing in earnest and with effect. They will wait, well disposed, for others to remedy the evil, that they may no longer have it to regret. At most, they give only a cheap vote, and a feeble countenance and God-speed, to the right, as it goes by them. There are nine hundred and ninety-nine patrons of virtue to one virtuous man. But it is easier to deal with the real possessor of a thing than with the temporary guardian of it.

All voting is a sort of gaming, like checkers or backgammon, with a slight moral tinge to it, a playing with right and wrong, with moral questions; and betting naturally accompanies it. The character of the voters is not staked. I cast my vote, perchance, as I think right; but I am not vitally concerned that that right should prevail. I am willing to leave it to the majority. Its obligation, therefore, never exceeds that of expediency. Even voting *for the right* is *doing* nothing for it. It is only expressing to men feebly your desire that it should prevail. A wise man will not leave the right to the mercy of chance, nor wish it to prevail through the power of the majority. There is but little virtue in the action of masses of men. When the majority shall at length vote for the abolition of slavery, it will be because they are indifferent to slavery, or because there is but little slavery left to be abolished by their vote. *They* will then be the only slaves. Only *his* vote can hasten the abolition of slavery who asserts his own freedom by his vote.

I hear of a convention to be held at Baltimore, or elsewhere, for the selection of a candidate for the Presidency, made up chiefly of editors, and men who are politicians by profession; but I think, what is it to any independent, intelligent, and respectable man what decision they may come to? Shall we not have the advantage of his wisdom and honesty, nevertheless? Can we not count upon some independent votes? Are there not many individuals in the country who do not attend conventions? But no: I find that the respectable man, so called, has immediately drifted from his position, and despairs of his country, when his country has more reason to despair of him. He forthwith adopts one of the candidates thus selected as the only *available* one, thus proving that he is himself *available* for any purposes of the demagogue. His vote is of no more worth than that of any unprincipled foreigner or hireling native, who may have been bought. O for a man who is a *man,* and, as my neighbor says, has a bone in his back which you cannot pass your hand through! Our statistics are at fault: the population has been returned too large. How many *men* are there to a square thousand miles in this country? Hardly one. Does not America offer any inducement for men to settle here? The American has dwindled into an Odd Fellow, — one who may be known by the development of his organ of gregariousness, and a manifest lack of intellect and cheerful self-reliance; whose first and chief concern, on coming into the world, is to see that the Almhouses are in good repair; and, before yet he has lawfully donned the virile garb, to collect a fund for the support of the widows and orphans that may be; who, in short, ventures to live only by the aid of the Mutual Insurance company, which has promised to bury him decently.

It is not a man's duty, as a matter of course, to devote himself to the eradication of any, even the most enormous wrong; he may still properly have other concerns to engage him; but it is his duty, at least, to wash his hands of it, and, if he gives it no thought longer, not to give it practically his support. If I devote myself to other pursuits and contemplations, I must first see, at least, that I do not pursue them sitting upon another man's shoulders. I must get off him first, that he may pursue his contemplations too. See what gross inconsistency is tolerated. I have heard some of my townsmen say, "I should like to have them order me out to help put down an insurrection of the slaves, or to march to Mexico; — see if I would go;" and yet these very men have each, directly by their allegiance, and so indirectly, at least, by their money, furnished a substitute. The soldier is applauded who refuses to serve in an unjust war by those who do not refuse to sustain the unjust government which makes the war; is applauded by those whose own act and authority he disregards and sets at naught; as if the state were penitent to that degree that it hired one to scourge it while it sinned, but not to that degree that it left off sinning for a moment. Thus, under the name of Order and Civil Government, we are all made at last to pay homage to and support our own meanness. After the first blush of sin comes its indifference; and from immoral it becomes, as it were, *un*moral, and not quite unnecessary to that life which we have made.

The broadest and most prevalent error requires the most disinterested virtue to sustain it. The slight reproach to which the virtue of patriotism is commonly liable, the noble are most likely to incur. Those who, while they disapprove of the character and measures of a government, yield to it their allegiance and support are undoubtedly its most conscientious supporters, and so frequently the most serious obstacles to reform. Some are petitioning the state to dissolve the Union, to disregard the requisitions of the President. Why do they not dissolve it themselves, — the union between themselves and the state, — and refuse to pay their quota into its treasury? Do not they stand in the same relation to the state that the state does to the Union? And have not the same reasons prevented the state from resisting the Union which have prevented them from resisting the state?

How can a man be satisfied to entertain an opinion merely, and enjoy *it?* Is there any enjoyment in it, if his opinion is that he is aggrieved? If you are cheated out of a single dollar by your neighbor, you do not rest satisfied with knowing that you are cheated, or with saying that you are cheated, or even with petitioning him to pay you your due; but you take effectual steps at once to obtain the full amount, and see that you are never cheated again. Action from principle, the perception and the performance of right, changes things and relations; it is essentially revolutionary, and does not consist wholly with anything which was. It not only divides states and churches, it divides families; ay, it divides the *individual* separating the diabolical in him from the divine.

Unjust laws exist: shall we be content to obey them, or shall we endeavor to amend them, and obey them until we have succeeded, or shall we transgress them at once? Men generally, under such a government as this, think that they ought to wait until they have persuaded the majority to alter them. They think that, if they should resist, the remedy would be worse than the evil. But it is the fault of the government itself that the remedy *is* worse than the evil. *It* makes it worse. Why is it not more apt to anticipate and provide for reform? Why does it not cherish its wise minority? Why does it cry and resist before it is hurt? Why does it not encourage its citizens to be on the alert to point out its faults, and *do* better than it would have them? Why does it always crucify Christ, and excommunicate Copernicus and Luther, and pronounce Washington and Franklin rebels?

One would think, that a deliberate and practical denial of its authority was the only offense never contemplated by government; else, why has it not assigned its definite, its suitable and proportionate penalty? If a man who has no property refuses but once to earn nine shillings for the state, he is put in prison for a period unlimited by any law that I know, and determined only by the discretion of those who placed him there; but if he should steal ninety times nine shillings from the state, he is soon permitted to go at large again.

If the injustice is part of the necessary friction of the machine of government, let it go, let it go: perchance it will wear smooth, — certainly the machine will wear out. If the injustice has a spring, or a pulley, or a rope, or a crank, exclusively for itself, then perhaps you may consider whether the remedy will not be worse than the evil; but if it is of such a nature that it requires you to be the agent of injustice to another, then, I say, break the law. Let your life be a counter friction to stop the machine. What I have to do is to see, at any rate, that I do not lend myself to the wrong which I condemn.

As for adopting the ways which the state has provided for remedying the evil, I know not of such ways. They take too much time, and a man's life will be gone. I have other affairs to attend to. I came into this world, not chiefly to make this a good place to live in, but to live in it, be it good or bad. A man has not everything to do, but something; and because he cannot do *everything,* it is not necessary that he should do *something* wrong. It is not my business to be petitioning the Governor or the Legislature any more than it is theirs to petition me; and if they should not hear my petition, what should I do then? But in this case the state has provided no way: its very Constitution is the evil. This may seem to be harsh and stubborn and unconciliatory; but it is to treat with the utmost kindness and consideration the only spirit that can appreciate or deserves it. So is all change for the better, like birth and death, which convulse the body.

I do not hesitate to say, that those who call themselves Abolitionists should at once effectually withdraw their support, both in person and property, from the government of Massachusetts and not wait till they constitute a majority of one, before they suffer the right to prevail through them. I think that it is enough if they have God on their side, without waiting for that other one. Morover, any man more right than his neighbors constitutes a majority of one already.

I meet this American government, or its representative, the state government, directly, and face to face, once a year — no more — in the person of its tax-gatherer; this is the only mode in which a man situated as I am necessarily meets it; and it then says distinctly, Recognize me; and the simplest, most effectual, and in the present posture of affairs, the indispensablest mode of treating with it on this head, of expressing your little satisfaction with and love for it, is to deny it then. My civil neighbor, the tax-gatherer, is the very man I have to deal with, — for it is, after all, with men and not with parchment that I quarrel, — and he has voluntarily chosen to be an agent of the government. How shall he ever know well what he is and does as an officer of the government, or as a man, until he is obliged to consider whether he shall treat me, his neighbor, for whom he has respect, as a neighbor and well-disposed man, or as a maniac and disturber of the peace, and see if he can get over this obstruction to his neighborliness without a ruder and more impetuous thought or speech corresponding with his action. I know this well, that if one thousand, if one hundred, if ten men whom I could name, — if ten *honest* men only, — ay, if *one* HONEST man, in this State of Massachusetts, *ceasing to hold slaves,* were actually to withdraw from his copartnership, and be locked up in the county jail therefor, it would be the abolition of slavery in America. For it matters not how small the beginning may seem to be: what is once well done is done forever. But we love better to talk about it: that we say is our mission. Reform keeps many scores of newspapers in its service, but not one man. If my esteemed neighbor, the State's ambassador, who will devote his days to the settlement of the question of human rights in the Council Chamber, instead of being threatened with the prisons of Carolina, were to sit down the prisoner of Massachusetts, the State which is so anxious to foist the sin of slavery upon her sister, — though at present she can discover only an act of inhospitality to be the ground of a quarrel with her, — the Legislature would not wholly waive the subject the following winter.

Under a government which imprisons any unjustly, the true place for a just man is also a prison. The proper place to-day, the only place which Massachusetts has provided for her freer and less desponding spirits, is in her prisons, to be put out and locked out of the State by her own act, as they have already put themselves out by their principles. It is there that the fugitive slave, and the Mexican prisoner on parole, and the Indian come to plead the wrongs of his race should find them; on that separate, but more free and honorable ground, where the State places those who are not *with* her, but *against* her, — the only house in a slave State in which a free man can abide with honor. If any think that their influence would be lost there, and their voices no longer afflict the ear of the State, that they would not be as an enemy within its walls, they do not know by how much truth is stronger than error, nor how much more eloquently and effectively he can combat injustice who has experienced a little in his own person. Cast your whole vote, not a strip of paper merely, but your whole influence. A minority is powerless while it conforms to the majority; it is not even a minority then; but it is irresistible when it clogs by its whole weight. If the alternative is to keep all just men in prison, or give up war and slavery, the State will not hesitate which to choose. If a thousand men were not to pay their tax-bills this year, that would not be a violent and bloody measure, as it would be to pay them, and enable the State to commit violence and shed innocent blood. This is, in fact, the definition of a peaceable revolution, if any such is possible. If the tax-gatherer, or any other public officer, asks me, as one has done, "But what shall I do?" my answer is, "If you really wish to do anything, resign your office." When the subject has refused allegiance, and the officer has resigned his office, then the revolution is accomplished. But even suppose blood should flow. Is there not a sort of blood shed when the conscience is wounded? Through this wound a man's real manhood and immortality flow out, and he bleeds to an everlasting death. I see this blood flowing now.

I have contemplated the imprisonment of the offender, rather than the seizure of his goods, — though both will serve the same purpose, — because they who assert the purest right, and consequently are most dangerous to a corrupt State, commonly have not spent much time in accumulating property. To such the State renders comparatively small service, and a slight tax is wont to appear exorbitant, particularly if they are obliged to earn it by special labor with their hands. If there were one who lived wholly without the use of money, the State itself would hesitate to demand it of him. But the rich man — not to make any invidious comparison — is always sold to the institution which makes him rich. Absolutely speaking, the more money, the less virtue; for money comes between a man and his objects, and obtains them for him; and it was certainly no great virtue to obtain it. It puts to rest many questions which he would otherwise be taxed to answer; while the only new question which it puts is the hard but superfluous one, how to spend it. Thus his moral ground is taken from under his feet. The opportunities of living are diminished in proportion as what are called the "means" are increased. The best thing a man can do for his culture when he is rich is to endeavor to carry out those schemes which he entertained when he was poor. Christ answered the Herodians according to their condition. "Show me the tribute-money," said he; — and one took a penny out of his pocket; — if you use money which has the image of Cæsar on it and which he has made current and valuable, that is, *if you are men of the State,* and gladly enjoy the advantages of Cæsar's government, then pay him back some of his own when he demands it. "Render therefore to Cæsar that which is Cæsar's, and to God those things which are God's," — leaving them no wiser than before as to which was which; for they did not wish to know.

When I converse with the freest of my neighbors, I perceive that, whatever they may say about the magnitude and seriousness of the question, and their regard for the public tranquillity, the long and the short of the matter is, that they cannot spare the protection of the existing government, and they dread the consequences to their property and families of disobedience to it. For my own part, I should not like to think that I ever rely on the protection of the State. But, if I deny the authority of the State when it presents its tax-bill, it will soon take and waste all my property, and so harass me and my children without end. This is hard. This makes it impossible for a man to live honestly, and at the same time comfortably, in outward respects. It will not be worth the while to accumulate property; that would be sure to go again. You must hire or squat somewhere, and raise but a small crop, and eat that soon. You must live within yourself, and depend upon yourself always tucked up and ready for a start, and not have many affairs. A man may grow rich in Turkey even, if he will be in all respects a good subject of the Turkish government. Confucius said: "If a state is governed by the principles of reason, poverty and misery are subjects of shame; if a state is not governed by the principles of reason, riches and honors are the subjects of shame." No: until I want the protection of Massachusetts to be extended to me in some distant Southern port, where my liberty is endangered, or until I am bent solely on building up an estate at home by peaceful enterprise, I can afford to refuse allegiance to Massachusetts, and her right to my property and life. It costs me less in every sense to incur the penalty of disobedience to the State than it would to obey. I should feel as if I were worth less in that case.

Some years ago, the State met me in behalf of the Church, and commanded me to pay a certain sum toward the support of a clergyman whose preaching my father attended, but never I myself. "Pay," it said, "or be locked up in the jail." I declined to pay, But, unfortunately, another man saw fit to pay it. I did not see why the schoolmaster should be taxed to support the priest, and not the priest the schoolmaster; for I was not the State's schoolmaster, but I supported myself by voluntary subscription. I did not see why the lyceum should not present its tax-bill, and have the State to back its demand, as well as the Church. However, at the request of the selectmen, I condescended to make some such statement as this in writing: — "Know all men by these presents, that I, Henry Thoreau, do not wish to be regarded as a member of any incorporated society which I have not joined." Thus I gave to the town clerk; and he has it. The State, having thus learned that I did not wish to be regarded as a member of that church, has never made a like demand on me since; though it said that it must adhere to its original presumption that time. If I had known how to name them, I should then have signed off in detail from all the societies which I never signed on to; but I did not know where to find a complete list.

I have paid no poll-tax for six years. I was put into a jail once on this account, for one night; and, as I stood considering the walls of solid stone, two or three feet thick, the door of wood and iron, a foot thick, and the iron grating which strained the light, I could not help being struck with the foolishness of that institution which treated me as if I were mere flesh and blood and bones, to be locked up. I wondered that it should have concluded at length that this was the best use it could put me to, and had never thought to avail itself of my services in some way. I saw that, if there was a wall of stone between me and my townsmen, there was a still more difficult one to climb or break through before they could get to be as free as I was. I did not for a moment feel confined, and the walls seemed a great waste of stone and mortar. I felt as if I alone of all my townsmen had paid my tax. They plainly did not know how to treat me, but behaved like persons who are underbred. In every threat and in every compliment there was a blunder; for they thought that my chief desire was to stand the other side of that stone wall. I could not but smile to see how industriously they locked the door on my meditations, which followed them out again without let or hindrance, and *they* were really all that was dangerous. As they could not reach me, they had resolved to punish my body; just as boys, if they cannot come at some person against whom they have a spite, will abuse his dog. I saw that the State was half-witted, that it was timid as a lone woman with her silver spoons, and that it did not know its friends from its foes, and I lost all my remaining respect for it, and pitied it.

Thus the State never intentionally confronts a man's sense, intellectual or moral, but only his body, his senses. It is not armed with superior wit or honesty, but with superior physical strength. I was not born to be forced. I will breathe after my own fashion. Let us see who is the strongest. What force has a multitude? They only can force me who obey a higher law than I. They force me to become like themselves. I do not hear of *men* being *forced* to live this way or that by masses of men. What sort of life were that to live? When I meet a government which says to me, "Your money or your life," why should I be in haste to give it my money? It may be in a great strait, and not know what to do: I cannot help that. It must help itself; do as I do. It is not worth the while to snivel about it. I am not responsible for the successful working of the machinery of society. I am not the son of the engineer. I perceive that, when an acorn and a chestnut fall side by side, the one does not remain inert to make way for the other, but both obey their own laws, and spring and grow and flourish as best they can, till one, perchance, overshadows and destroys the other. If a plant cannot live according to its nature, it dies; and so a man.

The night in prison was novel and interesting enough. The prisoners in their shirt-sleeves were enjoying a chat and the evening air in the doorway, when I entered. But the jailer said, "Come, boys, it is time to lock up;" and so they dispersed, and I heard the sound of their steps returning into the hollow apartments. My room-mate was introduced to me by the jailer as "a first-rate fellow and a clever man." When the door was locked, he showed me where to hang my hat, and how he managed matters there. The rooms were white-washed once a month; and this one, at least, was the whitest, most simply furnished, and probably the neatest apartment in the town. He naturally wanted to know where I came from, and what brought me there; and, when I told him, I asked him in my turn how he came there, presuming him to be an honest man, of course; and, as the world goes, I believe he was. "Why," said he, "they accuse me of burning a barn; but I never did it." As near as I could discover, he had probably gone to bed in a barn when drunk, and smoked his pipe there; and so a barn was burnt. He had the reputation of being a clever man, had been there some three months waiting for his trial to come on, and would have to wait as much longer; but he was quite domesticated and contented, since he got his board for nothing, and thought that he was well treated.

He occupied one window, and I the other; and I saw that if one stayed there long, his principal business would be to look out the window. I had soon read all the tracts that were left there, and examined where former prisoners had broken out, and where a grate had been sawed off, and heard the history of the various occupants of that room; for I found that even here there was a history and a gossip which never circulated beyond the walls of the jail. Probably this is the only house in the town where verses are composed, which are afterward printed in a circular form, but not published. I was shown quite a long list of verses which were composed by some young men who had been detected in an attempt to escape, who avenged themselves by singing them.

I pumped my fellow-prisoner as dry as I could, for fear I should never see him again; but at length he showed me which was my bed, and left me to blow out the lamp.

It was like traveling into a far country, such as I had never expected to behold, to lie there for one night. It seemed to me that I never had heard the town-clock strike before, nor the evening sounds of the village; for we slept with the windows open, which were inside the grating. It was to see my native village in the light of the Middle Ages, and our Concord was turned into a Rhine stream, and visions of knights and castles passed before me. They were the voices of old burghers that I heard in the streets. I was an involuntary spectator and auditor of whatever was done and said in the kitchen of the adjacent village-inn, — a wholly new and rare experience to me. It was a closer view of my native town. I was fairly inside of it. I never had seen its institutions before. This is one of its peculiar institutions; for it is a shire town. I began to comprehend what its inhabitants were about.

In the morning, our breakfasts were put through the hole in the door, in small oblong-square tin pans, made to fit, and holding a pint of chocolate, with brown bread, and an iron spoon. When they called for the vessels again, I was green enough to return what bread I had left; but my comrade seized it, and said that I should lay that up for lunch or dinner. Soon after he was let out to work at haying in a neighboring field, whither he went every day, and would not be back till noon; so he bade me good-day, saying that he doubted if he should see me again.

When I came out of prison, — for some one interfered, and paid that tax, — I did not perceive that great changes had taken place on the common, such as he observed who went in a youth and emerged a tottering and gray-headed man; and yet a change had to my eyes come over the scene, — the town, and State, and country, — greater than any that mere time could effect. I saw yet more distinctly the State in which I lived. I saw to what extent the people among whom I lived could be trusted as good neighbors and friends; that their friendship was for summer weather only; that they did not greatly propose to do right; that they were a distinct race from me by their prejudices and superstitions, as the Chinamen and Malays are; that in their sacrifices to humanity they ran no risks, not even to their property; that after all they were not so noble but they treated the thief as he had treated them, and hoped, by a certain outward observance and a few prayers, and by walking in a particular straight though useless path from time to time, to save their souls. This may be to judge my neighbors harshly; for I believe that many of them are not aware that they have such an institution as the jail in their village.

It was formerly the custom in our village, when a poor debtor came out of jail, for his acquaintances to salute him, looking through their fingers, which were crossed to represent the grating of a jail window, "How do ye do?" My neighbors did not thus salute me, but first looked at me, and then at one another, as if I had returned from a long journey. I was put into jail as I was going to the shoemaker's to get a shoe which was mended. When I was let out the next morning, I proceeded to finish my errand, and, having put on my mended shoe, joined a huckleberry party, who were impatient to put themselves under my conduct; and in half an hour, — for the horse was soon tackled, — was in the midst of a huckleberry field, on one of our highest hills, two miles off, and then the State was nowhere to be seen. This is the whole history of "My Prisons."

I have never declined paying the highway tax, because I am as desirous of being a good neighbor as I am of being a bad subject; and as for supporting schools, I am doing my part to educate my fellow-countrymen now. It is for no particular item in the tax-bill that I refuse to pay it. I simply wish to refuse allegiance to the State, to withdraw and stand aloof from it effectually. I do not care to trace the course of my dollar, if I could, till it buys a man or a musket to shoot with, — the dollar is innocent, — but I am concerned to trace the effects of my allegiance. In fact, I quietly declare war with the State, after my fashion, though I will still make what use and get what advantage of her I can, as is usual in such cases.

If others pay the tax which is demanded of me, from a sympathy with the State, they do but what they have already done in their own case, or rather they abet injustice to a greater extent than the State requires. If they pay the tax from a mistaken interest in the individual taxed, to save his property, or prevent his going to jail, it is because they have not considered wisely how far they let their private feelings interfere with the public good.

This, then, is my position at present. But one cannot be too much on his guard in such a case, lest his action be biased by obstinacy or an undue regard for the opinions of men. Let him see that he does only what belongs to himself and to the hour.

I think sometimes, Why, this people mean well, they are only ignorant; they would do better if they knew how: why give your neighbors this pain to treat you as they are not inclined to? But I think again, This is no reason why I should do as they do, or permit others to suffer much greater pain of a different kind. Again, I sometimes say to myself, When many millions of men, without heat, without ill will, without personal feeling of any kind, demand of you a few shillings only, without the possibility, such is their constitution, of retracting or altering their present demand, and without the possibility, on your side, of appeal to any other millions, why expose yourself to this overwhelming brute force? You do not resist cold and hunger, the winds and the waves, thus obstinately; you quietly submit to a thousand similar necessities. You do not put your head into the fire. But just in proportion as I regard this as not wholly a brute force, but partly a human force, and consider that I have relations to those millions as to so many millions of men, and not of mere brute or inanimate things, I see that appeal is possible, first and instantaneously, from them to the Maker of them, and, secondly, from them to themselves. But if I put my head deliberately into the fire, there is no appeal to fire or to the Maker of fire, and I have only myself to blame. If I could convince myself that I have any right to be satisfied with men as they are, and to treat them accordingly, and not according, in some respects, to my requisitions and expectations of what they and I ought to be, then, like a good Mussulman and fatalist, I should endeavor to be satisfied with things as they are, and say it is the will of God. And, above all, there is this difference between resisting this and a purely brute or natural force, that I can resist this with some effect; but I cannot expect, like Orpheus, to change the nature of the rocks and trees and beasts.

I do not wish to quarrel with any man or nation. I do not wish to split hairs, to make fine distinctions, or set myself up as better than my neighbors. I seek rather, I may say, even an excuse for conforming to the laws of the land. I am but too ready to conform to them. Indeed, I have reason to suspect myself on this head; and each year, as the tax-gatherer comes round, I find myself disposed to review the acts and position of the general and State governments, and the spirit of the people, to discover a pretext for conformity.

> We must affect our country as our parents,
> And if at any time we alienate
> Our love or industry from doing it honor,
> We must respect effects and teach the soul
> Matter of conscience and religion,
> And not desire of rule or benefit.

I believe that the State will soon be able to take all my work of this sort out of my hands, and then I shall be no better a patriot than my fellow-countrymen. Seen from a lower point of view, the Constitution, with all its faults, is very good; the law and the courts are very respectable; even this State and this American government are, in many respects, very admirable, and rare things, to be thankful for, such as a great many have described them; but seen from a point of view a little higher, they are what I have described them; seen from a higher still, and the highest, who shall say what they are, or that they are worth looking at or thinking of at all?

However, the government does not concern me much, and I shall bestow the fewest possible thoughts on it. It is not many moments that I live under a government, even in this world. If a man is thought-free, fancy-free, imagination-free, that which *is not* never for a long time appearing *to be* to him, unwise rulers or reformers cannot fatally interrupt him.

I know that most men think differently from myself; but those whose lives are by profession devoted to the study of these or kindred subjects content me as little as any. Statesmen and legislators, standing so completely within the institution, never distinctly and nakedly behold it. They speak of moving society, but have no resting-place without it. They may be men of a certain experience and discrimination, and have no doubt invented ingenious and even useful systems, for which we sincerely thank them; but all their wit and usefulness lie within certain not very wide limits. They are wont to forget that the world is not governed by policy and expediency. Webster never goes behind government, and so cannot speak with authority about it. His words are wisdom to those legislators who contemplate no essential reform in the existing government; but for thinkers, and those who legislate for all time, he never once glances at the subject. I know of those whose serene and wise speculations on this theme would soon reveal the limits of his mind's range and hospitality. Yet, compared with the cheap professions of most reformers, and the still cheaper wisdom and eloquence of politicians in general, his are almost the only sensible and valuable words, and we thank Heaven for him Comparatively, he is always strong, original, and, above all, practical. Still, his quality is not wisdom, but prudence. The lawyer's truth is not Truth, but consistency or a consistent expediency. Truth is always in harmony with herself, and is not concerned chiefly to reveal the justice that may consist with wrong-doing. He well deserves to be called, as he has been called, the Defender of the Constitution. There are really no blows to be given by him but defensive ones. He is not a leader, but a follower. His leaders are the men of '87. "I have never made an effort," he says, "and never propose to make an effort; I have never countenanced an effort, and never mean to countenance an effort, to disturb the arrangement as originally made, by which the various States came into the Union." Still thinking of the sanction which the Constitution gives to slavery, he says, "Because it was a part of the original compact, — let it stand." Notwithstanding his special acuteness and ability, *he* is unable to take a fact out of its merely political relations, and behold it as it lies absolutely to be disposed of by the intellect, — what, for instance, it behooves a man to do here in America to-day with regard to slavery, — but ventures, or is driven, to make some such desperate answer as the following, while professing to speak absolutely, and as a private man, — from which what new and singular code of social duties might be inferred? "The manner," say he, "in which the governments of those States where slavery exists are to regulate it is for their own consideration, under their responsibility to their constituents, to the general laws of pro-

priety, humanity, and justice, and to God. Associations formed elsewhere, springing from a feeling of humanity, or other cause, have
nothing whatever to do with it. They have never received any encouragement from me, and they never will." [1]

They who know of no purer sources of truth, who have traced
up its stream no higher, stand, and wisely stand, by the Bible and
the Constitution, and drink at it there with reverence and humility;
but they who behold where it comes trickling into this lake or that
pool, gird up their loins once more, and continue their pilgrimage
toward its fountainhead.

No man with a genius for legislation has appeared in America.
They are rare in the history of the world. There are orators, politicians,
and eloquent men, by the thousand; but the speaker has not yet
opened his mouth to speak who is capable of settling the much-vexed
questions of the day. We love eloquence for its own sake, and not for
any truth which it may utter, or any heroism it may inspire. Our
legislators have not yet learned the comparative value of free-trade
and of freedom, of union, and of rectitude, to a nation. They have no
genius or talent for comparatively humble questions of taxation and
finance, commerce and manufactures and agriculture. If we were left
solely to the wordy wit of legislators in Congress for our guidance,
uncorrected by the seasonable experience and the effectual complaints
of the people, America would not long retain her rank among the
nations. For eighteen hundred years, though perchance I have no
right to say it, the New Testament has been written; yet where is the
legislator who has wisdom and practical talent enough to avail himself
of the light which it sheds on the science of legislation?

The authority of government, even such as I am willing to submit
to, — for I will cheerfully obey those who know and can do better
than I, and in many things even those who neither know nor can do
so well, — is still an impure one: to be strictly just, it must have the
sanction and consent of the governed. It can have no pure right over
my person and property but what I concede to it. The progress from
an absolute to a limited monarchy, from a limited monarchy to a
democracy, is a progress toward a true respect for the individual.
Even the Chinese philosopher was wise enough to regard the individual as the basis of the empire. Is a democracy, such as we know it,

---

[1] These extracts have been inserted since the lecture was read.

the last improvement possible in government? Is it not possible to take a step further towards recognizing and organizing the rights of man? There will never be a really free and enlightened State until the State comes to recognize the individual as a higher and independent power, from which all its own power and authority are derived, and treats him accordingly. I please myself with imagining a State at last which can afford to be just to all men, and to treat the individual with respect as a neighbor; which even would not think it inconsistent with its own repose if a few were to live aloof from it, not meddling with it, nor embraced by it, who fulfilled all the duties of neighbors and fellow-men. A State which bore this kind of fruit, and suffered it to drop off as fast as it ripened, would prepare the way for a still more perfect and glorious State, which also I have imagined, but not yet anywhere seen.

# On Civil Disobedience

## HUGO BEDAU

I wish to record my appreciation to Dr. John H. Brown for several conversations which stimulated my thinking in the early stages of preparing this paper and also to the Committee of Non-violent Action for the literature it brought to my attention. Responsibility for the opinions expressed, of course, rests entirely with me.

This paper is to be presented in a symposium on "Political Obligation and Civil Disobedience" at the fifty-eighth annual meeting of the American Philosophical Association, Eastern Division, December 27, 1961.

Since I have been unable to find a suitably detailed analysis of what civil disobedience is and of its role in turning dissent into resistance, I have decided to try to provide such an analysis myself. This has left me with some space, but not much, to examine the problem of justifying this form of resistance to government.

From the *Journal of Philosophy* (October, 1961). Reprinted by permission.

I

1. A dissenter performs an act of civil disobedience only if he acts *illegally;* i.e., if he violates some positive law, because of (one of) the laws, policies, or decisions of his government which he finds objectionable. Acts of protest directed at government, no matter how conscientious or effective, in which no law is violated (as is usually the case with a poster parade, voluntary boycott, or refusal to accept government employment), are not acts of civil disobedience.[1] Civil disobedience, after all, is not just done; it is committed. It is always the sort of thing that can send one to jail.

As with any disobedience, it seems possible to distinguish between positive acts, which are the doing of something proscribed by law (e.g., trespassing on government property), and negative acts, which are the refusal to do something prescribed by law (e.g., not taking cover when directed to do so during an air raid drill). It has been suggested [2] that acts of the latter sort are almost always likely to be justified, perhaps on the ground that the consequences of abstaining from obedience can seldom be so disruptive as those of committing active disobedience. I am not convinced of this. For instance, widespread refusal of draft calls for military service would have a far greater effect on any "defense" establishment than would widespread trespassing on military bases. Nor do I see how doing something illegal by not going out of one's way to do something in particular is any more likely to be justified than doing something illegal by going out of one's way to do something in particular.

It is also possible to distinguish between those acts of dissent which, though illegal according to the authorities at hand, are believed by the dissenter to be within his legal rights as defined by the "fundamental law" or constitution as interpreted by the highest courts of the

[1] It has been suggested that work stoppages in arms factories are an ideal form of civil disobedience. But unless quitting a "defense" job is illegal, this is impossible. See Alan Lovell, "Direct Action," *New Left Review,* no. 8 (March–April, 1961): 20. As for the special problems of conscientious disobedience of military orders, which I have totally ignored, see Guenter Lewy, "Superior Orders; Nuclear Warfare, and the Dictates of Conscience," *American Political Science Review,* 55 (March, 1961): 3–23.

[2] A. C. Ewing, *The Individual, the State and World Government* (New York, 1947), p. 69. The terms "negative" and "positive" as used in the text are borrowed from Ewing.

land (e.g., prior to the recent Supreme Court decisions in the Wilkinson and Braden cases, the refusal to testify about one's political beliefs and associations when questioned by a Congressional committee, on the ground that the First Amendment protects silence on such matters), and those acts which are committed without any belief in their judicial vindication (e.g., helping an escaped slave to keep his freedom in a slave state in the period immediately following the Supreme Court's decision in the Dred Scott case). This distinction is of some interest because, in the former class of cases, the dissenter quite possibly does not think of himself as committing an act of civil disobedience at all. But it seems irrelevant that his dispute with the government takes the form of a dispute over the legitimacy of a certain policy or of the authority of a certain government agency. So long as the authority at hand may, as it must, be permitted to define at least provisionally what is legal or within the scope of its authority, defying it can qualify as civil disobedience. The government may, as a rule, decide to treat this class of cases more leniently than those where there cannot be any reasonable hope of judicial vindication, but that is another matter.

Since all civil disobedience involves illegal activity, it has usually been supposed [3] that such acts could not receive legal protection; i.e., that there could be a legal right of civil disobedience (or of any form of resistance to government). What has not been noticed is that, by extending a practice already in use, civil disobedience could be lawfully eliminated. The law has long managed to obviate much civil disobedience by clauses providing exemption for conscientious objectors. There is no logical reason why every law could not have a rider to the effect that anyone who violates it on conscientious grounds shall be exempt from prosecution and penalty. The way in which such a provision would tend to weaken habitual obedience of the law and thus create problems for the police and the courts is obvious. But the fact that no government is likely even to consider such a provision,

---

[3] See Ewing, *op. cit.*, p. 73, and David Spitz, "Democracy and the Problem of Civil Disobedience," *American Political Science Review,* 48 (June, 1954): 342. See also Franz Neumann, "On the Limits of Justifiable Disobedience," reprinted in his *The Democratic and the Authoritarian State* (Glencoe, 1958), p. 154; he refers to Article 947 of the Constitution of Hesse (1946), which provides for "the right and the duty" of "resistance to unconstitutionally exercised public authority."

human nature being what it is, does not show any purely logical defect in extending this sort of legal protection to civil disobedience.

2. There would clearly be something odd about a policeman's reporting that he had surprised several persons in the act of committing civil disobedience or about employing detectives to root out conspiracies to commit civil disobedience. For this would suggest, contrary to fact, that these illegal acts were an embarrassment to the dissenter and that he might wish them to be kept secret from the public and especially from the government. Usually, though not always, it is essential to the purpose of the dissenter that both the public and the government should know what he intends to do. At least, it is essential that the government know of his act if it is intended that the government shall change its policy because of the act. This is one reason why the authorities are customarily notified in advance by those intending to commit civil disobedience. More fundamental still is the fact that the dissenter views what he does as a civic act, an act that properly belongs to the public life of the community. This derives from the fact that he thinks of himself as acting to thwart some law, policy, etc., that deviates from the true purpose of government as he sees it. Thus, his act draws attention to something he thinks the whole community should be brought to consider, since the community has as much interest in the act as he does. For these reasons, civil disobedience is necessarily *public*.

3. Not every illegal act of public resistance to government, however, is an act of civil disobedience. Anytime the dissenter resists government by deliberately destroying property, endangering life and limb, inciting to riot (e.g., sabotage, assassination, street fighting), he has not committed *civil* disobedience. The pun on "civil" is essential; only *nonviolent* acts thus can qualify.[4] By "nonviolent act" one means, I take it, that the agent does not try to accomplish his aim either by initiating or by threatening violence, that he does not respond with violence or violent resistance during the course of his

---

[4] Bentham is typical of the classic philosophers from Bacon to Mill, all of whom tend to ignore civil disobedience. His sole conception of "open disobedience" to government is of "forcible" resistance, as though "open" meant something other than "public." See his *Fragment of Government* (1776), F. C. Montague, ed. (Oxford, 1931), pp. 147 f. Not even Thoreau, who seems to have coined the phrase "civil disobedience," stressed its nonviolent character. The matter has become obvious only since the writings of Gandhi. See his *Non-violent Resistance* (New York, [1951] 1961), pp. 3–4.

disobedience, regardless of the provocation he may have, and thus that he is prepared to suffer without defense the indignities and brutalities that often greet his act. Even if the reaction to his act is a violent one, whether by the police or by a hostile public, I do not think this negates the civility of his act; it is not a logical consequence of anyone's attempt to act nonviolently that anyone else should respond with violence.

4. The typical act of civil disobedience is not only directed against the government because of some objectionable law, policy, or decision and not only undertaken in order to frustrate that law, etc., but also so designed that the act itself does frustrate that law, etc. If this were the rule, no act could qualify for the title of civil disobedience unless it was the sort of act that, if it were committed by everyone (or even by a large minority), would hamper and perhaps prevent the government from enforcing the law, etc., at issue.

Here we meet an important distinction. Some acts of civil disobedience intend to achieve this aim by directly violating the objectionable law (e.g., refusing to register for the military draft), whereas other acts, like Thoreau's, intend to achieve this aim by violating some other law and are thus aimed at the objectionable law only indirectly (e.g., withholding from payment that portion of one's income taxes used to support the "defense" establishment). Since there are severe limitations to the circumstances in which certain laws are open to direct resistance by anyone except those who administer them (e.g., no ordinary citizen is in a position to resist directly his government's decision to launch a nuclear missile strike or to execute a condemned prisoner), it is only by acts of indirect resistance that it is possible for everyone to commit civil disobedience because of any of his government's laws. On the other hand, an act often allows of no more than a remote connection to the objectionable law, with the result that it appears ineffective and absurd. Hence, the preference among dissenters of cool head and stout heart for direct resistance.

What I have called "direct resistance" must not be confused with what is popularly called "direct action." Direct action is a special form of direct resistance, in which the dissenter uses his own body as the lever with which to pry loose the government's policy. Nonviolent direct action takes either of two forms: "nonviolent obstruction" and "nonviolent interjection." [5] Since the former involves a kind of physi-

---

[5] This distinction and terminology I have taken from Bradford Lyttle, *Essays on Nonviolent Action* (Chicago [1959]), pp. 30 f.

cal coercion, albeit passive (e.g., climbing onto construction equip-
ment and sitting there), it raises problems for those who scruple at
the least suggestion of physical force in the act of disobedience. Thus,
it is nonviolent interjection that is generally recognized to constitute
the paradigm of every aspect of civil disobedience. Perhaps the most
striking example in recent years was the voyage of The Golden Rule
in the spring of 1958 into the Central Pacific, to try to force the United
States government to abandon its nuclear-weapons testing program or
to deliberately expose several of its citizens to a probably fatal dosage
of radioactive fallout, since the crew intended to sail the ship directly
into the testing area.[6] The fashion in which such an act without involving any conceivable physical coercion on the government, might force
it to change (or at least to reappraise) its policy, is quite plain.

There is a difficulty, however, in treating such cases as definitive,
because not all illegal nonviolent public resistance to government
constitutes even token frustration of the objectionable law that occasions the resistance. There is a whole class of acts, undertaken in the
name of civil disobedience, which, even if they were widely practiced,
would in themselves constitute hardly more than a nuisance (e.g.,
trespassing at a nuclear-missile installation). These acts may well
serve as public witness to the integrity of the dissenter's convictions
and may well lead to the commission of other acts that will frustrate
the objectionable law. But overrunning a missile site with trespassers
who only trespass and refuse to cooperate in their own arrest cannot
really interfere with the construction of a single launching pad or
with the launching of a single missile. Therefore, such acts are often
just a harrassment and, at least to the bystander, somewhat inane. I
am inclined, therefore, to treat this class of cases almost as border-
line, even though it is one of the most popular kinds of civil disobedience at the present time in Great Britain and the United States.
Bertrand Russell has recently suggested,[7] apparently with this class
of cases in mind, that civil disobedience that aims at altering the
government's policy should be viewed essentially as "propaganda"
directed at an acquiescent and uninformed public. Now it may be that
the dissenter can derive incomparable propaganda advantage from
acts which are not themselves even a feeble frustration of the law,
policy, etc., that occasions them and which, even if widely practiced,

---

[6] See Albert Bigelow, *The Voyage of The Golden Rule* (New York, 1959).
[7] See his "Civil Disobedience," *New Statesman,* 61 (Feb. 17, 1961): 245 f.

would not in themselves bring a reversal of the government's position. But, once again, the remoteness of the connection between the disobedient act and the objectionable law lays such acts open to the charge of ineffectiveness and absurdity. Since, however, it is an empirical and not a logical question how effective such acts might be, they certainly can qualify as acts of civil disobedience.

Even among those acts of the former class which, in virtue of their structure, aim at frustrating the government's enforcement of the objectionable law, not all are undertaken in the hope of replacing that law with a better one or merely in this hope alone. The dissenter may act in such a way that he can thwart the application of the objectionable law only to himself (e.g., refusal to register for the military draft). At the other extreme, nonviolent resistance could even be undertaken with the intention of collapsing an entire government, as it has been claimed[8] the Hungarians under Francis Deak did a century ago against Austria. This latter class of cases is also somewhat border-line. Acting with intent to collapse the government obviously involves disloyalty, possibly sedition, and an unwillingness on the dissenter's part to acknowledge allegiance to that government and thus to accept the legal consequences of his act, including trial and imprisonment. Normally, committing civil disobedience does not involve acting with disloyal, seditious, traitorous, or rebellious intent, nor with intent to resist, even nonviolently, the legal consequences of the act.[9] I see no logical reason, however, why civil disobedience could not aim at what Thoreau called "peaceable revolution." [10]

It is also worth noticing at this point that the civil disobedient need not be an anarchist. Contrary to some opinions, the decision to resist nonviolently a certain law does not logically presuppose or entail the belief that all laws (or all this government's laws) ought to be resisted, or that governments and police forces are unnecessary, or that it is a sufficient condition for justifiably resisting the government on any occasion that it sanctions a manifestly unjust law. It may be that civil disobedience tends to encourage anarchism, as the

[8] Richard Gregg, *The Power of Nonviolence* (New York, 1944), pp. 19 f.

[9] Some of the views Irving Kristol and Robert Penn Warren express in "On Civil Disobedience and the Algerian War," *Yale Review,* 50 (Spring, 1961): 470 and 477, respectively, are quite remarkable in implying the contrary.

[10] "Civil Disobedience" (1849), *The Portable Thoreau,* Carl Bode, ed. (New York, 1947), p. 123.

classic Utilitarians believed, because respect for law may be weakened in the public at large (not to mention among the dissenters) even by an isolated act of resistance. Since it is true that habitual respect for the law is needed to allow the enforcement of manifestly just and beneficial laws, the conscientious dissenter will hesitate to undertake any act that would undermine this habit. But if worry about cultivating this habit figures prominently in government chancelleries, why is it that we continue to have incidents where even "democratic" governments complacently murder, kidnap, incite to rebel, lie, and break their solemn promises?

5. Civil disobedience is, finally, a *conscientious* act. That is, the dissenter proposes to justify his disobedience by an appeal to the incompatibility between his political circumstances and his moral convictions. Usually, this requires that he be convinced that it would be worse for everyone to suffer the consequences of the objectionable law than it would be for everyone to suffer the consequences of his (and, conceivably, of everyone else's) civil disobedience. This requirement is reminiscent of Utilitarianism and one of its later variants[11] in that what is involved is a weighing of consequences against one another. But it is different in that such weighing is regarded here not as providing the criterion of justifiable civil disobedience but only as a condition of its conscientiousness. For not every conscientious act is justified, i.e., the right thing for the agent to do. Conscientiousness also usually requires that the dissenter acknowledge that the law, no matter what it is, makes some claim on his obedience, no matter how readily this claim may be overridden by other claims. Only an anarchist could think that his resistance was conscientious when he knew that he had taken nothing into account to justify himself except the fact that by this law the government sanctioned manifest injustice.[12] Why anyone should think a law is objectionable enough to deserve his resistance and why he should think his resistance ought to be non-violent are quite independent considerations; there are any number of reasons why he might come to such conclusions. So the conscientious-

[11] See Bentham, *op. cit.*, pp. 211, 215, 220, 227, and Ernest Barker, *Principles of Social and Political Theory* (Oxford, 1951), p. 224.

[12] Thus, when it is said that a bill of attainder provides its victim with a sufficient condition for having "the right to resist," I suppose one would want to introduce some further considerations to determine when and how the agent ought to exercise this right. See Neumann, *op. cit.*, p. 158.

ness of the decision seems to lie in the way it is reached rather than in the nature of the convictions used to reach it.

It is not even necessary that the law because of which the dis-obedience is committed effect substantial injustice, violate basic rights, suffocate liberty, or otherwise work to the public disadvantage, though some such claim is almost invariably put forward. Though it may be highly improbable, there is no logical reason why a United States citizen could not commit acts of civil disobedience because of racial desegregation in the public schools, the Fifth Amendment or foreign economic aid. A government, after all, can be subjected to conscien-tious resistance on account of *any* of its laws, policies, or decisions; and if anyone can have the right to resist conscientiously whatever he chooses, everyone else can have an equal right. I am even doubtful whether a civil disobedient must justify his resistance by appeal to the belief that the government sanctions manifest injustice, etc. I do not see any contradiction in his having no interest in that issue and still believing that his act is justified. It is true that disobedience that is mainly and patently self-serving raises doubts about its conscientious-ness. But it is not a *logical* truth that people are easily self-deceived about their own motives, especially for those of their acts which bene-fit themselves. About the only moral convictions, therefore, we can assume in advance that a civil disobedient must have are that it is better to suffer violence than to inflict it and that law and order are not lightly to be disturbed. But since even these convictions need obtain only *ceteris paribus* (one need not, after all, be a Gandhian *Satyagrahi*), this is not saying much. Any number of circumstances might arise to override them, and there are any number of other con-victions one might have with which they could conflict. I can con-clude only and somewhat lamely that probably no one holds moral convictions that would rule out civil disobedience for him in every conceivable situation.

6. Are there specifiable political circumstances in which civil disobedience rather than another form of resistance or rather than no resistance at all is so unexceptionably justified that these circum-stances constitute, as it were, part of the necessary context of any such act? I am not sure. Whenever legal devices for redress of griev-ances or for orderly change of laws and government personnel do not exist at all (e.g., the predicament of the dissenter in a totalitarian state) or when these devices have been exhausted for the foreseeable

future (e.g., the predicament of the segregationist since the Supreme Court decision in Brown vs. Board of Education) or when it would take so much time to pursue these remedies that the objectionable law would meanwhile take its effect (e.g., the predicament of the crew of The Golden Rule), some sort of direct resistance to government is likely to be contemplated by the aggrieved parties. One is almost bound to insist that whenever such legal devices still obtain and civil disobedience or any other form of resistance is nevertheless committed, either the dissenter is acting irresponsibly, or his politics are anarchical, or both.[13] But even if these legal devices do not obtain, that fact alone does not ordinarily suffice to justify resistance[14] nor to determine whether it should be direct or indirect, violent or nonviolent.

7. In the light of the foregoing examination, I suggest the following definition: Anyone commits an act of civil disobedience if and only if he acts illegally, publicly, nonviolently, and conscientiously with the intent to frustrate (one of) the laws, policies, or decisions of his government.

## II

8. The radical possibility arises that whenever one is confronted by a law, one ought to disobey it — partly, as H. A. Prichard once suggested, because "after all the mere receipt of an order backed up by a threat seems, if anything, to give rise to the duty of resisting rather than of obeying" [15] but mainly just because "the certification of something as legally valid is not conclusive of the question of obedience." [16] That is, for a man to know that he ought to obey a certain law, policy, or decision of his government it is not sufficient if all he knows (or believes) is that the law, etc., is legally valid. This must be so, since "I ought to do $x$" cannot be deduced from "There is a valid law that applies to me and prescribes the doing of $x$." So anyone's

---

[13] Thus, I tend to agree with those who think that the absence of these legal devices is a necessary condition of any form of justifiable resistance. See Guenter Lewy, "Resistance to Tyranny," *Western Political Quarterly,* 13 (September, 1960): 585, 591 f.

[14] Probably it does, if the government in question professes "democratic" principles and if the civil disobedience is undertaken on behalf of policies implied by those principles. See Spitz, *op. cit.,* pp. 396 f.

[15] *Moral Obligation* (Oxford, 1949), p. 54.

[16] H. L. A. Hart, *The Concept of Law* (Oxford, 1961), p. 206.

obligation to obey any law is pretty clearly contingent on what the law happens to be. Seen from this point of view, the concern of classic philosophers, such as Locke, to establish a "right" of resistance of government is unnecessary (and, when one recalls how they invariably hedged this right with obstacles before anyone could be in circumstances to justify his exercise of that right, somewhat ironical as well). For if we take the view that legal obligation is radically contingent, there is no problem at all in answering the question, "How can anyone ever have a right to disobey the law?" The answer is simply, "Because no one ever ought to do something just because it is the law." Surely, it is because it is so often easy to see and to approve of what a law is designed to accomplish and to agree that it does, more or less, succeed, that one tends to overlook the heavy burden morality places on a law before it yields any authority to the law to guide one's conduct.

9. The problem of justifying one's decision to resist government arises because it is not sufficient to plead either any special defect of the objectionable law or the conscientiousness of one's decision. It may seem that one could not have a better reason for refusing to do what one's government orders than that one conscientiously believes it to be wrong. At least, it has been argued,[17] one cannot do any better than this and so is blameless. But we hesitate to allow that a man can know that he ought not to accept a certain policy of his government if all he knows is that he has conscientious scruples against it. It is logically possible that his moral convictions are most unfortunate, so that we would like nothing better than for anyone with his principles to fail in what he thinks he ought to do. His predicament (which is ours, too, of course) is that he cannot support his convictions and his estimate of his circumstances by appeal to some more objective and thus more authoritative appraisal, without also surrendering the opportunity to direct his own conduct. But it does not follow from the fact that a man cannot do more than what he conscientiously thinks he ought to do that he ought to do whatever he thinks he ought to do. The force of saying, "I ought to disobey this law" cannot be derived from "Obeying this law is inconsistent with my moral convictions." To enable the deduction obviously requires begging the question. The most we can say is that

---

[17] Richard Brandt, *Ethical Theory* (Englewood Cliffs, N.J., 1959), p. 291.

one has a right to conscientious disobedience; we need not and we cannot always go on to say that conscientious disobedience is the right thing to do. But being able to say the latter, and not just the former, is surely the main aim of trying to justify an act of disobedience.

Thus, it is possible that a government is sometimes right in having its way against the will of those who conscientiously disobey. So one cannot say, as some have,[18] that a government ought never to force a man to obey a law against his conscience. Perhaps one comes to the contrary view from supposing that no one's conscience could really advise him to disobey except in the name of justice, basic rights, freedom, or the general welfare and that all that could be at issue is the relatively unimportant question of whether he or the government is right about the availability of those benefits under the law in question, since no government worthy of the name would aim at anything other than these ends, and that, in those cases where he is mistaken, the harm involved in forcing his compliance is always greater than the harm of letting him disobey and take the legal consequences. This is a set of amiable but nevertheless false suppositions.

10. Thus, the insufficiency of a law for obedience (and of conscientious scruples for disobedience) forces one to look elsewhere if one is to specify a principle that would identify the sufficient and necessary conditions, applicable in all situations, under which one's obedience (or disobedience) is justified. Unfortunately, I do not see how any such principle could be produced, or that it would be of any use once it was available. Any principle that could do the job required, being a principle of conduct, would itself be open to the very kind of demurrers and controversy it was designed to settle. Second, there is no compelling reason for anyone to adopt any principle in advance of knowing exactly what it will require of him. Since the kind of principle at issue here is likely to be formulated in the chronically open-textured moral concepts of justice, rights, and the like, one cannot know. Thus, anyone who searches for such a principle or who thinks he has one in hand really only disguises from himself the fact that the only way he could use his principle is by tacitly deciding on each occasion either to interpret the principle so as to cover the situation he is in or to describe the situation so as to fit the principle.

[18] Ewing, *op. cit.,* p. 68, and also, it would appear, Spitz, *op. cit.,* p. 400.

This is why "the philosopher can offer no general rules which will enable a man to decide whether obedience or disobedience is the right course in a given case." [19]

11. The difficulties brought forward in the previous two sections do not bear particularly on civil disobedience; they apply to any resistance to government. They signify nothing more and nothing less than the fact that this kind of political behavior is bound to be morally relevant conduct and thus subject to the characteristic potentialities and risks of such conduct.

The question naturally arises whether there is anything special to be said on behalf of civil disobedience which perhaps puts it in a more favorable light than any of its alternatives, viz., violent resistance, obedience under legal public protest, furtive disobedience, or silent acquiescence. Many people evidently think so at present, since they reject these other alternatives out of hand. The first they usually reject because, even if they did not scruple at violence, which they do, they apparently have decided that it would not be successful in persuading their government or their fellow citizens to reexamine the objectionable law. They have also reasoned that violence would tend to excuse violent countermeasures, thereby crushing their capacity to continue the resistance. The other alternatives they dismiss either as ineffective or as something to be pursued only out of diffidence or cowardice in the face of the genuine dangers that active resistance can bring on the head of the dissenter. Their course they explain thus: events in which the government's laws, policies, decisions, etc., play a decisive role are so distressing that if not soon improved they will lead to disaster. Therefore, directly or indirectly, action must be taken which could be fairly widely practiced (or threatened) and which, if it were, would force the government to change its course. Since one has no path to the seats of authority or to the minds of one's countrymen other than open resistance and since the method of resistance must be consistent, as far as possible, with preserving respect for law and order, the only thing to do is to commit civil disobedience, and the sooner the better.

The major obstacle in the way of granting a privileged status to

---

[19] Ewing, *op. cit.,* p. 73. See also Bentham, *op. cit.,* p. 215; Barker, *op. cit.,* pp. 224 f.; and most recently S. I. Benn and R. S. Peters, *Social Principles and the Democratic State* (London, 1959), pp. 70 f.

such acts is that such status would rest on a series of empirical facts whose factuality is still in doubt. Is it true that a government can be brought to reverse its policy through civil disobedience alone? If so, what sort of government and what sort of policies? If not, under what circumstances can civil disobedience be effective? What sort of civil disobedience in general has the most chance of success? Is it false that a relatively bloodless coup is always less effective than civil disobedience? If the availability to the general public of a fairly clear-cut alternative, complete with step-by-step implementation, is necessary to the success of civil disobedience, can this condition always be satisfied in time? Is it really possible to influence the foreign relations of one nation through civil disobedience when there are serious and widespread doubts in the government and the public at large whether the dissenter's politics are acceptable to the other nation? These are a few of the familiar empirical questions that must be raised, and it is not too much to say that there is still responsible disagreement on the answers. The only way to get answers is to conduct actual experiments in civil disobedience. But it is one thing to commit such acts in order to help behavioral scientists get on with their work and another to commit them as though this work had been completed.

There is a regrettable failure on the part of dissenting minorities and those whom government has victimized to explore those situations in which civil disobedience might have some chance of success. Direct nonviolent resistance can often be conducted without interfering with community functions that no sane man would disrupt if he could avoid it. Speaking for myself, I think that, in such cases, civil disobedience would vastly improve the quality of individual participation in public affairs and perhaps accelerate the painfully slow and uncertain advance in the concern of governments for the aspirations of mankind.

# Limits to the Moral Claim
# in Civil Disobedience

HARRY PROSCH

In recent years non-violent civil disobedience to laws has become fairly widespread and well organized in America as part of the effort to eliminate or to change existing laws and practices that discriminate against Negroes. Although there may now be a slacking off of such demonstrations, inasmuch as the passage of the civil rights bill has made illegal much of what the demonstrations were directed against, we may still expect to see civil disobedience in this and in other forms in the future. The civil rights bill will not, of course, remove all the Negroes' frustrations, much less everyone else's.

Non-violent civil disobedience as such is not new, of course. In fact, it is at least as old as Socrates. We find (according to Plato's *Apology*) that Socrates at his trial reminded his fellow citizens that when the Thirty ordered him to go to Salamis to arrest Leon he did not comply. He simply went home. The context makes it clear that his disobedience was, however, disobedience to what he considered the illegal actions of civil officials, not to the laws.[1] From the *Crito* we gather that Socrates could not be convinced of the wisdom of disobeying laws — even poor ones and even in the face of death.[2] When Gandhi and his followers in our times practiced passive resistance on a wide scale as a means for gaining India's independence they were not practicing disobedience to laws so much as disobedience to foreign administrators whose legitimate authority was not commonly acknowledged in India.

But what has arisen in America has been non-violent disobedience to laws — and not only to outright discriminatory laws, but also to laws, such as the trespass law, which are not in themselves dis-

From *Ethics,* Vol. 75, pp. 103–111. Copyright 1965, University of Chicago. Reprinted by permission.

[1] Plato, "Apology," *The Dialogues of Plato,* trans. B. Jowett (2 vols.; New York: Random House, 1937), I, 145.

[2] Plato, "Crito," *ibid.,* pp. 434–38.

criminatory, but which may be used to buttress discriminatory laws and practices. Such disobedience invites, and even demands, our careful attention. The way in which it skitters along the border between moral persuasion and the use of force, between passivity and activity, and between respect for the rule of law and for something higher than the rule of law must intrigue the student of ethics. But the fact that many of its proponents seem to claim that it ought to be regarded as not only morally permissible but also, sometimes, even morally obligatory constitutes a pressing demand that we give it a serious analysis.

A moral claim cannot simply be ignored by supposedly fair-minded people. To ignore it would be to put their own supposed "fair-mindedness" into serious question — even in their own eyes. But, since civil disobedience is not a moral claim made only in words, but rather one made in actions, it demands analysis from everyone — whether fair-minded or not. We may stop our ears to mere words — or remain apathetic — and our silence does not necessarily constitute approval or disapproval. Our silence has neither squelched the claim nor granted it. But when the claim is made in action, our continued silence or apathy either strengthens or weakens the effectiveness of the claim, depending upon the situation. If the claim (the action) is being met with forceful opposition by the authorities or by others and we remain inactive, our very inactivity helps to stifle it out of existence. If, however, the claim (the action) is not being forcefully opposed, and we remain inactive, our inactivity helps to fortify its existence in the world. Thus whoever has not been for the civil rights demonstrators may turn out, in fact, to have been against them, and whoever has not been against them may turn out, in fact, to have been for them. An attempted action is like a "thing" which must either become established in the world or not, depending upon the nature of other actions which are or are not taken, whereas a word is not like a "thing" in this way — except in its character as an action. It is possible, in other words, to oppose the actions of writing or of speaking certain words — that is, to deny freedom of speech or of the press. But it is also possible to allow these words to exist as "things" — that is, to allow an action to be taken which sets these words forth into the world — but still to ignore the claim which they are making to an object or to a further action, but which they are not in themselves actually laying hold of. Non-violent civil disobedience, being a claim expressed in actions, not merely in words, demands therefore a consideration of its claim because it demands a decision for or against itself.

The most attractive moral rationale for non-violent civil dis-obedience seems to run something like this: some laws, or some practices buttressed by some laws, are unjust or wrong, and, in simply doing what these laws say you should not do — that is, in simply placing your body where they forbid it to be placed — you are only asking those who presumably believe in the justice of these laws whether or not they really believe in it. You are not coercing them by violence or the threat of violence. You are merely putting to them a question. And so your own hands remain clean. You are prepared to submit to their violence if their answer is "Yes." But the trick is that you are asking them in such a way that they will have to reply. Do they believe in the rightness of these laws firmly enough to con-tinue enforcing them upon people who keep coming back to be arrested or even beaten? They must either act or not act in the face of your challenge, and so they must return an answer.

The tactic you are using appears, on this view, to be a striking and very effective mode of moral persuasion. However, since the employment of arguments — rational, emotional, or some combina-tion — is not involved at its point of action, your opponents are not likely to identify your effort as an attempt at moral persuasion. They must rather tend to regard it as a power move on your part. There-fore, even though your action is non-violent, its first consequence must be to place you and your opponents in a state of war. For your op-ponents now have only the same sort of choice that an army has: that of allowing you to continue occupying the heights you have moved on to, or of applying force — dynamic, active, violent force — to throw you back off them. Your opponents cannot now uphold the laws which they value without the use of such violence. And to fail to uphold them is to capitulate to you — to allow you to win and so to allow their laws to become inoperative — *de facto* null and void. You have therefore literally forced them out of the possibility of con-tending with you in the non-violent arenas of moral persuasion (of the argumentative type )and of political maneuvering.

In terms of its practical impact, therefore, your tactic is basically a military one rather than a morally persuasive one — or even a political one. It is a contest of force, even though the only force *you* may be resorting to is that of the inertia of your own body. It could possibly also have a morally persuasive effect, if your opponents already half-suspected the moral righteousness of their own laws (at least subconsciously) and if the hard decision you are forcing them to make should result in their uncovering their more deeply held principles — and if also, of course, their deeper principles should happen to be the same as yours. If and when it is reasonable to suppose that all these conditions do prevail, then, at such a time and place, non-violent civil disobedience would, no doubt, be mutually recognized as a genuine mode of moral persuasion, and therefore also as justifiable. This "if" and "when" are, however, rather formidable. The chance of error in the assessment that these essential conditions do prevail in some particular instance is great. That your opponents stand in need of moral psychoanalytic therapy in the first place could only be a guess for most people. That, even if your opponents did need it, they might respond to your particular "treatment" could also be hardly more than a good guess. And that, if they did respond, they would respond in the way you wanted them to must constitute yet a third pure conjecture.

It is true that the eventual outcome of the argumentative forms of moral persuasion is also quite problematical. But the penalties for failure in such argumentative attempts are not as great as are the penalties for failure in this non-argumentative form. If this form fails, one has succeeded only in increasing the hostility of one's opponents toward one's views, and actually therefore in creating a greater obstacle to the moral re-evaluation one is ostensibly seeking. And then there is, in addition, the further considerable risk that "non-violence" may spill over into "violence" when it meets with the counterviolence which it has provoked if it has not been successful. This latter risk, in fact, might almost be said to be a tendency. History seems to show us that it is very hard to keep limited wars limited — especially when one or more of the contending armies are popular armies who popularly think of their enemies as morally deficient. "Whosoever taketh the sword," Christ might have said, "shall be condemned to use it."

In view of all these uncertainties and dangers, non-violent civil disobedience, thought of as a mode of moral persuasion, seems indeed to be a risky business. Not only are the chances of success not very good, due to the difficulty in knowing when the proper conditions for its success prevail, but the penalties for failure are rather severe.

When we note, therefore, that non-violent civil disobedience seems to be widely used and respected as a form of high moral endeavor by those who are apparently not unaware of its considerable risks, we should suspect there is something more to its moral rationale than its precarious usefulness as a means of moral persuasion. Why should one choose such a risky way to persuade? How can one morally justify this choice? If its only moral justification is its capacity to serve as an effective means of moral persuasion then it can be said to have little, if any. The moral rationale of non-violent civil disobedience requires another principle able to justify it as an action, regardless of its success or failure in moral persuasion. A principle fit to do this would then constitute its primary moral justification, and the additional fact that its non-violent form also leaves the door even slightly ajar for moral persuasion would then merely add to its moral attractiveness, rather than, in supposedly defining its moral purpose, actually condemn it.

It is not too difficult to identify the principle that constitutes such a primary moral justification for non-violent civil disobedience. Proponents of civil disobedience extol it in their songs and stories, their legends and their heroes. It is the simple and popular notion that it is morally right, and even heroic, to oppose unjust laws, to take a forceful stand in battle against them, and to overcome them, even at great sacrifice. This principle does, in fact, beckon to us all, because we all see to some extent that it is absurd to suppose that every law is *ipso facto* right — that no law can be subject to criticism. In fact, we all surely must be aware of some laws that we ourselves are critical of. But if laws, as such, can be subject to criticism then it naturally seems to us there must be something that is right in terms of which they can be criticized. This "something" must be then what is truly right, and laws which we are not able to square with it must be truly wrong. But even to follow or to act according to a wrong law is surely itself to do what is wrong. It must, therefore, seem right to us to disobey, to contend against, to try to overturn, in a word, to *fight* these wrong or unjust laws.

We therefore have to turn our inquiry into a more general one. We must investigate the moral adequacy of the principle common to any form of protest civil disobedience: It is right to use force in the attempt to nullify or to change unjust laws. Force is the most general term to use here, since, as we have seen, even non-violent disobedience involves a resort to force, and it is the rightness of the use of such a means as this against unjust laws which is the crucial issue, inasmuch as it is this use that distinguishes disobedience from other peaceful (rule-abiding) modes of opposition.

Since the rightness of the use of force hinges, in terms of this principle, on an opposition to unjust laws only (anarchism or despotism — a total rejection of the rule of law — is not presumably what is being advocated), let us begin by inquiring into the criteria for correctly or rightly applying the term "unjust" to laws. Here we may profit from the work of the language analysts in philosophy. If we are asking for the criteria for the application of a word, we must, as many of them have pointed out, seek for the shared, common, or public way of applying the word — a way which does, in fact, communicate with those who are using the language. Otherwise we would merely be trying to speak a private language, and so we would not be effectively calling anything anything.[3]

If this is true, our question then must be: do we have a way of deciding in a public fashion what laws to designate (what laws we ought to designate) unjust? It turns out that we have at least two ways, sometimes involved in each other, for deciding this in a public way — and also for agreeing publicly that we have decided it rightly. One way is by the argumentative forms of moral persuasion. And the other is through the operation of commonly accepted political processes. We are sometimes able to argue each other into an agreement that a certain law is unjust or wrong or bad and that it ought to be opposed. And we are sometimes able to accept a repudiation or change of a law which has been accomplished by what are publicly regarded as ordinary political processes — such as the repeal or modification of a law by a constitutionally legitimate legislative body or (in America) by a Supreme Court decision that a law is unconstitutional.

Neither of these two ways, however, can be what we seek; for although they are both public ways of designating laws as unjust, they are also, at the same time, public ways of changing such laws — and, moreover, changing them in peaceful or non-coercive ways. If we

---

[3] A good brief résumé and defense of the later Wittgenstein's views on the impossibility of a private language — even in terms of words like pain — is found in Norman Malcolm, "Wittgenstein's Philosophical Investigations," *The Philosophy of Mind,* ed. V. C. Chappell (Englewood Cliffs, N.J.: Prentice-Hall, Inc., 1962). See also Norman Malcolm, "Knowledge of Other Minds," *ibid.,* esp. p. 152.

could have achieved a public designation in one or the other of these ways, we would not find ourselves involved in the use of force to accomplish a change in the laws.

So our question must be sharpened into whether or not, when we are trying to change or oppose laws by force, we have a public or common way available to us for identifying these laws as unjust. And it should be obvious from what has been said that we do not have and that we cannot have. Our not having such a way defines our situation. Where force is resorted to, some individuals think the laws under fire are just and others think they are unjust — that is, think the laws should be designated "unjust." It is quite clear that these two groups are not using the same criteria for the application of the word. As a matter of fact they will still not agree on the criteria for its use even after one side wins. Such agreement is, by contrast, forthcoming from successful persuasion, and some sort of agreement arises from successful political action as well. We all do agree, for instance, that a law which has been repealed in a commonly accepted, legitimate manner is no longer a law that ought to be obeyed — in spite of the fact that many of us may not have been morally persuaded that it was a bad or unjust law. What we are morally persuaded of in common, in this case however, is that the methods used in securing the political decision were right or "proper" ones. Our agreement on these methods is, in fact, what constitutes our political community. To the extent that such methods are lacking, either anarchy or despotism is present. But when the defeat has not been a moral or political one, but merely a physical one, there is no agreement — even upon the fact of defeat. Defeat is regarded as only a strategic withdrawal — the fight is still in progress. This appears to be the case for instance, in the American South — even after a hundred years.

A resort to force is, of course, thoroughly understandable when deep and serious disagreements exist and when neither moral persuasion nor political methods seem equal to their resolution. But it can hardly be said in any common, disinterested, or objective way to be morally right or just. What is morally right or just seems to remain as controversial after the use of the force as it was before or during it, and it would therefore be a strange (or possibly only an emotive) use of the term *moral* to apply it to a method for dealing with a moral controversy which can be seen analytically to be incapable of achieving a moral resolution.

But this conclusion meets with considerable resistance from those who find themselves in a serious moral disagreement with what the laws provide, such as in the case of the civil-rights controversy. It still seems to such contestants that the cause for which they are fighting is just and right and that to fail to fight for it would be wrong since it would be, in effect, to acquiesce in the wrong, namely, in what the laws now provide. Somewhere behind such a "feeling," therefore, must hover the notion that public agreement on the criteria for the use of such a word as "unjust" is irrelevant and unnecessary, that everyone has his own moral principles and standards and that they are rendered neither more nor less right by being also in agreement with public criteria. Ethics must therefore be thought, however dimly, to admit somehow of private criteria for the application of its key words — or else it is thought that the whole enterprise is only emotive, that is, merely an elaborate conventional and ceremonial way of expressing our feelings (like saying "Ouch!" and "Yum! Yum!" only much more complicated). At least, since the contention that it is right to fight for the right (i.e., against the unjust) must, as we have seen, deny that public agreement is essential to labeling something unjust, it seems difficult to see what criteria other than these are left. Let us therefore examine our language more closely to see whether or not we are merely speaking a private language in ethics — or are merely using words emotively.

When someone says, "It is right to fight for the right," he could, on the view that public criteria for the use of his ethical words are inappropriate, mean (or express) nothing more than that he thinks (or feels) it is right to fight for the right. He could not mean that it is right, in some public sense of the word, for then, in the end, he would be holding that some public sense of the word "right" is possible after all, and he would be thrown back into seeking for this sense and therefore into seeking for the ways of achieving public criteria for words like "right" or "just." These ways would have to be, as we have seen, argumentative persuasion and/or political maneuvering — not at all fighting. So he must not be understood to be stating something having a genuine public meaning when he says it is right to fight for the right. And yet, if someone did make such a statement as this, would he, in fact, be understood to be only asserting (or expressing) something of his own feelings? Would he not also, as Charles Stevenson suggested with respect to the moral use of the word "good," be under-

stood to be inviting from others an agreement with him on his feelings? [4] Indeed, as this expression is in fact used, he might even be
understood by his hearers to be demanding, or at least contending
for, such an agreement. But whether or not we do actually contend, or
demand, or only invite an agreement with us from others by the use
of our moral words, it seems clear that to say something is (morally)
right is not the same as to say it is appetitively delicious — and that
one way it is not the same is that we seem to intend to be met with or
to induce an agreement with us when we say something is right,
whereas we do not seem to intend this when we say something is
delicious. When I state a principle of action is right, I will be understood by those acquainted with ordinary usage to propose not only
that *I* should follow it, but that men should — that it is a principle that
ought to be followed. And I will be understood to be asserting also,
therefore, that men should permit it to be followed, not just permit *me*
to follow it. Are we ever understood to be demanding a special privilege when we use ethical language? If we are ever so understood, are
we not understood then to be trying to conceal a wish for special
privilege behind a use of ethical language? Behind what are we con-
cealing it, if ethical language is not, in fact, understood to be a proposal for rules supposedly applicable to all? Only philosophers ever
seem to get mixed up about this aspect of ethical language. Men in
real moral controversies understand quite well what is set forth by their
opponents. To assert that something is right is to assert that everybody ought to permit it — if not to do it.

If this is what is involved in men's serious moral talk, it should
follow that no principle could then be fit to serve as an ethical principle — as a principle operative in an ethical system of coherent rights
and duties (moral obligations) — unless it is capable of becoming a
common principle of action. Let us ask, therefore, whether the principle that it is morally right to fight for the right is one which is capable
of becoming a common principle of action.

Since a fight, as such, necessarily entails crossing the will of others
in a forceful way, the best hope for finding that fighting for the right is
fit to be a common ethical principle lies in discovering some ends or
causes that are rationally or intelligibly justifiable and so are *potentially*

[4] Charles L. Stevenson, *Ethics and Language* (New Haven, Conn.: Yale
University Press, 1944), pp. 25, 26.

capable of becoming common. This was, as a matter of fact, how Kant
was able to make his merely formal categorical imperative also a
material one, useful in making distinctions between better and worse
ways of life.[5] It might seem that if there are some causes which are
really right as causes, then to fail to fight for them must really be
wrong. But the difficulty is that, even if we are sure that we have our
fingers on the really right ones, our opponents are also sure they have
their fingers on the really right ones, too; and, as long as we have
been unable to agree with each other upon which ends or causes are
the truly right ones, the principle that we ought all to fight for the
right ones would be far from providing us with a common principle
to live by. It could only be said to be common to us in an abstract
sense. Since we would be putting different concrete fillings in it
(battling for different causes), it could only lead us in practice to tear
each other apart in thoroughly unprincipled ways. And this would be
true even if we tried to amend the principle to take care of this objection and said, for instance: "It is right for everyone to fight for
whatever he really thinks is right." We would find this principle could
only defeat itself in the sort of action where it should presumably come
into play, namely, where there was something to fight for or against,
where we did not all agree upon what was right or just — other than
the principle that it was right for each of us to fight for what he thought
was right. If we really tried to grant our opponents the right to fight
us (which would be to grant them the power and the privilege of
fighting us), we would not be truly engaging in what the principle
said was right — a fight for the right. Either it is right to fight, or it is
not. If it is then we ought to *fight,* and it would be wrong to give up or
to lose the fight by restraining ourselves to some set of restrictive rules.
If it is right to fight for the right, it is surely wrong to fail to fight in

[5] Immanuel Kant, *The Fundamental Principles of the Metaphysics of
Ethics,* trans. T. K. Abbott (New York: Longmans, Green & Co., 1900), pp.
66–68; and Immanuel Kant, *The Metaphysical Principles of Virtue,* trans.
James Ellington (Indianapolis: Bobbs-Merrill Co., 1964), pp. 42, 43, 46, 114,
126. Here Kant's language, esp. p. 126, might even be interpreted as providing
at least a limited justification for precisely the kind of fights for the right
which are now current. He says, "Therefore, reconciliation (*placabilitas*) is a
duty of man, although it is not to be confused with the weak toleration of
wrongs (*ignava injuriarum patientia*) which renounces stern (*rigorosa*) measures to forestall continued wrongs by others. For that would be to throw
one's rights at the feet of others and to violate man's duty to himself." Kant
does, however, reject revolution elsewhere.

the way we find we have to fight in order to win. We could have no right, under this principle, to turn the fight into a mere contest and so risk failing to bring about the right. As dedicated fighters in a holy cause, we must in all consistency try for nothing less than the liquidation of our opponents — as fighters, at least. We cannot be dedicated to their perpetuation. We must not, therefore, grant them the right to fight us — if we can take it away. And conversely, of course, they must not grant us this right. So none of us could, in practice, actually follow such a principle. We would have to confess ourselves, therefore, as out of ethical relations altogether with our opponents in a fight for the right — we would have to admit that they would always have as much, and as little, reason to claim their actions were moral as we would. Being out of moral phase with each other, only God could be our judge, and the only morality our fight could have would be that of a medieval appeal to Heaven — a trial by arms. Most of us are no doubt sufficiently freed from superstition to recognize that in such a case it could only be the stronger who would win — or at most the more fortunate — not necessarily those who were more "right."

What this should mean to us is that we cannot moralize fighting. To restrain our fights by the principle of non-violence is admirable as an indication of a yearning for righteousness on our part, a desire for a morality which we somehow divine does not lie wholly in our fight-for-the-right itself. And it would also transform the fight into an attempt at moral persuasion, were the conditions mentioned earlier in this essay to prevail in some particular instance. But it does not in itself moralize war. A fight, a state of war, is not and cannot be a moral state. Either we govern our relations by notions of mutual rights (i.e., ethically), or we govern them by force. There is nothing in between.

Yet there is no doubt that we will all still — in spite of the calm analytical facts of the case — fight for the right, "as God gives us to see the right," when the chips are down and battle lines are drawn. What else indeed can we do? But it would be unintelligent to regard this fighting as anything more than a last resort when all else has failed — as a most regrettable and even tragic situation. We surely ought to restrain our primitive impulse to regard it as our supreme moment of truth — as a glorious and glamorous opportunity to flail about, cracking heads for a noble cause, filling our little lives with meaning in this manner and accomplishing the will of God. A struggle for the "right" may at some time become a sober and solemn necessity, born of the circumstances and laid upon us in spite of ourselves. But then the only joy in it, meet and proper for us to take, should be something akin to the peace the Stoics found in resignation. A true fight for the right should be for us not really a fight at all, but rather a quest for a common ground — a patient and unromantic effort to be reasonable and tolerable, persuasive and conciliatory, in an attempt to reach decisions which may have in them little more than the commonplace virtue of being common — at least in the mundane political sense. Short of having made this supreme effort, we shall not — if our analysis here has been sound — have kept our hands clean, regardless of whether we wage the fight thrust upon us by violent or by non-violent means.

# The Problem of Consistently Losing Minorities

## Civil Disobedience: Prerequisite for Democracy in Mass Society

### CHRISTIAN BAY

#### I

During a recent debate on the war in Vietnam an irate member of the audience demanded to know if I was in favor of civil disobedience. My reply was "Yes, on some occasions." He sat down in silence, with a broad grin. Nothing else that I said from then on was worth taking seriously, so far as he was concerned. I might as well have come out in favor of arson. And I am sure many in the audience felt as he did.

This widespread tendency to recoil from the very concept of disobedience, even passive and presumably nonviolent disobedience, in a society priding itself on its liberties, is a measure of the degree of stability, if not immunity to real social change, that has been achieved by the present socioeconomic and political system in the United States.

To the spiritual fathers of the American democracy, most notably John Locke and Thomas Jefferson, it seemed evident that any liberty-loving people should have the right to stage even a bloody revolution against a tyrannical government; by comparison, the remedy of nonviolent civil disobedience would seem a mild brew indeed.

Reprinted by permission of the publishers, Atherton Press, Inc. Copyright © 1967, Atherton Press, Inc., New York. All rights reserved.

Among the most forceful counter-norms, or norms tending to lead many of us to reject *a priori* the very thought of civil disobedience, is another Lockian principle: the sanctity of the rule of law. Spokesmen for our academic as well as our political and economic establishments are for obvious reasons far happier with this part of Locke's theory of civil government.

Now, the classical writings of our democratic heritage, not unlike the Bible or the classical Marxist literature, can be used to prove the legitimacy of almost anything, and therefore, more critically viewed, of almost nothing. This point should be particularly poignant for those who have followed, during the last decades, developments in research and theory in the field of political behavior. For reasons of convenience and perhaps of habit as well, it has remained orthodox for our colleagues to proclaim their fealty to our democratic way of life (some, indeed, seem to feel that we are entitled to force other nations, too, to be guided by our example); and this fealty has remained unshaken, by and large, by the wealth of data that have come forth to demonstrate the wide and growing gulf between most of the classical ideals of democracy and what goes on in its name in today's mass societies.

Let us return to the part of our democratic heritage of particular concern here: the insistence on the sanctity of the rule of law. Now, a strong case for exalting the law (and indirectly, the lawyer) can be made from my own political ground of commitment to no system but to the sanctity of life, and the freedoms necessary for living,[1] *insofar as* laws (and lawyers) are to operate to protect all human lives, with priority for those most badly in need of protection. But to claim a corresponding sanctity for the laws that we have today, which, as in *every* state to a considerable extent, operate in the service of those who are privileged and influential in our socioeconomic order, seems to me to constitute an outright fraud at the expense of all the political innocents, unless one can claim for oneself, too, the innocence of not knowing any significant part of our modern behavioral literature.

At best a claim can be made that general obedience to the law is a lesser evil than general disobedience, which could well lead to much violence and conceivably even to a return to a Hobbesian

---

[1] See below, section III. This position is developed at greater length in my *The Structure of Freedom* (New York, 1964, 1958).

state of nature. But this surely is a false issue, for no society has ever known either general obedience or general anarchy. Most of us have become trained, as generations of our ancestors have before us, to obey almost all laws almost by instinct, and certainly by habit if not by conviction. Others have become conditioned to breaking laws, frequently for reasons of stunted growth on account of emotional as well as socioeconomic deprivation.

Democracy has not yet been achieved, at least not in any real sense, as we shall see, in the modern world. If so, then the most familiar justifications demanding obedience to "democratically enacted" laws would seem to have no firm foundation. For the argument that every law represents the will of all, or the will of the majority, is empirically false; so is the argument that all laws aim at serving the common good. So is, as we have seen, the argument that disobedience to *any* law will promote anarchy.

Yet it obviously will not do, either, to assert that all laws can be ignored, or that any particular law can be obeyed or disobeyed as a matter of convenience. Nobody in his right mind will support all disobedience, however "civil," regardless of the issues involved. The question to be tackled, then, is not whether, but when and on what grounds civil disobedience can be justified.

My point of departure is essentially Locke's: respect for the rule of law, or for the democratic processes that produce our laws, clearly must be contingent on and limited by standards for judging either the caliber of these processes or the purposes they promote, or, more precisely, by standards for judging how well these processes promote the purpose of politics. The *fundamental* purpose of politics, as I see it, is not to perpetuate a given political order but to protect human life and basic human rights. It cannot, if I may rub the point in, be the legitimizing purpose of politics or of government to perpetuate a political order that is democratic in name but in fact serves primarily to bolster privileges, not to equalize rights — as does ours and surely every other political order achieved till now.

The course of my argument in the remainder of this chapter will be as follows: first (II) comes a definition and a discussion of the concept of civil disobedience; next (III) a very brief statement of my own normative position, affirming the value of freedom and, only secondarily, of democracy as an aim; and then (IV) a discussion of the increasing chasm between current realities and the classical aims of democracy. I shall next (V) try to show how an expansion of the role of civil disobedience would, if anything could, turn the trend around, so that we might hope to move toward rather than away from democracy; and, finally (VI), I shall argue how essential civil disobedience is for the liberation of the individual as a political citizen — as a man and as a sharer of the burdens and benefits of politics. Since "real" democracy would require "real" citizens, this argument, too, will support the case for civil disobedience as a prerequisite for achieving something approximating democracy in modern societies.

II

"Civil disobedience" will here refer to any act or process of public defiance of a law or policy enforced by established governmental authorities, insofar as the action is premeditated, understood by the actor(s) to be illegal or of contested legality, carried out and persisted in for limited public ends, and by way of carefully chosen and limited means.

The notion of *disobedience* presupposes the concept of a norm to be disobeyed; typically a legal norm, but in any event a norm which is assumed by *some* people in power to be authoritative in the sense that transgressions would be expected to lead to punishment in one form or another. Disobedience can be active or passive; it can be a matter of doing what is prohibited or of failing to do what is required. But mere noncompliance is not enough; the action or nonaction must be openly insisted on if it is to qualify as civil disobedience, as the concept is interpreted here. For example, failure to vote in a country in which there is a legal obligation to vote does not in itself constitute civil disobedience; one would have to state in public that one does not intend to comply with the particular law; typically but not necessarily, one would publicly encourage others, too, to disobey.

The act of disobedience must be illegal, or at least be deemed illegal by powerful adversaries, and the actor must know this, if it is to be considered an act of civil disobedience.[2] Note the distinction

[2] See Harrop A. Freeman, "Civil Disobedience," in *Civil Disobedience,* Harrop A. Freeman *et al.* (Santa Barbara, 1966).

between *conscientious objection* to military service and civil disobedience in countries that permit exemptions from otherwise obligatory service for reasons of conscience. The conscientious objector engages in civil disobedience only if he knowingly and explicitly objects to military service on grounds not recognized by the law, or in a country that makes no exceptions for reasons of conscience.

"Civil" is the more ambiguous of the two terms. At least five different meanings would appear plausible, and in this area it would seem reasonable to cast the net wide and consider each of the following meanings equally legitimate:

1. The reference can be to a recognition of general obligations of citizenship and thus to the legitimacy of the existing legal order as a whole; pains taken to limit defiance to a particular legal clause or policy, and/or to avoid violence, may (but need not) be construed as an affirmation of general citizenship duties.

2. "Civil" can be taken to refer to the opposite of "military," in a broad sense. The customary stress on nonviolence may be construed to signify either (a) a recognition of the state's claim to monopoly with respect to legitimate use of physical violence, or (b) a rejection of all physical violence as illegitimate or morally wrong under all circumstances regardless of purpose.

3. "Civil" can refer to the opposite of "uncivil" or "uncivilized"; acts of civil disobedience may seek to embody ideals of citizenship or morality that will inspire adversaries and/or onlookers, hopefully, toward more civilized behavior, or behavior more in harmony with the ideals that inspire a given campaign of civil disobedience.

4. "Civil" can also be taken to refer to public as distinct from private; as citizens we act in public. Acts of civil disobedience seek not only to affirm a principle in private, but to call public attention to the view that a principle of moral importance is held to be violated by a law or a policy sanctioned by public authorities.

5. "Civil" can suggest that the objective of obedience is to institute changes in the political system, affecting not only one individual's or group's liberties but the liberties of all citizens. A religious sect persisting in outlawed practices of worship (say, the Peyote cult among western American Indians, before the U.S. Supreme Court came to its rescue) may insist only on being left alone, or may at the same time consciously assert a principle to the effect that other sects, too, should enjoy the equivalent rights. Degrees of conscious-

ness about the wider implications of disobedient behavior are not well suited as conceptual demarcation lines, however, and it would seem most practical to include even very parochially motivated acts of disobedience within the scope of the concept of civil disobedience.

The ambiguities of the term "civil" are far from exhausted by this brief list, but the five meanings presented are probably among the more common. The chances are that most of those who practice civil disobedience think of their behavior as "civil" in a sense, whether articulated or not, which embraces more than one of these associations, and perhaps others as well.

Returning now to the definition with which we began, let us note, first, that acts of civil disobedience may be illegal and legal at the same time, in cases of conflict of laws. For example, disobedience campaigns have been conducted against state segregation laws in the American South, in the belief that under the Federal Constitution such acts of disobedience will *eventually* be deemed legal in the Federal courts.

The ends of civil disobedience must be public and limited, it is suggested. The ostensible aim cannot, within the reference proposed, be a private or business advantage; it must have *some* reference to a conception of justice or the common good. (This is not to deny, of course, that individual motives for engaging in civil disobedience at times may be neurotic or narrowly self-seeking, consciously or subconsciously.) The proclaimed ends must be limited, too; they must fall short of seeking the complete abolition of the existing legal system; those who want a "nonviolent revolution" may engage in civil disobedience, but they, too, proclaim specific, limited ends each time. Also, according to the usage recommended here, the proclaimed aims must fall short of intending the physical or moral destruction of adversaries, even if at times a calculable risk of casualties may be tolerated. The ends of civil disobedience must be potentially acceptable to those in the *role* of adversaries even if to current adversaries they may be anathema on psychological grounds.

Above all, the proclaimed ends of civil disobedience, as the concept is understood here, must be formulated with a view to making them appear morally legitimate to onlookers and to the public. Educational objectives prompt most civil disobedience campaigns, and are never wholly absent. If a trade union violates the law to gain equality or justice, in some sense, for their members, we may speak of civil disobedience, but not if a key position in the economic system tempts a union to violate the law for the purpose of extorting unreasonable privileges in return for obeying the law. A civil disobedience campaign can aim at destroying privileges considered unjust, but not at abolishing the right to equal protection of an already underprivileged minority group.

The "carefully chosen and limited means" of civil disobedience are calculated to achieve maximum efficiency in promoting the ends and also maximum economy in seeking to reduce as much as possible the cost of the struggle in terms of suffering and deprivation. True, Gandhi at times stressed the value of bearing or even seeking suffering, but he always wanted to avoid inflicting suffering on his adversaries or on third parties.

"Civil disobedience" should be kept apart from "nonviolent action." The latter concept by definition rules out violent acts while the former does not, as defined here.[3] Among some pacifist believers in civil disobedience it seems to be assumed that a complete commitment to nonviolence, even in the sense of avoiding the provocation of violence on the part of adversaries, is ethically superior to a more pragmatic attitude toward the possible use of violence. No such assumption is made here. "Carefully chosen and limited means" in the definition at the outset refers to choice of means rationally calculated to promote the limited ends. For many reasons it seems plausible that such rational calculation normally will suggest strenuous efforts toward either avoidance or reduction of violence. Civil disobedience activists and social scientists ought to be equally interested in research on the causation and consequences of violence and nonviolence under conditions of social conflict; the expansion of this type of knowledge would seem of crucial importance for achieving increasingly realistic calculations of the most effective and economic means toward the chosen ends of civil disobedience campaigns, and also toward determining when such campaigns are and when they are not likely to be successful.[4]

---

[3] An opposite view is adopted by Hugo A. Bedau, "On Civil Disobedience," *Journal of Philosophy,* LVIII (1961), 653–665; by Carl Cohen, "Essence and Ethics of Civil Disobedience," *The Nation,* CXCVIII (March 16, 1964), 257–262; and by Freeman, *op. cit.*

[4] My discussion in section II is adapted from my forthcoming article, "Civil Disobedience," in the *International Encyclopedia of the Social Sciences* (in press).

### III

My normative position is essentially a simple one, even if it, like any other normative position, raises complex issues in application. Man and his world are, after all, almost infinitely complex.

The primary purpose of politics and of government, I hold, is to protect human life, and to expand the sphere of freedoms securely enjoyed by the individual — all individuals, mind you, on an equal basis. If all are equally entitled to grow and live in freedom, then those currently most deprived, in every unequal society, must have the highest priority claim on protection by the state.

A different way of stating the same fundamental commitment is to say that governmental coercion — and governments are by their nature coercive — can be justified only to the extent that it in fact serves to reduce coercion; and physical violence and oppressive economic deprivation prior to other, less debilitating restraints.

If I may anticipate for a moment my argument in the next section, no political order achieved so far, and that goes for our western ways of government, too, has been justifiable in these terms, if reasonably strictly construed. Demands on government arising from the lesser pains and frustrations suffered by influentials have generally taken precedence over demands arising, or demands that *should* arise, from the more debilitating indignities suffered by the poor and the inarticulate — whose very deprivation (with its cultural and psychological aspects) in fact prevents them, except in exceedingly rare revolutionary situations, almost unthinkable in the privilege-entrenched North American political order, from playing any political role at all.

According to the classical ideals, democracy should be a commonwealth of political equals, who are free to advance the common good and also their own good by constitutional means — that is, by legislation, brought about by processes designed to make sure that the laws express the well-deliberated desires *and* needs of the people. I feel committed to the aim of achieving democracy in this ideal sense because such a system would, to the extent that it could be brought about, be hospitable to respect for life and for human rights on the basis of equality. It would be easy to obey, presumably, the laws enacted in an ideal democracy. I shall argue, however, that this ideal cannot be realized, or even appreciably advanced, without a much expanded role for civil disobedience, given our present political order.

IV

Many leading political theorists would have us believe that western democracy as we know it in the United States and Britain today comes about as close to perfection as can any political order that fallible human beings can hope to attain. Some would have us dismiss as senseless "extremism" any radical questioning of the merits of our political *status quo,* and have even proclaimed an "end of ideology."

The classical ideals of democracy (excepting, most notably, the rule of law) have been all but abandoned by some of these theorists, or at any rate have been restructured so that their commitment to democracy has become a commitment to uphold what essentially amounts to the *status quo.*[5] Now, Bertrand Russell has remarked somewhere that the ruler of Hobbe's state would be far worse than Hobbes himself imagined if the citizens were to be as meek and submissive as Hobbes wanted. It is a fundamental part of my own thesis that every political order tends to become more tyrannical the more submissive its citizens are. Western democracies probably form no exception to this rule. In fact, as de Tocqueville saw, a peculiar hazard of democracies is that citizens are brought not only to comply with authority edicts but to regard them as binding morally as well, since they claim to represent the people's will.[6]

Democratic governments, like all others, seek to isolate and emasculate radical dissenters. If the domestic methods of democratic governments have been less extreme and less brutal than those of most dictator regimes, this probably reflects the usual stability of established democratic regimes, more so than any real appreciation of the value of dissent and dialogue about political fundamentals. True, the right to dissent is proclaimed as one of the many political virtues of our system, so that radical dissenters must be tolerated to a considerable extent, but there are many safeguards against permitting a fair hearing for their views. States and indeed all large

[5] See, most notably, the last chapter in each of the following volumes: Bernard R. Berelson, Paul F. Lazarsfeld, and William N. McPhee, *Voting* (Chicago, 1954); Seymour Martin Lipset, *Political Man* (Garden City, 1960); and Gabriel A. Almond and Sidney Verba, *The Civic Culture* (Princeton, 1963).

[6] See Alexis de Tocqueville, *Democracy in America* (New York, 1954), Vintage Books ed., especially Vol. I, Chap. XV.

organizations, as numerous studies from Michels[7] on have shown, tend toward oligarchy and toward becoming instruments in the service of their respective oligarchies, at the expense of rank-and-file members.

The fact that the Anglo-Saxon democracies at most times have been able to dispense with the coarser methods of political repression, which in itself should be valued and indeed welcomed as a major achievement of our species, is at the same time a testimonial to the unlikelihood of any real changes taking place within the framework of established democracies. It is argued in our civics texts that the governing political parties in democracies tend to accept defeat at the polls gracefully because they know they may have a chance to come back to power again another time, if the rules of the democratic game are maintained. A fuller explanation of this willingness to abide by election results surely should include, however, especially in the United States but in most other democracies as well, the fact that not much is really at stake in elections, generally speaking, for the major interests. The tradition of "negative government" prior to Franklin Roosevelt made the United States government unable, even if it had been willing, to reduce the amount of socioeconomic injustice; and even after Roosevelt, though a trend toward "positive government" has been growing, and perhaps culminating with the early years of Lyndon Johnson, the division of powers, the conservatism of the mass media, the enormity of the economic power of the privileged strata, and a host of other circumstances have made it virtually impossible to expect government to become an instrument, even in part, for the interests of the downtrodden, or for the enlargement of human rights at the expense of privileges.

True, there have been proclaimed programs of Square Deal, New Freedom, New Deal, Fair Deal, New Frontier, and more recently, the Great Society. In its affluence America has been able to keep most of its underprivileged from actual starvation and has increased the opportunities for gifted or energetic young people of all classes and races. This has been done perhaps in part with lofty motives but probably also in part to attract votes and also, especially in recent decades, out of concern for America's image abroad; surely also in part as a means to forestall or reduce the incidence of acts of desperation like race riots, industrial violence, and the like.

[7] Robert Michels, *Political Parties* (Glencoe, 1949, 1915).

As Dahl has observed, democratic government, even an ideal democratic government, has no ready way of registering the intensity of feeling about public issues.[8] "One man, one vote" means equal weight for the concerned vote and the indifferent vote; for the intelligent and the foolish vote; for the vote in defense of elemental dignities of life and the vote in pursuit of added privileges for groups already favored. As David Truman has observed, however, in our democracy the potential existence of new groups and new coalitions does put some limits on what a government will do, even if elected by a wide margin.[9] But the trouble is, as most of our civic culture-championing pluralists fail to acknowledge, that the potential groups and coalitions a president or governor or mayor needs to worry about are rarely made up of the underprivileged — except, perhaps, if they are desperate to the point of being riot-prone, or intelligently led to the point of being prone to engage in civil disobedience. Normally, except in countries with strong political labor movements, the underprivileged have been made politically ineffective to the point of emasculation by their circumstances of life; coalitions of influentials and privileged are usually the only effective potential groups, and theirs are the interests that most executives prefer to appease rather than confront. As Murray Edelman puts it, in every conflict of interest between the many and the few, the many tend to be given symbolic gratification by way of democratic rhetoric and nice-sounding laws, while the few are given the tangible benefits, including a way of enforcing or not enforcing the laws that suit them.[10]

As Kolko and others have documented, the structure of economic wealth and power in this country has not been changed at all for the last half-century.[11] For all the slogans, Square Deal to Great Society, political influence remains in the hands of the economically strong while the poor remain inarticulate and largely without influence. Even the trade unions, though in the past they have served the economic interests of some categories of poor, are politically irrelevant

---

[8] Robert A. Dahl, *A Preface to Democratic Theory* (Chicago, 1963), Phoenix Books ed., especially pp. 48–50, 90 ff., and 134–135.

[9] David B. Truman, *The Governmental Process* (New York, 1951), *passim*.

[10] Murray Edelman, *The Symbolic Uses of Politics* (Urbana, 1964).

[11] Gabriel Kolko, *Wealth and Power in America* (New York, 1962).

today, having become guilds for the protection of their own shrinking number of members only, and uninterested in general issues of social justice, either domestically or internationally.

I am not out to castigate United States democracy as distinct from other democracies. My point is that the realities of western democracies keep stacking the cards in favor of the influentials and the privileged, who are therefore in a position to keep expanding their power and influence, while the underprivileged are becoming less and less able even to *think* and much less to act politically. The United States is merely the society in which this development has come the farthest, perhaps because the accumulation of private wealth has been and is larger than anywhere else. Ironically and significantly, the United States is also the modern nation most explicitly committed to the political principles of democracy, and has been for the longest time.

Democracy as we know it in the West has become, it would seem, an almost foolproof instrumentality to preserve the political and socioeconomic *status quo*. Orderly political change has become impracticable, I submit, except to the extent that citizens free themselves from their prevailing belief that democracy has already been achieved, and that the laws enacted in their society therefore must be obeyed.

Under conditions of democratic pluralism, an uncritical submission to the rule of law means not only the shunning of violence but also, in effect, the abandonment of all intelligent effort to work effectively for changing the system. For it means agreeing in advance to live by rules in fact operating to forestall the development of democracy in any real sense. These are the rules by which the powerful have become more powerful, and the powerless more emasculated, while only the appearances of democracy have been maintained — an ever more challenging task, incidentally, but a task to which our media of communication and indoctrination so far have proved equal. Thus the discrepancies between our rose-colored perceptions of a government "by the people" and the stark realities of poverty and oppression have kept on growing.

Apparently, stability has kept growing, too. But for the human factors of alienation and desperation, this process might continue indefinitely. But social pathologies were bound to grow below the surface. Not only common crimes but also disorderly attacks against "the system" are likely to occur to an increasing extent. They will be destructive of lives and property but will fail to promote more democratic realities. They may well tempt the present and future American governments to engage in increasingly reckless violence abroad, as a means of seeking to recover national unity, to avoid the alternative of reducing the domestic socioeconomic injustice at the root of national disunity.

V

All organizational leaders are troubled by the fact that, as Philip Selznick has put it, human beings can be recalcitrant rather than pliant instruments in their designs.[12] This goes for statesmen and political leaders as well. Dictators may have to rely on secret police and recurrent terror to prevent revolutions and *coups d'état*. Democratic statesmen in some ways have an easier time of it, as we have seen, as they normally can rely on a broad consensus affirming not only a faith in democracy as an ideal but a belief that democracy has been achieved and that all democratically enacted laws must be obeyed, and that whatever is done by democratically elected statesmen is legitimate. If Texas oilmen in effect are subsidized by all consumers of gasoline; if wars are fought to install aggressive satellite regimes on unwilling foreign nations; and so on: to the extent that people believe democracy has been achieved in their country they tend to become pliant rather than recalcitrant; they can be "managed."

Yet degrees of and extent of pliancy vary with issues and with events. Generally speaking, it is greater the less immediately the individual is affected by particular laws and policies — or rather, the less he is aware of being affected. A policy of supplying faraway foreign dictators with napalm and other achievements of American know-how for use against their rebellious compatriots is readily accepted as being in the national interest on the say-so of a president; it is only when sons and brothers and boy friends and husbands are sent off to kill and to risk their own lives far away that a policy may be questioned or even resisted.

On the other hand, these are precisely the situations in which strong feelings about the inherently superior righteousness of the

---

[12] Philip Selznick, *TVA and the Grass Roots* (Berkeley, 1949), pp. 252–253.

"democratic cause" are most easily developed, and an intelligent dialogue made most difficult.[13] At such times public witness by way of disobedient acts may be the only way to convey to the average citizen even an *awareness* of the existence of strongly felt dissent. In times of hero-worship, resistance to jingo sentiments must perhaps be heroically bold in order to become visible, lest the average citizen either remain unaware of the existence of dissent or else confuse opposition to a war with cowardice.

Ironically, the most striking example of bold and also effective resistance to legislation in recent American history had little to do with heroism. I refer to our experiment with Prohibition during the twenties. Let me stress that this is not an example of civil disobedience as defined in this paper, for the Volstead Act was usually evaded in secret, even if Clarence Darrow is said to have referred to bootleggers as fighters for American liberties and to have predicted the erection of statues to Al Capone in many a public park.[14] My point is simply that our own recent history testifies to the power of popular defiance to change a law.[15] This result is more likely to come about, presumably, the more widespread and determined the defiance, civil or not, of a particular law.

But there is little prospect, alas, that laws and policies supported by far more powerful economic interests — say the Vietnam war, or the continuing inequities in our school systems — can be changed by way of disobedience, civil or not. It takes knowledge, independence of livelihood, and certain skills in interpersonal relations to engage in civil disobedience. True, something has been and more will perhaps be accomplished in race relations, a field in which some acts of disobedience against some southern state laws have become almost respectable elsewhere in the nation, under the impact of a growing concern for America's image abroad in its confrontation with com-

[13] "The first casualty in every shooting war is common sense, and the second is free and open discussion," wrote James Reston in *The New York Times* of February 12, 1965, five days after the beginning of the United States bombing of North Vietnam.

[14] See Harry Elmer Barnes, *Prohibition Versus Civilization* (New York, 1932), pp. 71–72.

[15] In fact, Mr. Darrow is quoted as claiming that this "nullification," as he calls it, is a traditional American way of changing the law, *ibid*. See also Clarence Darrow and Victor S. Yerros, *The Prohibition Mania* (New York, 1927).

munist nations. But issues of war and peace are beyond the reach of most people, as are even more the underlying issues of an economic system which depends on preparation for war and serves to bolster and expand privileges instead of rights.

Our only hope, as I see it, is in education — that is, education toward intellectual and political independence for the individual. We badly need an education that enables and encourages each young citizen to think for himself about the proper aims of government, or the state, and to judge by his own standards to what extent the government of his own nation pursues those aims. Only to that extent should it have his support. To the extent that his government pursues illegitimate aims, in his judgment, or employs means subversive of and menacing to the values a just government must uphold, civil disobedience may well be the right response if acts of protest within the framework of existing legislation would be ineffective or take too long a time.[16] Or it may be the wrong response. My point is that a man is not educated to the point of political responsibility unless he can and will make this decision for himself.

And the most elementary requirement of political education, thus conceived, is liberation from the prevailing pluralist democratic myth, which claims a reverence for the Majesty of the Law — all laws! — on the ground that they have been democratically enacted. It is about time, I think, that political theorists, at least, free themselves from the stultifying grip of this myth, however convenient it may be as a rationalization for political inaction and, in my terms, political irresponsibility.

## VI

In psychological terms, attention to the functions of political opinions for the individual provides an additional ground for arguing that the individual should strive to become sovereign in the choice of his fundamental political commitments.

[16] "What I have to do is see, at any rate, that I do not lend myself to the wrong which I condemn. As for adopting the ways which the state has provided for remedying the evil, I know not of such ways. They take too much time, and a man's life will be gone." Henry David Thoreau, "Civil Disobedience," in his *Walden and Other Writings* (New York, 1950), Modern Library ed., pp. 644–645.

We are aware today of the wide extent to which government policies as well as public opinion are the outcome of neurotic anxieties and fears, which are difficult to diagnose with exactitude and are more difficult still to cure. Modern psychologists and political scientists have established in a general way how political opinions are developed to meet personality needs, and how the individual's ability to cope with anxieties at various levels determines his capacity for rationality and a realistic long-term assessment of his own good as well as the common good.[17] Most people are neurotic and conformist as well as rational, in varying mixtures; enlightened, civilized policies are unlikely to emanate from democratic processes except to the extent that influential leaders become capable of far-sighted rationality. Yet democratic competition for office and power almost invariably strengthens the neurotic aspects and lessens the rational aspects of political behavior; most electoral appeals, especially in times of crises when cool rationality is most needed, are directed to anxieties and paranoid sentiments rather than to reason or enlightened hopes.

The conscientious dissenter who cannot opt out of this system has no easy guide available for determining when to obey and when to disobey the law. There is no general solution to his dilemma, except to urge that he insist on protecting his own sanity and powers of reason, the autonomy of his own social conscience, and his own right to grow toward whatever moral stature or humanity he is capable of achieving. The criteria for concrete decisions to obey or disobey must depend on the nature of each situation, anticipating by careful inquiry and reflection the consequences of either obeying or disobeying; but they must also depend on each moral dissenter's personality and beliefs, especially his beliefs concerning priorities among evils or among good causes.

This open-endedness of the modern dilemma of civil disobedience fits well with Albert Camus's theory of rebellion as an individual responsibility: While only an active and pressing social conscience can bring an individual to full life as a human being, his responsibility for

[17] See especially Daniel Katz, "The Functional Approach to the Study of Attitudes," *Public Opinion Quarterly*, XXIV (1960), 163–204; and M. Brewster Smith, Jerome S. Bruner and Robert W. White, *Opinions and Personality* (New York, 1964). In this section, too, several paragraphs are adapted from my forthcoming article for the *International Encyclopedia, op. cit.*

action or inaction as a social being is strictly individual and lonesome. What is given, according to Camus, is only the immorality or inhumanity of a life of acquiescence in evil; he goes even further and argues that a commitment never to resist violence with violence amounts to such acquiescence, or "bourgeois nihilism." But he offers no guidelines for concrete political decisions.[18]

It is worth noting that legislation to legitimize certain grounds for conscientious objection to military service has tended to excuse only those who could prove they had no rational, politically articulate basis for objecting to becoming soldiers. In the United States as in other western democracies, only a religious basis for objection was recognized at the outset. To the extent that the courts or subsequent legislation have attempted to liberalize the rules, as has happened in the States and in other western nations, the tendency has been to lower the demand for evidence of church membership or religious orthodoxy of some kind, but to keep insisting that objection is no longer legitimate unless it remains apolitical, and condemns all past and future warfare indiscriminately.

For contrast, take Bertrand Russell's response when he was once chided on a British "Brain Trust" program over the BBC for having gone to jail for resisting World War I as a pacifist, while he had supported World War II, and now once again seemed prepared to object to the point of civil disobedience against preparations for a third world war. He said, "I want to pick my wars." This, in my view, is a simple but profound statement of responsible citizenship. What other human right can be more basic than the right to choose what cause, if any, to kill for and to die for?

Yet this, of course, is precisely the kind of human right that no government, dictatorial or democratic, wishes to grant. Legal recognition of politically motivated conscientious objection would hamper the pursuit of "tough" foreign policies in a way that religiously or pacifistically motivated objection will not. Any government can limit the influence of saints; far more dangerous to established privileges and policies are citizens who combine radical dissent with political know-how, or saintly aims like social justice, freedom, or peace with flexible tactics of protest inside and outside the law.

It seems to me that Camus's theory of rebellion has contributed at least two important thoughts toward a modern theory of civil

[18] Albert Camus, *The Rebel* (New York, 1958), especially Part V.

disobedience. One, which has been touched on already, is his view that a rigid adherence to nonviolent means of protest in some situations may amount to acquiescence in continued violence and oppression. For him as for the orthodox pacifists, violence is always the supreme evil; but to him it is in part an empirical question whether violence in given situations can be overcome or reduced by entirely nonviolent means (or, of course, by any combination of violent and nonviolent means). In my view and in Max Weber's terminology, he argues that an ethics of *a priori* duty must be supplanted by an ethic of responsibility, a responsibility for anticipating as full a range of consequences of alternative means of action as experience and research can establish, if there is time, before deciding on a course of action, nonviolent or in part violent.

It is precisely because the consequences of revolutionary activity are likely to be both violent and to a large extent unpredictable (especially with respect to the extent and duration of acts of violence) that Camus is so strongly in favor of rebellion, in his sense, as an alternative to revolution. His rebel is the piecemeal revolutionary — the politically responsible citizen who is committed to fight violence and oppression by the most *economic* means, i.e., he seeks to avoid the use of violence whenever possible, and above all to avoid the use of remedies that could be worse than the present evil — worse in terms of degrees and extent of violence suffered. With respect to his aims, Camus's rebel is related to the revolutionary in that he will be satisfied with nothing less than complete justice or a complete end to oppression, but he is apt to be less confident that this utopia can ever be fully realized. When it comes to his choice of means, Camus's rebel is identical with the type of responsible citizen extolled in these pages: the person who honors not the Rule of Law so much as the Rule of Justice, and who is prepared to support or commit civil disobedience against oppressive government or legislation.

If Camus has helped draw the demarcation line and develop the rationale for modern civil disobedience, as distinguished from revolutionary activity,[19] he has also, as a second contribution to a modern

---

[19] To distinguish the two concepts is not to say that the same person or movement cannot at the same time believe in civil disobedience and in revolution. For example, one may have proximate or short-range aims to be served by civil disobedience and yet believe in eventual revolution; or one may believe in revolution as an ultimate resort if results of civil disobedience are too limited or too slow.

theory of civil disobedience, been the first to articulate the psychological necessity of being a rebel, or a citizen in principle prepared to commit civil disobedience against oppressive laws and policies, if one is to achieve one's full human stature. Rebellion, as a manifestation of revulsion against injustice, is to Camus an essential dimension of the free man's life; only men who remain too neurotic, too stymied to develop a consciousness of their own humanity, their own solidarity with all men, can remain indifferent and passive when confronted with victims or perpetrators of injustice. In a cruelly competitive society, perhaps most men remain stymied, or in Camus's sense less than fully human; yet at all times there have been rebels, believers in obedience to their own principles as a higher necessity than obedience to the powers that be, or the laws with which these powers guard their interests. I have argued in this chapter that only a good supply of such individuals can help us come closer to the achievement of democracy; Camus argues that only such qualities in a man can help him achieve his own individuality as well as his own humanity.

But in our time, with its unprecedented technology, capable of bureaucratizing acts of murder, and of dehumanizing men who may make decisions about life or death for millions of fellow human beings, the more effective education of an expanding supply of rebels may well be our civilization's last hope of survival. Without thousands of young men able and willing to disobey calls to contribute to moral monstrosities like, for example, American warfare in Vietnam, where is there hope that the bureaucratized, consensus-manufacturing forces of destruction of the modern super-powers — the Leviathans of our time — can be checked before our civilization becomes engulfed in a third world war?

In the name of democracy a new kind of servitude has developed in the West. Witness the hundreds of thousands of men who, educationally unequipped to judge for themselves, have been shipped to a far-off land to kill and perhaps die for what they cheerfully believe is the cause of democracy, or at any rate their own nation's best interests. And witness the many admonitions to dissenters against the war policy that they limit their protests to legal channels, again in the name of democracy, lest its rules of order be violated. Naturally, only harmless, easily manageable forms of protest are desired; violence in contests for power at home is inveighed against with democratic moral fervor by the same leaders who look to violence as almost the only way to engage in contests for power abroad. Advocacy of force and violence at home is condemned, and so is advocacy *against* use of force and violence abroad, for both kinds of advocacy could menace the status quo.

Let me conclude by returning to the most fundamental argument of this essay: governments exist for the purpose of establishing and defending human rights, with the most basic rights, like protection against violence and starvation, taking precedence over less basic rights. The common good, according to this view, hinges on the good of the least favored individuals, taking into account also the prospects for those not yet born.

This or any similar type of basis for political obligation directed to the ends of politics, which relegates not only democracy but also respect for the law in all its alleged majesty to the status of means, takes the vestiges of the role of subject out of the role of citizen. It substitutes an ethics of individual responsibility for the probable results of one's political behavior, including law-abiding as well as legally obligated behavior, for an ethics of duty to subordinate conscience, knowledge, and individual judgment to existing legal norms, government directives, or a majority vote.

The judgments at Nuremberg and the wide attention given to the Eichmann trial in Jerusalem have increased acceptance for the view that the autonomy of the individual conscience is a vital resource in our modern technological and bureaucratized civilization. The "essence of totalitarian government, and perhaps the nature of every bureaucracy," writes Hannah Arendt, "is to make functionaries and mere cogs in the administrative machinery out of men, and thus to dehumanize them."[20] "Each time we obey an order from higher up, without evaluating and judging it in moral terms, there is the Eichmann within ourselves bending his neck," writes a reviewer of Arendt's book, and further observes: "Eichmann was neither intellectually nor morally worse equipped than most people . . . his fault was that he did not feel personally responsible for what his government did. In this respect he is not unique."[21]

The human race may never fully achieve democracy; no large

[20] *Eichmann in Jerusalem* (New York, 1963), p. 289.
[21] Jens Bjorneboe, "Eichmann i varre hjerter" ("Eichmann in our hearts"), *Orientering, Oslo* (December 18, 1965).

nation is likely to come very close to this exacting ideal, although
I believe it can be approximated in the foreseeable future in university
communities and perhaps in some other local communities. What is
important, if we value freedom for all on the basis of justice, is that
we move toward rather than away from democracy. For this purpose
our educational institutions must try to produce, I submit, men and
women less like Eichmann, and more like his opposite, more like
Camus's rebel. The rebel, or the believer in civil disobedience in the
fight against oppression, is to this writer the model of the responsible
citizen who wishes to promote democracy. What we don't need, in
my view, and what we are now oversupplied with, is the cheerful,
loyal, pliable, law-abiding, basically privatist type of citizen extolled
not only in our high school civics texts but in our professional civic
culture and end of ideology literature as well.

---

# On Violence

### ROBERT PAUL WOLFF

Everything I shall say in this essay has been said before, and much
of it seems to me to be obvious as well as unoriginal. I offer two
excuses for laying used goods before you. In the first place, I think
that what I have to say about violence is true. Now, there are many
ways to speak falsehood and only one way to speak truth. It follows,
as Kierkegaard pointed out, that the truth is likely to become boring.
On a subject as ancient and much discussed as ours today, we may
probably assume that a novel — and, hence, interesting — view of
violence is likely to be false.

But truth is not my sole excuse, for the subject before us suffers
from the same difficulty that Kant discerned in the area of metaphysics. After refuting the various claims that had been made to
transcendent rational knowledge of things-in-themselves, Kant remarked that the refutations had no lasting psychological effect on

From the *Journal of Philosophy* (October, 1969). Reprinted by permission.

true believers. The human mind, he concluded, possessed a natural dispostion to metaphysical speculation, which philosophy must perpetually keep in check. Somewhat analogously, men everywhere are prone to certain beliefs about the legitimacy of political authority, even though their beliefs are as groundless as metaphysical speculations. The most sophisticated of men persist in supposing that some valid distinction can be made between legitimate and illegitimate commands, on the basis of which they can draw a line, for example, between mere violence and the legitimate use of force. This lingering superstition is shared by those dissenters who call police actions or ghetto living conditions "violent"; for they are merely advancing competing legitimacy claims.

I shall set forth and defend *three* propositions about violence:

*First:* The concept of violence is inherently confused, as is the correlative concept of nonviolence; these and related concepts depend for their meaning in political discussions on the fundamental notion of legitimate authority, which is also inherently incoherent.

*Second:* It follows that a number of familiar questions are also confusions to which no coherent answers could ever be given, such as: when it is permissible to resort to violence in politics; whether the black movement and the student movement should be nonviolent; and whether anything good in politics is ever accomplished by violence.

*Finally:* The dispute over violence and nonviolence in contemporary American politics is ideological rhetoric designed either to halt change and justify the existing distribution of power and privilege or else to hasten change and justify a total redistribution of power and privilege.

Let us begin with the first proposition, which is essential to my entire discussion.

## I

The fundamental concepts of political philosophy are the concepts of power and authority.[1] Power in general is the ability to make

---

[1] What follows is a summary of analyses I have published elsewhere. The concept of political power is treated in Chapter III of *The Poverty of Liberalism* (Boston: Beacon Press, 1968). The concepts of legitimacy and authority are analyzed in my essay on "Political Philosophy" in Arthur Danto, ed., *The Harper Guide to Philosophy* (New York: Harper & Row, 1970).

and enforce decisions. Political power is the ability to make and enforce decisions about matters of major social importance. Thus the ability to dispose of my private income as I choose is a form of power, whereas the ability to make and enforce a decision about the disposition of some sizable portion of the tax receipts of the federal government is a form of *political* power. (So too is the ability to direct the decisions of a large private corporation; for the exercise of political power is not confined to the sphere of government.) A complete analysis of the concept of political power would involve a classification both of the means employed in the enforcing of decisions and of the scope and variety of questions about which decisions can be made.[2] It would also require an examination of the kinds of opposition against which the decision could be enforced. There is a very considerable difference between the ability a parliamentary majority has to enforce its decisions against the will of the minority and the ability of a rebel military clique to enforce its decisions against the Parliament as a whole.

Authority, by contrast with power, is not an ability but a right. It is the right to command and, correlatively, the right to be obeyed. Claims to authority are made in virtually every area of social life, and, in a remarkably high proportion of cases, the claims are accepted and acquiesced in by those over whom they are made. Parents claim the right to be obeyed by their children; husbands until quite recently claimed the right to be obeyed by their wives; popes claim the right to be obeyed by the laity and clergy; and of course, most notably, virtually all existing governments claim the right to be obeyed by their subjects.

A claim to authority must be sharply differentiated both from a threat or enticement and from a piece of advice. When the state commands, it usually threatens punishment for disobedience, and it may even on occasion offer a reward for compliance, but the command cannot be reduced to the mere threat or reward. What characteristically distinguishes a state from an occupying army or private party is its insistence, either explicit or implicit, on its *right* to be obeyed. By the same token, an authoritative command is not a mere recommendation. Authority says, "Do this!" not, "Let me suggest this for your consideration."

[2] See Robert A. Dahl, "The Concept of Power," *Behavioral Science* (July 1957), for just such a classification.

Claims to authority have been defended on a variety of grounds, most prominent among which are the appeal to God, to tradition, to expertise, to the laws of history, and to the consent of those commanded. We tend to forget that John Locke thought it worth while to devote the first of his *Two Treatises on Civil Government* to the claim that Europe's monarchs held their authority by right of primogenitural descent from Adam. It is common today to give lip service to the theory that authority derives from the consent of the governed, but most of us habitually accord *some* weight to any authority claim issuing from a group of men who regularly control the behavior of a population in a territory, particularly if the group tricks itself out with flags, uniforms, courts of law, and printed regulations.

Not all claims to authority are justified. Indeed, I shall suggest shortly that few if any are. Nevertheless, men regularly accept the authority claims asserted against them, and so we must distinguish a descriptive from a normative sense of the term. Let us use the term *"de facto* authority" to refer to *the ability to get one's authority claims accepted by those against whom they are asserted. "De jure* authority," then, will refer to *the right to command and to be obeyed.* Obviously, the concept of de jure authority is primary, and the concept of de facto authority is derivative.

Thus understood, de facto authority is a form of power, for it is a means by which its possessor can enforce his decisions. Indeed, as Max Weber — from whom much of this analysis is taken — has pointed out, de facto authority is the *principal* means on which states rely to carry out their decisions. Threats and inducements play an exceedingly important role in the enforcement of political decisions, to be sure, but a state that must depend upon them entirely will very soon suffer a crippling reduction in its effectiveness, which is to say, in its political power. Modern states especially require for the successful prosecution of their programs an extremely high level of coordination of the behavior of large numbers of individuals. The myth of legitimacy is the only efficient means available to the state for achieving that coordination.

*Force* is the ability to work some change in the world by the expenditure of physical effort. A man may root up a tree, move a stalled car, drive a nail, or restrain another man, *by force.* Force, in and of itself, is morally neutral. Physically speaking, there may be very little difference between the physical effort of a doctor who resets a dislocated shoulder and that of the ruffian who dislocated it.

Sometimes, of course, force is used to work some change in the body of another man — to punch him, shoot him, take out his appendix, hold his arms, or cut his hair. But there is in principle no significant distinction between these uses of force and those uses which involve changing some other part of the world about which he cares. A man who slips into a parking place for which I am heading inflicts an injury on me roughly as great as if he had jostled me in a crowd or stepped on my toe. If he destroys a work of art on which I have lavished my most intense creative efforts, he may harm me more than a physical assault would.

Force is a means to power, but it is not of course a guarantee of power. If I wish to elicit hard work from my employees, I can threaten them with the lash or tempt them with bonuses — both of which are employments of force — but if my workers prefer not to comply, my threats and inducements may be fruitless. It is a commonplace both of domestic and of international politics that the mere possession of a monopoly of force is no guarantee of political power. Those who fail to grasp this truth are repeatedly frustrated by the baffling inability of the strong to impose their will upon the weak.

There are, so far as I can see, *three* means or instruments by which power is exercised — three ways, that is to say, in which men enforce or carry out their social decisions. The first is *force,* the ability to rearrange the world in ways that other men find appealing or distasteful. In modern society, money is of course the principal measure, exchange medium, and symbol of force. The second instrument of power is de facto authority — the ability to elicit obedience, as opposed to mere compliance, from others. De facto authority frequently accrues to those with a preponderance of force, for men are fatally prone to suppose that he who can compel compliance deserves obedience. But, de facto authority does not reduce to the possession of a preponderance of force, for men habitually obey commands they know could not effectively be enforced. The third instrument of power is social opinion, or what might be called the "symbolic" use of force. When a runner competes in a race, he may want the first-prize money or the commercial endorsements that will come to the winner, or he may even just like blue ribbons — but he may also want the acclaim of the fans. Now, that acclaim is expressed by certain uses of force — by clapping of hands and cheering, which are physical acts. But its value to the runner is symbolic; he cherishes it as an expression of approval, not merely as a pleasing sound. To say that man is a social creature is not merely to say that he hangs out in groups, nor even to say that he engages in collective and cooperative enterprises for self-interested purposes; it is most importantly to say that he values symbolic interactions with other men and is influenced by them as well as by the ordinary exercise of force and by claims of authority. This point is important for our discussion, for, as we shall see, many persons who shrink from the use of force as an instrument of political power have no compunctions about the use of social opinion or what I have called the "symbolic" use of force. Anyone who has observed a progressive classroom run by a teacher with scruples of this sort will know that a day "in coventry" can be a far crueler punishment for an unruly ten-year old than a sharp rap on the knuckles with a ruler.

We come, finally, to the concept of violence. Strictly speaking, *violence is the illegitimate or unauthorized use of force to effect decisions against the will or desire of others.* Thus, murder is an act of violence, but capital punishment *by a legitimate state* is not; theft or extortion is violent, but the collection of taxes *by a legitimate state* is not. Clearly, on this interpretation the concept of violence is normative as well as descriptive, for it involves an implicit appeal to the principle of de jure legitimate authority. There is an associated sense of the term which is purely descriptive, relying on the descriptive notion of de facto authority. Violence in this latter sense is the use of force in ways that are proscribed or unauthorized by those who are generally accepted as the legitimate authorities in the territory. Descriptively speaking, the attack on Hitler's life during the second World War was an act of violence, but one might perfectly well deny that it was violent in the strict sense, on the grounds that Hitler's regime was illegitimate. On similar grounds, it is frequently said that police behavior toward workers or ghetto dwellers or demonstrators is violent even when it is clearly within the law, for the authority issuing the law is illegitimate.

It is common, but I think wrong-headed, to restrict the term "violence" to uses of force that involve bodily interference or the direct infliction of physical injury. Carrying a dean out of his office is said to be violent, but not seizing his office when he is absent and locking him out. Physically tearing a man's wallet from his pocket is "violent," but swindling him out of the same amount of money is not. There is a natural enough basis for this distinction. Most of us value our lives and physical well-being above other goods that we enjoy, and we tend therefore to view attacks or threats on our person as different in kind from other sorts of harm we might suffer. Nevertheless, the distinction is not sufficiently sharp to be of any analytical use, and, as we shall see later, it usually serves the ideological purpose of ruling out, as immoral or politically illegitimate, the only instrument of power that is available to certain social classes.

In its strict or normative sense, then, the concept of political violence depends upon the concept of de jure, or legitimate authority. If there is no such thing as legitimate political authority, then it is impossible to distinguish between legitimate and illegitimate uses of force. Now, of course, under any circumstances, we can distinguish between right and wrong, justified and unjustified, uses of force. Such a distinction belongs to moral philosophy in general, and our choice of the criteria by which we draw the distinction will depend on our theory of value and obligation. But the distinctive political concept of violence can be given a coherent meaning *only* by appeal to a doctrine of legitimate political authority.

On the basis of a lengthy reflection upon the concept of de jure legitimate authority, I have come to the conclusion that philosophical anarchism is true. That is to say, I believe that there is not, and there could not be, a state that has a right to command and whose subjects have a binding obligation to obey. I have defended this view in detail elsewhere, and I can only indicate here the grounds of my conviction.[3] Briefly, I think it can be shown that every man has a fundamental duty to be autonomous, in Kant's sense of the term. Each of us must make himself the author of his actions and take responsibility for them by refusing to act save on the basis of reasons he can see for himself to be good. Autonomy, thus understood, is in direct opposition to obedience, which is submission to the will of another, irrespective of reasons. Following Kant's usage, political obedience is heteronymy of the will.

Now, political theory offers us one great argument designed to make the autonomy of the individual compatible with submission to the putative authority of the state. In a democracy, it is claimed, the citizen is both law-giver and law-obeyer. Since he shares in the authorship of the laws, he submits to his own will in obeying them, and hence is autonomous, not heteronymous.

[3] See "Political Philosophy," in Danto, *op. cit.*

If this argument were valid, it would provide a genuine ground for a distinction between violent and nonviolent political actions. Violence would be a use of force proscribed by the laws or executive authority of a genuinely democratic state. The only possible justification of illegal or extralegal political acts would be a demonstration of the illegitimacy of the state, and this in turn would involve showing that the commands of the state were not expressions of the will of the people.

But the classic defense of democracy is *not* valid. For a variety of reasons, neither majority rule nor any other method of making decisions in the absence of unanimity can be shown to preserve the autonomy of the individual citizens. In a democracy, as in any state, obedience is heteronymy. The autonomous man is of necessity an anarchist. Consequently, there is no valid *political* criterion for the justified use of force. Legality is, by itself, no justification. Now, of course, there are all manner of utilitarian arguments for submitting to the state and its agents, even if the state's claim to legitimacy is unfounded. The laws may command actions that are in fact morally obligatory or whose effects promise to be beneficial. Widespread submission to law may bring about a high level of order, regularity, and predictability in social relationships which is valuable independently of the particular character of the acts commanded. But in and of themselves, the acts of police and the commands of legislatures have no peculiar legitimacy or sanction. Men everywhere and always impute authority to established governments, and they are always wrong to do so.

## II

The foregoing remarks are quite banal, to be sure. Very few serious students of politics will maintain either the democratic theory of legitimate authority or any alternatives to it. Nevertheless, like post-theological, demythologized Protestants who persist in raising prayers to a God they no longer believe in, modern men go on exhibiting a superstitious belief in the authority of the state. Consider, for example, a question now much debated: when is it permissible to resort to violence in politics? If "violence" is taken to mean an *unjustified* use of force, then the answer to the question is obviously *never*. If the use of force were permissible, it would not, by definition, be violence, and if it were violent, it would not, by definition, be permissible. If "violence" is taken in the strict sense to mean "an illegitimate or unauthorized use of force," then *every* political act, whether by private parties or by agents of the state, is violent, for there is no such thing as legitimate authority. If "violence" is construed in the restricted sense as "bodily interference or the direct infliction of physical harm," then the obvious but correct rule is to resort to violence when less harmful or costly means fail, providing always that the balance of good and evil produced is superior to that promised by any available alternative.

These answers are all trivial, but that is precisely my point. Once the concept of violence is seen to rest on the unfounded distinction between legitimate and illegitimate political authority, the question of the appropriateness of violence simply dissolves. It is mere superstition to describe a policeman's beating of a helpless suspect as "an excessive use of force" while characterizing an attack by a crowd on the policeman as "a resort to violence." The implication of such a distinction is that the policeman, as the duly appointed representative of a legitimate government, has a right to use physical force, although no right to use "excessive" force, whereas the crowd of private citizens has no right at all to use even moderate physical force. But there are no legitimate governments, hence no special rights attaching to soldiers, policemen, magistrates, or other law-enforcement agents, hence no coherent distinction between violence and the legitimate use of force.

Consider, as a particular example, the occupation of buildings and the student strike at Columbia University during April and May of 1968. The consequences of those acts have not yet played themselves out, but I think certain general conclusions can be drawn. First, the total harm done by the students and their supporters was very small in comparison with the good results that were achieved. A month of classwork was lost, along with many tempers and a good deal of sleep. Someone — it is still not clear who — burned the research notes of a history professor, an act which, I am happy to say, produced a universal revulsion shared even by the SDS. In the following year, a number of classes were momentarily disrupted by SDS activists in an unsuccessful attempt to repeat the triumph of the previous spring.

Against this, what benefits flowed from the protest? A reactionary and thoroughly unresponsive administration was forced to resign; an all-university Senate of students, professors, and administrators was created, the first such body at Columbia. A callous and antisocial policy of university expansion into the surrounding neighborhood was reversed; some at least of the university's ties with the military were loosened or severed; and an entire community of students and professors were forced to confront moral and political issues which till then they had managed to ignore.

Could these benefits have been won at less cost? Considering the small cost of the uprising, the question seems to me a bit finicky; nevertheless, the answer is clearly, No. The history of administrative intransigence and faculty apathy at Columbia makes it quite clear that nothing short of a dramatic act such as the seizure of buildings could have deposed the university administration and produced a university senate. In retrospect, the affair seems to have been a quite prudent and restrained use of force.

Assuming this assessment to be correct, it is tempting to conclude, "In the Columbia case, violence was justified." But this conclusion is *totally wrong,* for it implies that a line can be drawn between legitimate and illegitimate forms of protest, the latter being justified only under special conditions and when all else has failed. We would all agree, I think, that, under a dictatorship, men have the right to defy the state or even to attack its representatives when their interests are denied and their needs ignored — the only rule that binds them is the general caution against doing more harm than they accomplish good. My purpose here is simply to argue that a modern industrial democracy, whatever merits it may have, is in this regard no different from a dictatorship. No special authority attaches to the laws of a representative, majoritarian state; it is only superstition and the myth of legitimacy that invests the judge, the policeman, or the official with an exclusive right to the exercise of certain kinds of force.

In the light of these arguments, it should be obvious that I see no merit in the doctrine of nonviolence, nor do I believe that any special and complex justification is needed for what is usually called "civil disobedience." A commitment to nonviolence can be understood in two different senses, depending on the interpretation given to the concept of violence. If violence is understood in the strict sense as the political use of force in ways proscribed by a legitimate government, then of course the doctrine of nonviolence depends upon the assumption that there *are* or *could be* legitimate governments. Since I believe this assumption to be false, I can attribute no coherent meaning to this first conception of nonviolence.

If violence is understood, on the other hand, as the use of force to interfere with someone in a direct, bodily way or to injure him physically, then the doctrine of nonviolence is merely a subjective queasiness having no moral rationale. When you occupy the seats at a lunch counter for hours on end, thereby depriving the proprietor of the profits he would have made on ordinary sales during that time, you are taking money out of his pocket quite as effectively as if you had robbed his till or smashed his stock. If you persist in the sit-in until he goes into debt, loses his lunch counter, and takes a job as a day laborer, then you have done him a much greater injury than would be accomplished by a mere beating in a dark alley. He may deserve to be ruined, of course, but, if so, then he probably also deserves to be beaten. A penchant for such indirect coercion as a boycott or a sit-in is morally questionable, for it merely leaves the dirty work to the bank that forecloses on the mortgage or the policeman who carries out the eviction. Emotionally, the commitment to nonviolence is frequently a severely repressed expression of extreme hostility akin to the mortifications and self-flagellations of religious fanatics. Enough testimony has come from Black novelists and psychiatrists to make it clear that the philosophy of nonviolence is, for the American Negro, what Nietzsche called a "slave morality" — the principal difference is that, in traditional Christianity, God bears the guilt for inflicting pain on the wicked; in the social gospel, the law acts as the scourge.

The doctrine of civil disobedience is an American peculiarity growing out of the conflict between the authority claims of the state and the directly contradictory claims of individual conscience. In a futile attempt to deny and affirm the authority of the state simultaneously, a number of conscientious dissenters have claimed the right to disobey what they believe to be immoral laws, so long as they are prepared to submit to punishment by the state. A willingness to go to jail for one's beliefs is widely viewed in this country as evidence of moral sincerity, and even as a sort of argument for the position one is defending.

Now, tactically speaking, there is much to be said for legal martyrdom. As tyrannical governments are perpetually discovering, the sight of one's leader nailed to a cross has a marvelously bracing effect on the faithful members of a dissident sect. When the rulers are afflicted by the very principles they are violating, even the *threat* of self-sacrifice may force a government to its knees. But leaving tactics aside, no one has any moral obligation whatsoever to resist an unjust government openly rather than clandestinely. Nor has anyone a duty to invite and then to suffer unjust punishment. The choice is simple: if the law is right, follow it. If the law is wrong, evade it.

I think it is possible to understand why conscientious and morally concerned men should feel a compulsion to seek punishment for acts they genuinely believe to be right. Conscience is the echo of society's voice within us. The men of strongest and most independent conscience are, in a manner of speaking, just those who have most completely internalized this social voice, so that they hear and obey its commands even when no policeman compels their compliance. Ironically, it is these same men who are most likely to set themselves against the government in the name of ideals and principles to which they feel a higher loyalty. When a society violates the very principles it claims to hold, these men of conscience experience a terrible conflict. They are deeply committed to the principles society has taught them, principles they have truly come to believe. But they can be true to their beliefs only by setting themselves against the laws of the very society that has been their teacher and with whose authority they identify themselves. Such a conflict never occurs in men of weak conscience, who merely obey the law, however much it violates the moral precepts they have only imperfectly learned.

The pain of the conflict is too great to be borne; somehow, it must be alleviated. If the commitment to principle is weak, the individual submits, though he feels morally unclean for doing so. If the identification with society is weak, he rejects the society and becomes alienated, perhaps identifying with some other society. But if both conscience and identification are too strong to be broken, the only solution is to expiate the guilt by seeking social punishment for the breach of society's laws. Oddly enough, the expiation, instead of bringing them back into the fold of law-obeyers, makes it psychologically all the easier for them to continue their defiance of the state.

## III

The foregoing conclusions seem to reach far beyond what the argument warrants. The classical theory of political authority may indeed be inadequate; it may even be that the concept of legitimate authority is incoherent; but surely *some* genuine distinction can be drawn between a politics of reason, rules, and compromise on the one hand, and the resort to violent conflict on the other! Are the acts of a rioting mob different only in degree from the calm and orderly processes of a duly constituted court of law? Such a view partakes more of novelty than of truth!

Unless I very much misjudge my audience, most readers will respond roughly in this manner. There may be a few still willing to break a lance for sovereignty and legitimate authority, and a few, I hope, who agree immediately with what I have said, but the distinction between violence and nonviolence in politics is too familiar to be so easily discarded. In this third section of my essay, therefore, I shall try to discover what makes the distinction so plausible, even though it is — I insist — unfounded.

The customary distinction between violent and nonviolent modes of social interaction seems to me to rest on *two* genuine distinctions: the first is the *subjective* distinction between the regular or accepted and the irregular or unexpected uses of force; the second is the *objective* distinction between those interests which are central or vital to an individual and those which are secondary or peripheral.

Consider first the subjective distinction between regular and irregular uses of force in social interactions. It seems perfectly appropriate to us that a conflict between two men who desire the same piece of land should be settled in favor of the one who can pull more money out of his pocket. We consider it regular and orderly that the full weight of the police power of the state be placed behind that settlement in order to ensure that nothing upset it. On the other hand, we consider it violent and disorderly to resolve the dispute by a fist fight or a duel. Yet what is the difference between the use of money, which is one kind of force, and the use of fists, which is another? Well, if we do not appeal to the supposed legitimacy of financial transactions or to the putative authority of the law, then the principal difference is that we are accustomed to settling disputes with dollars and we are no longer accustomed to settling them with fists.

Imagine how barbaric, how unjust, how *violent,* it must seem, to someone unfamiliar with the beauties of capitalism, that a man's ability to obtain medical care for his children should depend solely on the contingency that some other man can make a profit from his productive labor! Is the Federal Government's seizure of my resources for the purpose of killing Asian peasants less violent than a bandit's extortion of tribute at gunpoint? Yet we are accustomed to the one and unaccustomed to the other.

The objective distinction between central and peripheral interests also shapes our conception of what is violent in politics. When my peripheral or secondary interests are at stake in a conflict, I quite naturally consider only a moderate use of force to be justified. Anything more, I will probably call "violence." What I tend to forget, of course, is that other parties to the conflict may find their primary interests challenged and, hence, may have a very different view of what is and is not violent. In the universities, for example, most of the student challenges have touched only on the peripheral interests of professors. No matter what is decided about ROTC, curriculum, the disposition of the endowment, or Black studies, the typical philosophy professor's life will be largely unchanged. His tenure, salary, working conditions, status, and family life remain the same. Hence he is likely to take a tolerant view of building seizures and sit-ins. But let a classroom be disrupted, and he cries out that violence has no place on campus. What he means is that force has been used in a way that touches one of his deeper concerns.

The concept of violence serves as a rhetorical device for proscribing those political uses of force which one considers inimical to one's central interests. Since different social groups have different central interests and can draw on different kinds of force, it follows that there are conflicting definitions of violence. Broadly speaking, in the United States today, there are four conceptions of violence corresponding to four distinct socioeconomic classes.

The first view is associated with the established financial and political interests in the country. It identifies the violent with the illegal, and condemns all challenges to the authority of the state and all assaults on the rights of property as beyond the limits of permissible politics. The older segments of the business community adopt this view, along with the military establishment and the local elites of middle America. Robert Taft was once a perfect symbol of this sector of opinion.

The second view is associated with the affluent, educated, technical and professional middle class in America, together with the new, rapidly growing, future-oriented sectors of the economy, such as the communications industry, electronics, etc. They accept, even welcome, dissent, demonstration, ferment, and — within limits — attacks on property in ghetto areas. They look with favor on civil disobedience and feel at ease with extralegal tactics of social change. Their interests are identified with what is new in American society, and they are confident of coming out on top in the competition for wealth and status within an economy built on the principle of reward for profitable performance.

The "liberals," as this group is normally called, can afford to encourage modes of dissent or disruption that do not challenge the economic and social arrangements on which their success is based. They will defend rent strikes, grape boycotts, or lunch-counter sit-ins with the argument that unemployment and starvation are a form of violence also. Since they are themselves in competition with the older elite for power and prestige, they tend to view student rebels and black militants as their allies, up to the point at which their own interests are attacked. But when tactics are used that threaten their positions in universities, in corporations, or in affluent suburbs, then the liberals cry *violence* also, and call for the police. A poignant example of this class is the liberal professor who cheers the student rebels as they seize the Administration building and then recoils in horror at the demand that he share his authority to determine curriculum and decide promotions.

The third view of violence is that held by working-class and lower middle-class Americans, those most often referred to as the "white backlash." They perceive the principal threat to their interests as coming from the bottom class of ghetto dwellers, welfare clients and nonunionized laborers who demand more living space, admission to union jobs with union wages, and a larger share of the social product. To this hard-pressed segment of American society, "violence" means street crime, ghetto riots, civil-rights marches into all-white neighborhoods, and antiwar attacks on the patriotic symbols of constituted authority with which backlash America identifies. Studies of the petty bourgeoisie in Weimar Germany suggest, and George Wallace's presidential campaign of 1968 confirms, that the lower middle class, when it finds itself pressed between inflationary prices and demands from the lower class, identifies its principal enemy as the lower class. So we find the classic political alliance of old established wealth with right-wing populist elements, both of which favor a

repressive response to attacks on authority and a strong governmental policy toward the "violence" of demands for change.

The fourth view of violence is the revolutionary counterdefinition
put forward by the outclass and its sympathizers within the liberal
wing of the established order. Two complementary rhetorical devices
are employed. First, the connotation of the term "violence" is accepted,
but the application of the term is reversed: police are violent, not
rioters; employers, not strikers; the American army, not the enemy.
In this way, an attack is mounted on the government's claim to possess
the right to rule. Secondly, the denotation of the term is held constant
and the connotation reversed. Violence is good, not bad; legitimate,
not illegitimate. It is, in Stokely Carmichael's great rhetorical flourish,
"as American as cherry pie." Since the outclass of rebels has scant
access to the instruments of power used by established social classes
— wealth, law, police power, legislation — it naturally seeks to
legitimize the riots, harassments, and street crime which are its only
weapons. Equally naturally, the rest of society labels such means
"violent" and suppresses them.

In the complex class struggle for wealth and power in America,
each of us must decide for himself which group he will identify with.
It is not my purpose here to urge one choice rather than another. My
sole aim is to argue that the concept of violence has no useful role
to play in the deliberations leading to that choice. Whatever other
considerations of utility and social justice one appeals to, no weight
should be given to the view that *some* uses of force are prima facie
ruled out as illegitimate and hence "violent" or that other uses of force
are prima facie ruled in as legitimate, or legal. Furthermore, in the
advancement of dissenting positions by illegal means, no special moral
merit attaches to the avoiding, as it were, of body contact. Physical
harm may be among the most serious injuries that can be done to an
opponent, but, if so, it differs only in degree and not in kind from the
injuries inflicted by so-called "nonviolent" techniques of political
action.

## IV

The myth of legitimate authority is the secular reincarnation of
that religious superstition which has finally ceased to play a significant

role in the affairs of men. Like Christianity, the worship of the state has its fundamentalists, its revisionists, its ecumenicists (or world-Federalists), and its theological rationale. The philosophical anarchist is the atheist of politics. I began my discussion with the observation that the belief in legitimacy, like the penchant for transcendent metaphysics, is an ineradicable irrationality of the human experience. However, the slow extinction of religious faith over the past two centuries may encourage us to hope that in time anarchism, like atheism, will become the accepted conviction of enlightened and rational men.

# The Idea of a Right to Revolution

## Ethics and Revolution

### HERBERT MARCUSE

I propose to discuss the relation between ethics and revolution by taking as guidance the following question: can a revolution be justified as right, as good, perhaps even as necessary, and justified not merely in political terms (as expedient for certain interests) but in ethical terms, that is to say, justified with respect to the human condition as such, to the potential of man in a given historical situation? This means that ethical terms such as "right" or "good" will be applied to political and social movements, with the hypothesis that the moral evaluation of such movements is (in a sense to be defined) more than subjective, more than a matter of preference. Under this hypothesis, "good" and "right" would mean serving to establish, to promote, or to extend human freedom and happiness in a commonwealth, regardless of the form of government. This preliminary definition combines individual and personal, private and public welfare. It tries to recapture a basic concept of classical political philosophy which has been all too often repressed, namely, that the end of government is not only the greatest possible freedom, but also the greatest possible happiness of man, that is to say, a life without fear and misery, and a life in peace.

Here we encounter the first vexing question, namely, who deter-

From *Ethics and Society* by Richard T. De George. Copyright © 1966 by The Kansas University Endowment Association. Reprinted by permission of Doubleday & Company, Inc.

mines, who can and by what right determine the general interest of a commonwealth, and thereby determine the range and limits of individual freedom and happiness, and the sacrifices imposed upon individual freedom and happiness in the name and on behalf of the commonwealth? For as long as the general and individual welfare do not immediately coincide, the latter will be *made* to conform with the former. And if we ask this question we are at once confronted with an equally serious and embarrassing problem: granted even that freedom is not only an individual and private affair, that it is rather determined by the society, by the state in which we live, what about happiness? Is the happiness of an individual his own private affair, or is it too, in a very definite sense, subject to the limitations and even the definitions imposed upon it by a commonwealth? The extreme position that human happiness is and must remain individual and the individual's own affair cannot be defended if we give it only a few minutes' thought. There are certainly modes and types of individual happiness which cannot be tolerated by any kind of commonwealth. It is perfectly possible — as a matter of fact we know it to be the fact — that the people who were the master torturers in the Hitler concentration camps were often quite happy doing their job. This is one of the many cases of individual happiness where we do not hesitate to say that it is not merely the individual himself who can be and who can remain the judge of his own happiness. We assume a tribunal which is (actually or morally) entitled to "define" individual happiness.

Now after these preliminary clarifications, let me define what I mean by "revolution." By "revolution" I understand the overthrow of a legally established government and constitution by a social class or movement with the aim of altering the social as well as the political structure. This definition excludes all military coups, palace revolutions, and "preventive" counterrevolutions (such as Fascism and Nazism) because they do not alter the basic social structure. If we define revolution in this way we can move one step forward by saying that such a radical and qualitative change implies violence. Peaceful revolutions, if there are such things, if there can be such things, do not present any problem. We can therefore reformulate the initial question by asking: is the revolutionary use of violence justifiable as a means for establishing or promoting human freedom and happiness? The question implies a very important assumption, namely, that there are rational criteria for determining the possibilities of human freedom and happiness available to a society in a specific historical situation. If there are no such rational criteria, it would be impossible to evaluate a political movement in terms of its chances to attain a greater extent or a higher degree of freedom and happiness in society.

But postulating the availability of rational standards and criteria for judging the given possibilities of human freedom and happiness means assuming that the ethical, moral standards are *historical* standards. If they are not, they remain meaningless abstractions. Applied to our question, this means that to claim an ethical and moral right, a revolutionary movement must be able to give rational grounds for its chances to grasp real possibilities of human freedom and happiness, and it must be able to demonstrate the adequacy of its means for obtaining this end. Only if the problem is placed in such a historical context, is it susceptible to rational discussion. Otherwise, only two positions remain open, namely, to reject a priori or to endorse a priori all revolution and revolutionary violence. Both positions, the affirmative as well as the negative one, offend against historical facts. It is, for example, meaningless to say that modern society *could* have come about without the English, American, and French Revolutions. It is also meaningless to say that all revolutionary violence had the same social function and consequences. The violence of the Civil Wars in seventeenth century England, the violence of the first French Revolution certainly had effects and consequences very different from those of the Bolshevik Revolution, and very different from the counter-revolutionary violence perpetrated by the Nazi and Fascist regimes. Moreover, the positions of a priori rejecting or a priori approving social and political violence would amount to sanctioning any change brought about in history, regardless of whether it would be in a progressive or regressive, liberating or enslaving direction.

A very brief glance at the historical development of our problem may facilitate the discussion. In classical political philosophy, revolutions were not considered as breaks of the historical continuum. Plato as well as Aristotle believed that revolutions were built into the very dynamic of politics, that they belonged to the historical and at the same time natural cycle of birth, growth and decay of political forms. In medieval and early modern philosophy the idea of a natural and divine order either outlawed all resistance to established government, or made resistance against tyranny not only a right but a moral duty and obligation. Then, in the sixteenth and seventeenth centuries, the practically unlimited right to resist a government, even to overthrow a government, was normally claimed by Protestant against Catholic, and by Catholic against Protestant regimes. A most characteristic reaction against these doctrines may be seen in the attitude towards revolution which we find in such different figures as Hobbes and Descartes, namely, that change is always to the worst. Leave the established social and political institutions as they are, for, no matter how bad they may be, the risk of overthrowing them is too great. Descartes, the great revolutionary in thought, was extremely conservative with respect to the "great public bodies." To them, doubt is not supposed to be extended, they are supposed to be left alone. At the same time, philosophers are strongly inclined to endorse a revolution once it has proved to be successful. Representative of this attitude is the case of Kant — certainly not a paragon of opportunism and expedience — who rejected the right of resistance and condemned revolt against established government, but added that, once a revolution has succeeded, a new legal government is established, and man owes obedience to the new revolutionary government just as he owed it to the government which was overthrown by the revolution.

On the other side of the fence, political theory and practice recognize historical situations in which violence becomes the necessary and essential element of progress. This concept is instrumental in the political theory and practice of totalitarian democracy. Robespierre calls for the "despotism of liberty" against the despotism of tyranny: in the fight for freedom, in the interest of the whole against the particular interests of oppression, terror may become a necessity and an obligation. Here, violence, revolutionary violence, appears not only as a political means but as a moral duty. The terror is defined as *counter*violence: it is "legitimate" only in defense against the oppressors and until they are defeated. Similarly, the Marxian concept of proletarian dictatorship is that of a transitional self-cancelling dictatorship; self-cancelling because it is supposed to last only as long as the power of the old ruling classes still combats the construction of the socialist society; after their defeat, the engines of repression were to be stopped. Here too, revolutionary violence is defined as counter-violence. The Marxian concept assumes that the old ruling classes would never voluntarily abdicate their position, that they would be the first to use violence against the revolution, and that revolutionary violence would be the defense against counterrevolutionary violence.

The theory of an educational, transitional dictatorship implies the paradoxical proposition that man must be "forced to be free." Political philosophy has always recognized the moral function of coercion (the coercive power of law, either above the sovereign or identical with the sovereign), but Rousseau provides a radically new justification. Coercion is necessitated by the immoral, repressive conditions under which men live. The basic idea is: how can slaves who do not even know they are slaves free themselves? How can they liberate themselves by their own power, by their own faculties? How can they spontaneously accomplish liberation? They must be taught and must be led to be free, and this the more so the more the society in which they live uses all available means in order to shape and preform their consciousness and to make it immune against possible alternatives. This idea of an educational, preparatory dictatorship has today become an integral element of revolution and of the justification of the revolutionary oppression. The dictatorships which began as revolutionary dictatorships and then perpetuated themselves claim to be in their very essence and structure transitional and preparatory for a stage at which they can be abolished by virtue of their own achievements.

The main argument against the notion of the transitional dictatorship is usually condensed in the question: who educates the educators? By what right do those who actually exercise the dictatorship speak in the name of freedom and happiness as general conditions? This argument by itself is not sufficient, because in a lesser degree it applies even to non-authoritarian societies, where the policy-making top layer is not constantly and effectively controlled from below. However, even if we concede that the majority of men are not yet free today, and that their liberation cannot be spontaneous, the question still remains whether the dictatorial means are adequate to attain the end, namely, liberation. In other words the question of a transitional dictatorship cannot be separated from the general question of whether there can be such a thing as a moral justification of suppression and violence in a revolution. I shall now briefly discuss this question.

The historical revolutions were usually advocated and started in the name of freedom, or rather in the name of greater freedom for more strata of the population. We must first examine this claim strictly on empirical grounds. Human freedom is not and never has been a static condition but an historical condition, a process which involves the radical alteration, and even negation, of established ways of life. The form and content of freedom change with every new stage in the development of civilization, which is man's increasing mastery of man and nature. In both modes, mastery means domination, control; more effective control of nature makes for more effective control of man. Obviously, the possibilities of human freedom and happiness in advanced industrial society today are in no way comparable with those available, even theoretically available, at preceding stages of history. Thus, with respect to the form, extent, degree and content of human freedom, we deal with strictly historical and changing conditions. We can say even more. Measured against the real possibilities of freedom, we always live in a state of relative unfreedom. The wide gap between real possibility and actuality, between the rational and the real has never been closed. Freedom always presupposes liberation, or a step from one state of freedom and unfreedom to a subsequent state. With the advance of technical progress, the later state is *potentially* (but by no means actually!) a *higher* stage, that is, quantitatively and qualitatively. But if this is the case, if freedom always presupposes liberation from unfree and unhappy conditions, it means that this liberation always offends against and ultimately subverts established and sanctioned institutions and interests. In history, they never abdicated voluntarily. Consequently, if and when freedom is a process of liberation, a transition from lower, more restricted forms of freedom to higher forms of freedom, then it always, not matter how, offends against the existing and established state of affairs. And precisely on this ground revolutionary violence has been most effectively justified as counterviolence, that is, as violence necessary in order to secure higher forms of freedom against the resistance of the established forms.

The ethics of revolution thus testifies to the clash and conflict of two historical rights: on the one side, the right of that which *is,* the established commonwealth on which the life and perhaps even the happiness of the individuals depend; and on the other side, the right of that which *can* be and perhaps even *ought* to be because it may reduce toil, misery, and injustice, provided always that this chance can be demonstrated as a real possibility. Such a demonstration must provide rational criteria; we can now add: these must be *historical* criteria. As such, they amount to an "historical calculus," namely, calculation of the chances of a future society as against the chances of the existing society with respect to human progress, that is to say, technical and material progress used in such a way that it increases individual freedom and happiness. Now if such an historical calculus is to have any rational basis, it must, on the one side, take into account the sacrifices exacted from the living generations on behalf of the established society, the established law and order, the number of victims made in defense of this society in war and peace, in the struggle for existence, individual and national. The calculus would further have to take into account the intellectual and material resources available to the society and the manner in which they are actually used with respect to their full capacity of satisfying vital human needs and pacifying the struggle for existence. On the other side, the historical calculus would have to project the chances of the contesting revolutionary movement of improving the prevailing conditions, namely, whether the revolutionary plan or program demonstrates the technical, material, and mental possibility of reducing the sacrifices and the number of victims. Even prior to the question as to the possibility of such a calculus (which, I believe, does exist), its inhuman quantifying character is evident. But its inhumanity is that of history itself, token of its empirical, rational foundation. No hypocrisy should from the beginning distort the examination. Nor is this brutal calculus an empty intellectual abstraction; in fact, at its decisive turns, history became such a calculated experiment.

The ethics of revolution, if there is such a thing, will therefore be in accordance not with absolute, but with historical standards. They do not cancel the validity of those general norms which formulate requirements for the progress of mankind toward humanity. No matter how rationally one may justify revolutionary means in terms of the demonstrable chance of obtaining freedom and happiness for future generations, and thereby justify violating existing rights and liberties and life itself, there are forms of violence and suppression which no revolutionary situation can justify because they negate the very end for which the revolution is a means. Such are arbitrary violence, cruelty, and indiscriminate terror. However, within the historical continuum, revolutions establish a moral and ethical code of their own and in this way become the origin, the fountainhead and source of new general norms and values. In fact some of today's most generally-professed values originated in revolutions, for example, the value of tolerance in the English Civil Wars, the inalienable rights of man in the American and French Revolutions. These ideas become an historical force, first as partial ideas, instruments of a revolutionary movement for specific political ends. Their realization originally involved violence; they then assumed not only partial political but general ethical validity and rejected violence. In this way, revolutions place themselves under ethical standards.

Violence per se has never been made a revolutionary value by the leaders of the historical revolutions. His contemporaries rejected Georges Sorel's attempt to cut the link between violence and reason, which was at the same time the attempt to free the class struggle from all ethical considerations. In comparing the violence of the class struggle in its revolutionary phase with the violence of military operations in war, he made the former subject to strategic calculations only: the end was the total defeat of the enemy; violence a means to attain this end — the relation between means and end was a technical one. Sorel's defense of violence this side of good and evil remained isolated from the revolutionary reality of his time; if he had any influence, it was on the side of the counterrevolution. Otherwise, violence was defended, not per se, but as part of rational suppression, suppression of counterrevolutionary activity, of established rights and privileges, and, for the society at large, of material and intellectual needs, that is, enforcement of austerity, rationing, censorship.

Now this suppression which includes violence is practiced in the interest of the objectives of the revolution, and these objectives are presented not only as political but also as moral values, ethical imperatives, namely greater freedom for the greater number of people. And in this sense the objectives and the ends of the revolution itself claim general validity and become subject to moral standards and evaluation.

Here we are confronted with the problem of all ethics, namely, the question as to the ultimate sanction of moral values. Or, in plain language, who or what determines the validity of ethical norms? The question becomes acute only with the secularization of the West; it was no problem in the Middle Ages as long as a transcendent sanction of ethics was accepted. The infidels could justly be exterminated, heretics could justly be burned — in spite of all protest. This was justice in terms of the prevailing values, which in turn were those of transcendent ethics. But today, where is the sanction of ethical values

— sanction not in terms of the enforcement but in terms of the acceptance of ethical values, the proof of their validity? Sanction today, it seems, rests mainly in a precarious and flexible syndrome of custom, fear, utility, and religion; flexible because, within the syndrome, there is a large range of change. I refer, for example, to the high degree of liberalization in sexual morality which we have witnessed during the last thirty years, or, to the easy suspension of practically all ethical values in so-called emergency situations. The sanction and validity of ethical norms is thus restricted to the normal state of affairs in social and political relations.

Now in terms of the normal established state of affairs, a revolution is by definition immoral; it offends against the right of the existing commonwealth; it permits and even demands deception, cunning, suppression, destruction of life and property, and so on. But a judgment by definition is an inadequate judgment. Ethical standards by virtue of their imperative claim transcend any given state of affairs, and they transcend it, not to any metaphysical entities but to the historical continuum in which every given state of affairs has emerged, by which every given state of affairs is defined, and in which every given state of affairs will be altered and surpassed by other states. And in the historical continuum which defines its place and function, the ethics of revolution appeal to an historical calculus. Can the intended new society, the society intended by the revolution, offer better chances for progress in freedom than the existing society? In the historical continuum, these chances can only be measured by going beyond the given state of affairs, going beyond it not simply into an abstract vacuum of speculation, but going beyond it by calculating the resources, intellectual as well as material, scientific as well as technical, available to a given society, and projecting the most rational ways of utilizing these resources. Now if such projection is possible, then it can yield objective criteria for judging revolutions as to their historical function in terms of progress or regression, in terms of the development of *humanitas*.

A preliminary answer is suggested by a glance at the historical process itself. Historically, the objective tendency of the great revolutions of the modern period was the enlargement of the social range of freedom and the enlargement of the satisfaction of needs. No matter how much the social interpretations of the English and French Revolutions may differ, they seem to agree in that a redistribution of the social wealth took place, so that previously less privileged or under-privileged classes were the beneficiaries of this change, economically and/or politically. In spite of subsequent periods of reaction and restoration, the result and objective function of these revolutions was the establishment of more liberal governments, a gradual democratization of society, and technical progress. I said "objective function" because this evaluation of the revolution is obviously a judgment ex post facto. The intention and ideology of the leaders of the revolution, and the drives of the masses may have had quite different aims and motives. By virtue of their objective function, these revolutions attained progress in the sense defined, namely, a demonstrable enlargement of the range of human freedom; they thus established, in spite of the terrible sacrifices exacted by them, an ethical right over and above all political justification.

But if such ethical right and its criteria are always and necessarily after the fact, it serves for nought and leaves us with the irrational choice of either a priori accepting or a priori rejecting all revolution. Now I submit that, while the historical function of a revolution becomes identifiable only after the fact, its prospective direction, progressive or regressive is, with the certainty of a reasonable *chance,* demonstrable *before* the fact — to the same degree to which the historical conditions of progress are demonstrable. For example, it could be demonstrated — and it was demonstrated before the fact — that the French Revolution of 1789 would give, in terms of the historical calculus, a better chance for the development of human freedom than the Ancien Régime. Contrariwise, it could be demonstrated, and was demonstrated long before the fact, that Fascist and National-Socialist regimes would do the exact opposite, namely, necessarily restrict the range of human freedom. Moreover, and I think this is a very important point, such demonstration of the historical *chances* before the fact becomes increasingly rational with the development of our scientific, technical, and material resources and capabilities, with our progress in the scientific mastery of man and nature. The possibilities and contents of freedom today are coming more and more under the control of man: they are becoming increasingly calculable. And with this advance in effective control and calculability, the inhuman distinction between violence and violence, sacrifice and sacrifice becomes increasingly rational. For throughout history, the happiness and freedom, and even the life of individuals, have been sacrificed. If we consider human life per se sacred under all conditions, the distinction is meaningless, and we have to admit that history is per se amoral and immoral, because it has never respected the sanctity of human life as such. But in fact we do distinguish between sacrifices which are legitimate and sacrifices which are not legitimate. This distinction is an historical one, and with this qualification, ethical standards are also applicable to violence.

Let me now recapitulate and reformulate. In absolute ethical terms, that is to say, in terms of suprahistorical validity, there is no justification for any suppression and sacrifice for the sake of future freedom and happiness, revolutionary or otherwise. But in historical terms we are confronted with a distinction and a decision. For suppression and sacrifice are daily exacted by all societies, and one cannot start — indeed I would like to say this with all possible emphasis — one cannot start becoming moral and ethical at an arbitrary but expedient point of cut off: the point of revolution. Who can quantify and who can compare the sacrifices exacted by an established society and those exacted by its subversion? Are ten thousand victims more ethical than twenty thousand? Such is in fact the inhuman arithmetic of history, and in this inhuman historical context operates the historical calculus. Calculable are the material and intellectual resources available, calculable are the productive and distributive facilities in a society, and the extent of unsatisfied vital needs and of satisfied non-vital needs. Quantifiable and calculable are the quantity and size of the labor force and of the population as a whole. That is the empirical material at the disposal of the historical calculus. And on the basis of this quantifiable material the question can be asked whether the available resources and capabilities are utilized most rationally, that is to say, with a view to the best possible satisfaction of needs under the priority of vital needs and with a minimum of toil, misery and injustice. If the analysis of a specific historical situation suggests a negative answer, if conditions exist in which technological rationality is impeded or even superseded by repressive political and social interests which define the general welfare, then the reversal of such conditions in favor of a more rational and human use of the available resources would also be a maximalization of the chance of progress in freedom. Consequently, a social and political movement in this direction would, in terms of the calculus, allow the presumption of historical justification. It can be no more than a presumption, subject to correction as the movement actually develops, reveals its potential and establishes new facts, or in other words, as it sustains or as it cuts the links between the means which the revolution employs and the end which it professes to attain.

And this leads to the last question which I want to raise here, namely, can the revolutionary end justify *all* means? Can we distinguish between rational and irrational, necessary and arbitrary, suppression? When can such suppression be called rational in terms of the objective of a respective revolution? I shall briefly illustrate the scope of this question by the Bolshevik Revolution. The professed objective of the Bolshevik Revolution was socialism. It implied the socialization of the means of production, the dictatorship of the proletariat as preparatory to a classless society. In the specific historical situation in which the Bolshevik Revolution occurred, socialism called for industrialization in competition with the advanced capitalist countries of the West, for the building up of the armed forces, and for propaganda on a global scale. Now can we apply a distinction between rational and irrational to these objectives and to the degree of suppression involved in them? In terms of the revolution, rational would be accelerated industrialization, the elimination of non-cooperative layers of management from the economy, the enforcement of work discipline, sacrifices in the satisfaction of needs imposed by the priority of heavy industry in the first stages of industrialization, and suspension of civil liberties if they were used for sabotaging these objectives. And we can reject, without long discussion, as not justifiable, even in terms of the revolution, the Moscow trials, the permanent terror, the concentration camps, and the dictatorship of the Party over the working classes. Further examination would require introducing into the discussion the situation of global coexistence; but time forbids us to do so. We have also made abstraction from the human element in the leadership of the revolution, that is to say, from the so-called historical individuals.

And here I want to add one remark. It seems to me characteristic that, the more calculable and the more controllable the technical apparatus of modern industrial society becomes, the more does the chance of human progress depend on the intellectual and moral qualities of the leaders, and on their willingness and ability to educate the controlled population and to make it recognize the possibility, nay, the necessity of pacification and humanization. For today, the technical apparatus of advanced industrial society is in itself authoritarian, requiring service, submission, subordination to the objective mechanism of the machine system, that is to say, submission to those who control the apparatus. Technology has been made into a powerful instrument of streamlined domination — the more powerful the more it proves its efficiency and delivers the goods. And as such, it serves the politics of domination.

I come to the conclusion. The means-end relation is the ethical problem of revolution. In one sense, the end justifies the means, namely, if they demonstrably serve human progress in freedom. This legitimate end, the only legitimate end, demands the creation of conditions which would facilitate and expedite its realization. And the creation of these conditions may justify sacrifices, as it has justified sacrifices throughout history. But this relation between means and ends is a dialectical one. The end must be operative in the repressive means for attaining the end. But no matter how rational, how necessary, how liberating — revolution involves violence. The non-violent history is the promise and possibility of a society which is still to be fought for. At present, the triumphant violence seems to be on the other side.

---

# Intelligence, Conscience, and the Right to Revolution

### SIDNEY HOOK

. . . I shall discuss a cluster of problems which may be called variations on a Jeffersonian theme. The theme is the nature and limits of democratic resistance to democratic authority. My conclusions will not be startling — originality in this sphere is almost always a sign of error — but I hope they will be of interest. At any rate, I console myself with Justice Holmes's observation that sometimes the

Reprinted by permission of The Regents of the University of California.

vindication of the obvious is more important than the elucidation of the obscure — especially when the obvious is challenged. Even tautologies have their uses when counterposed to absurdities.

In the summer of 1960, a Declaration concerning the Right of Insubordination in the Algerian War was signed and circulated in France by 121 intellectuals headed by Jean-Paul Sartre. It came to the defense of Frenchmen, in the army and without, who were being imprisoned, tried, and condemned for refusing to participate in the war and for having given direct aid to the Algerian rebels. It asked and answered affirmatively the questions whether "civic responsibility in certain circumstances becomes shameful submission" and whether or not there are "instances when the refusal to serve is a sacred duty, when 'treason' means the courageous respect of the truth." The government responded by taking certain measures against some of the signers, ranging from indictment of a few to banning some literary and dramatic personalities from state-controlled radio, television, and theater. The Declaration of the 121 set off a series of manifestos and counter-manifestos, some denouncing the signers as "professors of treason" and some denouncing the government for proceeding against them. It was more than the usual Parisian brouhaha, because some asserted that soldiers and recruits had been induced by the Declaration to desert. The repercussions of the Declaration were felt abroad, and some intellectuals in Italy and the United States expressed their solidarity with the signers.

Shortly thereafter in Great Britain, Bertrand Russell and some other leaders of the Aldermaston marchers called for a civil disobedience movement in protest against the decision of the Tory government to continue the policy of nuclear defense armament, originally introduced by the Labour government.

In our own country, in several parts of the South, in consequence of the desegregation decision, agitators abetted by some local officials called for both active and passive resistance to the legal directives of the courts to integrate the schools. Some of them made use of the same kind of language and type of argument which Northerners who violated the Fugitive Slave Laws a century ago had invoked to denounce the Constitution as "a compact with Hell." At the same time, Negro and white students carried out widespread sit-ins and sit-downs, violating local ordinances with the widely expressed approval of principled democrats who felt they were articulating the democratic conscience of the country.

Considered as a moral problem, the question of justification of revolution is comparatively simple, once we disentangle it from the mystical notion that submission to the will of a divine ruler requires submission to the will of the political rulers on earth. Indeed, such a notion is incompatible with a moral position on the generic question of political obedience. In principle a moral position must allow for the desirability of political revolution under certain conditions, even if on prudential grounds some practical decisions are left open. This is true even for those moral positions which regard the use of force or violence as intrinsically evil and wish to reduce it to a minimum. They cannot consistently condemn revolutionary action against oppressive government if there is good reason to believe that the costs in violence and human suffering of such action, broadly viewed, are less than the costs of the continued existence of the government. The problem is complicated by the fact that not all resistance to the specific evils of a government are intended to be revolutionary. The evil, however grave, may be episodic rather than systematic.

There are certain kinds of situation in which resistance to government, even when felt justified, is not intended to be an act, or part of an act, of total revolutionary overthrow. Antigone disobeyed the law without wishing to destroy the rule of Creon in behalf of another political order. She may have even felt some interest in preserving his rule. Analogously, the problem faced by a democrat in violating laws of a genuinely functioning democracy is much more difficult to resolve than when the problem is posed as an abstract ethical one independently of the individual's own political allegiance. Tyranny is tyranny, whether exercised by one man or by many, whether expressed through the arbitrary decision of a power-crazed maniac or through the considered decision of a majority pursuing some notion of the public good. But the *limits* of tyranny — the point at which disobedience is undertaken, the point of no return when disobedience turns to open resistance — cannot be laid down without reference to one's own political commitment. That is why it seems to me to be unrewarding to seek some general or universally valid answer to the *political* question concerning the justification of revolution on abstract ethical grounds alone.

Our own government was born in revolution, and the right to revolutionary overthrow of oppressive governments is enshrined as a natural right in the Declaration of Independence. Almost every line of this document assumes the validity of the democratic premises of a self-governing community. Its language could hardly be used by those who accepted absolute monarchy or benevolent despotism or the rule of an hereditary aristocracy as legitimate. It is axiomatic that anyone who takes as his point of departure its commitment to self-government cannot *in principle* be opposed to the revolutionary overthrow of an oppressive and tyrannical minority government anywhere, although he may conclude in specific cases that the occasion and times may make such action unwise. That is why democrats can hail and even encourage revolutions in Fascist, Communist, and other dictatorial countries and, without the slightest inconsistency, take vigorous measures to prevent totalitarians of any variety from overthrowing genuinely functioning democracies wherever they exist.

Why do I say that although a democrat *in principle* is justified in overthrowing a dictatorial regime, he may forgo advocating it? There are a number of obvious reasons, some of which may be made apparent by considering different types of situation. (1) Democrats may not be sure that they have sufficient strength and popular support to triumph; they may wish to avoid a *Putsch* which, even if successful, would require that they impose democracy in a country from above — as in some South American revolutions. Since such governments, established by a *Putsch* or by minority groups which declare themselves democratic, are usually unstable unless they transform themselves into dictatorships, democrats may wish to postpone action until they have built sufficient strength or sentiment to provide a majority consensus for the act of revolutionary overthrow. (2) But even when democrats are convinced that they have the majority of the population behind them, they may have reason to believe that the outcome is problematic because of the potential power of repression from internal or external mercenaries, better armed and more ruthless than the supporters of the revolution. Some of my Polish democratic friends, with poignant memories of what happened in Hungary when the West stood idly by as the Soviet soldiers, on direct orders from Khrushchev, slaughtered the freedom fighters, say that although the overwhelming majority of the Polish people oppose the minority Communist regime, few would ever dream of launching a revolution. Coming from gallant Poles, this is highly significant. (3) Even if the outcome is unproblematic, and there is good reason to believe that the democratic revolution against tyranny will triumph, democrats may regard the cost of victory as too heavy and wait for a more favorable course while continuing an outer and inner resistance.

None of these situations in any way affects the validity in principle of democratic revolutions in oppressive nondemocratic countries. But the question we are now concerned with is whether they have any bearing on the right to revolution or disobedience in *democratic* countries. Is there any implicit answer in the considerations so far offered? What does traditional political theory say? When we differentiate the problem of resistance to democratic authority by believers in democracy from the problem of resistance to undemocratic government, we cannot find much of a guide in the traditional solution offered in political theory to the question of the nature and limits of obedience to government.

The traditional solution was one in which the processes of democratic self-government were offered as the only reasonable alternative between unacceptable evils. We may recapitulate the argument as follows: there is a truth about revolutions in history, recognized not only by ancient thinkers but by the authors of the Declaration of Independence, that men "are more disposed to suffer, while evils are sufferable, than to right themselves by abolishing the forms to which they are accustomed." They knew that revolutions and civil wars are often terrible events in history — until recently they produced more terror and suffering than most wars. Our own Civil War, in which comparatively humane conventions of conflict were followed, was the bloodiest of all wars until that time. Ernest Renan once observed: "Happy is a people which inherits a revolution: woe to those who make it." This wisdom is as old as the human race. Hobbes was wrong in believing that a state of nature is usually marked by a war of all against all: it is only after law has been established and then breaks down, fragmenting the center of authority, that something approaching a war of all against all is likely to result. It was this realization which accounts for Aristotle's view that it is better for a bad law to be obeyed than by disobeying it to have all law brought into disrepute.

But how bad must a bad law be before Aristotle's counsel of prudence becomes a support of insufferable tyranny? Suppose a people accept a bad law in hopes of being able to change it by petition or the appeal to reason, but find "a long train of abuses and usurpations, pursuing invariably the same object, evinces a design to reduce them under absolute despotism" — what then? Here we must answer, as did the authors of the Declaration: "It is their right" to overthrow such governments. There is a limit to the blessings of law and order if they become the law of the hangman and the order of the grave.

How can we tell what laws of duly constituted authority to obey or to disobey? The second traditional position, sometimes evoked by the first, is that we should obey laws which conform with our conscience and disobey those which violate our conscience. This would be a wonderfully simple solution if only the conscience of the people spoke with one voice. But conscience, of all things, is an individual matter. One man's conscience is another man's abomination. There is hardly any important law to which some man's conscience has not taken and may not take exception. If it is conscience, and only conscience, which justifies a man in refusing to bear arms in defense of his country, why does not another man's conscience justify *him* in ridding the country of the first conscientious objector? If a man's conscience is the sole or sufficient authority for *his* action, how can it serve as an authority for *my* action, by what right can it deny, suppress, or ignore my conscience? The history of the deliverance of human conscience has shown that an indefinite multiplicity of actions, varying from the pitiless slaughter of harmless old women as witches to the odd refusal to wear bone buttons, has been justified in its name. On the other hand, some of our cruelest actions — and especially our neighbors' actions — seem to be accompanied by no twinge of conscience whatever. Some Biblical incidents, which outrage our moral sensibilities when we read about them today, seem to have left unmoved the conscience of even contemporary prophets. At any rate, if the law were to be obeyed only when it is authorized by our conscience, the result would be anarchy. And not the anarchy of the philosophical anarchists! Most philosophical anarchists quietly assume that there will always be a policeman on the corner protecting them from the ordinary varieties of anarchy, including unphilosophical larceny and worse.

How do we escape the dilemma between the acceptance of tyranny, on the one hand, and anarchy, on the other?

The traditional argument in favor of democracy is that it is a political system which enables us to avoid both horns of the dilemma. In a democracy the major policies of government rest directly or indirectly upon the freely given consent of the majority of the governed or their representatives. Every citizen who meets certain standard qualifications has a right to participate in the political process and to convince his neighbors of the justice and wisdom of the deliverance of his conscience. The hope is that in the course of the political process consciences would submit themselves *conscientiously* to public criticism and debate, and finally work out the reasonable compromises which permit those with different consciences to live and let live, if not to live and help live. Tyranny is avoided by virtue of the fact that when a law is considered unwise or unjust by a dissenter or nonconformist, and the means of inducing consent remain unimpaired, he is free to agitate for its amendment or repeal. Anarchy is avoided in that after the discussion is over, and the votes are counted, the decision of the majority is accepted and obeyed as law. To the question, then, whether anybody who accepts the principle of democratic self-government can believe in the right to a revolution in a democracy, the answer is obviously, "No."

I am saying something more, I believe, than what Justice Hand said when he wrote: "Revolutions are often 'right' but 'right to revolution' is a contradiction in terms, for a society which acknowledged it could not stop at tolerating conspiracies to overthrow it, but must include their execution." In this *legal* sense of "right," there can be no "right to revolution" in any system. What I am saying is that in the moral and political sense of "right," democratic theory and practice would be self-stultifying if they admitted a right to revolution in a democracy because the *faith* of the democrat is that all morally legitimate demands can sooner or later be realized through democratic processes without recourse to revolutionary violence. To a democrat there is a presumption of validity in any law passed by democratic process, in the sense that it commands a prima facie justified obedience. Its validity is comparable to the claim upon the assent of an individual who accepts scientific methods as the most reliable way of reaching truth, of any conclusion reached by these methods, even if later in the light of additional evidence the conclusion is modified or abandoned.

But this faith in the democratic process may be strained to the breaking point. It may be strained in two ways: by extremely unwise or oppressive substantive action, and by procedural violation. By substantive action, I mean that a democratic community may by due legal process adopt a measure so morally outrageous that some individuals say: "No matter how constitutional, we refuse to submit to this piece of legislation and will fight with *any* means to overthrow it." This was the position of the extreme abolitionists in the North who were prepared to approve even of secession from the Union to bring an end to slavery. At a great public meeting in the 1850's in Boston's Faneuil Hall in which the Constitution was called "a compact with Hell," a resolution was offered which declared: "Constitution or no Constitution, law or no law, we will not allow a fugitive slave to be taken in Massachusetts."

By procedural violations, I mean a situation in which the democratic rules of political process are so abridged that doubt arises whether the outcome does represent the democratic consensus. Here the objection to the procedural action usually follows hard on the disapproval of some substantive measure which was adopted or imposed by breaching democratic rules. We shall find this kind of situation the most difficult.

Positions polarize with respect to the morally legitimate mode of behavior incumbent upon the citizen of a self-governing community when its representative assembly, by due process, adopts a measure that seems violative of basic human values. One of these positions may be characterized as the position of absolutist democracy which holds that obedience to democratic law, good or bad, must be unqualified. It obviously differs from the position of Bill of Rights' absolutism which asserts that any law which violates any right in the Bill of Rights has no legitimacy. This is the position which Abraham Lincoln took in a famous address on "The Perpetuation of our Political Institutions."

> Let every American, every lover of liberty, every well wisher to his posterity swear by the blood of the Revolution, never to violate in the least particular, the laws of the country; and never to tolerate their violation by others . . . Let every man remember that to violate the law, is to trample on the blood of his father, and to tear the charter of his own, and his children's liberty. Let reverence for the laws be breathed by every American mother to the lisping baby that prattles on her lap — let it be taught in schools, in seminaries and in colleges; let it be written in primers, spelling books and Almanacs; let it be preached from the pulpit, proclaimed in legislative halls, and enforced in courts of justice. And, in short, let it become *the political religion* of the nation; and let the old and the young, the rich and the poor, the grave and the gay, of all sexes and tongues and colors and conditions, sacrifice unceasingly upon its altars. . . .
>
> When I so pressingly urge a strict observance of all the laws,

let me not be understood as saying there are no bad laws, nor that grievances may not arise, for the redress of which, no legal provisions have been made. I mean to say no such thing. But I do mean to say, that, although bad laws, if they exist, should be repealed as soon as possible, still while they continue in force, for the sake of example, they should be religiously observed. So also in unprovided cases. If such arise, let proper legal provisions be made for them with the least possible delay; but, till then, let them if not too intolerable, be borne with.

This is a very strong statement; it denies almost without qualification the primacy of moral principle over any political or legal decision made by duly constituted democratic authority. It does not distinguish between degree or occasion. For most laws which come from legislative chambers and governmental commissions, much can be said for this attitude, despite the needless extremism of the language. The consequences of the widespread violation of the Prohibition Amendment, by making crime a way of life and encouraging a cynical attitude towards law enforcement, were far more harmful to the community than the arbitrary and unjust restrictions which this ill-considered amendment placed upon the sumptuary habits of American citizens. A foolish traffic law usually works less hardship than would its widespread flouting. An unjust tax is to be deplored less than a tax strike. But suppose it is a matter which touches deeply not merely one's conscience but one's *reflective* conscience. What then? The law may command an action which outrages the strong feelings of a minority whose reasoned arguments and protests have been ignored. It was a situation of this kind which confronted those citizens of the North who, although opposed to slavery, were willing to suffer it so long as they were permitted to agitate against it, but who refused to obey the Fugitive Slave Act of September, 1850.

Here is a characteristic passage from Theodore Parker which expresses a not uncommon response by a man of religion to Lincoln's demand that all laws on the statute books be religiously obeyed and enforced.

Let me suppose a case which may happen here, and before long. A woman flies from South Carolina to Massachusetts to escape from bondage. Mr. Greatheart aids her in her escape, harbors and conceals her, and is brought to trial for it. The punishment is a fine of one thousand dollars and imprisonment for six months. I am drawn to serve as a juror and pass upon this offence. I may refuse to serve and be punished for that, leaving men with no scruples to take my place, or I may take the juror's oath to give a verdict according to the law and the testimony. The law is plain, let us suppose and the testimony conclusive. Greatheart himself confesses that he did the deed alleged, saving one ready to perish. The judge charges that, if the jurors are satisfied of that fact, then they must return that he is guilty. This is a nice matter. Here are two questions. The one put to me in my official capacity as juror is this, — "Did Greatheart aid the woman?" The other put to me in my natural character as man is this, — "Will you help to punish Greatheart with fine and imprisonment for helping a woman to obtain her unalienable rights?" If I have extinguished my manhood by my juror's oath, then I shall do my official business and find Greatheart guilty, and I shall seem to be a true man; but if I value my manhood, I shall answer after my natural duty to love a man and not hate him, to do him justice, not injustice, to allow him the natural rights he has not alienated, and shall say, "Not guilty." Then men will call me forsworn and a liar, but I think human nature will justify the verdict. . . .

This position was strongly condemned by a great many believers in constitutional democracy, especially by Justice Curtis, who was to write the dissenting opinion in the Dred Scott decision. And yet there is moral heroism in refusing to do the things which Parker describes which we would not like to see disappear from life. But how can a *democrat* defend such unlawful action? It seems to me he can defend it *only* if he willingly accepts the punishment entailed by his defiance of the law, only if he does not seek to escape or subvert or physically resist it. If he engages in any kind of resistance to the punitive processes of the law which follows upon his sentence of legal guilt, he has in principle embarked upon a policy of revolutionary overthrow. If he insists upon his moral right to overthrow the government because of its infamous laws, then he has abandoned the position of the principled democrat and must stand on God's law as he interprets it or on the moral right as he sees it. We may agree with him on the ground that we are both "God's angry men" come to bring his erring children to their senses, or we may, as secular humanists, speak up for human liberty against democratic power, but we cannot consistently do so on democratic grounds. Were the democratic process to result in laws which we regard as so morally iniquitous as to justify overt or implicit rebellion, we would have to conclude that men were incapable of self-government, that good government could not be achieved by democratic processes. To seek to overthrow a democratic government whose deliberative processes, attended by all the procedural safeguards of civil and political rights, results in a reign of terror against an innocent and helpless minority may certainly be morally justifiable. To do so in the name of democracy is usually a piece of suave hypocrisy or self-deception, and is to shift the meaning of democracy from a set of political procedures to a set of goals which might very well be achieved by other than democratic political procedures.

John Brown and others like him had the honesty of their fanaticism. They never pretended that they were violating and destroying the fabric of democracy in the name of democracy. For the history of democracy had shown them that justice, freedom, God's will — however they conceived it, mistakenly, as I believe, or not — could not be achieved by the democratic political process. They would have felt at home in a theocracy administered by their favorite sectarian luminaries. Thoreau, on the other hand, never saw the issue clearly. His theoretical position as expressed in his *Essay on Civil Disobedience* is thoroughly confused and muddled because it implies both that one can accept democracy as a political system and also believe that every citizen has a right to overthrow it if any law passed by a democracy violates his obligation to the right. Thoreau's practice was, however, compatible with the democratic position in that, refusing to pay taxes to be used to enforce laws he regarded as evil, he did not take to the hills but gladly and proudly went to jail. Under certain circumstances, if the penalty for the violation of a law were extreme enough, one can conceive a democrat violating the law and at the same time willingly forfeiting his life rather than weakening or betraying the structure of democratic law by flight or resistance. The argument which Socrates makes in the *Crito* is unanswerable and is binding on anyone who, despite his differences with the democratic community, still feels that he is a loyal member of that community and not at war with it. In war — national, civil or class war — one expects prisoners to attempt to escape. In Socrates' case, he carried matters a little far, not by his willingness to accept punishment, but by his insistence upon it. One gets the impression that he thought he was punishing the Athenians. And perhaps he was.

The situation is more complicated with respect to the violation of procedural principles of a democracy by its legislative or executive organs. For in such instances one may claim that beyond a *certain point* a democracy in violating its own democratic laws is moving into a condition of despotism which emboldens the democratic dissenter or rebel to proceed against it as he would against any despotism. According to some democrats, Lincoln violated the laws of democracy in suspending the writ of habeas corpus in states which were outside the immediate theater of war. One can conceive of many situations in which an unwise or corrupted democracy destroys its own institutional presuppositions. But so long as one still regards the community, despite its procedural lapses, as still functioning under a democratic political system, revolutionary opposition to it cannot be justified on democratic grounds.

It is at this point that we must recognize a distinction in principle between revolutionary violence and nonviolent civil disobedience, even though situations may arise which make it difficult *in practice* to draw the precise line. Although a democrat must condemn any kind of revolutionary violence, no matter how nobly motivated, he may condone, within certain narrowly prescribed limits, some forms of civil disobedience, Lincoln to the contrary notwithstanding. A situation may arise in which a democrat believes that a municipal or state law violates the fundamental law of the land. In a desire to test the local law — and it is a law because it is currently being enforced — a democrat may defy it in the way in which Norman Thomas defied the decrees laid down by "I-am-the-Law" Mayor Hague of Jersey City. Such situations are clear and simple. One may, however, go further. Even when such laws are upheld by the courts of highest instance, even in cases where federal laws have been held constitutionally valid, a democratic dissenter may, without inconsistency to his principles, disobey them provided he is prepared to accept the consequences. His justification lies in his hope that his act, and the acts of others, will serve as moral challenge and educational reinfluence on the attitudes of the majority. His very willingness to endure all sorts of hardships and their attendant deprivations normally arouses, when not compassion, second thoughts about the wisdom and justice of the law in question. That is why a sincere democrat who disobeys the law cannot whine or dodge or evade or fall back on the Fifth Amendment. Indeed, the very effectiveness of the violation of the law, in the intent of the dissenter, depends upon his being punished. Much worse than the punishment is to be ignored. I recall that during the war against Hitler, a group of conscientious objectors all crowding the age of sixty-five, led by Reverend A. J. Muste, publicly proclaimed their intention to defy the Registration Act. They gave up their valuable apartments, put their furniture in storage, made their farewells to their families, notified the newspapers — and awaited the federal marshal. But someone in Washington with a sense of humor or proportion completely ignored them. The expectant martyrs were furious, and spoke about the deception of the government in shockingly un-Christian terms.

Of course no one can lay down in advance at what precise point civil disobedience, especially mass civil disobedience, by disorganizing essential services, may lead to the destruction of the entire democratic process. This is something which cannot be settled by principled formulations. But any democrat who advocates or undertakes a policy of civil disobedience must take note of considerations of this order and, as a democrat, must always stop short this side of the line.

We must also qualify, in the interests of clarity, what was said above about the nonviolent character of civil disobedience. The absence of violence is normally evidence of the bona fides of those who publicly disobey a law, since it reveals the absence of revolutionary intention. But the judgment of the character and legitimacy of acts of civil disobedience must, in the end, depend not so much on whether the acts are nonviolent or not but on the consequences of those acts on the community. A nonviolent or passive act of disobedience which will result in starving a city or in deprivation of essential care may be much worse and less tolerable, from a democratic point of view, than a flurry of transient violence.

We are now in a position to apply some of the distinctions we have made to the situations from which we took our point of departure. On the assumption that Sartre and his group are democrats, and on the assumption that they are not merely expressing an opinion, the incitement to French soldiers to desert is incompatible with the existence of a democratic state if the Fifth Republic is considered democratic as most of the signers, but not Sartre, seem to believe. It is sometimes said that no government can tolerate incitement to desertion and insubordination among its military forces. This is an incipient revolutionary act. True, but that is not the point here. As democrats, we can see nothing wrong in inciting the soldiers of totalitarian states to come over to the camp of freedom. The question is restricted only to soldiers of a democratic state. Some of the signers have made loud protests against the halfhearted measures taken against them, and some of the extralegal sanctions invoked have, indeed, the touch of a French farce and an uncharacteristic logical inconsistency about them. There is also an air of *opéra bouffe* about the protests of some individuals against government sanctions on the ground that, although the government may have a right to shoot the signers, it has no right to prevent them from singing over the state-owned radio. Nonetheless, an important point is involved here. If the signers are guilty of incitement to desertion, they should be charged and proceeded against under due legal process. But *until* this is done, the imposition of other extralegal discriminatory sanctions against them cannot be justified, if they are not state officials bound by a code of professional conduct, for they have not yet been adjudged guilty.

One thing should be clear. If it is established that the declaration was an incitement to desertion and disobedience, I can see no democratic justification for protesting or refusing to accept the consequences of the violation of the law. One cannot with integrity — especially if one is a democrat — both defy a law of the democratic community, take bows and plaudits for a stand widely heralded as "heroic," and then run from the consequences of one's heroism. After all, a soldier who deserted on the strength of the appeal of these intellectuals might be court-martialed and shot. How can those who issued the appeal to him responsibly claim immunity for actions which their appeal brought about?

The discussion precipitated by the case of the French intellectuals revealed some curious — even startling — misconceptions about the nature of democracy by individuals who regard themselves as committed to democratic principles. In a supporting statement drawn up by some Italian intellectuals, which was endorsed by some of their American confreres, it was asserted that "The right to disobedience . . . is the essence of democracy. It is an extreme right, to be exercised only in extreme circumstances." The inadequacy of this radical political innocence is apparent on its face. A strange essence, this right to disobedience! The essence of anything is found, not in extreme circumstances, where is it difficult to tell whether we are dealing with a phenomenon which belongs to the class whose essence we are defining, but in its normal and ordinary state. As well say that the essence of humanity is to be found in the extreme, borderline cases in which we do not know whether to classify an animal as belonging to Homo sapiens or to the lower primates. To make the right to disobedience "essential" to democracy is to conceive of democracy as a state of permanent civil war, except possibly on the assumption that men have angelic natures, so that their disagreement with the decisions of the majority never goes beyond the limits of philosophic discourse. But not even the "real" angels of sacred theology, judging by the story of Lucifer, are that angelic!

In explaining what he means by this peculiar concept of the essence of democracy, the author of the supporting Declaration, Nicola Chiaromonte, writes: "The principle of disobedience . . . is implicit in the very essence of democracy in the sense that, if democracy rests on an ever renewed act of *spontaneous* obedience to law, the moment the act becomes in all conscience impossible, is also the moment both of revolt and of the end of democracy."

This is false and horrendous doctrine. It logically implies that a democracy is impossible unless it rests on unanimous and spontaneous obedience to law. If such a situation existed, we should have no need of the state or of laws with any penal sanction whatsoever. A democracy rests upon the freely given consent of the majority of the governed, after full, fair, and free discussion and criticism. The obedience to the laws of a democracy by a democrat need not be spontaneous in the least. It can be as reluctant as one pleases, so long as they are obeyed — with the exception of the carefully circumscribed acts of civil disobedience. The Spanish Loyalist government was no less democratic because Franco regarded revolt against it as a matter of conscience. Signor Chiaromonte, like so many other well-intentioned persons — whether Christian or humanist, anarchist or pacifist — assumes that only men of good faith have consciences, and that by definition the conscience of all men of good faith is at least compatible with, if not the same as, his own.

The instance of the conscientious objector to war is more familiar to us. Those who oppose *any* kind of war on religious grounds do not feel bound by any overriding commitment to the values of democracy, even in situations where democracy can survive only by means of a defensive war. They feel about war — any war — the way John Brown felt about slavery, but happily, unlike John Brown, they cannot consistently engage in any violent action in behalf of their cause. Modern democracies try to accommodate these religious dissenters as much as possible by giving them an opportunity to perform non-military service. Where any kind of service is refused, they *may* be held accountable if their refusals are too widespread and dangerous to be ignored and the prospects of democratic survival weakened. It is — or should be — one of the great merits of democratic government that it respects and tries to accommodate *as far as possible* the scruples of those who believe that their relation to God "involves duties superior to those arising from any human relation," but, as we have seen, we cannot absolutize this belief. As democrats we cannot suffer it to go beyond the line set by reflective morality and the necessity of safeguarding the whole structure of other democratic freedoms.

The instances of nonreligious violators of laws and obligations relating to military defense should be treated no differently, if their moral convictions against any war are sincere. To the extent that they are principled democrats, we can rely on their setting limits on the scale of their own civil disobedience. This may not be true for some groups who are engaging in the practice of civil disobedience in behalf of unilateral disarmament and who are prepared, however reluctantly, to sacrifice free institutions to the risk of a nuclear war in their defense. Since, in the extreme situation posed by the threat of war, they are disposed to surrender democracy, they may be tempted to encourage the transformation of a movement of civil disobedience into one of revolution if this were the only means which seemed available to prevent war. For this reason nonpacifist civil disobedience movements are as a rule far more dangerous than purely pacifist ones.

Those who are currently engaged in violating the federal laws relating to desegregation in education are probably not very much concerned whether their behavior is consistent with democratic principles or not. To the extent that this opposition is articulate, one gathers that some Southern editors and political figures believe that in resisting the law they are upholding the Constitution against the Supreme Court. The ruffians who have been threatening parents willing to send their children to desegregated schools are something else again. The law must be enforced against them. But enforcement, although necessary, is not enough. If disorders continue, they cannot be attributed exclusively to agitators but to principled resentment against the law. The task of the over-all democratic community is to convince those who feel that they are fighting *for* democracy in fighting *against* the law, that they are mistaken in this belief and that the spirit of democratic community, whose basic principle is equality of concern for all individuals to develop themselves as persons, requires the abandonment of unjust and arbitrary discriminations against any group of citizens.

The sit-in and sit-down strikes of students, since they have not been accompanied by violence and since they have ended happily in some Southern towns and cities, are the best illustrations of a kind of civil disobedience undertaken in the name of democracy to reeducate a community to the significance of the democratic way of political life. It may be that those who yielded did so out of convenience or business considerations. No matter. Habit, use, and wont will gradually put down taproots to nourish the frail blossoms of social equality which until now have withered in the climate of hate and fear. Nonetheless, it must be acknowledged that civil disobedience is at best a danger to a democracy, even when in small doses it may have some healthy medicinal effect. It can be legitimately undertaken only when the action is sustained by a great moral principle implicit in the democratic process, and only when there is no great danger it will be a preface to riot and civil war, or imperil the functioning of democratic political life.

There is such a thing as social timing in human affairs. Properly regarded, it enables one to strike a blow for human liberation which will echo in the hearts and minds of even those against whom it is directed. If social timing is disregarded, then, no matter how exalted the motive behind the action, it may shatter all bonds of community and have disastrous effects upon the cause of freedom. A half-century ago, the Southern sit-ins and sit-downs would have resulted in a series of bloody disasters. What Gandhi accomplished against the British could not have had the same effect at the time against a Nazi or Communist or Japanese military regime, because British democracy had already reached a point where its colonial possessions troubled the sensibilities and conscience of its citizens.

One may contrast the civil disobedience of the sit-in and sit-down strikes against racial segregation in the United States with the kind of sit-in and sit-down strikes conducted by the left-wing Socialist party of Japan in recent years. Seizing upon the phrase "the dictatorship of the majority," from some misremembered context in the lessons of their American teachers of the Occupation, and fearful of the fancied consequences of legislation proposed by the majority party in the Japanese Diet, they mobilized their partisans time and again to prevent the speaker from opening the session and by locked-arm tactics prevented the ministers and leading members of the opposing party from attending to their legislative functions. Even if their grievances had been legitimate, and their fears of unwise legislation justified, by their tactics they did far more damage to the faltering, uncertain traditions of democratic process in Japan than what would have resulted from the enactment of the measures they proposed. We must therefore distinguish between the tactic of civil disobedience as part of a calculated strategy to destroy the political democratic process — Communists too pose as pacifists and civil libertarian absolutists! — and civil disobedience undertaken with a kind of religious veneration for the values of democracy and which inspires by its openness and self-sacrifice community rethinking of the issues involved.

All this may strike enthusiasts, who identify good causes only with their own causes, as hedging the right to civil disobedience about with too many restrictions and cautions to make it a powerful means of social protest and change. But I submit that democratic theory requires that these limitations be put upon it, whereas common sense tells us that the effectiveness of civil disobedience in raising the standards of democratic practice is, beyond a certain point, inversely proportional to its frequency.

Lest I be misunderstood, I should like to repeat that nothing I have written about civil disobedience implies that there is an obligation on the moral and religious dissenter to accept the authority of the political system of democracy blindly, to forgo his moral claims to defy the entire structure of the democratic ethos on the grounds that it imperils some sacred value or some assurance of salvation which for him is beyond price and commands an *unpostponable* allegiance. In other words, if individuals refuse to play within the rules of the democratic game on the ground that these rules are too frivolous for the great stakes at issue, they are free to act as if they are at war with the democratic community. By the same token, democrats are just as free to crush them if they resort to war instead of argument. Despite Lincoln's words in praise of democracy as a political religion, his moral sensibilities rejected the absolutism which makes a fetish of any set of political institutions independently of their fruits. Facing the grim threat of rebellion which he believed both politically and morally unjustified, he nonetheless acknowledged in his First Inaugural, "If by the mere force of numbers a majority should deprive a minority of any clearly written constitutional right, it might in a moral point of view justify revolution — certainly would if such a right were a vital one."

I am not asserting that in such historical situations of conflict, when conscience is arrayed against conscience, both sides are equally justified merely because they stake their lives on the outcome. One or another side may be hasty, partial, or mistaken about what their needs and interests are, and the consequences of the different methods of gratifying them. The faith of the democrat in this juncture of disagreement is one with the faith of all liberal civilization. It is that so long as the processes of reflective inquiry are kept open, what seems to be an ultimate or inarbitrable conflict of interest and value may prove to be negotiable — at the very least, that mutual agreement can be established that there are some lesser evils in the situation which are preferable to the risks of mutual destruction. If and when such conflicts are not negotiable, if it is true that the reflective good of one side is incompatible with the reflective good of the other, what is shown is *not* that the moral values at issue are devoid of objectivity but that they lack universality, not that they are relativistic, in the sense that they are arbitrary and subjective, but that they are relational — that is to say, related to the kind of creatures we are or may become.

At any rate, whether the alleged antinomies of "ultimate" moral conflict can be resolved by this theory of objective relativism, the freedom or liberty which is inherent in the theory and practice of democracy is not the liberty to do anything one's conscience dictates. A surprisingly large number of generous spirits have been misled by this notion. No less a thinker than Lord Acton, in his *History of Freedom*, gives currency to this illusion of noble but naïve minds. He writes: "Liberty is the assurance that every man shall be protected in doing what he believes his duty, against the influence of authority and majorities, custom and opinion." This would entail our protecting the actions of madmen and fools, and invite perpetual war between conflicting fanaticisms. The only duty which can make a legitimate claim to overarching authority in a democratic community is the duty to accept the test of all the rational methods that can be brought to bear on our value claims.

These value claims may be legion, and when intelligence tests them, it can only do so in the light of commonly shared values which grow out of common interests. Although these too may be questioned at any given time they possess the working authority of experience. None is final. A democratic society is more congenial than other societies to the recognition of a plurality of values. It is also more vulnerable than other societies in virtue of the potential conflicts latent in such plurality. That is why the perpetuation of the rationale of the democratic process becomes of primary importance to all who cherish the ideal of an open society with plural values, even when they differ among themselves concerning the order and hierarchy of values. Religious freedom was originally born as a consequence of the impotence of religious persecution. But, once having tasted the fruits of religious toleration, even the believer in the "true" religion — whatever it may be — is likely to accept religious freedom as intrinsically justified and not merely as a hedge against possible persecution or as a means of converting unbelievers.

There is a corresponding moral extension — not displacement — from individuals and individual values to society when it is considered as a set of arrangements which nurtures and cherishes individuals and individual values. The good life cannot be pursued independently of the good society because a bad society can make the good life impossible. Failure to recognize this sometimes leads to very strange pronouncements. Consider, for example, the avowal of E. M. Forster that "if I had to choose between betraying my country and betraying my friend, I hope I should have the guts to betray my country."

This paradoxical remark is Forster's way of saying that personal relations should come first in the order of our moral allegiances, and that social and political systems are ultimately to be tested by the character of the personal relations they make possible and not by production figures, rates of economic growth, and the mythologies of progress. To the extent that a democracy is truly committed to an equality of concern for all human beings to develop themselves to the fullest reach of their personalities, it is the faces which men turn to their neighbors in everyday life which carry the message of their faith rather than the cold and remote promises of their ideology.

Taken unqualifiedly, however, Forster's remark violates the very spirit which he strove to articulate. Surely his dictum does not apply to any country, any friend. Suppose the country a democracy, worthy of the two cheers which is top score for Forster for anything short of the City of God or brotherly love. Suppose the country a democracy which regards the individual as possessing intrinsic worth, and which views the quality of personal relations as the test of all social institutions. Suppose the country a democracy which encourages variety and permits criticism. Does this not make an enormous difference to the decision of which to betray — country or friend? And suppose one's friend — something hard to imagine but conceivable — turns out to be a Quisling, a Fuchs, a Hiss, prepared to open the gates of the open society to its deadly foes — foes of every value Forster holds dear. Would Forster still pray to have the guts to betray his country rather than his friend? I very much doubt it. In betraying his country he would be betraying many more friends, who are no less deserving of his concern, than the one who creates the dilemma. Nor is it necessary to paint countries in black-and-white contrasts to recognize that it is the direction in which they are moving which counts.

The days of Epicurus, who could cultivate his friendships and his garden in independence of the world, are gone forever. There is no longer any distinction between Greek and barbarian. We are all Greeks, and underlying all other differences is whether we are to live in a free society or a totalitarian one. To profess an indifference to the good society in behalf of the pursuit of the good life for ourselves and our friends indicates an indifference to the lives of others which is sure to be revenged upon us and our descendants. It is not necessary, even if it were possible, to love all men, but in a democracy it is necessary to respect every man until he forfeits our respect.

This poses for us the last great problem. Its theoretical roots are as tangled and deep as its practical sweep is troublesome and wide. What attitude should the democratic community take toward political groups which invoke democratic rights and privileges in order to destroy the entire system that makes these rights and privileges possible? What action, if any, should a democratic community take toward any minority that proposes, if and when it comes to power, to make forever impossible the opportunity of any other minority to become a majority through peaceful and orderly means, by destroying all the rights of the Bill of Rights and instituting a reign of terror?

This problem is posed in a unique way by twentieth-century totalitarianism — Fascism, Nazism, and Communism. Once these totalitarian movements come to power, the system of terror they establish cannot be overthrown except by war — which every humane person, for obvious reasons, would like to avoid. Liberal and democratic opinion has often proved helpless or inept in meeting the danger. The errors which Kerensky made with regard to the Bolsheviks were repeated by the Weimar Republic with regard to the Nazis. I have discussed elsewhere the cluster of problems connected with the defense of democracy against the varieties of totalitarian attack, but one important problem keeps recurring and deserves extended analysis.

Let us rehearse a few preliminary distinctions in order to determine their bearing on the main problem. One of the great differences between the Fascist and Communist totalitarian movements today is that although both are equally hostile to democratic government, the latter are affiliated with a foreign power and serve as organized fifth columnists of the Kremlin, coordinating their activities at the behest of the Soviet Union with the Communist strategy for world domination.

In the United States, as distinct from some European countries, the Communist movement is not and has never been a domestic danger. It has never even acquired a mass character. But the Communist party and its immediate periphery — consisting of individuals under its discipline, but technically not members — are tied to the international Soviet apparatus in multiple ways. Their chief task is to infiltrate into key sensitive and influential posts in government, trade unions, cooperatives, and peace movements in order to do the bidding of the Kremlin on appropriate occasions. The evidence of this is massive and overwhelming. For this and other reasons, I believe that the Smith Act should be recast or amended, since repeal is impracticable, in order to bring Communist organizational activities, and not its propaganda, under the scope of the law.

This still leaves the chief theoretical question to which I wish to address myself. There are Communists who are quite independent in their notions of how to destroy the open society. They are not affiliated with the Kremlin, and may even be at odds with it on points of sectarian doctrine. There are other types of native totalitarianism, proud of their indigenous character, whose leaders, despite their rhetoric about Americanism, are vehemently opposed to democracy and wish to destroy it. What should the attitude of democrats be toward them if they avoid overt organization and merely teach and preach the necessity for the overthrow of democracy and the establishment of a dictatorship?

The current interpretation of the doctrine of "clear and present danger," referred to in the first chapter, is somewhat vague. I would restate the doctrine in order to make juries, not judges, determiners both of the facts which define the danger and of the specific consequences of the words used. Substantially, this position expresses the point of view of enlightened common sense, as well as the basic Jeffersonian philosophy which is a foe of all absolutism.

It is this Jeffersonian position I wish to contrast with a recurrent view which argues that in principle a democracy is justified in denying political privileges to those who would destroy it. This view has recently been restated with great ingenuity by Professor Ernest van den Haag, and argues that a democracy not merely is justified in repressing groups which *act* or *organize* to overthrow it by violence but is justified in principle in denying the right of political organization to any group that proposes to destroy democracy by peaceful means.

The argument runs as follows. Belief in democracy is belief in a system of self-government. This entails the political right and power of its citizens to control and change the government in accordance with their desires. Consequently, the functioning of a democracy is subject to two limitations. Although the citizens may delegate power to the government to rule for a limited period of time, they cannot surrender this power permanently. The government must always return at some point for a renewal of its mandate. Citizens cannot elect to abandon the power of election. Second, the power of the government must be so limited that it cannot deprive citizens of their right to replace it, and cannot suppress those liberties of speech, press, and assembly which are essential to the exercise of that right.

> The fathers of our Constitution were successful in protecting us against a government that might keep itself in power by taking away our rights. Less attention was paid to the possibility that some citizens might *give away* their democratic birthright and invite others to do so, as large groups abroad have done. Yet if our right to choose the government freely is *inalienable,* then we are not entitled to *give* the right away any more than the government is entitled to *take* it away. We cannot then elect a government that does not recognize the right of the people to oust it peacefully or that denies the necessary civil liberties. Nor, if freedom is to be inalienable, can invitations to alienate it be recognized as a legitimate part of the democratic process.

This is another way of saying that in a democracy, once it has been established, the one thing that is not open to popular decision is the principle of popular decision itself. Otherwise, so it is claimed, democracy would be self-stultifying. Leonard Nelson, a great German philosopher in the Platonic tradition, came precisely to this conclusion. He argued that democracy was self-defeating because it was based on the self-contradictory principle that all basic policies be decided by majority vote. This made it possible for the majority to vote to abolish majority rule — which is absurd. The argument I am considering denies the contradiction by refusing to allow the use of our political freedom to abolish it. It restricts the application of the majority principle so that the principle itself is not subject to decision. It asserts that one freedom — to give up freedom — must be precluded at *any* time, if freedom is to be preserved at *all* times.

The argument draws an analogy between the freedom of an individual voluntarily to become a slave and the freedom of citizens in a democracy to sacrifice their rights to a dictatorship, and denies the legitimacy of both. Once we abolish involuntary servitude, we cannot permit individuals to alienate their freedom by entering into voluntary servitude. We maximize the amount of desirable freedom in the world by denying them this one freedom. Similarly, once we establish democracy, we cannot permit citizens to alienate their political freedom. In this way, we maximize their freedom of political choice by denying them this one choice. After all, John Stuart Mill himself admitted that the principle of freedom cannot require that a man "should be free not to be free. It is not freedom to be allowed to alienate his freedom."

The argument continues:

> . . . by installing a government which is to be the irremovable and total master of their fate, those voting to become *voluntary* political slaves would necessarily compel some of their fellows into *involuntary* servitude. They would not only irreversibly mortgage their own future; they would also deprive of political freedom those who want to keep it. . . .
>
> Nor is this all. Any vote by which we abdicate our right to future free election also robs our children of their heritage of freedom. To allow citizens to vote against democracy is to allow them to sell their children into slavery. . . .
>
> Our heritage permits us forever to elect and to replace governments as we see fit. Our fiduciary duty requires us to keep this sacred trust intact for our children, to protect it against those who want to rob us of it by violence, as well as against those who want to

seduce us to give it away. It is not ours to give. Hence, we have no business voting it away and no one has any business trying to corrupt us into doing so. We ought not to permit advocacy of the ballot to extinguish democracy any more than we can allow advocacy of resort to violence. For the end, the surrender of power to a group which would not recognize the right of our children to oust it, is vicious in itself regardless of the means used. And the means are tainted by the vice of the illicit end. To advocate violence to overthrow a democratic government is to propose illegal means for an illegal end. To advocate a vote to overthrow democracy is to advocate an illegal end to be achieved by means that lose their legitimate character to the extent to which they are used for that end.

These arguments express the *absolutist* position on democracy. They make explicit what is implicit in the thought of many conservative critics of democracy. They have considerable weight, but at best, where valid, they add up to an argument *for* retaining democracy, not an argument against permitting *agitation* for the destruction of democracy.

This may be more apparent when we consider some analogous situations. Those who believe in tolerance must, if they are sincere, be opposed to intolerance. To be opposed to intolerance certainly requires that any *acts* of intolerance be prevented or punished; it may even require that incitement to intolerance, when this threatens to eventuate into intolerant action, may be prevented or punished. But does it require that those who propose that our policy of tolerance should be abolished for a policy of intolerance — and give reasons for it — should be prevented or punished for making such proposals? I do not think so. We may condemn them as foolish or even immoral, but we cannot prevent or punish them for making the proposal without abandoning our own principle of tolerance.

Let us concretize this with an example drawn from religious history. Those who believe in religious freedom extend to all religious groups, within the limits of existing moral principles, freedom to practice their religion. In the past some Catholic theologians have asserted that if and when believing Catholics constitute a majority of the population, they would be justified in denying to false and heretical religions the freedom to proselytize as well as their freedom from taxation. Such action was alleged to be in consonance with their doctrine that it is wrong to permit apostles of false religions to propagate for their faith and thus endanger the eternal salvation of the souls of believers in the true faith. This doctrine had fateful consequences for the Jesuits in Japan in the seventeenth century. The Japanese were, and still are, very tolerant of religious differences. When they discovered that the Jesuits, whom they had previously welcomed, actually believed that Christianity, as they interpreted it, was the only true religion, and that under certain circumstances, this warranted the true believers denying religious freedom to heretics and infidels, they turned on the Jesuits and exterminated them. Religious freedom was only for those who believed in religious freedom.

Today it is denied that this notion of principled intolerance is canonic Catholic doctrine, and some prelates have been excommunicated for professing similar views. But as far as the logic of the situation is concerned, there is no inconsistency in tolerating the expression of all religious opinions including the *opinion,* as distinct from current practice, that the true religious faith justifies in the future repression of religious error. Such an opinion is undoubtedly a powerful reason for not subscribing to such a religion; by itself it is not a sufficient ground for legal interdictment of the profession of the religion. If a group promises some day to interfere with our religious freedom but scrupulously refrains from doing so now, our duty is to agitate and educate to prevent them from winning political power to carry out their threat to our religious freedom. It is not to violate their religious freedom now.

Is the situation any different with respect to belief in democracy? Must a democracy make the democratic principle an unchallengeable axiom in political thought? The faith of democracy rests upon the belief that the interests which divide men may be more successfully settled to their mutual satisfaction by popular debate, discussion, and the give and take of peaceful negotiation than by anarchy or despotism. Shall this faith itself be made sacrosanct, immune to critical inquiry? Shall we, in the name of democracy, refuse to permit democracy to be judged for fear of losing it forever? Grant that the fear and danger are there. Is the only way of meeting it the conversion of a democratic principle into an absolute presupposition? If it is, in what way does a democracy of this sort logically differ from a form of despotism — however enlightened or benevolent? We are told that "when necessary we must restrict the people's rule to conserve their liberty." Is this not equivalent to abandoning the majority principle and substituting the rule of the watchful minority who must set themselves up as the perpetual guardians of the liberties of their wards — the people? Politically, this reformulates the position of Rousseau that, if necessary, individuals and, for that matter, the entire people, since numbers are irrelevant here, must be "forced to be free" — the premise or seed of a new authoritarianism.

Is it permissible for a majority to alienate the freedom of a minority together with its own? No, not if one believes in freedom. But if the majority does not believe in freedom, even though as a minority we may fiercely complain and forcibly resist it, we cannot charge it with inconsistency. If the majority does believe in freedom, and prevents the minority which wishes to alienate its own and others' freedom from doing so, the minority in this instance has the same formal right to complaint and can take the same risk of action. There is no logical inconsistency here either.

Every majority decision in a democracy decides something, good or bad, to which by definition the minority is opposed. But we are not discussing what is specifically good or bad, but only the legitimacy of the majority action, under the democratic rules, in voting into office those who will destroy democracy. If a democracy behaves this way, it would establish, for those who believe in personal freedom, sufficient evidence of the inadequacy of a democratic system to preserve human freedom and a decent social order. It does not justify them in asserting that a true democracy consists in preventing the majority from doing what is foolish or unwise. If this were to be construed as democracy, we should have to regard Plato as a democrat-something, which would be dismissed as absurd in the light of customary usage.

The same considerations hold in considering the argument that the surrender of democracy by any majority is "undemocratic" because it binds future generations. No decision irrevocably binds future generations. The decision to uphold a democratic system does not obligate future generations to preserve it; the decision to surrender it does not prevent future generations from restoring it.

Any political system which accepts the premise that a people must be forced to be free seems to me to be psychologically defective. Freedom — like loyalty, like love — by the very nature of the human emotions involved, cannot be commanded. Those who are prevented from expressing their wish to challenge democracy will not thereby cease wishing and feeling. They will be driven to express their determination to transform the system of democracy by hypocritical professions of strengthening it.

Despite asseverations to the contrary, the danger that a people which has once enjoyed democracy will voluntarily vote a totalitarian regime into power, although always present, seen in the perspective of history has rarely been acute. Historically, there is no clear example in which the majority of a self-governing people entrusted its destiny to a dictator who declared that he would end their liberties in the future. Neither Bolshevism nor Fascism came to power through the vicissitudes of the free political process. Although Hitler reached the chancellorship by constitutional means, the Nazi party received a majority only after a campaign in which it unloosened a reign of terror against its political opponents. Nonetheless, instances can be cited of communities living in comparative freedom which voluntarily voted to place themselves under the heel of dictatorships. The plebiscite by which the Saar voted to rejoin a Nazi Germany rather than affiliate with a democratic France or remain independent shows that the spirit of nationalism may be stronger than allegiance to democracy. Today in Italy and France a complex pattern of fear, hate, and myth may prove stronger than both the spirit of nationalism and the love of freedom. Although improbable, the situation is not inconceivable.

Nonetheless, it is not necessary to make a religious absolute out of any set of political institutions and place them beyond the reach of criticism and change. The greatness, the nobility of the American Revolution lies in the fact that it was conceived as an experiment in liberty. Until the thought of the American Enlightenment challenged the view, it was assumed, on the basis of the record of human ignorance, folly, and cruelty in history, that men were born either to rule or to be ruled. It was the daring hypothesis of the philosopher-statesmen of the American Republic that if given an opportunity, under conditions in which they had free access to information and in which traditions of free speech and press prevailed, men could be trusted to govern themselves. "I have no fear," wrote Jefferson, "but that the result of our experiment will be, that men may be trusted to govern themselves without a master. Could the contrary of this be proved, I should conclude either that there is no God, or that He is a malevolent being."

Events have so far confirmed this faith, although it has come near to failing. But it cannot be finally confirmed, because self-government is a *continuing experiment* facing new challenges which are created by the very successes of the past, challenges which require more and more resourcefulness, more and better education, and a commitment as deep and sustained as that which inspired those who left us our heritage of freedom.

Jefferson and those who fought to make the American experiment in freedom succeed staked not only their faith in God and human intelligence, they staked their very lives. Creative intelligence, courage to think and act on a world scale, and a passion for human freedom cannot guarantee the survival of liberal civilization today, but they are our best hope.

The world we live in is far removed from Jefferson's. The dangers to peace and to freedom are more massive and dreadful than he ever conceived them. Only those who refuse to see can deny that the threatening tides of Communist totalitarianism threaten to engulf the remaining islands of freedom — West Berlin, West Germany, Western Europe. They are already lapping at the shores of the Western Hemisphere, not far from the North American mainland. The prospects of conflict are so fearful that one can observe in Europe and in Great Britain, and even in the United States, a growing mood which defines our choice as limited to universal destruction, if we resist Communist aggression, or surrender to Communism if we do not resist. These alternatives are neither exclusive nor exhaustive — not exclusive, because surrender does not guarantee survival; not exhaustive, because there is an entire gamut of possibilities that remain to be explored which, without sacrificing human freedom, can preserve peace.

In moments of crisis, however, there are those who are prepared to abandon the experiment of freedom and self-government for the sake of survival at any price and at all costs in human infamy. They say that if the defense of freedom imperils peace, then better life under Communist despotism, with all its evils, than the risk of destruction. To which, I reply, invoking in all humility the values of the Jeffersonian tradition: those who will never risk their lives for freedom will surely lose their freedom without surely saving their lives; that unless we prize something in life which is more precious than mere life, we have renounced the human estate, that in our precarious world, intelligence and courage have proved to have greater survival value than hysterical fear; and that if we continue to place our trust in them, we are justified, in Jefferson's words, "to disdain despair, encourage trial, and nourish hope."

# PART FOUR

---

# OBLIGATION
# AND DISSENT
# IN TIME OF WAR

# Introduction

The problems of obligation and dissent in time of war are many and extremely varied. But they all arise in a time of great crisis, when things seem distorted and exaggerated. In wartime moral problems in politics become especially acute and agonizing, in some instances because the time to decide is short, as with the young man wrestling with whether he ought to fight; or because the conditions for moral decision making are otherwise severe, as is often the situation of prisoners of war. Such conditions are always difficult because the stakes of war are overwhelmingly high. One's life and the life of one's political community may well be at stake.

As a result, theories and problems of obligation and dissent in time of war present fascinating cases of morality in regard to politics in extremis, cases unusually hard in time or place or in consequences. They receive here a harsh test. Since no political theory made for only sunny days is worth much, we cannot ignore the tests and the problems of war.

More important though, moral issues in politics cannot ignore the special case of war and its aftermath because war creates some of the most acute problems of obligation. In our time this process is obvious. As the Indochina War has dragged on, we have frequently come face to face with problems of obligation and dissent. For some of America's younger citizens these issues of obligation and dissent in time of war represent not special cases in a special situation, but common cases in an ordinary situation. For them the "ordinary" world of peace is a vague memory, or scarcely even that.

We will investigate three questions of morality in politics raised by war. First, we will consider pacifism, again a living issue. J. Narveson's careful, analytical attempt to refute the logical and empirical basis for a pacifist stand is countered by the M. J. Whitman essay specifically attacking Narveson. Both pieces represent real attempts to consider pacifism seriously as a moral position, substituting argument for the rhetoric and counter-rhetoric that usually hopelessly clouds this important issue.

A second issue, perhaps the most fascinating, is that of prisoners of war. What is their obligation? Are they obligated to the military, to their political community, to their families, to their fellow prisoners, to whom? This issue lives for prisoners in Vietnam today, as it did for Captain Bucher of the Pueblo. In a real sense, the issues of obligation of the POW camp are those of society as a whole, only in more severe circumstances, and are thus inescapable even if few of us will ever have to actually endure becoming POWs.

In their articles Professors Walzer and Fowler consider several points of view. Grappling with largely common moral problems regarding POWs, their pieces form a debate on many of the key issues.

Finally, several pieces treat an issue of tremendous personal concern to many young men today, conscientious objection and selective conscientious objection. Both Quentin Quade's and the late John Courtney Murray's essays explore with caution and insight the difficult moral issues involved in reconciling individual moral and political beliefs and obligations to a general political community. Both opt for conscientious and even selective conscientious objection, but only after an examination that fully explores, doubts, and acknowledges differing positions.

Together these three issue areas: pacifism, prisoners of war, conscientious objection, hardly constitute all the vital moral issues involved in the politics of war. None for instance directly confronts the question of whether war can ever be morally right, though of course both the pacifism and the selective conscientious objection discussions do not ignore this matter. Nonetheless, these three issues do focus on the specific problem of this book, obligation and dissent with regard to war. As such, they are a summons to all of us to struggle to understand what ought to be in the ever fascinating, ever complex realm of the political.

# Pacifism

## Pacifism: A Philosophical Analysis

### JAN NARVESON

Several different doctrines have been called "pacifism," and it is impossible to say anything cogent about it without saying which of them one has in mind. I must begin by making it clear, then, that I am limiting the discussion of pacifism to a rather narrow band of doctrines, further distinctions among which will be brought out below. By "pacifism," I do *not* mean the theory that violence is evil. With appropriate restrictions, this is a view that every person with any pretensions to morality doubtless holds: nobody thinks that we have a right to inflict pain wantonly on other people. The pacifist goes a very long step further. *His* belief is not only that violence is evil but also that it is morally wrong to use force to resist, punish, or prevent violence. This further step makes pacifism a radical moral doctrine. What I shall try to establish below is that it is in fact, more than merely radical — it is actually incoherent because self-contradictory in its fundamental intent. I shall also suggest that several moral attitudes and psychological views which have tended to be associated with pacifism as I have defined it do not have any necessary connection with that doctrine. Most proponents of pacifism, I shall argue, have tended to confuse these different doctrines, and that confusion is probably what accounts for such popularity as pacifism has had.

It is next in order to point out that the pacifistic attitude is a

From *Ethics,* Vol. 75, pp. 259–271. Copyright 1965, University of Chicago. Reprinted by permission.

matter of degree, and this in two respects. In the first place, there is the question: how much violence should not be resisted, and what degree of force is one not entitled to use in resisting, punishing, or preventing it? Answers to this question will make a lot of difference. For example, everyone would agree that there are limits to the kind and degree of force with which a particular degree of violence is to be met: we do not have a right to kill someone for rapping us on the ribs, for example, and yet there is no tendency toward pacifism in this. We might go further and maintain, for example, that capital punishment, even for the crime of murder, is unjustified without doing so on pacifist grounds. Again, the pacifist should say just what sort of a reaction constitutes a forcible or violent one. If somebody attacks me with his fists and I pin his arms to his body with wrestling holds which restrict him but cause him no pain, is that all right in the pacifist's book? And again, many non-pacifists could consistently maintain that we should avoid, to the extent that it is possible, inflicting a like pain on those who attempt to inflict pain on us. It is unnecessary to be a pacifist merely in order to deny the moral soundness of the principle, "an eye for an eye and a tooth for a tooth." We need a clarification, then, from the pacifist as to just how far he is and is not willing to go. But this need should already make us pause, for surely the pacifist cannot draw these lines in a merely arbitrary manner. It is his reasons for drawing the ones he does that count, and these are what I propose to discuss below.

The second matter of degree in respect of which the pacifist must specify his doctrine concerns the question: who ought not to resist violence with force? For example, there are pacifists who would only claim that they themselves ought not to. Others would say that only pacifists ought not to, or that all persons of a certain type, where the type is not specified in terms of belief or non-belief in pacifism, ought not to resist violence with force. And, finally, there are those who hold that everyone ought not to do so. We shall see that considerations about this second variable doom some forms of pacifism to contradiction.

My general program will be to show that (1) only the doctrine that everyone ought not to resist violence with force is of philosophical interest among those doctrines known as "pacifism"; (2) that doctrine, if advanced as a moral doctrine, is logically untenable; and (3) the reasons for the popularity of pacifism rest on failure to see exactly what the doctrine is. The things which pacifism wishes to accomplish, insofar as they are worth accomplishing, can be managed on the basis of quite ordinary and conservative moral principles.

Let us begin by being precise about the kind of moral force the principle of pacifism is intended to have. One good way to do this is to consider what it is intended to deny. What would non-pacifists, which I suppose includes most people, say of a man who followed Christ's suggestion and, when unaccountably slapped, simply turned the other cheek? They might say that such a man is either a fool or a saint. Or they might say, "It's all very well for him to do that, but it's not for me"; or they might simply shrug their shoulders and say, "Well, it takes all kinds, doesn't it?" But they would *not* say that a man who did that ought to be punished in some way; they would not even say that he had done anything wrong. In fact, as I have mentioned, they would more likely than not find something admirable about it. The point, then, is this: the non-pacifist does *not* say that it is your *duty* to resist violence with force. The non-pacifist is merely saying that there's nothing wrong with doing so, that one has every right to do so if he is so inclined. Whether we wish to add that a person would be foolish or silly to do so is quite another question, one on which the non-pacifist does not *need* to take any particular position.

Consequently, a genuine pacifist cannot merely say that we may, if we wish, prefer not to resist violence with force. Nor can he merely say that there is something admirable or saintly about not doing so, for, as pointed out above, the non-pacifist could perfectly well agree with that. He must say, instead, that, for whatever class of people he thinks it applies to, there is something positively wrong about meeting violence with force. He must say that, insofar as the people to whom his principle applies resort to force, they are committing a breach of moral duty — a very serious thing to say. Just how serious, we shall ere long see.

Next, we must understand what the implications of holding pacifism as a moral principle are, and the first such implication requiring our attention concerns the matter of the size of the class of people to which it is supposed to apply. It will be of interest to discuss two of the four possibilities previously listed, I think. The first is that in which the pacifist says that only pacifists have the duty of pacifism. Let us see what this amounts to.

If we say that the principle of pacifism is the principle that all and only pacifists have a duty of not opposing violence with force, we get into a very odd situation. For suppose we ask ourselves, "Very well, which people are the pacifists then?" The answer will have to be "All those people who believe that pacifists have the duty not to meet violence with force." But surely one could believe that a certain class of people, whom we shall call "pacifists," have the duty not to meet violence with force without believing that one ought not, oneself, to meet violence with force. That is to say, the "principle" that pacifists ought to avoid meeting violence with force, is circular: it presupposes that one already knows who the pacifists are. Yet this is precisely what that statement of the principle is supposed to answer! We are supposed to be able to say that anybody who believes that principle is a pacifist; yet, as we have seen, a person could very well believe that a certain class of people called "pacifists" ought not to meet violence with force without believing that he himself ought not to meet violence with force. Thus everyone could be a "pacifist" in the sense of believing that statement and yet no one believe that he *himself* (or anyone in particular) ought to avoid meeting violence with force. Consequently, pacifism cannot be specified in that way. A pacifist must be a person who believes either that he himself (at least) ought not to meet force with force or that some larger class of persons, perhaps everyone, ought not to meet force with force. He would then be believing something definite, and we are then in a position to ask why.

Incidentally, it is worth mentioning that when people say things such as "Only pacifists have the duty of pacifism," "Only Catholics have the duties of Catholicism," and, in general, "Only *X*-ists have the duties of *X*-ism" they probably are falling into a trap which catches a good many people. It is, namely, the mistake of supposing that what it *is* to have a certain duty is to *believe* that you have a certain duty. The untenability of this is parallel to the untenability of the previously mentioned attempt to say what pacifism is. For, if having a duty is believing that you have a certain duty, the question arises, *"What* does such a person believe?" The answer that must be given if we follow this analysis would then be, "He believes that he believes that he has a certain duty"; and so on, ad infinitum.

On the other hand, one might believe that having a duty does not consist in believing that one has and yet believe that only those people really have the duty who believe that they have it. But in that case, we would, being conscientious, perhaps want to ask the question, "Well, *ought* I to believe that I have that duty, or oughtn't I?" If you say that the answer is "Yes," the reason cannot be that you already do believe it, for you are asking whether you *should*. On the other hand, the answer "No" or "It doesn't make any difference — it's up to you," implies that there is really no reason for doing the thing in question at all. In short, asking whether I ought to believe that I have a duty to do *x*, is equivalent to asking whether I should *do x*. A person might very well believe that he ought to do *x* but be wrong. It might be the case that he really ought *not* to do *x;* in that case the fact that he believes he ought to do *x,* far from being a reason why he ought to do it, is a reason for us to point out his error. It also, of course, presupposes that he has some reason other than his belief for thinking it is his duty to do *x*.

Having cleared this red herring out of the way, we must consider the view of those who believe that they themselves have a duty of pacifism and ask ourselves the question: what general kind of reason must a person have for supposing a certain type of act to be *his* duty, in a moral sense? Now, one answer he might give is that pacifism as such is a duty, that is, that meeting violence with force is, as such, wrong. In that case, however, what he thinks is not merely that *he* has this duty, but that *everyone* has this duty.

Now he might object, "Well, but no; I don't mean that everyone has it. For instance, if a man is defending, not himself, but *other* people, such as his wife and children, then he has a right to meet violence with force." Now this, of course, would be a very important qualification to his principle and one of a kind which we will be discussing in a moment. Meanwhile, however, we may point out that he evidently still thinks that, if it weren't for certain more important duties, everyone would have a duty to avoid meeting violence with force. In other words, he then believes that, other things being equal, one ought not to meet violence with force. He believes, to put it yet another way, that if one does meet violence with force, one must have a special excuse or justification of a moral kind; then he may want to give some account of just which excuses and justifications would do. Nevertheless, he is now holding a general principle.

Suppose, however, he holds that no one *else* has this duty of pacifism, that only he himself ought not to meet force with force, although it is quite all right for others to do so. Now if this is what our man feels, we may continue to call him a "pacifist," in a somewhat attenuated sense, but he is then no longer holding pacifism as a *moral* principle or, indeed, as a principle at all.[1] For now his disinclination for violence is essentially just a matter of taste. I like pistachio ice cream, but I wouldn't dream of saying that other people have a duty to eat it; similarly, this man just doesn't *like* to meet force with force, although he wouldn't dream of insisting that others act as he does. And this is a secondary sense of "pacifism" first, because pacifism has always been advocated on moral grounds and, second, because non-pacifists can easily have this same feeling. A person might very well feel squeamish, for example, about using force, even in self-defense, or he might not be able to bring himself to use it even if he wants to. But none of these has anything to do with asserting pacifism to be a duty. Moreover, a mere attitude could hardly license a man to refuse military service if it were required of him, or to join ban-the-bomb crusades, and so forth. (I fear, however, that such attitudes have sometimes caused people to do those things.)

And, in turn, it is similarly impossible to claim that your support of pacifism is a moral one if your position is that a certain selection of people, but no one else, ought not to meet force with force, even though you are unprepared to offer any reason whatever for this selection. Suppose, for example, that you hold that only the Arapahoes, or only the Chinese, or only people more than six feet high have this "duty." If such were the case, and no reasons offered at all, we could only conclude that you had a very peculiar attitude toward the Arapahoes, or whatever, but we would hardly want to say that you had a moral principle. Your "principle" amounts to saying that these particular individuals happen to have the duty of pacifism just because they are the individuals they are, and this, as Bentham would say, is the "negation of all principles." Of course, if you meant that somehow the property of being over six feet tall *makes* it your duty not to use violence, then you have a principle, all right, but a very queer one indeed unless you can give some further reasons. Again, it would not be possible to distinguish this from a sheer attitude.

Pacifism, then, must be the principle that the use of force to meet

---

[1] Compare, for example, K. Baier, *The Moral Point of View* (Cornell, 1958), p. 191.

force is wrong *as such,* that is, that nobody may do so unless he has a special justification.

There is another way in which one might advocate a sort of "pacifism," however, which we must also dispose of before getting to the main point. One might argue that pacifism is desirable as a tactic: that, as a matter of fact, some good end, such as the reduction of violence itself, is to be achieved by "turning the other cheek." For example, if it were the case that turning the other cheek caused the offender to break down and repent, then that would be a very good reason for behaving "pacifistically." If unilateral disarmament causes the other side to disarm, then certainly unilateral disarmament would be a desirable policy. But note that its desirability, if this is the argument, is due to the fact that peace is desirable, a moral position which anybody can take, pacifist or no, plus the purely contingent fact that this policy causes the other side to disarm, that is, it brings about peace.

And, of course, that's the catch. If one attempts to support pacifism because of its probable effects, then one's position depends on what the effects are. Determining what they are is a purely empirical matter, and, consequently, one could not possibly be a pacifist as a matter of pure principle if his reasons for supporting pacifism are merely tactical. One must, in this case, submit one's opinions to the governance of fact.

It is not part of my intention to discuss matters of fact, as such, but it is worthwhile to point out that the general history of the human race certainly offers no support for the supposition that turning the other cheek always produces good effects on the aggressor. Some aggressors, such as the Nazis, were apparently just "egged on" by the "pacifist" attitude of their victims. Some of the S.S. men apparently became curious to see just how much torture the victim would put up with before he began to resist. Furthermore, there is the possibility that, while pacifism might work against some people (one might cite the British, against whom pacifism in India was apparently rather successful — but the British are comparatively nice people), it might fail against others (e.g., the Nazis).

A further point about holding pacifism to be desirable as a tactic is that this could not easily support the position that pacifism is a *duty.* The question whether we have no *right* to fight back can hardly be settled by noting that not to fight back might cause the aggressor to stop fighting. To prove that a policy is a desirable one because it works is not to prove that it is *obligatory* to follow it. We surely need considerations a good deal less tenuous than this to prove such a momentous contention as that we have no *right* to resist.

It appears, then, that to hold the pacifist position as a genuine, full-blooded moral principle is to hold that nobody has a right to fight back when attacked, that fighting back is inherently evil, as such. It means that we are all mistaken in supposing that we have a right of self-protection. And, of course, this is an extreme and extraordinary position in any case. It appears to mean, for instance, that we have no right to punish criminals, that all of our machinery of criminal justice is, in fact, unjust. Robbers, murderers, rapists, and miscellaneous delinquents ought, on this theory, to be let loose.

Now, the pacifist's first move, upon hearing this, will be to claim that he has been misrepresented. He might say that it is only one's *self* that one has no right to defend, and that one may legitimately fight in order to defend other people. This qualification cannot be made by those pacifists who qualify as conscientious objectors, however, for the latter are refusing to defend their fellow citizens and not merely themselves. But this is comparatively trivial when we contemplate the next objection to this amended version of the theory. Let us now ask ourselves what it is about attacks on *other* people which could possibly justify *us* in defending them, while we are not justified in defending ourselves? It cannot be the mere fact that they are other people than ourselves, for, of course, everyone is a different person from everyone else, and if such a consideration could ever of itself justify anything at all it could also justify anything whatever. That mere difference of person, as such, is of no moral importance, is a presupposition of anything that can possibly pretend to be a moral theory.

Instead of such idle nonsense, then, the pacifist would have to mention some specific characteristic which every *other* person has which we lack and which justifies us in defending them. But this, alas, is impossible, for, while there may be some interesting difference between *me,* on the one hand, and everyone else, on the other, the pacifist is not merely addressing himself to me. On the contrary, as we have seen, he has to address himself to everyone. He is claiming that each person has no right to defend himself, although he does have a right to defend other people. And, therefore, what is needed is a characteristic which distinguishes *each* person from everyone else, and not just *me* from everyone else — which is plainly self-contradictory.

If the reader does not yet see why the "characteristic" of being identical with oneself cannot be used to support a moral theory, let him reflect that the proposition "Everyone is identical with himself" is a trivial truth — as clear an example of an analytic proposition as there could possibly be. But a statement of moral principle is not a trivial truth; it is a substantive moral assertion. But non-tautologous statements, as everyone knows, cannot logically be derived from tautologies, and, consequently, the fact that everyone is identical with himself cannot possibly be used to prove a moral position.

Again, then, the pacifist must retreat in order to avoid talking idle nonsense. His next move, now, might be to say that we have a right to defend all those who are not able to defend themselves. Big, grown-up men who are able to defend themselves ought not to do so, but they ought to defend mere helpless children who are unable to defend themselves.

This last, very queer theory could give rise to some amusing logical gymnastics. For instance, what about groups of people? If a group of people who cannot defend themselves singly can defend themselves together, then when it has grown to that size ought it to stop defending itself? If so, then every time a person *can* defend someone else, he would form with the person being defended a "defensive unit" which was able to defend itself, and thus would by his very presence debar himself from making the defense. At this rate, no one will ever get defended, it seems: the defenseless people by definition cannot defend themselves, while those who can defend them would enable the group consisting of the defenders and the defended to defend themselves, and hence they would be obliged not to do so.

Such reflections, however, are merely curious shadows of a much more fundamental and serious logical problem. This arises when we begin to ask: but why should even defenseless people be defended? If resisting violence is inherently evil, then how can it suddenly become permissible when we use it on behalf of other people? The fact that they are defenseless cannot possibly account for this, for it follows from the theory in question, that everyone ought to put himself in the position of people who are defenseless by refusing to defend himself. This type of pacifist, in short, is using the very characteristic (namely, being in a state of not defending oneself) which he wishes to encourage in others as a reason for denying it in the case of those who already have it (namely, the defenseless). This is indeed self-contradictory.

To attempt to be consistent, at least, the pacifist is forced to accept the characterization of him at which we tentatively arrived. He must indeed say that no one ought ever to be defended against attack. The right of self-defense can be denied coherently only if the right of defense, in general, is denied. This in itself is an important conclusion.

It must be borne in mind, by the way, that I have not said anything to take exception to the man who simply does not wish to defend himself. So long as he does not attempt to make his pacifism into a principle, one cannot accuse him of any inconsistency, however much one might wish to say that he is foolish or eccentric. It is solely with moral principles that I am concerned here.

We now come to the last and most fundamental problem of all. If we ask ourselves what the point of pacifism is, what gets it going, so to speak, the answer is, of course, obvious enough: opposition to violence. The pacifist is generally thought of as the man who is so much opposed to violence that he will not even use it to defend himself or anyone else. And it is precisely this characterization which I wish to show is, far from being plausible, morally inconsistent.

To begin with, we may note something which at first glance may seem merely to be a matter of fact, albeit one which should worry the pacifist, in our latest characterization of him. I refer to the commonplace observation that, generally speaking, we measure a man's degree of opposition to something by the amount of effort he is willing to put forth against it. A man could hardly be said to be dead set against something if he is not willing to lift a finger to keep it from going on. A person who claims to be completely opposed to something yet does nothing to prevent it would ordinarily be said to be a hypocrite.

As facts, however, we cannot make too much of these. The pacifist could claim to be willing to go to any length, short of violence, to prevent violence. He might, for instance, stand out in the cold all day long handing out leaflets (as I have known some to do), and this would surely argue for the sincerity of his beliefs.

But would it really?

Let us ask ourselves, one final time, what we are claiming when we claim that violence is morally wrong and unjust. We are, in the first place, claiming that a person *has no right* to indulge in it, as such (meaning that he has no right to indulge in it, *unless* he has an over-riding justification). But what do we mean when we say that he has no right to indulge in it? Violence, of the type we are considering, is a two-termed affair: one does violence *to* somebody, one cannot simply "do violence." It might be oneself, of course, but we are not primarily interested in those cases, for what makes it wrong to commit violence is that it harms the people to whom it is done. To say that it is wrong is to say that those to whom it is done have a right *not* to have it done to them. (This must again be qualified by pointing out that this is so only if they have done nothing to merit having that right abridged.)

Yet what could that right to their own security, which people have, possibly consist in, if not a right at least to defend themselves from whatever violence might be offered them? But lest the reader think that this is a gratuitous assumption, note carefully the reason why having a right involves having a right to be defended from breaches of that right. It is because the prevention of infractions of that right is precisely what one has a right to when one has a right at all. A right just *is* a status justifying preventive action. To say that you have a right to $X$ but that no one has any justification whatever for preventing people from depriving you of it, is self-contradictory. If you claim a right to $X$, then to describe some action as an act of depriving you of $X$, is logically to imply that its absence is one of the things that you have a right to.

Thus far it does not follow logically that we have a right to use force in our own or anyone's defense. What does follow logically is that one has a right to whatever may be necessary to prevent infringements of his right. One might at first suppose that the universe *could* be so constructed that it is never necessary to use force to prevent people who are bent on getting something from getting it.

Yet even this is not so, for when we speak of "force" in the sense in which pacifism is concerned with it, we do not mean merely physical "force." To call an action a use of force is not merely to make a reference to the laws of mechanics. On the contrary, it is to describe whatever is being done as being a means to the infliction on somebody of something (ordinarily physical) which he does not want done to him; and the same is true for "force" in the sense in which it applies to war, assault and battery, and the like.

The proper contrary of "force" in this connection is "rational persuasion." Naturally, one way there *might* be of getting somebody not to do something he has no right to do is to convince him he ought not to do it or that it is not in his interest to do it. But it is inconsistent, I suggest, to argue that rational persuasion is the only morally permissible method of preventing violence. A pragmatic reason for this is easy enough to point to: violent people are too busy being violent to be reasonable. We cannot engage in rational persuasion unless the enemy is willing to sit down and talk; but what if he isn't? One cannot contend that every human being can be persuaded to sit down and talk before he strikes, for this is not something we can determine just by reasoning: it is a question of observation, certainly. But these points are not strictly relevant any-way, for our question is not the empirical question of whether there is some handy way which can always be used to get a person to sit down and discuss moral philosophy when he is about to murder you. Our question is: *if* force is the only way to prevent violence in a given case, is its use justified *in that case?* This is a purely moral question which we can discuss without any special reference to matters of fact. And, moreover, it is precisely this question which we should have to discuss with the would-be violator. The point is that if a person can be rationally persuaded that he ought not to engage in violence, then precisely what he would be rationally persuaded of if we were to succeed would be the proposition that the use of force is justifiable to prevent him from doing so. For note that if we were to argue that only rational persuasion is permissible as a means of preventing him, we would have to face the question: do we mean *attempted* rational persuasion, or *successful* rational persuasion, that is, rational persuasion which really does succeed in preventing him from acting? Attempted rational persuasion might fail (if only be-cause the opponent is unreasonable), and then what? To argue that we have a right to use rational persuasion which also succeeds (i.e., we have a right to its success as well as to its use) is to imply that we have a right to prevent him from performing the act. But this, in turn, means that, if attempts at rational persuasion fail, we have a right to the use of force. Thus what we have a right to, if we ever have a *right* to anything, is not merely the use of rational persuasion to keep people from depriving you of the thing to which you have the right. We do indeed have a right to that, but we also have a right to anything else that might be necessary (other things being equal) to prevent the deprivation from occurring. And it is a logical truth, not merely a contingent one, that what *might* be necessary is *force*. (If merely saying something could miraculously deprive someone of the ability to carry through a course of action, then those speech-acts would be called a type of force, if a very mysterious one. And we could properly begin to oppose their use for precisely the same reasons as we now oppose violence.)

What this all adds up to, then, is that *if* we have any right at all, we have a right to use force to prevent the deprivation of the thing to which we are said to have a right. But the pacifist, of *all* people, is the one most concerned to insist that we do have some rights, namely, the right not to have violence done to us. This is logically implied in asserting it to be a duty on everyone's part to avoid violence. And this is why the pacifist's position is self-contradictory. In saying that violence is wrong, one is at the same time saying that people have a right to its prevention, by force if necessary. Whether and to what extent it may be necessary is a question of fact, but, since it is a question of fact only, the *moral* right to use force on some possible occasions is established.

We now have an answer to the question. How much force does a given threat of violence justify for preventive purposes? The answer, in a word, is "Enough." That the answer is this simple may at first sight seem implausible. One might suppose that some elaborate equation between the aggressive and the preventive force is needed: the punishment be proportionate to the crime. But this is a misunderstanding. In the first place, prevention and punishment are not the same, even if punishment is thought to be directed mainly toward prevention. The punishment of a particular crime logically cannot prevent *that* instance of the crime, since it presupposes that it has already been performed; and punishment need not involve the use of any violence at all, although law-enforcement officers in some places have a nasty tendency to assume the contrary. But preventive force is another matter. If a man threatens to kill me, it is desirable, of course, for me to try to prevent this by the use of the least amount of force sufficient to do the job. But I am justified even in killing him *if* necessary. This much, I suppose, is obvious to most people. But suppose his threat is much smaller: suppose that he is merely pestering me, which is a very mild form of aggression indeed. Would I be justified in killing him to prevent this, under any circumstances whatever?

Suppose that I call the police and they take out a warrant against him, and suppose that when the police come, he puts up a struggle. He pulls a knife or a gun, let us say, and the police shoot him in the ensuing battle. Has my right to the prevention of his annoying me extended to killing him? Well, not exactly, since the immediate threat in response to which he is killed is a threat to the lives of the policemen. Yet my annoyer may never have contemplated real violence. It is an unfortunate case of unpremeditated escalation. But this is precisely what makes the contention that one is justified in using enough force to do the job, whatever amount that may be, to prevent action which violates a right less alarming than at first sight it seems. For it is difficult to envisage a reason why extreme force is needed to prevent mild threats from realization except by way of escalation, and escalation automatically justifies increased use of preventive force.

The existence of laws, police, courts, and more or less civilized modes of behavior on the part of most of the populace naturally affects the answer to the question of how much force is necessary. One of the purposes of a legal system of justice is surely to make the use of force by individuals very much less necessary than it would otherwise be. If we try to think back to a "state of nature" situation, we shall have much less difficulty envisaging the need for large amounts of force to prevent small threats of violence. Here Hobbes' contention that in such a state every man has a right to the life of every other becomes understandable. He was, I suggest, relying on the same principle as I have argued for here: that one has a right to use as much force as necessary to defend one's rights, which include the right of safety of person.

I have said that the duty to avoid violence is only a duty, other things being equal. We might arrive at the same conclusion as we have above by asking the question: which "other things" might count as being *un*equal? The answer to this is that whatever else they may be, the purpose of preventing violence from being done is necessarily one of these justifying conditions. That the use of force is never justified to prevent initial violence being done to one logically implies that there is nothing wrong with initial violence. We cannot characterize it as being wrong if preventive violence is not simultaneously being characterized as justifiable.

We often think of pacifists as being gentle and idealistic souls, which in its way is true enough. What I have been concerned to show is that they are also confused. If they attempt to formulate their position using our standard concepts of rights, their position involves a contradiction: violence is wrong, *and* it is wrong to resist it. But the right to resist is precisely what having a right of safety of person is, if it is anything at all.

Could the position be reformulated with a less "committal" concept of rights? I do not think so. It has been suggested[2] that the pacifist need not talk in terms of this "kind" of rights. He can affirm, according to this suggestion, simply that neither the aggressors nor the defenders "have" rights to what they do, that to affirm their not having them is simply to be against the use of force, without this entailing the readiness to use force if necessary to protect the said rights. But this will not do, I believe. For I have not maintained that having a right, or believing that one has a right, entails a *readiness* to defend that right. One has a perfect right not to resist violence to oneself if one is so inclined. But our question has been whether self-defense is justifiable, and not whether one's belief that violence is wrong entails a willingness or readiness to use it. My contention has been that such a belief does entail the justifiability of using it. If one came upon a community in which no sort of violence was ever resisted and it was claimed in that community that the non-resistance was a matter of conscience, we should have to conclude, I think, not that this was a community of saints, but rather that this community lacked the concept of justice — or perhaps that their nervous systems were oddly different from ours.

The true test of the pacifist comes, of course, when he is called upon to assist in the protection of the safety of other persons and not just of himself. For while he is, as I have said, surely entitled to be pacific about his own person if he is so inclined, he is not entitled to be so about the safety of others. It is here that the test of principles comes out. People have a tendency to brand conscientious objectors as cowards or traitors, but this is not quite fair. They are acting as if they were cowards or traitors, but claiming to do so on principle.

---

[2] I owe this suggestion to my colleague, Leslie Armour.

It is not surprising if a community should fail to understand such "principles," for the test of adherence to a principle is willingness to act on it, and the appropriate action, if one believes a certain thing to be grossly wrong, is to takes steps to prevent or resist it. Thus people who assess conscientious objection as cowardice or worse are taking an understandable step: from an intuitive feeling that the pacifist does not really believe what he is saying they infer that his actions (or inaction) must be due to cowardice. What I am suggesting is that this is not correct: The actions are due, not to cowardice, but to confusion.

I have not addressed myself specifically to the question whether, for instance, conscription is morally justifiable, given that the war effort on behalf of which it is invoked is genuinely justifiable. Now, war efforts very often aren't justifiable (indeed, since at least one of the parties to each war must be an aggressor, a minimum of 50 per cent of war efforts must be unjustifiable); but if they ever are, is it then justifiable to conscript soldiers? In closing, I would suggest an answer which may seem surprising in view of my arguments a few pages back. My answer is that it is, but that in the case of conscientious objectors, the only justifiable means of getting them to comply is rational persuasion.

The reason is that, in showing that self-defense is morally justifiable, one has not simultaneously shown that the defense of other people is morally *obligatory*. The kinds of arguments needed to show that an act is obligatory are quite different from those which merely show that it is justified. And, since what has been shown is that self-defense is justifiable and not obligatory, the only conclusion that can be immediately inferred from this is that defense of others is also justifiable and not obligatory. Would it be possible to show that the defense of others (at least in some circumstances) is obligatory and not merely justifiable, without at the same time showing that self-defense is obligatory and not merely justifiable?

The only thing I can suggest here is that the answer requires us to speculate about the obligations of living in a community. If a community expects its members to assist in the common defense when necessary, it can make this clear to people and give them their choice either to be prepared to meet this obligation or to live somewhere else. But a community of pacifists would also be quite conceivable, a community in which no citizen could expect the others to defend him as a part of their community responsibilities. One might not care to live in such a community, but then, a pacifist might not care to live in our sort. When the community is a whole nation of present-day size, it is much more difficult to put the issue clearly to each citizen in advance. But the upshot of it is that (1) the issue depends upon what sort of community we conceive ourselves to have; (2) we do not have clearly formed views on this point; (3) there is no basic moral duty to defend others; (4) we therefore have no direct right to force people to become soldiers in time of justified wars; (5) but we do have a right to deny many basic community services to people who will not assist us in time of need by contributing the force of their arms; and so (6) the only thing to do is to try to argue conscientious objectors into assistance, pointing to all of the above factors and leaving them their choice.

Too much can easily be made of the issue of conscription *versus* voluntary service in time of war. (In time of peace, we have another issue altogether; my arguments here apply only when there is clear justification for defensive measures.) It must be remembered that there is a limit to what law can do in "requiring" compliance, and the pacifist is precisely the person who cannot be reached by the ordinary methods of the law, since he has made up his mind not to be moved by force. The philosophical difference lies, not in the question of whether compliance is ultimately voluntary, since with all laws it to some extent must be, but in the moral status which military service is presumed to have. The draft is morally justifiable if the defense of persons is considered a basic obligation of the citizen. In contemporary communities, it seems to me that there is good reason for giving it that status.

Many questions remain to be discussed, but I hope to have exposed the most fundamental issues surrounding this question and to have shown that the pacifist's central position is untenable.

# Is Pacifism Self-Contradictory?

### M. JAY WHITMAN

Jan Narveson argues[1] that pacifism, as a moral doctrine, is self-contradictory. The only doctrine Professor Narveson finds of philosophical interest among those commonly known as "pacifism" is the doctrine that no one ought to resist violence with physical force. He continues: "To hold the pacifist position as a genuine, full-blooded moral principle is to hold that nobody has a right to fight back when attacked, that fighting back is inherently evil, as such, . . . [and] that we are all mistaken in supposing that we have a right of self-protection."[2] Narveson concludes that the pacifist can deny the right of self-defense consistently only if he denies the right of defense in general. For, when we claim that violence is morally wrong, we are claiming that a person *has no right* to indulge in it. But a right *is* precisely a status justifying preventive action. To say that you have a right to freedom from violence, but that no one has any justification for preventing people from depriving you of it, is thus (he contends) self-contradictory. I shall show that, although the pacifists may be wrong, their position is not self-contradictory in the light of their probable use of priority rules and their probable conception of what it means to possess a moral right.

### I

Narveson's charge of self-contradiction is too strong because he fails to allow for the fact that pacifists can and do use rules of priority in making moral judgments. As he suggests, the pacifist is one who believes we are under the strictest of moral obligations never to employ physical force. The pacifist will maintain that physical force of any species will *always* lead to substantive evils and that our one

From *Ethics*, Vol. 76, pp. 307–308. Copyright 1966, University of Chicago. Reprinted by permission.
[1] "Pacifism: A Philosophical Analysis," *Ethics*, LXXV, No. 4 (July, 1965), 259–71.
[2] *Ibid.*, p. 264.

supreme moral obligation is to the negative part of the principle of benevolence (i.e., we ought never to do evil). The pacifist position, in other words, is "evil ought never to be done, 'though the heavens fall.' " In cases of conflict between two strict moral obligations, the pacifist must employ some priority rule. Specifically, he would hold that the strict obligation never to do evil (and therefore never to use physical force) must always take priority over the other strict obligations of contract, justice, and the like. For example, a democratic government may agree with the pacifist that the use of physical force very often leads to substantive evils. Nevertheless, it may still send military forces to war because the government thinks that the strict obligations of contract (e.g., international alliances) take priority, in that particular situation, over the strict obligation not to do evil. The pacifist strongly disagrees, arguing that the obligations of negative benevolence must *always* be prior; that we should never go to war because the use of physical force is itself a substantive evil and inevitably leads to greater substantive evil than any other immoral act; and that our supreme moral obligation is never to do evil or, if we must choose between evils, never to choose the greater. So, given the pacifist's rock-hard priority rule, he can consistently maintain the right to freedom from physical force while denying the right of defense.

This is not to say the pacifist is correct, only that he is not self-contradictory. Strict priority rules are difficult to defend in practice. One who asserts "Do $X$, 'though the heavens fall,' " generally believes that doing $X$ is the best way to keep the heavens from falling. And it may be that, if the firmament were ever to fall, even the most orthodox pacifist would be tempted to change his priority rule. We all use priority rules (more or less consistently) to decide conflicts between our strict obligations. The pacifist, although he may be wrong in being too doctrinaire, is not subject to Narveson's charge of self-contradiction if he employs his strict priority rule consistently.

## II

But Narveson holds that he cannot apply it consistently, because having a right (says he) is precisely being in a position which justifies preventive physical action in defense of that right. But this the pacifist may flatly, and rightly, deny. He argues that strict moral obligations confer corresponding rights to have those obligations fulfilled; but he could never agree that all such rights are precisely statuses justifying preventive action of the sort Narveson suggests. In the case of certain contractual obligations where there is an enforcement clause involved, it may be the case that the violation of a right entails preventive or retributive physical action, if necessary. But it is by no means clear that all strict obligations are of such a contractual, enforcement-clause sort. Likewise, it is by no means clear that the rights implied by all strict moral obligations are precisely statuses justifying preventive action. The pacifist would hold, I think quite plausibly, that one whose right is violated has a moral grievance against the transgressor, but not necessarily a license to use whatever means possible to obtain redress or to defend against the transgression. For example, we have a strict right to be told the truth under most normal circumstances. If someone tells us a lie, we may have a moral grievance against him. This griev-ance may be later manifested in many ways, for example, scolding, future distrust, etc.; but very rarely would this grievance entitle the aggrieved to a physical defense of his right. If the right transgressed were a contractual right — and the contract involved the stipulation that it is to be enforced by whatever means necessary — the remedy might take the form of physical force. But our right to be told the truth — and many of our other rights — are rarely of this sort; and even if they were, the pacifist would not enter into such contracts. Thus, unless Narveson intends to maintain some general contract theory of obligation, complete with enforcement clause, he will be unable to hold that the strict obligations to tell the truth, to do justice, not to do evil, etc., if violated, entail per se moral grievances identical with statuses justifying preventive physical actions. Narveson's argu-ment has an unsound premise, without which the pacifist's self-contra-diction cannot be proved.

# Selective Conscientious Objection

## War and Conscience

### JOHN COURTNEY MURRAY, S.J.

The nation is confronted today with the issue of selective conscientious objection, conscientious objection to particular wars or, as it is sometimes called, discretionary armed service.

The theoretical implications of the issue are complex and subtle. The issue raises the whole question of war as a political act and the means whereby it should be confined within the moral universe. The issue also raises the question of the status of the private conscience in the face of public law and national policy. In fact, the whole relation of the person to society is involved in this issue. Moreover, the practical implications of the issue are far reaching. Selective conscientious objection, as Gordon Zahn has pointed out, is an "explosive principle." If once admitted with regard to the issue of war, the consequences of the principle might run to great lengths in the civil community.

My brief comments on this far-reaching principle are here directed, for reasons that will appear, both to the academic community, especially the student community, and to the political community and its representatives.

A personal note may be permissible here. During the deliberations of the President's Advisory Commission on Selective Service, on which I was privileged to serve, I undertook to advocate that the revised statute should extend the provisions of the present statute to include

Reprinted by permission of Western Maryland College. From the text of a commencement address.

not only the absolute pacifist but also the relative pacifist; that the grounds for the status of conscientious objector should be not only religiously or non-religiously motivated opposition to participation in war in all forms, but also to similarly motivated opposition to participation in particular wars.

This position was rejected by the majority of the Commission. No Presidential recommendation was made to the Congress on the issue. There is evidence that the Congress is not sympathetic to the position of the selective objector and is not inclined to accept it. This does not mean that the issue has been satisfactorily settled. The public argument goes on and must go on. It is much too late in the day to defend the theory of General Hershey that "the conscientious objector by my theory is best handled if no one hears of him." The issue is before the country and it must be kept there.

It is true that the issue has been raised by a small number of people, chiefly in the academic community — students, seminarians, professors, not to speak of ministers of religion. But this group of citizens is socially significant. It must be heard and it must be talked to. I recognize that in many respects the issue has been raised rather badly, in ways that betray misunderstandings. Moreover, mistakes have been made about the mode of handling the issue. Nevertheless, the student community is to be praised for having raised a profound moral issue that has been too long disregarded in American life.

The American attitude toward war has tended to oscillate between absolute pacifism in peacetime and extremes of ferocity in wartime. Prevalent in American society has been an abstract ethic, conceived either in religious or in secularized terms, which condemns all war as immoral. No nation has the *jus ad bellum*. On the other hand, when a concrete historical situation creates the necessity for war, no ethic governs its conduct. There are no moral criteria operative to control the uses of force. There is no *jus in bello*. One may pursue hostilities to the military objective of unconditional surrender, and the nation may escalate the use of force to the paroxysm of violence of which Hiroshima and Nagasaki are forever the symbols, even though they were prepared for by the fire-bomb raids on Tokyo and by the saturation bombing of German cities. And all this use of violence can somehow be justified by slogans that were as simplistic as the principles of absolute pacifism.

These extreme alternatives are no longer tolerable. Our nation must make its way to some discriminating doctrine — moral, political, and military — on the uses of force. Perhaps the contemporary agitation in the academic community over selective conscientious objection may help in this direction. It has contributed to a revival of the traditional doctrine of the just war, whose origins were in Augustine and which was elaborated by the medieval Schoolmen and furthered by international jurists in the Scholastic tradition and by others in the later tradition of Grotius.

This doctrine has long been neglected, even by the churches; now we begin to witness its revival. We are also beginning to realize that it is not a sectarian doctrine. It is not exclusively Roman Catholic; in certain forms of its presentation, it is not even Christian. It emerges in the minds of all men of reason and good will when they face two inevitable questions. First, what are the norms that govern recourse to the violence of war? Second, what are the norms that govern the measure of violence to be used in war? In other words, when is war rightful, and what is rightful in war? One may indeed refuse the questions, but this is a form of moral abdication, which would likewise be fatal to civilization. If one does face the questions, one must arrive at the just war doctrine in its classical form, or at some analogue or surrogate, conceived in other terms.

The essential significance of the traditional doctrine is that it insists, first, that military decisions are a species of political decisions, and second, that political decisions must be viewed, not simply in the perspective of politics as an exercise of power, but of morality and theology in some valid sense. If military and political decisions are not so viewed, the result is the degradation of those who make them and the destruction of the human community.

My conclusion here is that we all owe some debt of gratitude to those who, by raising the issue of selective conscientious objection, have undertaken to transform the tragic conflict in South Vietnam into an issue, not simply of political decision and military strategy, but of moral judgment as well.

The mention of South Vietnam leads me to my second point. The issue of selective conscientious objection has been raised in the midst of the war in Southeast Asia. Therefore, there is danger lest the issue be muddled and confused, or even misused and abused. In South Vietnam we see war stripped of all the false sanctities with which we managed to invest World War I and World War II, and to a lesser extent even Korea. The South Vietnamese war is not a crusade. There is not even a villain of the piece, as the Kaiser was, or Hitler, or Hirohito. Not even Ho Chi Minh or Mao Tse-tung can be cast in the role of the man in the black hat. We have no easy justifying slogans. We cannot cry, "On to Hanoi," as we cried "On to Berlin" and "On to Tokyo." This war does not raise the massive issue of national survival. It is a limited military action for limited political aims. As we view it in the press or on television it almost seems to fulfill Hobbes's vision of human life in the state of pure nature, "nasty, brutish, and short" except that the war in South Vietnam will not be short. In the face of the reality of it, all our ancient simplisms fail us. The American people are uncomfortable, baffled, and even resentful and angry.

To state the problem quite coldly, the war in South Vietnam is subject to opposition on political and military grounds, and also on grounds of national interest. This opposition has been voiced, and voiced in passionate terms. It has evoked a response in the name of patriotism that is also passionate. Consequently, in this context, it is difficult to raise the moral issue of selective conscientious objection. There are even some to whom it seems dangerous to let the issue be raised at all.

At this juncture I venture to make a recommendation in the common interest of good public argument. The issue of selective conscientious objection must be distinguished from the issue of the justice of the South Vietnam war. If this distinction is not made and enforced in argument, the result will be confusion and the clash of passions. The necessary public argument will degenerate into a useless and harmful quarrel. The distinction can be made. I make it myself. I advocate selective conscientious objection in the name of the traditional moral doctrine on war and also in the name of traditional American political doctrine on the rights of conscience. I am also prepared to make the case for the American military presence and action in South Vietnam.

I hasten to add that I can just about make the moral case. But so it always is. The morality of war can never be more than marginal. The issue of war can never be portrayed in black and white. Moral judgment on the issue must be reached by a balance of many factors. To argue about the morality of war inevitably leads one into gray areas. This is the point that was excellently made by Mr. Secretary Vance in his thoughtful address to the Annual Convention of the

Episcopal Diocese of West Virginia on May 6th, 1967. It is evident here that our national tradition of confused moral thought on the uses of force does us a great disservice. It results in a polarization of opinion that makes communication among citizens difficult or even impossible. As Mr. Vance said, "In America today one of the greatest barriers to understanding is the very nature of the dialogue which has developed over the issue of Vietnam. It is heated and intolerant. The lines on both sides are too sharply drawn." I agree.

By the same token rational argument about selective conscientious objection will be impossible if public opinion is polarized by all the passions that have been aroused by the South Vietnam war. The two issues, I repeat, can and must be separated.

Another difficulty confronts us here. The issue about conscientious objection seems to have been drawn between the academic community and the political community — if you will, between poets and politicians, between scientists and statesmen, between humanists and men of affairs, between the churches and the secular world. It is, therefore, no accident that the dialogue at the present moment is in a miserable state. One may seek the reason for the fact in the differences in the climate of thought and feeling that prevail in the two distinct communities, academic and political. In consequence of this difference in climate each community, in a different way, can become the victim of the intellectual and moral vice that is known as the selective perception of reality.

It has been observed that the commitment of the intellectual today is not simply to the search for truth, but also to the betterment of the world — to the eradication of evil and to the creation of conditions of human dignity, first among which is peace. One might say that he has assumed a prophetic role, not unlike that of the churches. This is most laudable. The danger is lest the very strength of the moral commitment — to peace and against war — may foreclose inquiry into the military and political facts of the contemporary world — the naked facts of power situations and the requirements of law and order in an imperfect world, which may justify recourse to the arbitrament of arms. The problem is compounded if the so-called "norms of nonconformism" begin to operate. In that case opposition to war becomes the test of commitment to the ideals of the academic community.

On the other hand, the politician is no prophet. He may and should wish to shape the world unto the common desire of the heart of man which is peace with freedom and justice. But he is obliged to regard the world as an arena in which historical alternatives are always limited. He must face enduring problems, which may seem intractable, and which demand continuing decisions and acts. His actions cannot be based on absolute certainties or on considerations of the ideal, but on a careful balancing and choosing between the relativities that are before him.

In a word, for the prophets and for the intellectual, war is simply evil. For the politician it may well appear to be the lesser evil. This too is a conscientious position, but it is very different from the prophetic position, even though the choice of the lesser evil is part of the human pursuit of the good. In any event, it is not surprising that the politician and the prophet fail to communicate. It must also be remembered that the politician creates the situation within which the prophetic voice may be safely heard. There is much wisdom in the statement of Paul Ramsey: "The right of pacifist conscientious objection can be granted for the fostering of the consciences of free men, only because in national emergencies there are a sufficient number of individuals whose political discretion has been instructed in the need to repel, and the justice of repelling, injury to the common good."

I might add a practical point. The intellectual, whether he be student or professor, sets a premium on being provocative. His task is to challenge all certainties, especially easy certainties, and therefore to challenge the authorities on which certainties may depend. He wants evidence, not authority, and he sets a high value on dissent. All this is excellent and necessary. But there is danger in thrusting this scale of evaluation into the political community. It is not merely that the intellectual provokes reaction; he provokes an over-reaction on the part of the representatives of the political community, and thus he may easily defeat his own cause.

The advocacy of selective conscientious objection in the midst of the South Vietnamese war is provocative, and the political response to it has been an over-reaction. If you want the evidence you need only read the record of the hearings in the Congress, both Senate and House, on the revision of the Selective Service Act, when the issue of conscientious objection was brought up. The claim that the selective objector should be recognized was met with the response that all conscientious objection should be abolished.

All this amounts simply to saying that we face a most difficult issue. It might be of some value to try to locate some of the sources of the difficulty. Strictly on grounds of moral argument, the right conscientiously to object to participation in a particular war is incontestable. I shall not argue this issue. The practical question before all of us is how to get the moral validity of this right understood and how to get the right itself legally recognized, declared in statutory law. (I leave aside the question whether the right is a human right, which ought to receive sanction in the Bill of Rights as a constitutional right.)

I have made one practical suggestion already. The issue of selective conscientious objection must be argued on its own merits. It is not a question of whether one is for or against the war in Vietnam, for or against selective service, much less for or against killing other people. The worst thing that could happen would be to use the issue of conscientious objection as a tactical weapon for political opposition to the war in Vietnam or to the general course of American foreign policy. This would not be good morality and it would be worse politics. Perhaps the central practical question might be put in this way: do the conditions exist which make possible the responsible exercise of a right of selective conscientious objection? The existence of these conditions is the prerequisite for granting legal status to the right itself.

There are two major conditions. The first is an exact understanding of the just-war doctrine, and the second is respect for what Socrates called "the conscience of the laws." I offer two examples, from among many, where these conditions were not observed.

Not long ago a young man in an anti-Vietnam protest on television declared that he would be willing to fight in Vietnam if he knew that the war there was just, but since he did not know, he was obliged to protest its immorality. This young man clearly did not understand the just-war doctrine and he did not understand what Socrates meant by the "conscience of the laws."

Similarly, in a statement issued by a Seminarians' Conference on the Draft held not long ago in Cambridge, there appears this statement: "The spirit of these principles [of the just-war doctrine] demands that every war be opposed until or unless it can be morally justified in relation to these principles." Socrates would not have agreed with this statement nor do I. The dear seminarians have got it backward.

The root of the error here may be simply described as a failure to understand that provision of the just-war doctrine which requires that a war should be "declared." This is not simply a nice piece of legalism, the prescription of a sheer technicality. Behind the provision lies a whole philosophy of the State as a moral and political agent. The provision implies the recognition of the authority of the political community by established political processes to make decisions about the course of its action in history, to muster behind these decisions the united efforts of the community, and to publicize these decisions before the world.

If there is to be a political community, capable of being a moral agent in the international community, there must be some way of publicly identifying the nation's decisions. These decisions must be declared to be the decisions of the community. Therefore, if the decision is for war, the war must be declared. This declaration is a moral and political act. It states a decision conscientiously arrived at in the interests of the international common good. It submits the decision to the judgment of mankind. Moreover, when the decision-making processes of the community have been employed and a decision has been reached, at least a preliminary measure of internal authority must be conceded by the citizens to this decision, even by those citizens who dissent from it. This, at least in part, is what Socrates meant by respect for the "conscience of the laws." This is why in the just-war theory it has always been maintained that the presumption stands for the decision of the community as officially declared. He who dissents from the decision must accept the burden of proof.

The truth, therefore, is contrary to the statement of the seminarians. The citizen is to concede the justness of the common political decision, made in behalf of the nation, unless and until he is sure in his own mind that the decision is unjust, for reasons that he in turn must be ready convincingly to declare. The burden of proof is on him, not on the government or the administration or the nation as a whole. He does not and may not resign his conscience into the keeping of the State, but he must recognize that the State too has its conscience which informs its laws and decisions. When his personal conscience clashes with the conscience of the laws, his personal decision is his alone. It is valid for him, and he must follow it. But in doing so he still stands within the community and is subject to its judgment as already declared.

Only if conceived in these terms can the inevitable tension

between the person and the community be properly a tension of the moral order. Otherwise, it will degenerate into a mere power struggle between arbitrary authority and an aggregate of individuals, each of whom claims to be the final arbiter of right and wrong.

This is the line of reasoning which led me to argue before the National Advisory Commission on Selective Service that one who applies for the status of selective conscientious objector should be obliged to state his case before a competent panel of judges. I was also following the suggestion of Ralph Potter that the concession of status to the selective objector might help to upgrade the level of moral and political discourse in this country. It is presently lamentably low. On the other hand, Paul Ramsey has recently suggested that the matter works the other way round. "A considerable upgrading of the level of political discourse in America is among the conditions of the possibility of granting selective conscientious objection. At least the two things can and may and must go together." He adds rather sadly: "The signs of the times are not propitious for either." I agree.

Those who urge the just-war doctrine as the ground for selective conscientious objection must understand the doctrine itself. They may not naïvely or cynically employ it as a device for opting out from under the legitimate decisions of the political community, or as a tactic for political opposition to particular wars. Rightly understood, this doctrine is not an invitation to pacifism, and still less to civil disobedience. There is a further requisite for legal recognition of selective conscientious objection. It is the prior recognition of the difference between moral objection to a particular war and political opposition to a particular war. This seems to be the sticking point for the political community. It brings into question the whole ethos of our society in the matter of the uses of force.

Historically, we have been disposed to regard the intuitive verdict of the absolute pacifist that all wars are wrong as having the force of a moral imperative. The same moral force is not conceded to the judgment of the conscientious man, religious or not, who makes a reflective and discriminating judgment on the war in front of him. The general disposition is to say that objection to particular wars is and can only be political and, therefore, cannot entitle anyone to the status of conscientious objector.

Here again there is a misunderstanding of the just-war doctrine.

In fact there seems to be a misunderstanding of the very nature of moral reasoning. The just-war doctrine starts from the moral principle that the order of justice and law cannot be left without adequate means for its own defense, including the use of force. The doctrine further holds that the use of force is subject to certain conditions and its justice depends on certain circumstances. The investigation of the fulfillment of these conditions leads the conscientious man to a consideration of certain political and military factors in a given situation. There is the issue of aggression, the issue of the measure of force to be employed in resisting it, the issue of probable success, the issue of the balance of good and evil that will be the outcome. The fact that his judgment must take account of military and political factors does not make the judgment purely political. It is a judgment reached within a moral universe, and the final reason for it is of the moral order.

There is some subtlety to this argument. But that is not, I think, the reason why the political community refuses to assimilate or accept it. The reasons are of the practical order. The immediate reason is the enormous difficulty of administering a statute that would provide for selective conscientious objection. The deeper reason is the perennial problem of the erroneous conscience. It may be easily illustrated.

Suppose a young man comes forward and says: "I refuse to serve in this war on grounds of the Nuremberg principle." Conversation discloses that he has not the foggiest idea what the Nuremberg principle really is. Or suppose he understands the principle and says: "I refuse to serve because in this war the United States is committing war crimes." The fact may be, as it is in South Vietnam, that this allegation is false. Or suppose he says, "I refuse to serve because the United States is the aggressor in this war." This reason again may be demonstrably false. What then is the tribunal to do?

Here perhaps we come to the heart of the difficulty and I have only two things to say. First, unless the right to selective objection is granted to possibly erroneous consciences it will not be granted at all. The State will have to abide by the principle of the Seeger case, which does not require that the objection be the truth but that it be truly held. One must follow the logic of an argument wherever it leads. On the other hand, the political community cannot be blamed for harboring the fear that if the right to selective objection is acknowledged in these sweeping terms, it might possibly lead to anarchy, to the breakdown of society, and to the paralysis of public policy.

Second, the reality of this fear imposes a further burden on the consciences of those who would appeal to freedom of conscience. Selective objection is not a trivial matter. As Ralph Potter has said: "The nation is ultimately a moral community. To challenge its well-established policies as illegal, immoral, and unjust is to pose a threat, the seriousness of which seems at times to escape the critics themselves, whether by the callowness of youth or the callousness of usage." It must be recognized that society will defend itself against this threat, if it be carelessly wielded.

The solution can only be the cultivation of political discretion throughout the populace, not least in the student and academic community. A manifold work of moral and political intelligence is called for. No political society can be founded on the principle that absolute rights are to be accorded to the individual conscience, and to all individual consciences, even when they are in error. This is rank individualism and to hold it would reveal a misunderstanding of the very nature of the political community. On the other hand, the political community is bound to respect conscience. But the fulfillment of this obligation supposes that the consciences of the citizens are themselves formed and informed.

Therefore, the final question may be whether there is abroad in the land a sufficient measure of moral and political discretion, in such wise that the Congress could, under safeguard of the national security, acknowledge the right of discretionary armed service. To cultivate this power of discretion is a task for all of us.

---

# Selective Conscientious Objection
# and Political Obligation

QUENTIN L. QUADE

The question of selective conscientious objection has become a significant political problem for this nation. Articulate persons and groups are seeking it as a policy for the United States; other articulate groups wish to prevent its becoming a policy. Free men, following free consciences, in a society that calls itself free and proclaims freedom its goal; the primordial and intrinsic need of government to govern and in governing to bind universally the governed — such are the generic ingredients of the present conflict. Reconciliation of these values-in-conflict is possible if we perceive that one *depends* upon the other, and one *exists* for the other.

It is my contention that the question of selective conscientious objection is, in its essentials, a modern form of a classic and recurring political problem; that despite this, much discussion on both sides of the issue has lacked political awareness; that the result has often been irrelevant argument, true to the American tradition of non-political discourse about politics; that it is necessary to attempt a reconstruction of the argument in fully political terms; that it is possible to do so, and once done that the problem is susceptible to rational and tolerable resolution.

Proponents of selective conscientious objection in effect ask the government to adopt a policy which would allow some individuals under certain circumstances to be exempted from other policies of the government — in this case, some wars. But war is a thing nation-states do. When a nation through its regular channels of decision decides to go to war, this decision is a national policy, not essentially unlike other policies established through legislative processes, judicial decrees, or executive order. As such, the policy of war is usually thought of as a policy with much the same character as other policies, i.e., universally binding on all citizens. In this traditional view, the

From *A Conflict of Loyalties* edited by James Finn, copyright © 1968, by Western Publishing Company, Inc., reprinted by permission of The Bobbs-Merrill Company, Inc.

citizen is obliged to follow the policy (which has about it at least a procedural legitimacy) even while he may be trying to change it. Implicit in this "accepting even while opposing" is a prior, more fundamental judgment that the political system is itself a value worth supporting.

Advocates of selective conscientious objection say that in war, at least, procedurally legitimate policy need not always be followed, that indeed citizens have a *right* to diverge from it, to avoid its repercussions. In this form the present debate is an absolutely basic one, for it demands that we once again examine root issues of politics: what is the character of political decision, particularly in a democratic situation; what is the meaning of political obligation; how does individual conscience relate to societal value judgment?

A classic political problem it is. Yet, as I have suggested and, hopefully, will demonstrate, much of the discussion surrounding it has been relatively unproductive. This is so largely because both sides have tried to strip the problem of its political character, and to carry on the argument at the level of pure, sharply contradictory, yet seldom intersecting abstractions. Differing in the values they have chosen, each side has tended to identify a single value as not only prime but exclusive. Where values are exclusive, politics does not exist. Politics serves to find resolution among conflicting values. Selective conscientious objection needs to be seen as a problem involving multiple values, none of which should be ignored or destroyed but, rather, all of which should be integrated into one acceptable decision.

### SCO — SOME PROBLEMS WITH ITS FRIENDS

I think the beauty of the Gospel story of the Pharisee and the Publican is that no one except the Lord Himself can call another man a Pharisee without automatically becoming one himself. Accordingly, I certainly will not brand as Pharisees those who contend that the issue of war and military service is practically the only anguish- and virtue-generating political issue which ever arises; and, in this view, because anguish- and virtue-generating, not even truly a political issue. But I do propose that many of these commentators seem to think that their concern over this matter gives them some sort of monopoly on indignation. No such monopoly exists. It depends on what and whose ox. . . .

A number of responsible journals have published articles and editorials strongly favoring selective conscientious objection that will serve as illustrations. *Christianity and Crisis* is justly considered a leading Protestant journal of opinion. But in an editorial otherwise marked by considerable prudential strength, Roger L. Shinn slips into two common and related difficulties. First, he portrays the responsibility for military service as a somehow unique burden, and a burden somehow more ethically charged than others. Second, and companion to the first, he tries to distinguish between politics involving moral choices (and thus pregnant with the possibility of conscientious objection) and politics involving non-moral choices (and thus not susceptible to conscientious objection).

Acknowledging the fact that not all who disagree with this or that policy can be permitted to act out this disagreement, Shinn writes:

> Everybody finds himself in the minority on some public questions, but he conforms. We [proponents of selective conscientious objection] are asking for the right to reject governmental policy on the grounds not simply of opinion but of conscience.
>
> We think it is possible to make some distinctions between moral and political judgments. If a man says, "I think this war is not the most effective way to serve the national interest," he would not be a conscientious objector. If he says, "I profoundly believe that this war is morally evil," he probably is a conscientious objector.[1]

There are genuine distinctions to be made, but in each case Shinn makes the wrong one, in my view. What is the difference between "grounds of opinion" and "grounds of conscience"? Conscience reflects on "opinions" or judgments one makes and brings forth new opinions and judgments. One can properly differentiate degrees of intensity with which opinions or convictions are held, and the degree of diligence displayed in arriving at a position, but the opinion on a policy's rightness is a judgment of the conscience in any case.

When someone says the policy in question is "not the most effective way . . . ," is he really saying something different from the man who says the policy is "morally evil"? Again, the genuine distinction, if there is to be one at all, is in the intensity of the critique. Both statements are in fact and inescapably statements about the morality of the policy. The question of "effectiveness" in pursuit of "national interest" has indeed two clear moral dimensions: effective-

---

[1] *Christianity and Crisis,* April 3, 1967, p. 63.

ness concerns the utility of means; the content of national interest speaks of the value ends or goals.

Thus the man (if he is himself conscious) who says "I think this war is not the most effective way . . ." is stating a conscientious objection quite as surely as his verbally more impassioned counterpart. The relevant distinction, therefore, is not that one speaks "morally" and the other "politically" — speaking politically is always to portray some vision of the human good — but precisely that one may be speaking with much greater passion, intensity, and subjective need.

This is itself of crucial importance politically, and an enlightened political system will be more sensitive and responsive to the more anguished voice. But it is not true, seemingly, that one voice is the voice of morality and the other some kind of non-moral, "political" expression.

*Commonweal,* a journal published by Catholic laymen, succumbs to a similar analytic malaise:

> If a political draftee objects to a particular war on the grounds that it involves widespread torture or genocide, his decision seems clearly a moral one, even if he should have to make some elementary political judgments to define or ascertain the facts. If a potential draftee objects to a particular war on the grounds that it is causing evil disproportionate to whatever good might emerge from it, then he is probably applying a somewhat sophisticated political analysis to the situation; and locating the specifically moral element in his objection becomes much more difficult.[2]

This seems passing strange from a journal which on the same page champions members of ". . . religious traditions whose moral teachings on warfare are based on the distinction between just and unjust wars, *and whose normal method for reaching moral conclusions involves a prudential examination of the actual circumstances of any action.*" (Emphasis added.) The confusion runs very deep. Again, a true distinction seems to be portrayed in the lengthy quotation above, but it is not the one sought by the editorialist. While he seeks a non-existent distinction between moral and political (thus conscientious and non-conscientious) objection, what he actually

[2] "The Draft and Conscience," *Commonweal,* April 21, 1967, p. 140.

portrays is a distinction of moral methods, a distinction between ways of judging the right, a distinction probably best described as that between a deontological ethic and an ethic of consequences.

*Commonweal* also states, in the same editorial, that "Participation in warfare is clearly recognized as ultimate and exceptional among the many demands a nation puts on citizens. It would be easy to draw the line between exemptions from this particular obligation [military service] and exemptions from obligations such as payment of taxes." "Clearly recognized" by whom? Ultimate? Exceptional? Indeed, by degrees. And like any class of obligations, "exceptional" from any other. Is it really so easy to draw the line, even between apparently easy cases such as military service and taxes? J. Bracken Lee appeared not to think so, when he sought to hold back the portion of his tax liability destined to be used for foreign aid. And Joan Baez appears to agree that it is not so easy, as she seeks to subtract from her taxes those monies that would go for war.

Even if it were easy to draw the line between what seem to be easy cases, what of the countless matters of principle (somebody's principle) which crop up in politics every day? Not all men who oppose racial desegregation are simply expedient cynics. To believe in essential racial superiority is, in my judgment, flatly wrong. But it is a position that can be truly, if wrongly, held. And, as this country painfully knows, it is a position which can and does generate truly conscientious objection to national policy. Nor are all men who oppose welfare legislation just selfish beings spewing out smoke-screens of moral indignation behind which to clip their coupons. I believe that Social Security is a work of social justice. But some men truly believe it to be a corruption of human existence, and their opposition to it is a matter of conscience in the most complete sense.

War, though grievous, is not the only cause of grief. And there are not political choices which are moral choices and then political choices which are just — well, "political" choices. Political choosing — what should be done, here, now, for the human community — *is* moral choosing. The choice may be good or bad, enlightened or blind, on important or trivial matters, socially disruptive or inoffensive, based on intense conviction or clouded uncertainty — but a moral choice it is. Indeed, there is something peculiarly self-defeating in a *Commonweal* or *Christianity and Crisis* attempt to put matters of war in a separate category. For this tends to rob them of moral force when they turn their attention to other issues of equal significance, such as distribution of wealth internationally or civil rights domestically. If war is a uniquely moral matter, how do they claim to enunciate moral guidelines in other areas?

By portraying the case of war and military service as unique, the proponents of selective conscientious objection are able to dismiss easily one of the major criticisms: that to provide for selective conscientious objection would be to invite general disobedience to laws. Because in the advocates' eyes the case is unique, it would not constitute a precedent for others in society. As I have suggested above, the claim for uniqueness is a weak one, and the notion that it would not serve as a precedent is highly questionable also. Those who reject the possibility of selective conscientious objection serving as a precedent for other types of selective exemption could take a lesson in logic and straightforwardness from Gordon Zahn. Professor Zahn characteristically entitles an essay on selective conscientious objection "An Explosive Principle." After endorsing the principle completely, he proceeds to draw what to him is an obvious corollary: "conscientious objection to taxation," i.e., to that part of one's tax liability which would be devoted to the war from which one had already been exempted.[3]

Another major problem in the political thinking among selective conscientious objection advocates is this: they repeatedly indicate that the nation should adopt selective conscientious objection as a policy simply because, in the abstract, it is so clearly a good in itself. Men should follow their consciences — therefore, let there be selective conscientious objection; just-war theory teaches that some wars may be unjust — therefore . . . ; men should be men before being Americans — therefore . . . One may agree profoundly that conscience should be obeyed, that some wars (including ours) may be unjust, and that men should not succumb to national egomania. But none of these points is an integral basis for a national policy. Each of the points is a value which is abstractly good, but which is only a *part* of the total social equation that goes into policy. An abstract value does not constitute an imperative for society, even though it may for the individual. What are the other values which might be impacted upon by implementing this one? What would be the cost (in terms of values)

[3] *Worldview*, March, 1967, p. 6.

if this provision were enacted? These are questions which political society legitimately asks before deciding on any policy's desirability.

Gordon Zahn illustrates this direct movement from one value to policy, in the essay mentioned above, when he says that anyone who is convinced the war in question is unjust ". . . must refuse active and direct participation in the injustice. If this nation is sincere in its democratic pretensions . . . the right of the individual to make such a refusal must be respected *and supported,* even by those who do not share that adverse moral judgment concerning the war." Grant that the individual should obey his conscience — but how does his decision serve as a directive to "this nation," which while properly concerned with the objector's conscience must necessarily have other concerns simultaneously?

In an editorial entitled "The Selective Conscientious Objector" the Jesuit journal, *America,* evidenced a confusion. "Every man is obliged to follow his conscience. Yet, under current legislation, there is no legal protection for the young man who, though not an absolute pacifist, is forbidden by his conscience to fight in the Vietnam war." [4] Again, the presumption is that the individual's need to follow his conscience is equivalent to a directive to society to enact a selective conscientious objection provision. The individual's need *should* clearly serve as advisory to society as it considers policy, but society cannot be *bound* by it. Following conscience is a recognized good in this society, indeed a good of a very high order, related to other values such as freedom of speech and religion. But even goods as basic as these are not translatable directly into policy. We weigh, balance, and judge them, we constrict and expand them in their action dimensions according to circumstances — and we do this because we understand that each of them is a *good among goods.*

Other attempts to demonstrate the policy validity of selective conscientious objection by straight deductions from an abstract premise are equally problematical. In another *Christianity and Crisis* editorial, one of America's most prominent theologians, Harvey G. Cox, stated: "Also, it is now time for our draft procedures to recognize the rights of conscientious objectors who, although they are not pacifists, nevertheless have moral objections [is there some other kind of objection?] to fighting in some particular war. As Roger L. Shinn

---

[4] *America,* July 22, 1967, p. 73.

has argued in these pages before, ". . . selective objection would be a natural extension of our present recognition of the rights of the [universal] conscientious objector. . . ." [5] It is a natural extension in the logic of conscience, I would agree, but it is certainly not a natural or automatic political extension. Selective and universal conscientious objection are alike, or naturally related, in one respect: they both involve negative moral judgments of a relatively intense kind. But in this they are like serious objections to any national policy.

They are quite unlike each other, however, in a crucial respect: the universal conscientious objector's opposition to war is not a critique of his own government in any specific respect, but is a general rejection of one proclivity of all nation-states. In that sense, it is almost a pre-political judgment. But the selective conscientious objector by definition is criticizing *his* government on *this* policy *now* — and whatever else this may be, let us understand that it is indeed a political judgment. One may advocate a policy of selective conscientious objection, as I do, but not simply on the grounds that it would be a logical and natural extension of present protections for the universal objector.

In looking over these points, the central problem is fairly clear; many of the commentators have not reconciled themselves to a political framework for thinking and speaking on political matters. In his essay "Is Freedom Is a Fantasy" [6] Everett E. Gendler states that the present requirement for conscientious objection — that the objection be to all wars — represents ". . . an absolutist demand which strikes me as a denial of full freedom of conscience to religious Jews, religious Catholics . . ." and others who believe ". . . that the essence of respect for their conscience is precisely a *sometime* nay-saying." "Denial of full freedom of conscience" — in terms of acting out the dictates of private conscience, that is in the nature of political existence. There are no "full freedoms" in this sense, and there are no abstract values the logic of which can be taken to infinity in the realm of action.

Another set of arguments for selective conscientious objection made by its supporters is drawn by analogy from two historical situations which are presumed to be instructive to the present circumstances

---

[5] *Christianity and Crisis,* April 17, 1967, pp. 73–74.
[6] *Worldview,* February, 1967, pp. 7–8.

of the United States. The first of these is the Nuremberg War Tribunals precedent, which many people see as logically demanding a selective objection law. Typical of such views are those expressed by Graham R. Hodges, Pastor, Emmanuel Congregational Church, Watertown, N.Y. As quoted in *Commonweal,* he said, "In the Nuremberg convictions we contend that the individual, not the state, is final arbiter of conscience. Now, by refusing selective conscientious objection we are saying to American youth, 'The state, not the individual, is the final arbiter of conscience.' " [7] And Michael Harrington has written that "It has even been asserted by the United States Government in the Nuremberg trials that, in certain cases, murderous orders are so obviously immoral as to create a universal obligation of disobedience with the force of positive law." [8]

Leaving aside the large and real question of whether Nuremberg ultimately made sense, what is its meaning, its instruction for the present problem in the United States? If Nuremberg taught that in some situations men should say no to their governments, this was hardly new or news. One can conceive of countless cases in which the individual should refuse to act, even if martyrdom is the alternative. Concretely, Dachau, for example, would seem clearly to be an instance where individuals should have refused to implement the extermination orders. But note: this is an instruction to the individual to disobey the most inhumane commands; it offers no clear lesson to a society on how it should treat the disobedient. Its lesson to society is a systematic one: do not let madness achieve institutional control.

Moreover, Dachau, and all of Nuremberg for that matter, is too easy and obvious a case to be very useful for present purposes. Its analogic relevance to current or likely future wars of the United States seems to me radically limited, despite the Bertrand Russell Tribunal's attempt to equate the two (which strikes me as somewhat comparable to the recent Soviet comparison of Israeli and Nazi policies). Individual American field commanders may order or countenance clearly heinous acts, but is overall policy likely to order or condone them? If that possibility seriously exists, the task of conscience is to permeate the policy structure *before* decision, for it will

[7] *Commonweal,* June 2, 1967, p. 306.
[8] "Moral Objection and Political Opposition," *Worldview,* March, 1967, p. 6.

certainly be too late after. We need to note that most Germans so instructed did carry out the orders we so readily and rightly condemn; we need to note that Stalin had no difficulty recruiting thousands and thousands of OGPU and NKVD operatives to carry out similar policies of liquidation.

When one looks at Nuremberg in this manner, it is easier to see its meaning. That meaning surely was not simply to tell us that conscientious men should refuse orders in some situations. Nuremberg's central message, in my judgment, is one for society at large: there are no limits on the evil possible under a regime which has gathered total control as the modern totalitarian systems have been able to do. Nuremberg is, in short, a plea to maintain the strength of non-authoritarian systems.

Nuremberg is used to show that there *ought* to be a selective conscientious objector provision. But the British exemption from military service of selective objectors during World War II is offered as evidence of the *feasibility* of such a policy for the United States.

The *Commonweal* editorial to which I have referred typifies the use made of British experience: "The British, even during the bombardment by Nazi Germany, managed to exempt from military service those men who admitted they might fight in certain wars but could not morally fight in this one." [9] On its face, the British case proves nothing except that under some conditions *a* nation might be able to allow selective conscientious objection. Even preliminary analysis indicates that attempts to draw much more meaning from it in order to apply it to the United States would be rather dubious: of all wars in which a nation might try selective objection, World War II would certainly be among the easiest, especially for Britons. Of all the nations that might try it, Britain was probably ideal in terms of political homogeneity, lawfulness, martial tradition, and so forth. This suggests to me, at least, that Britain's policy is of limited relevance to present-day United States, engaged for the foreseeable future in conflicts intrinsically blurred, and with ample evidence of internal political incoherence far greater than Britain, circa 1940–41.

While an argument can be made for selective conscientious objection as a policy for the United States, it should be clear that the argument has been inadequately developed by most of its friends so

[9] *Commonweal*, April 21, 1967, p. 140.

far. They have wrongly portrayed the case as unique in the political order; they have distorted the relationship of politics and morality; they have failed to confront and accommodate satisfactorily the values which conflict with the value of conscience-following; and they have relied on quite doubtful analogies to support their case.

With friends like these, selective conscientious objection may well need no enemies. But it has some, nonetheless.

### SCO — SOME PROBLEMS WITH ITS ENEMIES

Perhaps the most important direct attack upon the wisdom of selective conscientious objection was that contained in the *Report of the National Advisory Commission on Selective Service,* issued in February, 1967. The reasoning expressed in this statement is, in its own way, as lacking in a sense of the political as are most of the pro-selective exemption positions examined above.

The Commission considered two recommendations for selective conscientious objection provisions offered by minority elements within the Commission. The first of these is like most such proposals, in that its essence is simply to remove objection to "war in any form" from present requirements for conscientious objection, and let objector status be sought on the basis of conscientious objection to a particular war.

It argued that the traditions of this country recognize that the justice of war and its prosecution are always in question — may or may not be just; and that the individual citizen, in addition to policy-makers, is obliged to judge the justice of particular war. This citizen obviously may judge conscientiously contrary to his government and if he does he should not be forced to violate his conscience by bearing arms. For the rest, the selective objector would do as the universal objector presently does: convince a panel that his judgment was "truly held," and accept alternative service.

The second minority recommendation was significantly different. Those who sought exemption from combatant service should be quite automatically excused, but only after accepting a very rigorous option: service ". . . in a noncombatant military capacity, under conditions of hardship and even of hazard, and perhaps for a longer period (for example, 3 years)." [10]

[10] *Report of the National Advisory Commission on Selective Service* (Washington: United States Government Printing Office, 1967), p. 50.

These two recommendations for a selective conscientious provision are both seemingly policy conclusions drawn from explicit or implicit just-war theorizing: since wars or their conduct could be unjust, and since the responsible individual might conclude on this question differently from his government, therefore provide for that individual the conscience or integrity safeguard of selective conscientious objection status.

The Commission's majority rejected both proposals. As the Report states, "The majority of the Commission did not agree with either the premise or the conclusions of the minority." [11] The majority put forth five arguments against selective conscientious objection.

First, they state that the status of conscientious objector ". . . can properly be applied only to those who are opposed to all killing of human beings. . . ." Either the Commission here means that a person could not conscientiously object to killing in a particular situation (which seems analytically false, for most of us who can conceive acceptable grounds for killing would certainly object conscientiously to killing in general) or the statement is a simple tautology. In either case, it lacks persuasiveness. "It is one thing to deal in law with a person who believes he is responding to a moral imperative outside of himself when he opposes all killing. It is another to accord a special status to a person who believes there is a moral imperative which tells him he can kill under some circumstances and not kill under others."

Indeed, as I argued above, they are quite different things. But nowhere does the Commission explain what differences they are alluding to and, most importantly, nowhere do they tell us what in the difference constitutes a refutation of the validity of selective conscientious objection.

"Secondly, the majority holds that so-called selective pacifism is essentially a political question of support or nonsupport of a war and cannot be judged in terms of special moral imperatives. Political opposition to a particular war should be expressed through recognized democratic processes and should claim no special right of exemption from democratic decisions." This clearly illustrates the failure of the Commission to maintain analytic rigor and to sustain a political framework. There is a sense in which the Commission's first point here is correct: conscientious objection to a particular war

[11] *Idem.*

*is* a political question in a way the universal pacifist's rejection of all war is not. The universal pacifist's critique, as we saw earlier, is not distinctively aimed at his own nation's policies, and his claim to exemption is not in that sense a political question. The selective objector just as clearly seeks his exemption because of a critical judgment he has made about his nation's policy, and this is a political question. But in no way does this lessen the fact that the stance of the selective conscientious objector is a position of moral force equal to that of the universal pacifist. In no way is the internal moral imperative any less for this man.

Thus the Commission falls prey to the standard confusion: that somewhere, somehow there are *political* postures, and then there are *moral* postures. The real truth illustrated here, of course, is that the political conviction (on anything of significance) is itself an ethical position, a judgment about human values. This confusion pervades the entire debate on selective conscientious objection, and is significantly responsible for the nonproductiveness of the argument thus far.

The second part of this second point is absolutely correct — but it yielded the wrong conclusion and illustrates once again the nonpolitical context of the Commission's thinking. I submit that it is transparently true that opposition to a particular war should use regular democratic processes, and that such opposition can "claim no special right" to be exempted from political discussions. But this does not constitute an argument against selective conscientious objection either. It is an argument only against proclaiming that selective conscientious objection is a *right* deriving from some self-defining source. As such, it in no sense refutes the possible *policy desirability* of granting selective conscientious objector status on the political grounds of its being, on balance, a social good. The advocates, as we saw earlier, have tended to call their policy recommendation a right, and thereby have distorted the argument. Then, with something approaching absolute predictability, the opponents use the distortion as the basis of discussion and declare that there is no such right. Their declaration is correct; it is also politically irrelevant.

"Third, in the majority view, legal recognition of selective pacifism could open the doors to a general theory of selective disobedience to law, which could quickly tear down the fabric of government; the distinction is dim between a person conscientiously opposed to payment of a particular tax."

In the second half of this sentence the Commission displays a truer political insight than most selective objection supporters have demonstrated. As shown previously, there are simply no grounds for asserting that the only political matters which pose serious conscience problems are those involving war. *Laissez-faire* proponents of yesterday and today did and do believe that government involvement in the economy is not only tactically questionable but morally wrong. To many people, miscegenation creates not just a burden for the offspring but is additionally a sin against God. If the test of conscience is that a belief be sincerely held — rather than objectively right — there is indeed a dim distinction between conscientious objection to a particular war and a similar objection to any other policy judged to be abominable.

But all of this, while true enough, is only an analytic, abstract point. If selective conscientious objector status were granted and *if* a person who conscientiously objected to another policy — e.g., taxation for Social Security — stated that he, too, should be exempted from these taxes in view of the selective objection precedent, he would be on good logical grounds. And if in fact the selective objection provision were seized upon by large numbers as a precedent for selective exemption from many kinds of policy, as could in fact happen, *then* one could argue against selective objection that it threatened the "fabric of government" and was accordingly invalid because too dangerous.

But that is the point. In its third argument, the Commission used as a conclusive political consideration the totally abstract *possibility* that selective conscientious objection *might* lead to general disobedience to law. Indeed, it might. But if selective objection advocates are mistaken in dismissing out of hand the question of anarchic potential — and they are — the Commission is equally wrong in using this anarchic potential as if its dimensions were an established fact, a fact from which conclusions can readily be drawn. Both sides are confusing abstract logical possibilities with political reality. Analytically, all one can possibly say is that a selective objection provision is not essentially different from selective exemption to any class of policy to which people seriously object, and that therefore it *could* constitute an anarchic precedent. But there is no intrinsic reason for saying that it would constitute such a precedent, and the *would* is the politically relevant category.

As I will suggest, one can recognize the abstract potential of a selective conscientious objection law, and then do a variety of things to test the likely repercussions of its adoption. What *could* happen? This is relatively lacking in political significance. What *would* happen if it were adopted? This is a pertinent question.

"Fourth, the majority of the Commission was unable to see the morality of a proposition which would permit the selective pacifist to avoid combat service by performing noncombat service in support of a war which he had theoretically concluded to be unjust." If the alternative service offered the selective conscientious objector is entirely military and would thus in some sense be directly supporting the combatants, this point probably has considerable validity. But it excludes for no stated reason other forms of alternative service, with no direct military connections, which would recognize the moral depth of one's objection.

And the fifth argument suffers from the ills of the third and fourth. "Finally, the majority felt that a legal recognition of selective pacifism could be disruptive to the morale and effectiveness of the Armed Forces." *Could* be? Well, certainly it could be. But would it? The point is that it is possible to gather some data on what the repercussions would be. It is not necessary to rely simply on intuitive estimates of abstract possibilities. "A determination of the justness or unjustness of any war could only be made within the context of that war itself." If the individual had to determine the justice of the war, this ". . . could put a burden heretofore unknown on the man in uniform and even on the brink of combat, with results that could well be disastrous to him, to his unit and to the entire military tradition."

If you want to destroy a suggestion, reduce it to its absurd conclusion, even though you know not all ideas have to be pushed to their conclusions. This is essentially what the Commission has done here. One need only conjure up a vision of a Marine platoon, twenty yards from the enemy, the platoon sergeant shouting "Charge!" — and five members of the platoon reply "Sorry, we conscientiously object to this war, or this phase of it, at this moment." But to see the impossibility of tolerating such a situation as this does not in itself show the impossibility of selective conscientious objection for persons at some moment prior to combat or, more likely, prior to entrance into the service.

Summarily, it may be said that the Report is something less than a model of prudential, political judgment. Its authors saw fit to issue a judgment on a political question without thinking seriously in a political sense. They did not, for example, remark on the multiplicity of values involved in the issue, they did not note the very real societal good that would be achieved if it were judged possible to grant selective conscientious objection status in this country. They did not articulate the value of preserving conscientious integrity *in action* if feasible. They saw clearly the primary possible social evil that could result from a selective objection provision. And because they saw this essentially in isolation — that is, without the competition of contrary values — they were able to move quite easily, because abstractly, to a rejection of selective conscientious objection.

They were able to move easily, but ineffectively, and unpolitically.

### TOWARD RECONSTRUCTION AND RESOLUTION

The problem of selective conscientious objection should be seen for what it is: a recurrence in contemporary dress of the inherent political problem of man with limitless aspirations confronting the necessary reality of political limitation. When the current problem is viewed in categories as old as political man himself, one can begin to see the path to a tolerable resolution of the conflict also. This kind of difficulty triggers the beginning of the political process, not the end of society or any segment of it — unless the segment in the dispute so alienates itself or is so alienated from the rest of society as to become irreconcilable. This could happen if the segment were to become completely egoistic, refusing to perceive the other values present and refusing to see the necessity for society reigning through its political agencies. Or this could happen if those same agencies were to become completely frozen in their posture and failed to see also the values proposed by the disenchanted element. It is a central function of the democratic process to avoid this kind of apocalyptic development and find the way toward political reconciliation. The first and in a way most important step is to reconstruct the terms of the argument. What are the values placed in conflict by the selective conscientious objection proposal? What are the rewards and costs of alternative actions?

Wars may be just or unjust. In a democratic nation and in an age of personalism, not just the formal policy-makers but each citizen has the opportunity and obligation to judge matters of national policy, including war. But clearly, the individual may judge differently from the majority or the government. Further, there is, of course, no guarantee that the majority or the government will be right in its judgment. If the nation goes to war, should it provide military exemption for the citizen who conscientiously judges the war to be unjust?

The abstract good proposed is obvious enough: to relieve this person from the unhappy choices of serving a cause he considers immoral or going to jail for following his conscience. But the problem is this: in its essence, war is a national policy akin to other policies. It is in the character of political society that decisions (policies) made by the legitimate authorities are binding on all men in society. Indeed, looked at from one point of view, the state exists precisely to bring uniform social action to areas in which conflicting values are at issue. To war or not, and how to war if doing so — these are political questions which demand *an* answer, in the same sense that to have Medicare or not demands *an* answer, not an infinite series of individual responses which constitute no policy at all.

This, then, is the second and competing value which all but the anarchist will recognize: it is good to maintain the health, vitality, and effectiveness of the state itself, which brings order and stability to its society, and frees its members by so doing. If, therefore, a selective conscientious objector statute would in some clear and significant sense endanger this government's ability to do what governments exist to do, one would have to weigh the values in some either/or relationship — that to choose one would be practically to exclude the other. To choose a selective conscientious objection statute would be to abandon political stability; to opt for political stability would be *ipso facto* to exclude selective conscientious objection. If the only choices before us were those, the choice for me would be easy (as it was for the Commission): in no sense do I think the value of selective conscientious objection comparable to the value of political effectiveness and order.

But this is a Hobbesian view of the alternatives and, I think, a wrong one. Not every conflict need become Armageddon. Genuine either/or situations do arise, but in general it is an objective and a responsibility of democratic politics to avoid them, to find a hierarchy among competing values rather than reduce all to one, to harmonize multiple goods rather than mute one in the name of the other. And this objective is possible in the present case, it seems. We need to begin by asking if the good of a selective conscientious objector provision can in some manner be achieved without introducing an unacceptable probability of anarchistic repercussions.

That the individual is or should be conscience-bound is not a part of the dispute. What is a part of the dispute is the role political obligation *perceived as a human value* should play in forming that conscience. If an individual concludes that a policy of his nation — a war, let us say — is absolutely untenable; and if all the available means of changing it have been fruitless and give promise of fruitlessness in the future; then presumably he must withdraw from the existing situation, and accept the consequences of so doing. He ought only to be sure that a recognition of his obligations to society was part of his conscientious makeup in coming to his conclusion. He must understand also that his decision was *his,* and will not likely serve as an instruction to his society. Nor is there any reason why it should, if the government has been as careful in its judgmental process as he was.

But presumably this conscientious person, like Socrates, even if driven to the extreme of some form of political martyrdom over the disputed policy, would not seek to sunder his society simply on the grounds of *this* policy dispute. For what he took to be horrendous error on this policy would not in itself mean that the political system itself was erroneous. If, then, his complaint was confined to a particular policy, he presumably would do nothing to endanger the health of political society.

He would seek to do this momentous thing — sunder the political fabric — only if he concluded, again circumspectly, that the system itself had become irretrievably corrupted. And even then, if he were fully conscientious, he would judge the system's corruption only comparatively, only, in a word, with an eye to the alternative: he would ask, as Carl Lotus Becker once asked, "How *new* will the better world be?" Destroy a system if you wish — neither I nor anyone can say that this should never be done. But be honest enough to explain the future, and demonstrate its superiority.

And what of political society? What are its obligations to those within itself whose consciences are deeply troubled by policy? Clearly, it has no obligation to be tyrannized by the objecting voices in its midst. But it is obliged to strive for that same circumspection of judgment which the objector must seek. It is obliged to see that serious criticism of its political actions is a warning signal itself, a signal to re-examine, re-think, and re-evaluate the policy it has espoused.

And more important, even if that policy should be reaffirmed, it is obliged to seek avenues of accommodation and reconciliation with those disenchanted elements in its body. This it should do both because the political good ought to be insofar as possible a good for all, and because in its own interest it needs to understand the destructive potential of alienated parts of the political community.

The present problem is a case of this type. Multiple goods are in conflict and priorities must be established among them. But even if the priorities are set, and set as I see them, with society's prerogatives recognized as prime, the point is that priority does not mean exclusivity.

Even if there is no right to selective conscientious objection from military service (any more than there is a right to conscientious objection to civil rights laws) perhaps society should grant it as a privilege. Maybe selective conscientious objection *could* be adopted because it is possible to do it without establishing a serious precedent for general disobedience of the law. Maybe, under these circumstances, it *should* be done because it can be without great disruption and because, as we have seen, there is a real good to be achieved by such a policy.

To say these things is only to say that it is time to move the question of selective objection from its seeming apocalyptic dimensions into what in fact it is: a prudential question, posed to a democratic system, which asks that system to appraise the goods and bads and to decide, on balance, *whether it should be done.*

If the selective objection problem is approached in this way, significant progress can be made. First, regarding the value it would have for society, these points are fairly clear: a serious source of community disgruntlement would be removed; a segment of society would find the area of its self-definition expanded; society would provide itself and the world at large a new demonstration of American belief in self-specification.

But what of the costs, or counter-values? Clarity does not exist here, as the earlier critical sections have indicated. Some argue that there would be no real cost; but we have seen that within the notion of selective objection there is a potential for social disruption. Others assert that the cost is clearly too high — that selective objection would unleash and aggravate ever-present anarchistic tendencies within society. But we have seen that while this exists as a possibility, there is no compelling reason for believing that it would inevitably transpire.

In short, on the matter of costs, there seems to be an analytic and argumentative impasse.

What needs to be done, accordingly, is to probe empirically these various possibilities, to better ascertain the likely costs in order to better judge the real costs of such a program. The tools exist: public opinion surveys have considerable utility for identifying future actions. Within the national pool of service-eligible men, surveys could seek answers to such broad questions as these: how many young men would be likely to apply for selective objector status; more important, what would be the impact (in terms of morale or esprit) of such a provision on those in service and those likely to serve in the future? With this kind of data available, one could judge more rationally whether selective objection would have a seriously debilitating impact on the services, and whether it would impair the capacity of the services to perform their functions.

Using a national sample representative of all adolescent and adult citizens, surveys could then turn to another and perhaps more important series of questions: what would be the effect of selective objection to military service on people with other, non-military conscientious complaints against national policy? To what extent, if any, would such a provision constitute a precedent-at-large for disobedience to law? How many Negroes, for example, would respond to it in this way? Or how many Southerners would feel justified by it in trying to exempt themselves from the strictures of civil rights legislation?

These are the kinds of questions one needs to answer in order to judge with reasonable intelligence the costs of the selective conscientious objection proposal. And it is not necessary to rely simply on intuitive judgment. The devices for obtaining relatively hard knowledge exist, and we have some obligation to use them.

My own intuitive judgment would be that selective objection could be adopted by this nation without serious social disruption, and therefore, given the values which can be obtained by it, I would urge that such a provision be enacted. But first there should be the kind of attitude surveys suggested here. If these bear out the presumption that expected repercussions would be tolerable, then appropriate legislation should be adopted. If the point is to influence Congressional and Administration thinking before the next review of draft legislation, then perhaps private groups and foundations should undertake the opinion surveying suggested above.

What have I suggested? Fundamentally, that the question of selective conscientious objection has become a political problem: should the United States adopt such a practice? Further, that, like any political question, no rational answer for this one exists *a priori,* despite the fact that most commentators on both sides have acted as if the matter were self-evident.

In the absence of a self-evident (one-value) resolution, it is necessary to identify and assess the several values which are in conflict, and to establish priorities among them. In the case at hand the values are clear enough, and for me at least the priorities are clear also. But it is not enough to identify the prime value and simply snuff out the secondary one. It is necessary to try to maintain them both, and to gauge the intensity of their conflict. In this case it seems likely that the secondary value can be supported without seriously endangering the higher one. If this be the case, the prudent polity will do so, even at some price of social turbulence.

The foregoing points are essentially analytic: they can be seen simply through reflection on the character of the problem in the context of democratic politics. Before moving to adoption of the proposal, however, the prudent polity will inform itself empirically regarding likely repercussions.

Such a formula is a political response to a real problem confronting society. Its logic is not the logic of spinning off the abstract implications of a single value. Rather its logic is the logic of politics, in which several values must be interwoven and harmonized even while recognizing and articulating the fact that not all values are of equal importance. It presupposes some considerable wisdom on all sides: wisdom in the polity inclining it to accommodate its estranged elements; and wisdom on the part of the estranged inclining them to see the value of political order (the very cradle of justice *and* freedom) and its corollary of political obligation. It is easier, I think, for society to harden and suppress; just as it may be easier for the disenchanted to go the distance to complete alienation and irreconcilability. But it would not be wiser, nor more virtuous.

# Prisoners of War

## Prisoners of War: Does the Fight
## Continue After the Battle?

MICHAEL WALZER

### I.  REFUGEES AND PRISONERS OF WAR

Just beyond the state there is a kind of limbo, a strange world this side of the hell of war, whose members are deprived of the relative security of political or social membership. Different sorts of people live there, mostly for indefinite periods of time, people who have been expelled from their state or otherwise deprived of legal rights, people whose state has been defeated in war and occupied or who have been separated somehow from its jurisdiction. Among the residents, two groups endure conditions paradigmatic for all the others: refugees, deprived of their rights by persecution; and prisoners of war, separated from their state by captivity. The two are very different, since refugees are stateless persons, radically dependent on their hosts and unable to look backward to any protecting authority, while prisoners remain citizens still and receive such protection as their states can provide. However distant and isolated they may be from their home country, their captivity is (hopefully) temporary; both captives and captors may one day be required to account for their behavior. Nevertheless, prisoners and refugees belong alike to the limbo world. They cannot expect effective help from any organized society; they do not know when, if ever, they will be "at home" again; they are compelled to

From *The American Political Science Review* (September 1969). Reprinted by permission of The American Political Science Association.

reconstruct or redefine their obligations without reference, or without clearcut reference, to authoritative laws and commands.

Refugees face their hosts with a special kind of helplessness and pathos, but also with an unaccountable and peculiar freedom. They are men free of all allegiance except to other men, without political obligations, at least without obligations to any state in the world of states. And their condition testifies to the wretchedness of such freedom.[1] Frightening as it may be to the authorities (at least, the authoriies generally profess to be frightened), it is far more so to the refugees themselves. Until they are given a home, they have a right to do whatever they can to save themselves, within limits imposed only by their humanity and the relations they form with particular other people. But in fact they can do painfully little, and theirs is a freedom any of us would speedily exchange for membership and protection, despite the restraints these impose. The value of the state as an inclusive community, the importance of even the most minimal kinds of social solidarity and legal definition — these are never more clear than when we regard ourselves as possible participants in the limbo of statelessness.

The prisoner, on the other hand, is doubly unfree, since he is not set loose from his former allegiance, or so he is told, by his captivity. If he is forced to face his captors, bound or at gunpoint, he must also look over his shoulder to the authorities of his own state. He is required continually to balance the obligations he knows he once had, and may still have, as a citizen and soldier, against the more immediate threats and coercions of his captors — and perhaps also against his new obligations to the society of prisoners. What should he do? It is never easy to say. If the statelessness of a refugee is frightening, so is the citizenship of a prisoner of war. To regard ourselves as possible captives is to learn how oppressive political obligations can be. Even limbo, as we shall see, has its temptations.

## II. THE CONDITION OF PRISONERS OF WAR

Captivity can be conceived in two different ways: first, as the termination of combat for an individual soldier, the imposition by the captor and the acceptance by the captive, of a total quarantine for the

---

[1] For a brilliant discussion of the problem of statelessness, see Hannah Arendt, *The Origins of Totalitarianism* (New York, 1958), Ch. 9.

duration of the war; secondly, as the termination of one sort of combat and its replacement by another sort, where the fighting is relatively circumscribed and its conditions radically unequal.[2] Both of these are modern conceptions; both depend on the recognition of the prisoner as a moral and legal person, possessed of certain rights, entitled at the very least to be kept and provided for by what the lawyers call "the detaining power." The prisoner is "detained," and that means that whatever else is done to him or with him during his detention, he cannot be killed or enslaved. Not so very long ago, a prisoner was thought to have forfeited his life by his surrender. Then his slavery was justified as the end result of an exchange made possible solely by the benevolence of his captor, an exchange of life for perpetual service. On that view, captivity was in no sense a status within which a man might be more or less secure even if impotent. Prisoners were rapidly converted into dead men or living slaves, and the choice between these two conditions was only secondarily their own.[3] (In practice, during the early modern period, prisoners were often required simply to join the army of their captors, common soldiers being little more than chattel anyway.) Today, a prisoner can expect to remain a prisoner for as long as the war lasts, and then he can expect to be released. In the interim between capture and release, he is forced into a relation with his captors unlike that of slave and master, though not entirely unlike it, and into a relation with his fellow prisoners unlike that of any normal political (or military) association. The prison or prison camp is the scene of a new society, which exists precariously in the shadow of the detaining power and whose members feel the pull of their previous political commitments, not least because these are likely to be their future commitments as well.

This new society of prisoners exists by virtue of, or at least in accordance with, international law. Its members have even been called,

---

[2] See G. S. Pugh, "Prisoners at War: The P.O.W. Battleground," 60 *Dickenson Law Review* 123–138 (1956), and "The Code of Conduct," 56 *Columbia Law Review* 678–707 (1956). The best book on the nature and laws of captivity is William E. S. Flory, *Prisoners of War: A Study in the Development of International Law* (Washington, 1942).

[3] Hugo Grotius, writing in the early seventeenth century, still defended the right of enslavement, *De Jure Belli ac Pacis,* Book III, Chapter 14, Section 9. The decisive theoretical critiques of this idea are by Montesquieu, *The Spirit of the Laws,* Book IV, Chapter 2, and Rousseau, *The Social Contract,* Book I, Chapter 4.

by a serene theorist of the nineteenth century, "citizens of the world."[4] The world is, unfortunately, not so organized that citizenship in it is much of a benefit — as stateless persons have learned over and over again in the past 30 years. But the name does serve to suggest something very important, if true: that prisoners are no longer at war. It presses us toward the first of the two conceptions of captivity. For the war is being fought by citizens of this state and of that one, and citizens of the world, even if they hold dual citizenship in one of the belligerent states, are presumably exempt from the compulsions of the struggle. The rules of quarantine replace the code of battle, and this replacement is not merely legal, but moral as well; it frees the prisoner from all obligations to continue the war.

The same replacement would seem to be implied by the conventional practice of "surrendering" or "giving up," though this has sometimes been denied. In the *Code of Conduct* for US soldiers issued by President Eisenhower in 1955, it is said that soldiers must never surrender "of their own free will." [5] If it were possible for soldiers to surrender in any other way, the act might indeed have no moral consequences. But unless the *Code* is intended to bar surrender altogether — and then its subsequent provisions, which deal with the conduct of prisoners, would be superfluous — the phrase "of their own free will" is very odd. The authors presumably want to say that only extreme duress and the threat of imminent death are acceptable reasons for surrender, but that does not mean that the act of surrendering can never be a decision of the men who surrender or an agreement between them and their captors.[6] It most often is a decision, and it is probably

---

[4] James Lorimer, *Institutes of the Law of Nations* (London, 1884), Volume II, p. 72. The whole passage is excellent and should be consulted.

[5] The *Code of Conduct* is the most important official statement on how U.S. soldiers are to behave when overpowered by an enemy, and I will refer to it frequently below. At the time it was issued, its legal status was unclear (see Pugh, "The Code of Conduct"), but it has recently been described, in the aftermath of the *Pueblo* incident, as "only a guideline." Violations of the articles of the *Code* do not constitute a criminal offense: *New York Times,* December 29, 1968. It is presumably still the opinion of the authorities that they constitute a moral offense, and the *Code* continues to play a very important part in the training of US soldiers.

[6] Something must be said here about the difficult problem of coercion, though to deal with it in even a minimally adequate way would require another essay. The common and plausible view is that no man is morally bound to fulfill a contract or commitment he was coerced into making. Since the word "coerced" is usually taken to mean "forced by violence or the threat of violence,"

always an (implicit) agreement. Even when no decision seems possible, as when the sailors of a sunken ship are simultaneously rescued and captured, it can probably be assumed that the prisoners agree to their captivity, if only for the sake of their rescue, and that they approve of the general practice of taking prisoners. In battle or in the aftermath of battle, surrender usually involves a more explicit judgment and choice on the part of the men surrendering, a judgment of their own continuing effectiveness as soldiers and of the risks they face, a choice to fight on or not. And this is in some sense a free choice, though it is made under varying degrees of duress, since soldiers can and have been known to accept enormous risks and even fight to the death. Surrender is precisely a way of choosing not to take enormous risks and not to fight to the death. It takes the conventional form of an agreement not to fight at all, to "give up" fighting, in return for life itself and then benevolent quarantine.

This agreement obviously requires a second party; surrender must be accepted as well as offered, and armies can refuse, though no longer lawfully, to take prisoners. Clearly, there would be a positive incentive to refuse if surrender were thought to involve no commitment to cease (and not to resume) fighting, just as there would be a positive incentive to fight to the death if the acceptance of surrender were not viewed as a commitment to one or another form of quarantine. Surrender as a social practice is only possible in the absence of these two incentives, that is, it is only possible when it is conceived as a mutual engagement with moral consequences. This conception is clearly reflected in international law, which requires benevolence of captors and simultaneously deprives a prisoner of all combatant rights.[7] If he kills a prison

---

surrender would appear to have no moral validity. But it might be argued against this that the definition of coercion depends or ought to depend on the situation of the individual said to be coerced, and that in the context of war, violence exercised in accordance with the laws of war is not coercive. Surrender is a social practice designed to accommodate the human difficulties of war; it can't be judged by conventions appropriate to other, and very different, settings. This calls into question the dictionary definition and ordinary usage of the word "coercion." But there are only two alternatives, neither of them attractive: either to suggest that no morally binding agreements are possible in wartime, or to accept Hobbes' argument that "Covenants entered into by fear . . . are obligatory" (an argument Hobbes explicitly applied to prisoners of war — see *Leviathan*, Chapter XIV).

[7] See the discussion in Pugh, "The Code of Conduct," pp. 682–683, 690n., and Eric Williams' introduction to *The Escapers* (London, 1953), p. 15.

guard, for example, the act is murder and not war, for he has given up fighting and thereby reassumed some of those civilian obligations which are suspended for soldiers in the face of an enemy.

The essence of surrender is the agreement not to fight, and this agreement may not require quarantine at all. In the days when officers were also gentlemen and aristocrats, it was perfectly normal to release a prisoner on parole, that is, to accept his word that he would not rejoin the fighting and then to permit him personal freedom of movement, even to permit him to go home. This is only possible on a very strict view of surrender, which holds the captives temporarily free of political allegiance and so able to make arrangements on their own behalf: "separated for the time being from any political community, they . . . belong to humanity and to themselves." [8] Eighteenth and nineteenth century lawyers argued — and their arguments were for a time widely accepted — that if a prisoner did return home on parole, his home state could not force him to fight again or in any way require him to violate his faith.[9] This clearly implies that the prisoner did not break faith when he gave parole in the first place; it grants that he belonged at that moment in time "to himself." Perhaps that is a status which aristocrats resume more readily than other men; nevertheless, its recognition is, I think, an extraordinary tribute to the liberality of eighteenth and nineteenth century states, or of some of them, and of their lawyers and philosophers. Modern states, whether liberal or not, are not inclined to grant a similar recognition. Most of them, including the United States, deny prisoners the right to give their parole (except under very restricted circumstances and for short periods of time). International law has been adjusted so as to deny validity to any parole arrangement contrary to the laws or regulations of the prisoner's home state.[10] Very occasionally the old ethic is rediscovered. Thus, a small number of captured American soldiers gave their parole to the Japanese in the Philippines during World War II, and "these paroles were recognized by the US as prohibiting military and other resistance to the

[8] Lorimer, *op. cit.*, II, 72.

[9] See the British *Manual of Military Law* (1884): "A State has no power to force its subjects to act contrary to their parole." Quoted in Flory, *op. cit.*, p. 123.

[10] Geneva Convention I, Article 21; for a discussion of contemporary law on parole arrangements, see Morris Greenspan, *The Modern Law of Land Warfare* (Berkeley, 1959), pp. 108–110.

Japanese on the part of the individuals concerned." [11] But such agreements are rare in this century and today the *Code of Conduct* explicitly declares that prisoners must not give their parole to their captors. Prisoners, it would appear, never belong, or are never admitted to belong, merely "to humanity and to themselves."

It is perfectly understandable that the state should continue to claim the allegiance and support of prisoners. It is even in the interests of the prisoners that it should do so — up to a point. They have no wish to be abandoned, however uneasy they may be about their "obligations." Nor does the state make its claim very effectively, since it has no immediate control over the persons of the prisoners and is unable to offer any but the most minimal guidance as to their everyday behavior in the radically new society of the prison camp. The claims of the state are still enormously important; they point toward the second and at present (in this country and more clearly in some others) the official view of the status of captives and the moral meaning of captivity. On this view, prisoners of war must regard themselves as combatants even after their capture, full-fledged members of a state at war, a state in trouble, needful of all the men it has, unwilling to yield the services of anyone except to death itself. The prisoner, so the *Code of Conduct* tells him, is an "American fighting man" (Article I). He must refuse any sort of cooperation with his captors and seek continually to escape. By implication, he must also help whenever he can to organize mass escapes, to maintain a resistance network in the camp, to harrass the enemy, spy on him and sabotage his behind-the-lines operations. He must always act so as to require as many guards as possible. It is a little hard to see why any state at war would maintain prisoners who actually did or tried to do all these things, and insofar as the *Code* requires them, it is not entirely consistent with the idea of benevolent quarantine. This is partly because it was designed as a response to North Korean and Chinese captors who paid little regard to that idea, but it also reflects, as did the actions of the North Koreans and Chinese, an extension of state sovereignty and an attempt at ideological control which amount to a denial that individuals can ever move, even partially, out of the range of political action and supervision. There simply is no space, it suggests, that might be called limbo, where quarantine is possible and a certain human passivity morally justified.

[11] Pugh, "The Code of Conduct," p. 683n.

Contemporary international law, as codified in the Geneva Conventions (1949), does not require the passivity of prisoners; indeed, it provides carefully and at considerable length for attempted escapes, though not for any other kind of resistance.[12] But it is not unfair to argue that the most humane provisions of the present code — for example, the rule that prisoners captured while trying to escape cannot be punished, but only detained more strictly, and that only for a short time — are rooted in the expectation that the vast majority of prisoners will not resume or make any attempt to resume their combatant roles. And that is an expectation most often realized in practice, despite the wishes of the governments whose citizens are imprisoned. The erosion of the idea of benevolent quarantine has come largely from the other side, from captors and not from captives, as one might expect; for if combat is resumed, it is the captors who have every advantage. Still, prisoners have chosen to fight on, sometimes in response to the coercive acts of the enemy, sometimes on their own initiative, and it is worth asking whether there is any justice at all in the increasingly strong presumption of their home states that they ought to do so.

Article III of the U.S. *Code of Conduct* requires that American soldiers, if captured, must "continue to resist by all means available." This is its most extreme provision, though the ambiguous word "resist" was carefully chosen. Mr. Carter Burgess, Assistant Secretary of Defense, argued at the time the *Code* was adopted that physical resistance (which is barred by Geneva Convention I, article 82) was not required of prisoners, but only mental resistance to political indoctrination.[13] That is hardly made clear by the *Code* itself, and the lack of clarity was presumably intentional, since the wording was long debated. One legal critic of the *Code* has pointed out that unless it is read as a call for resistance "by all *legitimate* means available," prisoners "would be encouraged to commit acts that may be war crimes or at least contrary to the spirit of the Geneva Conventions." [14] Needless to say, their captors would be similarly encouraged.

The *Code* was adopted in the immediate aftermath of the Korean

[12] Geneva Convention I, Articles 42, 91–93; see Greenspan, *op. cit.*, pp. 135–137.

[13] Carter L. Burgess, "Prisoners of War," 56 *Columbia Law Review* 676–677 (1956).

[14] Pugh, "The Code of Conduct," p. 690.

War, a struggle in which the noncombatant status of prisoners was undermined by both sides, though most dangerously and cruelly, judging from the available evidence, by the North Koreans and Chinese.[15] In prison camps north and south of the battleline, a new kind of war went on for the minds, that is, for the loyalty and political commitment, of the prisoners. To some extent, this was a war that could be fought within the limits set by the Geneva Convention. But one of its most ominous results was that in the American-run camps, where the Conventions were fairly rigorously observed, and in contrast to the Communist camps where they were not, resistance was amazingly successful. At one point, major sections of the camp on Koje Island were entirely controlled by North Korean prisoners, who even captured and for several days held the American commander of the camp. It quickly became clear that "measures permitted under the Geneva Conventions would not completely destroy the Communist organization within the compounds." The North Korean prisoners could no longer be regarded, or treated, "as passive human beings in need of care and protection. . . ." [16]

General Mark Clark's comment on the Koje mutiny suggests what American officials learned from this incident: ". . . my experience," he wrote, "had been with *old-fashioned* wars in which prisoners were people to be fed, housed, clothed, and guarded, nothing more. Never had I experienced a situation in which prisoners remained combatants and carried out orders smuggled to them from the enemy high command." [17] Only a few years later President Eisenhower brought American policies up to date by issuing the *Code of Conduct,* recommended to him in a Defense Department report entitled "P.O.W. — The Fight Continues After the Battle." [18] The *Code* was explicitly intended to provide a secure moral basis for resistance to the indoctrination of prisoners as this had been practiced by the North Koreans and Chinese. But its careful ambiguity suggests that it was also intended to encourage action on the scale of the Koje mutiny. What

[15] But see W. Burchett, *Koje Unscreened* (Peking, 1953).

[16] Pugh, "Prisoners at War," citing UN Command Reports, p. 131. A complete account of the Koje mutiny, from the American point of view, can be found in Hal Vetter, *Mutiny on Koje Island* (Tokyo, 1965).

[17] Quoted in Vetter, *Mutiny,* p. 10 (emphasis added).

[18] Report by the Secretary of Defense's Advisory Committee on Prisoners of War, August, 1955.

happens then to the "old-fashioned" notion that prisoners must be maintained and guarded and nothing more? Surely there would be some value in reiterating that notion, rather than merely conceding its antiquity.

### III.  OBLIGATIONS AND FORMS OF RESISTANCE

On the other hand, when serious pressure is put on prisoners to collaborate with the enemy, either by supplying military information or expressions of political support, we do want "our" soldiers (at least) to refuse and resist. It is important to understand just what is involved in such refusals: they don't represent a continuation of the war so much as an unwillingness to enlist or be enlisted on the other side; they are a defense of all that is implied by the idea of quarantine. Prisoners refusing to collaborate are also, of course, refusing to "sell out" their comrades or their recent comrades and to betray their country. But the obligations which they thus acknowledge and sustain are minimal in character. They can most readily be expressed in the negative: not to inform, not to confess, not to collaborate, and so on. I don't mean to suggest that they are for that reason easy to sustain. Whether they are easy or hard (or impossible) to sustain depends on the actions of the enemy. They are significantly different, however, from obligations that lend themselves to positive statement: to try to escape, to harrass, to sabotage, and so on. In practice, most states attempt legal enforcement only of negative obligations. Prisoners who collaborate with the enemy may be charged after the war with misconduct or even with treason, but not prisoners who refuse to join escape organizations.[19] Treason obviously requires some overt act of "aid and comfort," so mere refusals to participate in escape or harrassment attempts don't qualify. But the inability and unwillingness of states to enforce positive obligations has other reasons, which call into question their very status as obligations.

Negative and positive obligations (I mean the two adjectives merely as rough indications of certain sorts of actions and refusals to

---

[19]Rebecca West reports on the trials of several British prisoners of war for treason in *The Meaning of Treason* (London, 1947). For a complete review of judicial treatment of prisoner misconduct, see "Misconduct in the Prison Camp: A Survey of the Law and an Analysis of the Korean Cases," 56 *Columbia Law Review* 709–794 (1956).

act) are mediated very differently to the individual soldier. Negative obligations are his as an individual, a member, let us assume a willing member, of a particular state or of its army, and they clearly survive temporary separation from either. In captivity (as out of it) these obligations may be over-ridden, or they may be violated in extenuating circumstances. Refusals to collaborate, for example, may endanger the society of prisoners as a whole or some of its individual members, and then the man who is being pressed to perform this or that service must weigh relative evils and make a difficult and painful decision. It is important to stress the word "must," for whatever decision he comes to, he is faithful only if he takes into account his obligation not to act so as to injure his country or endanger his comrades-in-arms.

Similarly, in those cases where a prisoner collaborates under duress, he is later judged, and rightly so, by the integrity of his resistance as long as it lasts, that is, by his own manifest sense of his obligations. I cannot say, and I am not sure any free man can say, what constitutes an adequate manifestation.[20] Once a prisoner has done what he can on behalf of his home state, by refusal, evasion, or deceit, and can resist no more, his fellow citizens can only mourn with him, and not condemn, the disloyal or degrading acts he is driven to perform. Some manifestation of resistance there must be, however, so long as the prisoner regards himself and hopes to be regarded as a citizen. Negative obligations survive every separation except explicit renunciation, which is only possible under certain conditions and which terminates citizenship. They are paralleled, it should be added,

---

[20] The courts must say something, however, and what they have said is discussed in "Coercion: A Defense to Misconduct while a Prisoner of War," 29 *Indiana Law Journal* 603–621 (1954). In passing judgment on prisoners who have given military information, it is worth noting the finding of army experts after World War II: "It is virtually impossible for anyone to resist a determined interrogator." Cited in "P.O.W. — The Fight Continues After the Battle," p. 61. For a full discussion of this problem, see Albert D. Biderman's careful study of the behavior of American prisoners in Korea, *March to Calumny* (New York, 1963).

The whole question has recently been reopened because of the *Pueblo* case, and considerably complicated by the fact that the sailors of the *Pueblo* were imprisoned by a state with which the United States was not at war. They were thus formally unprotected by the Geneva Conventions and entirely without any sense of when or whether they might be returned to the United States. Perhaps for this reason, but also because of increased American sensitivity to the plight of prisoners, their "confessions" were not thought by the Secretary of the Navy to warrant court martial proceedings.

by the obligations of the home state to provide protection whenever it can, to protest every breach of the rules and agreements that make for benevolent quarantine, and to do nothing and demand nothing of its soldiers that might prompt or seem to excuse the coercion of prisoners.

Positive obligations belong to the individual as one of a group of citizens or soldiers. This can be a group of conscripts, whose members are designated as falling under one or another law or legitimate command, or a group of volunteers mutually engaged in some enterprise of value to the larger society. It seems most unlikely, in either case, that positive obligations survive clear-cut (even if temporary) separation from the group. The prisoner is alone and on his own, or he is the member of a new society, and while he remains in an important sense a citizen, he can no longer be regarded as a servant of the state. For he is cut off from the group support and organizational structure that once made his service possible. Positive obligations can be reinstated by joining an escape organization or a resistance network in the prison camp. But such reinstatements are actually commitments to a new group, and the precise relation of the new group to the larger society, the state or the army, is radically unclear. It seems unlikely that the state's right to conscript, for example, can ever devolve to an association of prisoners though such groups have sometimes claimed that right. A kind of rough and ready conscription may, of course, be effective in a camp where an escape organization has widespread support. There are many examples of this sort of thing in prison camp literature: certain kinds of minor helpfulness have often been required of prisoners who have no personal interest in escaping. It is less their patriotism that one appeals to at such moments, however, than their loyalty to fellow prisoners.

This appeal to the others may or may not be successful. That will depend on the nature of the society of prisoners as a whole (which may in turn depend on the nature of the state and army from which the prisoners come) or on the character of the personal relations involved. But it is clear that no prisoner has a positive obligation *to the state or army* to work and take risks for the escape of himself and others or for the harrassment of the enemy. Unless he actually commits himself to such purposes, he has what must be called a perfect right to "enjoy" his quarantine and to sit out the war — so long as doing so involves no conflict with his other obligations.

There are obligations, however, in addition to those positive and negative duties owed or said to be owed to the state, despite the prisoner's separation from the state. Captivity is not only a separation; it also brings men together and does so under conditions that make their cooperation both vitally necessary and extremely difficult. It can't accurately be said that anyone joins the society of prisoners willingly, even though there is a sense, as I've already argued, in which their surrender is a voluntary act. But that society can be organized on a consensual basis, and probably ought to be, either by intelligent officers who recognize that their own authority survives in a tenuous way, if at all, or in the absence of officers and in accordance with the Geneva Conventions' provisions for enlisted men's camps, by the election of representatives.[21] The political organization of the prison camp, whatever form it takes, considerably simplifies the moral life of the prisoners. It makes possible, for example, the rationing of available food, clothing and medical supplies. It also permits communal decisions on whether or not to support escape attempts, when these involve, as they often do, predictable reprisals against the whole society.[22]

Even when the society of prisoners cannot be politically organized, obligatory ties are likely to develop between a particular prisoner and each or any of his fellows. Shared suffering is a powerful bond among men and seems to entail — though I cannot specify the method of the entailment — very strong positive obligations to mutual assistance. These bonds seem to arise among groups of men assembled with or without regard to their previous citizenship, though they may be stronger or given practical effect more quickly among prisoners with common political and social commitments.[23] There may be some sense, that is, in which the new society is parasitic on the old. Nevertheless, these new obligations are owed to other prisoners and not to

[21] Geneva Convention I, Article 79. Resistance groups within the camp can also be organized democratically; thus an American group in Korea, one of whose members is quoted in Biderman, *March to Calumny*, p. 171: "We . . . agreed there would be no such thing as a leader. Before we would do anything, it would go before a vote and the majority would rule."

[22] These decisions can be informally made, as in the camp described by A. J. Evans in his memoir of World War I, *The Escaping Club* (London, 1922), pp. 180–181: "Escaping came before everything, and was an excuse for any discomforts which one or two members might bring on the rest of the community. If you wished for help, almost any man in the fort would have helped you blindly, regardless of consequences."

[23] P. R. Reid discussed some of the problems that arose in the multinational camp that the Germans ran for confirmed escapers at Colditz in World War II, in *Escape from Colditz* (New York, 1956).

the state from which they come. When the US *Code of Conduct* requires captured soldiers to "keep faith with their fellow prisoners" (Article IV), it does little more than point to the specific context within which obligations have to be negotiated. It does not strengthen the ties, nor determine their precise character. And insofar as the obligations of prisoners to each other are enforced, later on, in state or army courts, this must be by virtue of a kind of proxy from the (now dissolved) society of prisoners.[24] Such enforcement can be justified, at least in part, by the need to prevent acts of private revenge, but not by the unqualified assertion that the state's writ runs in limbo.

### THE OBLIGATION TO TRY TO ESCAPE

We do admire prisoners who actively resist their captors, and such men were thought admirable even before the ideological struggles of the present day provided new motives for continuing the fight after the battle. There is a large literature, dating chiefly from the two World Wars, which documents and celebrates the efforts of prisoners of war to escape and harass the enemy. And this literature suggests that such efforts have been felt as obligations, at least by a minority of the prisoners. Moreover, the detaining powers expect (some) prisoners to try to escape; their military authorities often regard the attempt as honorable and clearly accept the necessity of establishing a secure quarantine. Thus General Clark's statement of the "old-fashioned" view: that prisoners must be maintained "and guarded." The same sense has worked itself into international law, as I have already indicated. But it is worth stressing again that the security of the right to try to escape (which is implied by the rule against punishing escapees and obviously does not include a right to succeed in the attempt) is dependent on the relative infrequency of its exercise. If attempts to escape are common, if whole camps are organized for the sole purpose of facilitating escape, as were many British officers' camps during the two World Wars,[25] then benevolent quarantine will

[24] Sometimes prisoners set up their own courts in the camp, but these are not encouraged by the authorities on either side. See Pugh, "The Code of Conduct," pp. 683n. and 702.

[25] ". . . nearly everyone was working in some way on the X (escape) organization," Paul Brickhill, *The Great Escape* (New York 1967) p. 42; ". . . we pooled our knowledge. The camp was nothing less than an escaping club," Evans, *op. cit.,* p. 68. (The best books on escape are almost invariably written by British officers.)

almost certainly break down. Its cost to the captors will simply be too high, and they can argue that they had reckoned on a much lower cost when they accepted the surrender of the men in question. Thus the attempts of states like our own to require soldiers to "make every effort to escape" (Article III of the *Code of Conduct*) might well be disastrous for the soldiers, if they took the requirement more seriously than in fact they do. When we admire the men who "make every effort," we are really admiring heroes. It seems best to say of them, whatever they say of themselves, that their efforts are above and beyond the call of duty.

Escape is heroic only in part because of the physical risks involved, though these can be considerable, as a famous incident from World War II makes clear. In 1944, some 80 British officers escaped through a tunnel from the German camp at Sagan. All but three were eventually recaptured, and 50 were shot, apparently on direct orders from Hitler. Under the international laws of war, these executions constituted murder, and after the war the men who carried them out were tried and, some of them, executed in their turn.[26] That surely was justice done, yet it is hard to imagine a detaining power that would not go to considerable lengths to deter such mass escapes — for they tie down large numbers of troops, demoralize the civilian population, and, if successful, supply valuable information to the enemy. Hopefully, prisoners will not again have to anticipate Nazi brutality. But something less than that (and how much less can never be known) must be regarded as a normal risk. There is more involved, however, in the heroism of escape. Once a prisoner gets out of the camp, he is likely to have to spend weeks behind enemy lines, hiding or in disguise, constantly in danger, expecting discovery and arrest at every moment, able to trust no one, often without adequate food and shelter. For many men the strain must be unbearable, worse than anything that happens in battle. No prisoner can be obligated to undergo such an exacting test of his nerves and his endurance. Escape is precisely the sort of action that a man must choose for himself.

But perhaps this is not always true. In one of the best of the many books on escape, Aidan Crawley, an RAF officer captured during World War II, later a Labor MP and Undersecretary of State for Air, argues "that should a prisoner see a reasonable chance of

[26] Brickhill, *op. cit.*, pp. 211–223.

escape, it [is] his duty to take it. Suppose a prisoner had been abandoned by his guard and deliberately sought captivity again, he would have been the equivalent of a deserter." [27] Perhaps so, but in this example, it should be noted, captivity is ended without any effort by the prisoner himself. Whether he then resumes his former military role is hard to say. It is certainly possible, but if we imagine such a man seeking refuge in the home of a friendly farmer and remaining there for the rest of the war, I doubt that we would have to say, or want to say, that he had deserted. Crawley attempts to argue that there was a duty to attempt escape even when a prisoner was securely held in a camp, but he fails to argue this with much conviction. And in fact, despite the military ethic, the sense of an obligation to escape does not seem to have been widely or deeply felt, though it is almost always acknowledged in the memoir literature. "I am sure," writes one of the bravest of British escapers, "that the majority of the men who sought to escape did it for self-preservation. Instinctively, unconsciously, they felt that resignation [to an indefinite imprisonment] meant not physical, but mental death. . . ." [28] But what of the men who did not feel this way, who decided that they could make a worthwhile life even in the prison camp?

Crawley provides one of the most sympathetic accounts of these men, and he is worth quoting at length:

> From the first moment of captivity . . . there began in every prisoner's mind a conflict which lasted often until the day of liberation. Should he, or should he not try to escape? Ought he to spend his time in what would almost certainly be fruitless endeavor, or should he use it to equip himself to be a better citizen later on? There were many who from the start decided on the course of self-improvement. With great force they argued that, however heroic escape might appear, the odds against success [were] so enormous that the realistic and truly patriotic thing to do was to put the idea out of their minds. . . . To every thinking man, the wisdom of spending years in hopeless effort must at some time have seemed questionable and no one could blame those who decided escape was not worthwhile. Provided they stuck to their guns and held their

[27] *Escape from Germany* (New York, 1956), p. 8
[28] Reid, *op. cit.*, p. 35.

point of view with tolerance, they were often most valuable members of the community.[29]

To call such refusals "patriotic" is to put a good construction on them, but not necessarily the only good, or the best, construction. Refusal to escape might also express a man's sense of belonging, now, "to humanity and to himself," or his sense of personal obligations to family and friends. It might express his solidarity with his fellow prisoners, or with some of them doomed to remain in the camp for the duration of the war and in need, perhaps, of his help building a decent community.[30] And it might express his human fear or his relief at finding himself relatively safe and far from the battlefield. Surely if a man makes himself "a valuable member of the (prison) community," even these latter reasons need not be judged any more harshly than the others.

Curiously enough, one of the best arguments on behalf of escape, even mass escape, is that the attempt is itself of value to the society of prisoners. Crawley has once again put the argument very well:

> Most important of all, the effort to escape preserved the morale of the prisoners themselves. One of the great difficulties of prison life was that almost all effort, apart from the business of feeding and existing, was directed to goals which could be achieved only in the indefinite future. The mere fact that in preparing for a mass escape hundreds of people were co-operating in an enterprise which held the prospect of an immediate result was the best tonic a prison camp could have. In building a tunnel, making clothes, forging papers, or preparing maps, men took part in a common effort and once again got the feeling of serving a community.[31]

It may be that this new community is parasitic upon the old: that escape can be a common enterprise of the prisoners only because it is

---

[29] *Op. cit.*, p. 7.

[30] Exactly what this means and how such a community can be built are the main concerns of J. Davidson Ketchum's fine sociological study, *Ruhleben: A Prison Camp Society* (Toronto, 1965). In his postscript to this book, Robert MacLeod argues that the "prevalence of the idea of escape" may be a sign of group disintegration (or, presumably, of social underdevelopment), p. 353. But it is important to note that Ruhleben was a camp for enemy aliens, not soldiers.

[31] *Op. cit.*, pp. 9–10.

an enterprise of value to the state and army from which they commonly come. But this is not necessarily so. In Pierre Boule's novel (and in the better film by David Lean), *The Bridge Over the River Kwai,* the common enterprise of the prisoners is not of value to their state.[32] On the contrary, it poses a serious threat and even requires a military response. Yet it has an effect, and a plausible effect within the novel and the film, identical to that which Crawley describes. In the River Kwai case, the obligations that may arise to work on the bridge, and to work strenuously, are owed to one's fellow prisoners and to no one and nothing else. There is a certain absurdity in the spectacle of hundreds of men working with such zeal on a bridge that they "really" (as members of the conventional world, citizens and soldiers) don't want built. But this is an absurdity always possible in limbo, and it is the achievement of the novel and film to have evoked it. Nor is it clear that enterprises of more conventional value are very much less absurd. The extraordinary discipline and skill, the zeal and the sheer genius, that went into the British escape from Sagan were surely out of all proportion to its salutary effects upon the British war effort. George Harsh nicely summed up "the great escape" when he wrote of the prisoners involved that "they proved for all posterity that men, working together, can dig a damned deep hole in the ground. . . ." [33] Yes, they did prove that, and that hole was their triumph over captivity, their human triumph, as was the bridge for another group of men; and they dug it first of all for each other.

CONCLUSION

In limbo obligations are, by and large, not given, not established by any sovereign state, not waiting for discovery; they must be improvised. Attempts to specify them that go beyond those negative obligations which all citizens share are likely to be impositions on the freedom of the men involved and sometimes a cruel threat to their security. That is why they are largely ignored by the prisoners. Citizens and soldiers, safe or relatively safe among their comrades, have every right to hope that prisoners will form some sort of society, find an

[32] They are forced, in violation of the Geneva Conventions, to build a bridge which is of military value to the enemy.
[33] "Introduction" to Brickhill, *op. cit.,* p. 9.

effective way of making collective decisions, and remain faithful to one another. Armies have every right to train their soldiers to behave in that way. But to insist that this is what prisoners ought to do is to say nothing more than that they owe this much to one another, and finally it is up to the prisoners to say that themselves. Citizens and soldiers, and presidents and generals, may also hope that some of the prisoners will be heroes, that they will discover uncommon resources of courage and endurance, and unilaterally re-establish obligations that in fact have lapsed. But such heroism, it must be recognized, is also a denial of captivity, perhaps even a refusal of benevolent quarantine, and so a potential threat to the status of all those prisoners who don't choose to be heroes. All the more reason, then, that heroism should not be demanded by those of us who cannot expect to feel its consequences.

The fight does not continue after the battle, not for the men who have been captured, unless they choose together to fight on and accept the risks that choice involves. They have every right to choose differently, and this is what most of them do, opting for benevolent quarantine whenever it is offered. It is the responsibility of civilized men to insist that it always be offered and to repudiate decisively and without compromise the very idea of a "total war" to be fought within as without the bounds of the prison camp. The requirements of humanity are clear enough: detaining authorities must assume, and the prisoners' home states must give them reason to assume, that prisoners are not combatants and are no longer required by their citizenship to fight. Then they may safely be treated, and then they ought to be treated, if not like "citizens of the world," at least like men entitled to rest for a while in limbo.

# Obligation and Prisoners of War

## ROBERT BOOTH FOWLER

By now the dispute, once so intense, over the behavior of American prisoners of war during the Korean War has faded; but the many issues raised then have not. Numerous propaganda films, real or fake, involving American POWs held in North Vietnam and, particularly, the actions of Captain Bucher and the crew of the Pueblo, make this only too embarassingly clear. There is a major gap between the official standards for United States' military personnel when captured and actions taken by some of them. What should be done about this gap is a living question and it is the purpose of this essay to suggest that this practical problem involves serious normative questions that any proposed solution must take into account.[1]

Several normative questions have been raised by the actions of American POWs, in the last twenty years. What does it mean to be obligated to one nation when one is the military prisoner of another? What behavior is permitted? How much may one collaborate and how hard ought one to try to escape? How is one to balance obligation to one's nation, which may demand attempts to escape, with obligations to one's family, which may caution quiescence or even active collaboration for the purposes of survival? The questions are many, but perhaps the biggest is whether there should be any standards at all.

The answer of the United States government is spelled out very firmly — and obviously theoretically — in its military regulations appropriate to POWs. The famous Military Code of Conduct of 1955 provides a series of uniform standards of behavior for captured American soldiers.[2] One is permitted to "Give only name, rank, service number, and date of birth" and is commanded to "evade answering any questions to the utmost of my [one's] ability." Moreover, one is to "make no oral or written statements disloyal to my [one's] country and its allies or harmful to their cause" and is to accept no "special favors" while attempting to "resist by all means available" and making "every effort to escape."

---

[1] Michael Walzer started me thinking about the problems considered in this paper and he has continued me thinking about them. His is an influence I am happy to be able to acknowledge. It is large.

[2] See the appendix in this paper for the full Code.

All this is commanded in fully general, universal language whose absoluteness is unmistakable. Nonetheless, from the beginning, the legal status of the Code was vague, leaving the impression that it was not intended to be law, but only a guideline whose purpose was educational.[3] This has been the case, but it remains the basic standard upheld by the armed forces for POWs. Behind it lies the legal Universal Code of Military Justice whose provisions regarding POWs are in line with the Code of Conduct.[4]

Though previously they had been assumed by the military, these standards were put into a formal code of conduct and into the training programs because of American POW experience in the Korean War. Though this was unquestionably the cause, there is still no agreement as yet on the nature and significance of that experience. It has been charged that collaboration of all sorts was rampant and resistance minimal among American POWs in Korea, that one POW in three was guilty of some sort of unacceptable collaboration, and one in seven of serious collaboration such as writing anti-American propaganda.[5] On the other hand, the military charged only 4.3% with unacceptable collaboration and other crimes and far fewer than that percentage were ever actually convicted of any crime in POW camps.[6]

Either way, there was more collaboration than the official figures, if probably less than the alarmist total, and the amount was a revelation to the military establishment. The shock was intensified because though it is inaccurate to claim that collaboration has not occurred often before among POWs, including Americans, clearly the collaboration of Americans in Korea exceeded the amount in recent wars in which America has participated, a pattern that was duplicated by the record of British soldiers in Korea.[7]

Though the collaboration was especially dramatic, the lack of

---

[3] George S. Prugh, Jr., "The Code of Conduct for the Armed Forces," 56 *Columbia Law Review* (1956), p. 706; n.a., "Note: Misconduct in the Prison Camp: A Survey of the Law and an Analysis of the Korean Cases," 56 *Columbia Law Review* (1956), p. 716; Carter L. Burgess, "Prisoners of War: Forward," 56 *Columbia Law Review* (1956), p. 676.

[4] "Note: Misconduct," pp. 715–716 and 742 and ff.

[5] Eugene Kinkead, *In Every War But One* (New York: W. W. Norton & Co., 1959), pp. 16 and 34.

[6] Albert D. Biderman, *March To Calumny* (New York: Macmillan Co.), pp. 28 and 37.

[7] Biderman, *op. cit.,* pp. 17, 19–23, and 67; Rebecca West, *The New Meaning of Treason* (New York: Viking, 1964), pp. 76–77, 83–85, 100, and 249–250.

substantial resistance, such as escape attempts and raising difficulties for the captors, was by far more widespread. However, every camp had at least one resistance organization; there were quite a number of heroes of resistance in the American camps; special camps were set up for the large number of American POWs who were especially troublesome to their captors. Such resistance has been lost sight of.[8] But in general, the American POWs chose to follow "the path of least resistance" rather than give their captors a hard time. This was far from what the military expected even though other POW experiences suggest that the desire for survival and the force of inertia make such passivity a common result.[9]

Alarm at the Korean developments, then, produced the formalization of the traditional standards. But what fragmentary evidence we have of American Vietnam POWs' collaboration and certainly what definite evidence we have of the Pueblo crew's suggest that it has made little difference. Despite this, the military response has consisted of pretending that its traditional standards are being upheld by almost all captured Americans. Despite the clearly profound shock in the upper military ranks over what some United States POWs did in Korea, in the end only a fraction of the 10,000 Americans who returned from North Korea were publicly considered guilty of collaboration, and considerably fewer brought to trial. This happened despite the Army's original beliefs that a much larger number had collaborated, which no one denies, least of all the POWs themselves — and, after all, they were there.[10]

The military's beliefs never changed. Rather, it chose to adhere to high criteria of evidence before making formal charges, partly in response to public opinion which opposed much action against POWs, as in the Pueblo case.[11] In the end, the decision has been to pursue only the worst cases, pretending that the rest never happened.

The Pueblo crew could not be overlooked. In this case the military regulations were not applied because the crew were supposedly not POWs; instead, they were proclaimed "illegal detainees," a category invented for the awkward situation. Even then, some punishment

[8] Biderman, *op. cit.,* p. 60; Kinkead, *op. cit.,* ch. 13; "Note: Misconduct," p. 729.
[9] Kinkead, *op. cit.,* p. 130; Aidan Crawley, *Escape From Germany* (New York: Simon & Schuster, 1956), p. 3.
[10] Biderman, *op. cit.,* pp. 66–67 and 61; Kinkead, *op. cit.,* p. 73.
[11] Kinkead, *op. cit.,* chs. 3–6.

was proposed for Captain Bucher and several of his crew by the Court of Inquiry, only to be quashed by higher levels, including the Secretary of the Navy, until in effect nothing was done about behavior that flagrantly violated traditional and formal military standards, including the Code of Conduct, regarding collaboration and resistance.

Whether a different policy would make a substantial impact on POW behavior in the future is uncertain. It deterrence is to be the aim of punishment, it would seem that a policy of widespread, swift, and, possibly severe penalties ought to be applied to collaborators, a policy which is definitely beyond what the armed forces feel they can apply.[12] It is perhaps naive to think that high morale and proper behavior in the special environment of a POW, far from home, can be ensured by memories of punishments learned about in basic training. Even if this did succeed, one might question a policy that could work with most POWs only under fear of punishment.[13]

In any case, neither of the actual military responses comes to grips with the normative and practical problems of the current situation; abstract rule pronouncements ignored in practice do nothing to help solve the problem. Nor will continued inaction by the military produce a future solution.

One might begin by wondering if a POW, assuming he is politically obligated to the United States,[14] should be morally required to fulfill the high admonitions of active resistance and attempts at escape called for in the Code of Conduct. To contend that he must is really to suggest that the POW is obligated to continue fighting a war by all means possible. Yet by definition a POW is no longer a soldier, but a captured soldier.

According to United States military rules, however, the POW is by definition in the same military status during captivity that he was before captivity. The Code of Conduct indicates that the POW remains "a fighting man." This would appear to be official policy,[15] but it is a highly dubious one, apparently neither adhered to by POWs nor enforced.

---

[12] "Note: Misconduct," pp. 791–792.

[13] "Note: Coercion: A Defense to Misconduct . . ." 29 *Indiana Law Journal* (1954), p. 614.

[14] A big assumption perhaps, but one necessary here and one which cannot be considered here.

[15] "Note: Misconduct," p. 714; Prugh, *op. cit.,* p. 688; Michael Walzer, "Prisoners of War: Does the Fight Continue After the Battle," manuscript, p. 10; forthcoming, *Am. Political Science Review*.

One must grant that POWs are hardly civilians. On the other hand, they are not exactly soldiers either because soldiers are armed with weapons and are expected to use them to kill an enemy; that is what we mean by a soldier in military terms. But captured soldiers are not so armed. They have weapons, to be sure, but not military ones. Even if we define a soldier as one who is expected to use all and any physical means to destroy an enemy, the armed forces themselves do not appear to require this of a POW.[16] Thus, POWs can hardly be treated or viewed as soldiers in any conventional sense.

Yet we should not interpret the act of surrender "as the agreement not to fight"[17] — a view that in justifying not treating POWs as soldiers would sacrifice reality. Even when formal surrendering of numbers of men has taken place in recent wars this has not necessarily meant agreeing not to fight. More important, the individual, however captured, enters into no contract; rather, the tide suddenly turns and he is captured or he quickly chooses captivity and life over death, a choice which, if it is an "agreement" at all, is much more basic than that which would consider whether or not to fight in the future.

Nonetheless, despite the POWs' actual status as unarmed "soldiers" and despite the greater psychological disarmament possible in our time in which any man may be made to talk, the military rules insist that men behave as fierce resistants, as if they were ordinary soldiers. POWs basically have little chance under such arrangements, if their captors decide that they will pay with death. Struggle on the battlefields themselves is sometimes between sides that are not equal; but there is no battle for long when one side is largely helpless.

Moreover, alarm has been raised at "making the captive a prisoner at war rather than of war" on other grounds, grounds of desiring to limit war wherever possible.[18] But criticizing the United States' armed forces for their attitude that a POW is a soldier is not enough; battles require two sides, and the American POW experience in Korea suggests that captor nations can be the really guilty party. Stressing the importance of getting captor nations to cease warring in POW camps, then, is right,[19] though it is also probably futile.

Our military standards also err in assuming that the POW has

---

[16] "Note: Misconduct," p. 787.

[17] Walzer, *op. cit.*, p. 8.

[18] George Prugh; "Prisoners of War: The POW Background, 60 *Dickinson Law Review* (1956), pp. 125, 123–124, 126–138; Walzer, *op. cit.*, p. 10.

[19] Prugh, *op. cit.*, pp. 136–138.

fundamentally only one obligation, to the nation, as specified in military guidelines. However, in reality moral life for POWs is infinitely more complicated. Substantial collaboration in Korea resulted from men's efforts to contact and then join their families.[20] Are POWs' obligations to their families to be ignored? One's obligation to other POWs, which even the Code of Conduct mentions, was Captain Bucher's dilemma. Adherence to the rules might have cost him the lives of several of his men. It also might not have, but Bucher was caught in a human situation of conflicting moral obligations. Dismissing him as a coward is to miss this essential point.

To establish the POW dilemma as one of conflicting moral obligations is not to excuse any act in which a POW may engage; far from it. But it is to eliminate the simple-minded reduction to patriotic vs. weak American POWs and all other such Manichean dualities which have marred the debate too much,[21] and have led to heated disputes about whether or not the records of the supposedly tough Marines or the Turks in Korea showed that softness of the average Army man was the problem.[22]

Nor is this to suggest that our moral expectations of POWs ought to be tailored precisely to their behavior patterns, based on their choices among several obligations. What is need not be the precise delimitor of what ought to be, but it is at least a way of illustrating sharply that men's obligations and actual behavior are usually infinitely more complex than standardized moral formulas would wish. If one desires an effective moral code for POWs one must at least explore how they have acted morally; that is, one must know of their felt (and real) multiple obligations.

Specifically, knowledge of multiple and possibly conflicting obligations among POWs does not justify collaboration beyond the more elementary forms. Some of these are, after all, provided for by the military itself: provisions in the Code of Conduct which allow for the giving of name, rank, etc., the well understood policies that allow a soldier to become a POW under certain circumstances instead of fighting to death, the policies that allow a prisoner to cooperate in sleeping where told, eating when told. Such minimal collaboration is accepted and justified normally and properly.

---

[20] Biderman, *op. cit.*, pp. 46–47.
[21] Kinkead, *op. cit.*, chs. 13 and 15.
[22] *Ibid.*, pp. 163–164 and ch. 14; Biderman, *op. cit.*, pp. 156–165.

Yet there will be genuine moral conflict for at least some POWs. Sometimes higher collaboration will be insisted upon by their captors, even on penalty of death. Can it really be argued that POWs ought not to collaborate in order to preserve their lives and/or fulfill other moral obligations they may have incurred?

One cannot escape the problem in practice by simply avoiding communication with one's captors beyond that permitted in the Code of Conduct. It has been argued that to avoid collaboration silence is the best tactic, but this will not do not only because the psychology is debatable, but also because prisoners can be made to talk even if they are willing to die.[23]

The question must be faced. Perhaps the best answer that can be given is an acceptance that POWs may have to sacrifice their lives on some occasions rather than extensively collaborate; they may have to, owing national obligation or obligations to fellow prisoners. However, this ought to be asked of them only in specific circumstances established beforehand, and only in very limited cases. Perhaps only collaboration involving the transmission of information to an enemy that would threaten the national security in a major way or collaboration that would seriously harm fellow POWs must be absolutely forbidden.

Of course, no formal or declared transfer of loyalty and obligation would be permissible, regardless of treatment a POW received. How a POW is treated does not negate an obligation already owed; obligation owed to one nation cannot be transferred no matter how nice the captors are. Prisoner of war is a temporary status (usually) and, in any case, political obligation cannot be based solely on the present. Surely what men have done in the past, what political and other obligations they owe when captured, may not be lightly dismissed.

Again, whatever is forbidden must be made clear and specific, as far as this is possible, since the American POW experience in Korea showed that confusion and uncertainty about standards can be costly.[24] This is not to say that degree of duress and coercion should not figure into an assessment of POWs' collaborative acts when punishment is being considered later. It should, as should conflicting obligations; but so also should the acts committed, some of

[23] Biderman, *op. cit.*, pp. 236–237.
[24] *Ibid.*, pp. 264–265.

which are not at all acceptable, unless political obligation to the nation is to be just a phrase.[25]

To some, heroism "should not be demanded by those of us who cannot expect to feel its consequences."[26] I agree: heroism should only be demanded when its consequences would affect us (as in protecting national security) or when its consequences would affect our fellows, (as in protecting other POWs). The other general heroic demands of the Code of Conduct ought to be scrapped.

The question of accepting death to fulfill the Code's standards applies much more seriously to the other half of its requirements, those of active resistance as earlier defined. Indeed, here the Code really has its cutting edge, which was particularly and substantially ignored by POWs in Korea and, to a considerable extent, by the crew of the Pueblo. Should a POW be expected to follow the Code's exhortation to resist aggressively the enemy's control over him and his camp, to escape if possible, and to generally make life as difficult as possible for his captor, whatever the costs?

The best way to look at this side is to consider the escape issue in particular. This is part of the whole controversy regarding American POWs in Korea since not one escaped from a permanent base camp and got back to allied territory. For some this is a sign of the appalling performance of American POWs, of their weakness, allegedly shown most blatantly by the POW camps' lack of barbed wire fences because they were not needed.[27] Others point out that there were escapes and that their failure has more to do with other factors like the difficulty of terrain and language than with American softness.[28] Although there were many escapes, for example, in British Air Force POW camps in World War II, few men got back to allied territory, only a small minority of POWs concentrated on escaping, and the Nazis went quite far in treating POWs as provided for in the Geneva Convention, which was ignored by the North Koreans and Chinese in the Korean War, but which facilitated escapes.[29]

Still, the question of what should be remains. Although there

---

[25] Relevant here are: "Note: Misconduct," pp. 724, 722, and 769–771 and "Note: Coercion," p. 612.

[26] Walzer, *op. cit.*, p. 29.

[27] Kinkead, *op. cit.*, pp. 16–17; Biderman, *op. cit.*, p. 72.

[28] Biderman, *op. cit.*, ch. 6.

[29] Crawley, *op. cit.*, pp. x, 3, and 33.

seems no doubt that attempts to escape often serve a useful military purpose in tying up opposition troops and are useful in morale,[30] why need they be required or even urged? Because a POW is obligated to his nation? This can be shown much more usefully by his upholding collaboration standards; anything else is just toying with death which would inevitably mean the sacrifice of future fulfillment of a man's obligations to the state, not to mention obligations to family or friends. Acts leading to his death may well jeopardize the life or quality of life of his fellow POWs via reprisals. What applies to escapes applies to other forms of active resistance as well. They are not necessary, though if men wish to engage in them or in escapes and they will not hurt their fellows seriously, they should feel free to do so. This should be a realm of individual moral choice[31] and the Code of Conduct ought to be revised accordingly.

This view, however, ought not be adopted without awareness that there are important objections. Some complain that without resistance POW camps will fall apart internally, subjecting men to an aloneness which might promote major collaboration. This is the contention that escapes and active resistance are positively related to morale. Certainly escapes have sometimes been community-like and community-building affairs.[32] Perhaps the lack of escapes and acts of defiance in our camps in Korea may explain the evidence that there was little community among POWs there which may have contributed, in turn, to the degree of collaboration as well as a lack of concern for fellow POWs.[33] But the captor nation will have much to do with the state of morale and community in any POW camp; Germany permitted a life-style that allowed communities to be built; China was wiser. Thus resistance may be only futile, even in terms of building effective communities.

Moreover, the Korean War experience should teach us that the days of community in POW camps are now probably over, given a smart captor nation. Certainly it is past time to stop looking toward POW camps as possible places to achieve any communitarian ideal; they may have been fertile territory for that occasionally,[34] but they

---

[30] *Ibid.,* ch. 1 and p. 131.

[31] Walzer, *op. cit.,* p. 23.

[32] E.g., cf. Crawley, *op. cit.,* p. x and passim.

[33] Kinkead, *op. cit.,* pp. 148–150, 154, and 130.

[34] Cf. J. Davidson Ketchum, *Ruhleben: A Prison Camp Society* (Toronto: University of Toronto Press, 1965) (an alien camp).

were always short-lived artificial communities, in which conditions were good, and in which their captors played a coöperative game.[35] These days appear past.

Another argument against my view regarding escape and active resistance is that, whatever the effect on community and morale in relation to collaboration, lowering or eliminating standards will lead to the collapse of any limits on behavior, and directly to a situation where collaboration will run rampant. This contention remains totally unproved; and there seems little reason to believe that it would be correct. After all, one may view the Korean POW and the Pueblo crew records in two ways. One may be shocked at the extent of the collaboration. But it is at least as reasonable, and I would contend more so, to be impressed with the low amount of collaboration, particularly in Korea. After all, few defected (only 21 out of 10,000) and only small minorities engaged in blatant collaboration. To be sure, escapes and active resistance were not frequent. Still, the record is only bad to those who expect that men, obligated or not, will fail to behave as ordinary humans.

Even if one is shocked by the POWs' actions, it does not follow that lowering standards for resistance will make things worse. There is some evidence, indeed, that awareness of high standards led to demoralization in Korea, more collaboration, and less resistance, when the inevitable gap between standards and behavior was widely noted by the POWs. That is, the camp conditions may have been favorable to collaboration in part just because the men knew that very high standards were expected of them.[36]

Now the contention that the result of lowering standards for resistance will lead to a collapse altogether of moral norms for POWs makes no sense as a normative argument. Lowering standards is not abolishing them, and the two should not be confused. Some standards would remain: collaboration standards regarding national security information, regarding endangering fellow POWs, and, of course, regarding outright defection. Moreover, it may well be that the very conception of moral standards governing POWs would be strengthened rather than sacrificed by lowering the demands. More "realistically," they would have a better chance to be followed, and thus there might be more overall respect for the idea of rules.

[35] *Ibid.*, pp. 272, 173–174, and ix–x.
[36] Part of Biderman's claim.

Another possible related objection to my proposals is that they provide for situation ethics, which, especially in a POW camp, would lead to the creation of a Hobbesian state of war among the men. They would lead to anarchy, inevitably followed by tyrannies, whereas the present arrangement via the Code of Conduct, providing a series of firm, general rules, mitigates against this outcome.[37] This is a real objection, though in part the dreary dispute between situational and absolutist ethical ideals is unreal. No situation ethics is without vague, general standards that are absolute and no absolute ethics can easily, indeed conceivably, be made very specific in differing situations.

Still, there is a genuine difference of degree in my approach that would shift toward a situation ethics in POW camps. As with any situation ethics arrangement, but especially here, the objection is that in such difficult circumstances young, vulnerable men, will be left adrift morally and thus easy prey to those within the POW ranks who might seek to dominate, persecute, and exploit them. There is then a distinct chance of the creation of gangs or tyrants among the prisoners, as well portrayed in the movie "King Rat."

This is a real possibility; but as an empirical contention it too is speculative. Unquestionably in any real world social situation, power and influence will be unevenly distributed and some men will follow others. Cooperation, if not coerced, is perfectly consistent with individual moral choice and responsibility. Indeed, it is mandatory for my proposal as well as the regulations of the Code of Conduct, both of which insist that one is to consider one's fellow POWs. How much coercion there might be instead of free cooperation, and thus how much breaking down of individual choice within the camp remains to be seen.

On the other side, it is surely preposterous in the light of the Korean experience to propose that the present system is much guarantee against the emergence of a Hobbesian or tyrannical situation. It failed there; why should it not in the future? Perhaps in no arrangement in which officers are often separated from the men, conditions are not easy, and the enemy seeks to promote social disorganization among POWs, can some degree of the Hobbesian situation be prevented. But I see no reason my proposals would be certain to create such a reality.

Another objection is more normative, and bothersome. The

[37] Suggested to me by Richard Flannery.

whole emphasis of my argument is on building an environment in which POWs can survive and fulfill their multiple and possibly conflicting obligations to as great a degree as possible, sometimes at the sacrifice of what has been traditionally considered honorable behavior among POWs, specifically, in remaining inflexibly true to one's country at the cost of one's life, and willingly jeopardizing one's life to escape or actively resist. My approach might be seen as legitimizing the idea that life is more important than national obligation.

Traditional honor in this sense is deemphasized. However, this is not something for which we should apologize. In most circumstances, surely life is more important than national honor, especially when life gives the possibility of fulfilling a man's other obligations — he has much else to "honor" besides the state — as well as that owed to the state in the future, which, after all, is reserved to the living.

Limits remain. Men, if obliged, must be prepared to die for their nation and POWs must be flatly prohibited, even at the cost of their lives, from certain special activities. Obligation must be visible, in the end, if it exists.

Although there are objections, they do not seem decisive; therefore requirements for active resistance and escape ought to be dropped. There are two great advantages; my proposals go far toward treating a POW as a complex moral and individual being. My view considers the POW as a complex moral being because it understands that men need leeway in deciding how they will act morally; they have differing and sometimes conflicting obligations, and should decide for themselves whether this allows them to try to escape or actively resist. My view also considers the POW as an individual moral being just by allowing him to make as many of the choices for his own behavior as may be possible in a POW camp, within the specified limits regarding collaboration. He is no longer a soldier with orders to follow, but a soldier unarmed, a man with moral choices to make.

Periodic formal announcements might be made by the United States government stating that this is our policy, that our POWs are not under many specific injunctions regarding collaboration and resistance, and that therefore many of the acts POWs may commit, or fail to commit, are not to be taken seriously as indicators of loyalty or disloyalty. We should not assume that just because our government says such acts should be ignored, they will be;[38] yet any propaganda

[38] "Note: Coercion," pp. 611–612.

losses would surely be more than compensated for by possible gains in POW lives or reduced suffering.

Again, this is not to abandon all standards. POWs' behavior should be checked when they return to see if it shows they adhered to the proposed collaboration limits. Those whose behavior deviated from the generous contours of the standards or who could not offer adequate justifications for behavior that appeared to do so should be appropriately punished. In this way we would at last acknowledge that the POW is a man.

### APPENDIX

## *Code of Conduct*    (Biderman, p. 279)

### I

I am an American fighting man. I serve in the forces which guard my country and our way of life. I am prepared to give my life in their defense.

### II

I will never surrender of my own free will. If in command I will never surrender my men while they still have the means to resist.

### III

If I am captured I will continue to resist by all means available. I will make every effort to escape and aid others to escape. I will accept neither parole nor special favors from the enemy.

### IV

If I become a prisoner of war, I will keep faith with my fellow prisoners. I will give no information or take part in any action which might be harmful to my comrades. If I am senior, I will take command. If not, I will obey the lawful orders of those appointed over me and will back them up in every way.

### V

When questioned, should I become a prisoner of war, I am bound to give only name, rank, service number, and date of birth. I will evade answering further questions to the utmost of my ability. I will make no oral or written statements disloyal to my country and its allies or harmful to their cause.

## VI

I will never forget that I am an American fighting man, responsible for my actions, and dedicated to the principles which made my country free. I will trust in my God and in the United States of America.